Gospels, Jesus, and Christian Origins

Gospels, Jesus, and Christian Origins

Collected Essays

William O. Walker, Jr.

POLEBRIDGE PRESS
Salem, Oregon

Dedication

This collection of essays is dedicated, with great appreciation, to:

Austin College, Duke University, and Trinity University—
three outstanding institutions of higher education where I
was privileged to serve as a member of the faculty, beginning
in 1954 and ending with my retirement in 2002

My numerous supportive and helpful colleagues in these
institutions and particularly to those in the Trinity University
Department of Religion during my forty years of service
with them

The approximately five thousand talented and challenging
students who were in my classes between 1954 and 2002

I couldn't have dreamed of a more enjoyable, a more stimulating,
or a more richly rewarding career than that which was provided
by these institutions, colleagues, and students!

Cover and interior design by Robaire Ream

Library of Congress Cataloging-in-Publication Data
Walker, William O., Jr., 1930-
  [Essays. Selections]
  Gospels, Jesus, and Christian origins : collected essays / By William O.
Walker Jr.
     pages cm
  Includes bibliographical references and index.
  ISBN 978-1-59815-168-8 (alk. paper)
  1. Bible. Gospels--Criticism, interpretation, etc. 2. Bible. Gospels--
Hermeneutics. 3. Jesus Christ. I. Title.
  BS2555.52.W35 2016
  226'.06--dc23
                                                          2015031911

Contents

Preface

All of the essays in this collection except one were published between 1966 and 2009 in various scholarly journals and *Festschriften*. The one that has not previously been published—"The Lukan Nativity Story and Isaiah 7:14: Some Additional Evidence for Intertextuality"—was completed in 2014. Except for minor editing to bring them into conformity with the Polebridge Press format and style, the correction of some typographical errors, and the re-wording of a few sentences in the interest of greater clarity, the essays appear in the present volume exactly as they were originally published. Unfortunately, this has meant retaining the gender-specific language (e.g., "he" rather than "he or she," "man" rather than "human") that was prevalent in decades past.

All except three of the essays in this collection were written in the 1960s, 1970s, or 1980s—that is, more than a quarter of a century ago. The reason for this is simple: beginning in the 1970s, my scholarly interest increasingly focused less on the gospels and more on the Pauline letters (most of my publications since 1988 were included either in my *Interpolations in the Pauline Letters* [JSNTSup 213; London and New York: Sheffield Academic Press, 2001] or in my *Paul and His Legacy: Collected Essays* [Salem, OR: Polebridge Press, 2015]).

I have enjoyed working back through materials that I wrote during a span of more than forty years. In some instances, I wish I had expressed myself more clearly, cogently or comprehensively. For example, in "The Quest for the Historical Jesus: A Discussion of Methodology," I made no mention of the "criterion of embarrassment," which assumes that any item in the gospels—for example, Jesus' crucifixion or his baptism by John—that would have created theological problems for early Christians or been "embarrassing" to them has a high claim to authenticity because Christians would have been unlikely to create such items. Although it is impossible to be *certain* whether a particular item would have been problematic or "embarrassing" to early Christians, a rather high degree of probability is sometimes possible.

For the most part, I am still in agreement with the views I articulated in years past. At one point in particular, however, my thinking has changed. I am now much less confident that any type of "quest for the historical Jesus" can produce positive results than I was when I wrote "The Quest for the Historical Jesus: A Discussion of Methodology" in the mid-1960s. Indeed, it is now my judgment that we can actually know *very little* about the life and teaching of Jesus. Moreover, as regards the Synoptic Problem, I have become increasingly persuaded not only that it *has not* been solved but also that it probably *never will* be solved.

I am grateful to Larry Alexander, publisher of Polebridge Press, for accepting my proposal to publish this collection of essays, and no words of mine can adequately express my appreciation to the team of Cassandra Farrin, Char Matejovsky, and Robaire Ream for the skillful and highly professional way in which they have moved my materials through the process of publication. It is to them that I attribute much of the quality of this volume; whatever problems there are, however, should be laid at my door.

My thanks to the following journals, publishers, and individuals for permission to include previously published materials in this volume:

- *Anglican Theological Review*: "The Quest for the Historical Jesus: A Discussion of Methodology."
- *New Testament Studies* (Cambridge University Press): "The Lord's Prayer in Matthew and in John"; and "The Son of Man Question and the Synoptic Problem."
- *Journal for the Study of the New Testament* (Sage Publications): "John 1:43–51 and 'The Son of Man' in the Fourth Gospel."
- *Journal of Biblical Literature*: "The Origin of the Son of Man Concept As Applied to Jesus"; "Jesus and the Tax Collectors"; and "Postcrucifixion Appearances and Christian Origins."
- *The Catholic Biblical Quarterly*: "The Kingdom of the Son of Man and the Kingdom of the Father in Matthew: An Exercise in *Redaktionsgeschichte*"; "A Method for Identifying

Redactional Passages in Matthew on Functional and Linguistic Grounds"; and "The Son of Man: Some Recent Developments."

- *The Journal of Higher Criticism*: "Κύριος and Ἐπιστάτης as Translations of *Rabbi/Rabbouni*."
- *The Journal of Religion*: "Christian Origins and Resurrection Faith."
- Abingdon Press (The United Methodist Publishing House): "Demythologizing and Christology"; and "An Unexamined Presupposition in Studies of the Synoptic Problem."
- Mercer University Press: "'Nazareth': A Clue to Synoptic Relationships?"
- Allan J. McNicol, David B. Peabody, and J. Samuel Subramanian: "Martha and Mary in the Third and Fourth Gospels: An Exercise in Source Criticism."

Abbreviations

1,2 Cor	1,2 Corinthians
1 Esdr	1 Esdras
1,2,3,4 Kgdms	1,2,3,4 Kingdoms
1,2 Kgs	1,2 Kings
4 Macc	4 Maccabees
1,2 Pet	1,2 Peter
1QS	Serek Hayaḥad *or* Rule of the Community
1,2 Sam	1,2 Samuel
4QFlor	*Florilegium*, also *Midrash on Eschatology*ᵃ
AB	Anchor Bible
ABD	*Anchor Bible Dictionary*. Edited by D. N. Freedman. 6 vols. New York, 1992
AGJU	Arbeiten zur Geschichte des antiken Judentums und das Urchristentum
ASTI	*Annual of the Swedish Theological Institute*
AThR	*Anglican Theological Review*
Bar	Baruch
BAR	Biblical Archaeology Review
Barn.	Barnabas
BETL	Bibliotheca Ephemeridum Theologicarum Lovaniensium
BJRL	*Bulletin of the John Rylands Library of Manchester*
BR	*Biblical Research*
BZNW	Beihefte zur Zeitschrift für die neutestamentliche Wissenschaft
CBQ	*The Catholic Biblical Quarterly*
CBQMS	Catholic Biblical Quarterly Monograph Series
ChrCent	*Christian Century*
CGTC	Cambridge Greek Testament Commentary
CJT	*Canadian Journal of Theology*
D	Codex Claromontanus
Dan	Daniel
Deut	Deuteronomy

Did	Didache
DL	*Deutsche Literaturzeitung*
EDNT	*Exegetical Dictionary of the New Testament*. 3 vols. Edited by Horst Balz and Gerhard Schneider. Grand Rapids, 1990–93
Eph	Ephesians
ETL	*Ephemerides Theologicae Lovanienses*
EvT	*Evangelische Theologie*
Exod	Exodus
ExpTim	*The Expository Times*
Ezek	Ezekiel
F	Codex Augiensis
FB	Forschung zur Bibel
FBBS	Facet Books, Biblical Series
FRLANT	Forschungen zur Religion und Literatur des Alten und Neuen Testaments
Gal	Galatians
Gen	Genesis
Heb	Hebrews
Hist. eccl.	Eusebius, *Historia ecclesiastica*
HTR	*Harvard Theological Review*
IB	*The Interpreter's Bible*. Edited by George A. Buttrick *et al.* 12 vols. New York, 1951–57
IDB	*The Interpreter's Dictionary of the Bible*. Edited by George A. Buttrick. 4 vols. Nashville, 1962
IDBSup	*The Interpreter's Dictionary of the Bible: Supplementary Volume*, Ed. Keith Crim. Nashville, 1976
Int	*Interpretation*
Isa	Isaiah
Jas	James
JBL	*Journal of Biblical Literature*
JBR	*Journal of Bible and Religion*
Jer	Jeremiah
JTC	*Journal for Theology and the Church*
JJS	*Journal of Jewish Studies*
Josh	Joshua

JQR	*Jewish Quarterly Review*
JR	*Journal of Religion*
JSNT	*Journal for the Study of the New Testament*
JSNTSup	Journal for the Study of the New Testament: Supplement Series
JTC	*Journal for Theology and the Church*
JTS	*Journal of Theological Studies*
Judg	Judges
KBANT	Kommentare und Beiträge zum Alten und Neuen Testament
Mal	Malachi
Matt	Matthew
MSS	manuscripts
NCB	New Century Bible
NIB	*The New Interpreter's Bible.* Edited by Leander E. Keck *et al.* 12 vols. Nashville, 1994–2004.
NovT	*Novum Testamentum*
NovTSup	Supplements to Novum Testament
NTS	*New Testament Studies*
Num	Numbers
ÖTK	Ökumenischer Taschenbuch-Kommentar
Phil	Philippians
PRSt	*Perspectives in Religious Studies*
Ps(s)	Psalm(s)
Pss. Sol.	*Psalms of Solomon*
Q	Quelle
Rev	Revelation
RL	*Religion in Life*
Rom	Romans
SBLMS	Society of Biblical Literature Monograph Series
SBLSP	*Society of Biblical Literature Seminar Papers*
SBT	Studies in Biblical Theology
Sir	Sirach
SJT	*Scottish Journal of Theology*
SNTSMS	Society for New Testament Studies Monograph Series
ST	*Studia Theologica*

Str-B	Strack, H. L., and P. Billerbeck. *Kommentar zum Neuen Testament aus Talmud und Midrasch*. 6 vols. Munich, 1922–1961
StudNeot	*Studia Neotestamentica*
TDNT	*Theological Dictionary of the New Testament*. Edited by G. Kittel and G. Friedrich. Translated G. W. Bromiley. 10 vols. Grand Rapids, 1964–1976
TLZ	*Theologische Literaturzeitung*
TQ	*Theologische Quartalschrift*
TRu	*Theologische Rundschau*
TUSR	Trinity University Studies in Religion
TZ	*Theologische Zeitschrift*
USQR	*Union Seminary Quarterly Review*
Zech	Zechariah
ZNW	*Zeitschrift für die neutestamentliche Wissenschaft und die Kunde der älteren Kirche*
ZTK	*Zeitschrift für Theologie und Kirche*

PART ONE

Methodological Issues

Chapter 1

The Quest for
the Historical Jesus

A Discussion of Methodology

I

What is today known as "the old quest for the historical Jesus"
was abandoned by the mainstream of European New Testament
scholarship and theology in the early years of the twentieth century. The death of this movement, which represented an attempt
to recover through critical historical research the Jesus of history
as he really was before the early church transformed him into the
biblical Christ or the later church produced the Christ of Christian
orthodoxy, can be attributed primarily to four causes. *In the first
place*, Martin Kähler and later the Form Critics argued that the
Gospel materials were essentially "kerygmatic," not biographical,
in nature and that the original oral transmission and use of the
traditions within the Church ruled out the possibility of their use
as biographical sources.[1] *In the second place*, Wilhelm Dilthey and
others observed that objective, presuppositionless historiography
is impossible, that all history is interpreted history, that historical
facts have no independent and objective reality apart from their
significance for those persons who are somehow involved in or
affected by them, and, therefore, that the Jesus of history can be

"The Quest for the Historical Jesus: A Discussion of Methodology." *AThR*
51,1 (Jan 1969) 38–56. Copyright © 1969 Corporation of the *Anglican Theological Review*. Reprinted with permission.

1. See Kähler, *So-Called Historical Jesus* (first published in German in
1896). For major presentations of the application of Form Criticism to the
study of the Gospels, see, e.g. Dibelius, *From Tradition to Gospel* (first published in German in 1919) and Bultmann, *History of the Synoptic Tradition*
(first published in German in 1921).

known only as he has been interpreted, never as a bare historical fact.[2] *In the third place*, Albert Schweitzer and, in a somewhat different way, the History of Religions School asserted that the first-century Palestinian-Jewish Jesus was not necessarily intelligible and relevant to the modern world and that he had been made to appear intelligible and relevant only by an unconscious "modernizing" on the part of the questers.[3] *In the fourth place*, Martin Kähler and later the so-called Dialectical Theologians maintained that the proper object of Christian faith is not the Jesus reconstructed by critical historical research, but rather the Christ proclaimed in the kerygma, and that faith should never be at the mercy of the shifting results of historical criticism.[4]

As a result, many scholars—and Rudolf Bultmann articulated this viewpoint most forcefully—came to insist that the quest for the historical Jesus was both historically impossible and theologically illegitimate.[5] Bultmann himself has consistently warned against basing Christian faith upon the results of historical research, but he has nevertheless always stressed the necessity of

---

2. Wilhelm Dilthey lived from 1833 until 1911; a short selection of his writings on the problem of history is available in English in Dilthey, *Pattern & Meaning in History*.

3. See Schweitzer, *Quest of the Historical Jesus* (first published in German in 1906 and translated into English in 1910). For one example of the treatment of the historical Jesus by the History of Religions School, see Bousset, *Kyrios Christos* (first published in 1913 and revised in 1921).

4. See Kähler, *So-Called Historical Jesus*. The position of the Dialectical Theologians has recently been expressed again by Karl Barth ("Recapitulation Number Three," 75): "To me it is significant that present-day Old Testament scholars, especially in regard to the old yet always new theme of 'faith and history,' are on the whole on much better ground than the authoritative New Testament men, who to my amazement have armed themselves with swords and staves and once again undertaken the search for the 'historical Jesus'—a search in which I now as before prefer not to participate."

5. See, for example, Bultmann, "Die Bedeutung des geschichtlichen Jesus für die Theologie des Paulus," 208, where he asserts that "one may not go back behind the kerygma, using it as a 'source', in order to reconstruct a 'historical Jesus' with his 'messianic consciousness', his 'inwardness' or his 'heroism'," for "that would be precisely the Christ according to the flesh, who is gone," and it is "not the historical Jesus, but Jesus Christ, the proclaimed," who is the Lord (translation mine).

the *fact* of the Jesus of history as the starting point of Christian faith, and he has acknowledged that *some* historical information about Jesus is ascertainable and that this information has significance for Christian faith.[6] By the middle of the twentieth century, however, certain of Bultmann's former pupils began to express the fear that Bultmann's general skepticism and disinterest regarding the details of Jesus' history might lead to a docetic or mythological view of Jesus, and so what is known as "the new quest for the historical Jesus" began.[7]

The essential differences between the new quest and the old are two. The first difference is that the new quest has no intention of creating a "biography" or a comprehensive picture of Jesus, for it recognizes full well that the New Testament materials in their final literary form are direct expressions only of the faith of the various authors, that they reflect indirectly the corporate life and developing faith of the first-century Christian communities,

---

6. For a recent statement by Bultmann regarding the historical Jesus, see his response to scholars who have resumed the quest for the historical Jesus: "The Primitive Christian Kerygma and the Historical Jesus" (this essay was first delivered as a lecture in 1959 and published in German in 1960).

7. Ernst Käsemann first proposed this new quest in a paper read at the reunion of former Marburg students on October 20, 1953; the paper was first published in *ZTK* 51 (1954) 125–53, and is now available in English translation: Käsemann, "Problem of the Historical Jesus." More recently, however, Käsemann has increasingly disassociated himself from the new quest, explicitly refusing to base faith and Christian theology on what historical research can establish about the pre-Easter Jesus of History; cf. J. M. Robinson, "Recent Debate on the 'New Quest,'" 201; also Käsemann, "Die Anfänge christlicher Theologie." The new quest has been pursued primarily by Ernst Fuchs and Gerhard Ebeling. A number of Fuchs' writings are now available in English in his *Studies of the Historical Jesus*. Ebeling's thought is set forth in English in *Nature of Faith; Word and Faith; Theology and Proclamation;* and *Problem of Historicity*. Bornkamm has written the only full-length treatment to date of the historical Jesus as reconstructed through the methodology of the new quest: *Jesus of Nazareth*. Robinson has surveyed the new quest in his book, *A New Quest of the Historical Jesus*, which was enlarged and translated into German as *Kerygma und historischer Jesus*; the bulk of the additional material contained in this German edition is available in English as "Formal Structure of Jesus' Message"; cf. also Robinson's "Recent Debate on the 'New Quest.'"

and that they can be used, therefore, only with extreme caution as sources for the actual history of Jesus; rather, the new quest seeks to establish the probable authenticity of particular episodes, sayings, and motifs that are reported in the gospels and, on the basis of these, to depict as accurately and comprehensively as possible the characteristic message and activity of Jesus. A second difference is that the new quest, unlike the old, is concerned to demonstrate the continuity, not the discontinuity, between the Jesus of history and the Christ of Christian faith.

II

Inasmuch as the gospel traditions in their present form appear to be the end product of a long and complicated process of selection, transmission, reinterpretation, adaptation, alteration, and even creation within the early church, a great deal of attention has been devoted to the problem of establishing criteria for distinguishing between "authentic" materials (i.e., materials that actually go back to the historical Jesus) and "inauthentic" materials (i.e., materials that derive from the needs and concerns of the early Church).

The earliest such criterion, first proposed more than half a century ago by F. C. Burkitt,[8] is *the criterion of attestation in multiple sources* or, as it is sometimes labeled, a kind of cross-section criterion.[9] This criterion suggests that when a particular tradition or motif appears independently in all or most of the sources underlying the Synoptic Gospels (usually assumed to be Mark and "Q," and perhaps "M" and "L" as well), then that tradition or motif is likely authentic. Harvey K. McArthur thinks that this criterion, while it is not infallible, "is the most objective of the proposed criteria and one which will undoubtedly have a permanent place in the task of Gospel research," and he commends British scholars for "their regular and faithful use of this criterion" as opposed to the Bultmannians, who "do not display any great interest in this

---

8. Burkitt, *Gospel History and Its Transmission.*
9. See, e.g., T. W. Manson, *Teaching of Jesus,* 10–11; Dahl, "Problem of the Historical Jesus," 153–54; Fuller, *Critical Introduction to the New Testament,* 97–98; and Perrin, *Rediscovering the Teaching of Jesus,* 45–47.

multiple-attestation criterion, apparently preferring more esoteric guides."[10]

The value of this criterion of attestation in multiple sources is called into serious question, however, by the fact that the whole problem of the literary relationships among the Synoptic Gospels, as well as that of the validity of the "Q" hypothesis, has recently been re-opened by several scholars.[11] It is at least possible that Matthew, not Mark, was the earliest gospel and that there never was any "Q." If so, then this criterion, at least in its usual form, may not be as useful as McArthur and others think. At best, indeed, it can only lead us behind the sources to a common tradition, not necessarily the historical Jesus himself, for it can no longer be maintained seriously that the materials in Mark and "Q," for example, derive directly or second-hand from eye-witness testimony.[12]

Another kind of "cross-section" criterion was formulated and used by C. H. Dodd.[13] It is what might be called *the criterion of attestation in multiple forms*. If a tradition or motif appears in more than one literary form (pronouncement stories, parables, sayings, etc.), then that tradition or motif is likely authentic. Here, the presumption is that the tradition in question antedates the particular forms in which it appears. McArthur suggests that this criterion "has some value in distinguishing comparatively early from comparatively late traditions, but it is not as decisive as that of multiple attestation by a number of sources."[14]

The chief difficulty with this criterion of attestation in multiple forms, however, is its assumption that the Gospel writers exercised very little real creative and artistic literary and theo-

---

10. McArthur, "Basic Issues," 48.

11. See, e.g., Farmer, *Synoptic Problem: A Critical Analysis*.

12. For the view that the testimony of the Apostle Peter stands behind the Gospel of Mark, see, e.g., T. W. Manson, "Foundation of the Synoptic Tradition." For the view that "Q" was the work of the Apostle Matthew, see, e.g., T. W. Manson, "Gospel according to St. Matthew."

13. Dodd first used this criterion in his Cambridge lectures on "Earliest Sources for the Life of Jesus" (1937) and then made extensive use of it in his book, *History and the Gospel*, 91–101.

14. McArthur, "Basic Issues," 50.

logical skill in the composition of their Gospels and were, in fact, little more than editors or compilers, who transmitted the various traditions essentially as they received them. Recent studies in *Redaktionsgeschichte* point rather to the conclusion that each of the Gospels bears the distinctive literary and theological mark of its own author throughout all the traditions and literary forms contained in it.[15]

A third criterion has been proposed by Joachim Jeremias,[16] with reference to the earlier work of C. F. Burney. This is *the linguistic criterion*. As summarized by Reginald H. Fuller, this criterion asserts that:

> any saying of Jesus, if it is authentic, should exhibit Aramaic features, and if it has the structure of Aramaic Poetry this increases the presumption that the saying is authentic. Of course the earliest Aramaic-speaking church could also have used poetic forms, and certainly its creation would undoubtedly exhibit Aramaic linguistic features, just as the authentic logia of Jesus. … Hence this criterion of Aramaic linguistic features cannot be used alone. … But the linguistic criterion has special value in enabling us to eliminate later additions to logia. This is especially true of the parables, where it is quite easy to peel off the later interpretations and applications of the church.[17]

Jeremias himself has often tended to assume that the establishment of an Aramaic original proves the authenticity of a tradition.[18] As Fuller and others have pointed out, however, such establishment *per se* only locates the tradition within the context of the Aramaic-

---

15. See, e.g., Perrin, "Wredestrasse Becomes the Hauptstrasse," 296–300.

16. Jeremias, "Kennzeichen der *ipsissima vox* Jesu," 86–93.

17. Fuller, *New Testament in Current Study*, 33–34; cf. also his *Foundations of New Testament Christology*, 18, and *Critical Introduction to the New Testament*, 97. For a treatment of the Aramaic poetic forms, see Burney, *Poetry of Our Lord*.

18. See, e.g., Jeremias, *Eucharistic Words of Jesus*, 173–203, though the tendency is not so pronounced in this third edition as it was in the first and second.

speaking church.[19] Matthew Black carries the linguistic criterion further, including as indications of authenticity such phenomena as presumed faulty translations from Aramaic into Greek, variant translations of the same saying in two separate lines of tradition, and the appearance, upon re-translation of a saying into Aramaic, of assonance and rhyme.[20]

This linguistic criterion assumes that the Greek materials in the Gospels can be translated fairly accurately into their alleged Aramaic originals, and this, despite the painstaking labors of Jeremias, Black, and others, is a highly dubious assumption. Furthermore, it may well be the case that many features of the gospel traditions that are sometimes regarded as "Aramaisms" or "Semiticisms" are simply common forms of expression in the *koine* Greek of the first-century Graeco-Roman world or that they should be attributed to the literary influence of the Septuagint or other Greek-language literature of the Jews. Finally, the idea that an Aramaic version of a tradition is necessarily more primitive than a Greek version cannot simply be assumed, for a form of Jewish Christianity appears to have continued long after the translation of the Aramaic traditions into Greek, and this late Jewish Christianity could have made many changes in the earlier traditions.

Jeremias has also proposed a fourth criterion: *the environmental criterion*.[21] This criterion assumes that a saying is "authentic" if it reflects the social and domestic customs, the agricultural processes, and the religious practices and views of first-century Palestine.

This environmental criterion, however, like the linguistic criterion, cannot authenticate a tradition; it can only root the tradition within Palestinian Christianity. Many apparent reflections of

---

19. Fuller, *New Testament in Current Study*, 33–34, and *A Critical Introduction to the New Testament*, 97.

20. Black, *Aramaic Approach*.

21. Jeremias, "Kennzeichen der *ipsissima vox* Jesu," 86–93; cf. also his *Problem of the Historical Jesus*, 16–17. This criterion, like the linguistic criterion, is employed particularly in his *Parables of Jesus* and *Eucharistic Words of Jesus*.

Palestinian life, however, may be derived from the Old Testament or other Jewish literature or reflect merely an acquaintance of sorts with the area on the part of a writer or transmitter of the tradition.

A fifth criterion, which has been most thoroughly developed and utilized by Rudolf Bultmann and other Form Critics,[22] is *the criterion of the tendencies of the developing tradition.* By observing the way in which Mark's material has been altered in Matthew and Luke, and by noting the use of "Q" in Matthew and Luke, it is possible to detect certain "tendencies of the developing tradition"; these can be traced further in some cases by an investigation of the Fourth Gospel and particularly the apocryphal gospels.

> When once the laws governing such transmission of tradition are established we may assume that these laws prevailed also in the case of Mark and in the collection of the *Logia.* Then, it is frequently possible to attempt provisionally to reconstruct a literary form older than the one lying before us. The ability to make the necessary distinctions can be developed by studying the general laws that govern popular transmission of stories and traditions in other instances, for example, in the case of folk tales, anecdotes, and folk songs.[23]

McArthur summarizes the most common of these "tendencies of the developing tradition" as follows:

1. Changes in place, time, and sequence of incidents were made without serious historical concern.
2. The beginnings and endings of narratives were subjected to the greatest change; or, conversely, the central section of an incident remained the most stable.
3. Sayings of Jesus changed less than narrative material.
4. Names tended to be added to narratives.
5. Aramaisms tended to disappear.[24]

---

22. See, e.g., Bultmann, "New Approach to the Synoptic Problem," esp. p. 41; cf. also his "Study of the Synoptic Gospels," esp. pp. 32–35.

23. Bultmann, "New Approach to the Synoptic Problem," 41.

24. McArthur, "Basic Issues," 49.

Bultmann observes that the fundamental character of particular narratives remains the same, "but the details are subject to the control of fancy and are usually made more explicit and definite"; moreover, indirect discourse tends to become direct quotation, and there appears the inclination to "impose a schematic idea" upon such features of the tradition as Jesus' activity and the identity and intent of his opponents.[25]

As McArthur points out, however, these "tendencies of the developing tradition" indicate "what happens on the average; they cannot state categorically what must happen in a specific instance." Moreover, he notes "that the tendencies listed here have been identified from a study of the written tradition and its developments," and the same tendencies "may not have been applicable in precisely the same manner during the development of the oral tradition."[26] Indeed, the question must be raised here: How far do the Form Critics propose to go in removing everything from the tradition that could be attributed to the alleged "tendencies of the developing tradition"? In a great many instances, the traditions could be reduced to absolutely nothing! It must also be observed (as Bultmann admits in principle but not always in practice) that this criterion of the tendencies of the developing tradition cannot demonstrate the authenticity of a tradition, but can at best only recover an early form (perhaps even the earliest form) of the tradition, which may or may not derive from the historical Jesus. Finally, this criterion, like that of attestation in multiple sources, is based upon a particular view of the literary relationships among the Synoptic Gospels (i.e., the view that Mark and probably "Q" served as sources for Matthew and Luke), and this view is today being called into question by an increasing number of scholars. Indeed, it is a well-known fact that in many cases the Markan version of a particular tradition actually contains more detail than the Matthean and Lukan parallels, and this fact tends to discredit either one of the so-called "tendencies" proposed by Bultmann or the priority of Mark.

---

25. Bultmann, "Study of the Synoptic Gospels," 32–35.
26. McArthur, "Basic Issues," 49.

The most frequently cited criterion today is what might be called *the criterion of distinctiveness or dissimilarity*. As first formulated by Bultmann in his treatment of the parables, this criterion asserts that "we can only count on possessing a genuine similitude of Jesus where, on the one hand, expression is given to the contrast between Jewish morality and piety and the distinctive eschatological temper which characterized the preaching of Jesus; and where on the other hand we find no specifically Christian features."[27]

Ernst Käsemann later applied essentially the same criterion to the tradition as a whole, observing that "in only one case do we have more or less safe ground under our feet: when there are no grounds either for deriving a tradition from Judaism or for ascribing it to primitive Christianity."[28] The same point has been stressed by many others, including Hans Conzelmann,[29] Harvey K. McArthur,[30] Heinz Zahrnt,[31] Reginald H. Fuller,[32] and Norman Perrin.[33] As summarized by Fuller, this criterion asserts that:

> we can, for historical purposes, eliminate from the sayings of Jesus anything which clearly presupposes the post-Easter situation, and which reflects the faith of the post-Easter church. For here the presumption is that their *Sitz im Leben*, their creative milieu, is in the life of the church, and not in the life of Jesus. Secondly, we can eliminate any material which can be paralleled in contemporary Judaism, for here too the presumption is that the sayings in question have (historically speaking) been erroneously attributed to Jesus. This material would include sayings which are paralleled in Jewish

---

27. Bultmann, *History of the Synoptic Tradition*, 205; cf. also his *Jesus and the Word*, 12–13.

28. Käsemann, "Problem of the Historical Jesus," 37.

29. Conzelmann, "Jesus Christus," col. 623.

30. McArthur, "Basic Issues," 50–51.

31. Zahrnt, *Historical Jesus*, 107.

32. Fuller, *New Testament in Current Study*, 33; see also his *Foundations of New Testament Christology*, 18, and *Critical Introduction to the New Testament*, 96–97.

33. Perrin, *Rediscovering the Teaching of Jesus*, 39–43.

apocalyptic and Rabbinic tradition. Of course these methods are not foolproof, and one cannot help feeling that German scholars often proceed as if they were. They yield no complete certainty, for on some points Jesus could have agreed with the post-Easter church; but usually, in a saying of this class, the post-Easter situation is clearly reflected. Jesus might also have quoted or used with approval Rabbinic teaching. The most we can claim for this method of elimination is that it provides a safer course than [Ethelbert] Stauffer's principle of *in dubio pro tradito*. It may result in a reduction of the available historical data, but at least it should be reliable enough as far as it goes; and actually it turns out that it does go far enough for our purposes.[34]

Oscar Cullmann suggests the same criterion in a more positive form: sayings of Jesus which contradict the tendencies of the early church can be accepted as authentic.[35] Joachim Jeremias has demonstrated an effective use of this criterion of distinctiveness or dissimilarity in many of his works,[36] and it forms the real basis for Norman Perrin's recent book, *Rediscovering the Teaching of Jesus*.[37]

The use of this criterion of distinctiveness or dissimilarity encounters at least two difficulties, however. In the first place, the assumption that materials that *clearly* reflect the post-Easter situation or the faith of the post-Easter church should be eliminated is frequently interpreted in such a way as to mean that materials that *might* reflect the post-Easter situation or the faith of the post-Easter church are inauthentic. In the second place, as even its proponents agree, this criterion eliminates all but a bare minimum of material and, in the process, undoubtedly eliminates a great deal of authentic material; indeed, it may well be that the authentic

---

34. Fuller, *New Testament in Current Study*, 33.

35. Cullmann, *Salvation in History*, 189.

36. See, e.g., his discussion of the phrase, "Amen, I say to you …" in Jeremias, "Kennzeichen der *ippsissima vox* Jesu," 90–91; cf. also his investigation of the use of *abba* in addressing God in his *Central Message of the New Testament*, 9–30.

37. Perrin, *Rediscovering the Teaching of Jesus*.

material (or some of the authentic material) that is thus eliminated constitutes the most characteristic features of the authentic Jesus tradition. Unique features are not necessarily the most character-istic features, and only an exaggerated presupposition regard-ing the "uniqueness" of Jesus would assert that the message of Jesus, for example, must be distinguished sharply from both first-century Judaism and primitive Christianity. As a matter of fact, if everything "Jewish" and everything "Christian" is eliminated in the Jesus tradition, then nothing is left. Hence, even those who propose this criterion grant that it must be used with caution and not in isolation from the other criteria.

Yet another criterion, closely associated with the last, has been suggested by Käsemann; it is what might be called *the criterion of modification*, and it asserts that "we have more or less safe ground under our feet" when we can show that "Jewish Christianity has mitigated or modified the received tradition, as having found it too bold for its taste."[38] An example of this might be the say-ing about adultery. Mark 10:11–12 reads: "And he said to them, 'Whoever divorces his wife and marries another commits adul-tery against her; and if she divorces her husband and marries another, she commits adultery.'" The parallel in Luke 16:18 is similar: "Everyone who divorces his wife and marries another commits adultery, and he who marries a woman divorced from her husband commits adultery." In Matthew 5:32, however, there is a significant difference: "But I say to you that everyone who divorces his wife, except on the ground of unchastity, makes her an adulteress; and whoever marries a divorced woman commits adultery." Here, the presumption is that the phrase, "except on the ground of unchastity," has been added by the church in order to mitigate the original stipulation of Jesus.

The difficulty with this criterion of modification is that it as-sumes the ability to determine whether, when, and by whom the traditions in question were modified. It may be that no conscious modification was ever made in a given instance and that what

---

38. Käsemann, "Problem of the Historical Jesus," 37; cf. also Perrin, *Rediscovering the Teaching of Jesus*, 39–43.

appear to be variant versions of the same tradition actually represent originally different traditions. Moreover, traditions generally assumed to have been modified by Jewish Christianity because it found them too radical may, in fact, have been modified by Hellenistic Christianity for precisely the same reason, or for the opposite reason. Indeed, it may be that the so-called "modified" version actually derives from Jesus himself and that the church produced the more "radical" version; there seems to be no question but that some early Christians were more "radical" or "bold" (or perhaps the proper term is more "rigid") in certain respects than was Jesus himself.

An eighth and final criterion has been proposed by Charles Edwin Carlston,[39] though it was earlier used by Bultmann.[40] This is *the criterion of consistency or coherence*. If a tradition reflects the social, political, ecclesiastical, and linguistic conditions prevailing during Jesus' lifetime and, more importantly, if the tradition fits "reasonably well into the eschatologically based demand for repentance that was characteristic of Jesus' message,"[41] then that tradition may very well be authentic. As McArthur expresses it, once a critically assured minimum of authentic material has been established with a high degree of probability by means of other criteria, "it may be possible that materials previously rejected can be reclaimed because of their congruity with elements in the established base."[42] Nils Alstrup Dahl proposes the more ambitious goal of "harmonizing the maximum of the tradition with the critically assured minimum to the highest degree possible, in order step by step to approach more closely to the historical Jesus."[43] This criterion of consistency or coherence has been used to good effect by Joachim Jeremias.[44]

---

39. Carlston, "*Positive* Criterion of Authenticity?" Cf. also Perrin, *Rediscovering the Teaching of Jesus*, 43–45.

40. Bultmann, *History of the Synoptic Tradition*, 105, 125; note the constant use of this criterion in his *Jesus and the Word*.

41. Carlston, "*Positive* Criterion of Authenticity?" 34.

42. McArthur, "Basic Issues," 51.

43. Dahl, "Problem of the Historical Jesus," 156.

44. See, e.g., Jeremias, *Unknown Sayings of Jesus*, 30.

The most obvious weakness of this criterion, apart from questions about the "critically assured minimum" to be established by means of other criteria, is the probability that if the early church did, in fact, create traditions about Jesus (and it surely did), it would have attempted, at least for the most part, to create such traditions as would fit "reasonably well" into the general picture of Jesus that it had received through the prior traditions.

So much, then, for the criteria that have been proposed for distinguishing between the authentic and the inauthentic elements in the Gospel tradition.

III

No one, of course, would argue that any one of these criteria, taken alone, is decisive except, perhaps, in a negative sense. The appeal is generally to the cumulative weight of the criteria as a whole or to some combination of criteria. Fuller, for example, offers a rather typical summary of the appropriate use of the various criteria:

> The quest of the historical Jesus should be seen as part of and as the end-process of the study of the whole history of the gospel tradition. That study is an attempt to assign to their proper place in the history of the tradition the various strata: first, redaction, then primary sources, then oral tradition, Hellenistic and Palestinian, then finally, the authentic Jesus tradition. The appropriate criteria must be applied at each successive stage.
>
> 1. The redaction. This is established from the criteria furnished by source criticism and by the redactio-historical method (K. L. Schmidt).
> 2. Primary sources. These are established by source criticism.
> 3. Hellenistic and Palestinian oral tradition. This is established by the cross-section method applied to the primary sources (Burkitt), by form criticism (Bultmann, Dibelius), by the cross-section method applied to the oral forms (Dodd), and by the linguistic and environmental tests (Jeremias, Black).

4. The authentic Jesus tradition. This is established by the criteria of distinctiveness.

5. The criterion of consistency (Carlston) can then be employed to confirm the results at each stage, and to recover for the Jesus tradition some of the material which had been provisionally rejected by the test of distinctiveness.[45]

My own view is that these criteria can by no means be disregarded; indeed, they serve a very useful purpose. Nevertheless, primarily because of the often unexamined presuppositions that underlie them, they must be employed with great caution, and, for the reasons already mentioned, they produce extremely meager and tenuous results.[46] Perhaps the greatest difficulty of all, however is that the whole methodology and the very aims presupposed in the use of such criteria are themselves highly dubious or at least self-limiting. The method is the "atomistic" or "inductive" one of attempting to authenticate isolated bits of tradition, then of piecing these together in such a way as to be able to say something about the characteristic message and activity of the historical Jesus. In principle, this approach begs the real question, which is "whether we may detect only characteristic individual features or whether it is possible to give a scientific description of the life of Jesus founded on objective arguments."[47] Is this "atomistic" or "inductive" approach the only live option today, or is it possible that some kind of "holistic" or "deductive" approach would be more realistic and appropriate and useful?

Contemporary scholarship has tended simply to accept without question the view that the collapse of the nineteenth-century quest rules out the possibility of any future pursuit of that quest's goal, which was to form, on purely historical grounds, a

---

45. Fuller, *Critical Introduction to the New Testament*, 98.

46. See Fuller, *Critical Introduction to the New Testament*, 99–103, for a representative list of passages representing the authentic Jesus tradition as reconstructed on the basis of these criteria and a summary of the authentic Jesus tradition; cf. also Perrin, *Rediscovering the Teaching of Jesus*.

47. Dahl, "Problem of the Historical Jesus," 157.

comprehensive, consistent, and convincing picture of the historical Jesus. It seems to me, however, that the failure of the nineteenth-century quest may have resulted not from the impossibility of its intent, or even from the invalidity of its general methodological presuppositions and procedures, but rather from the fact that "it set too directly and rashly toward its goal,"[48] without first carrying out a thorough literary, form-critical, and tradition-historical analysis of the gospel materials.

I am suggesting, in short, that what is today called "the new quest for the historical Jesus" actually represents an untenable "halfway house" between the historical skepticism and unconcern of the Bultmannian "school" and the uncritical naïveté of the nineteenth-century quest and that its results are, and inevitably must be, unsatisfying both to the theologian and to the historian. For my own part, I should prefer either of the two so-called "extremes"—either Bultmannian skepticism and unconcern or "liberal" naïveté—to this middle "atomistic" position. In actual fact, however, I am proposing a return to a sobered version of the old quest or, as W. D. Davies has put it, a "resumption of the old quest on a new level."[49] Such a quest can learn much from the results to date of the new quest, and it can utilize the criteria that have been suggested, but it will attempt to go much further along the road toward the reconstruction, on purely historical grounds, of a comprehensive, consistent, and convincing picture of the historical Jesus.

This call for a resumption of the old quest is not new, of course. In various ways, it has been sounded by such eminent scholars as T. W. Manson,[50] Joachim Jeremias,[51] W. D. Davis,[52] and Nils Alstrup Dahl.[53] And of course there are many who have never

---

48. Dahl, "Problem of the Historical Jesus," 156.

49. Davies, "A Quest to Be Resumed," 71.

50. T. W. Manson, "Quest of the Historical Jesus—Continued"; cf. also his "Life of Jesus."

51. Jeremias, "Present Position in the Controversy."

52. Davies, "A Quest to Be Resumed."

53. Dahl, "Problem of the Historical Jesus."

abandoned the old quest.[54] Most of the men who call for a resumption of the old quest, and many of those who have never abandoned it, are motivated in large part by theological considerations: they want to establish a historical basis and object for Christian faith. It is highly significant, however, that they seek to recover the historical Jesus through the general methods of secular historiography and, at least in theory, are unwilling to allow their theological convictions to govern their historical conclusions. My own concern at this point, it should be noted, is essentially historical, not theological.

IV

It is true, of course, that the obstacles to a resumption of the quest are numerous and formidable. *In the first place*, the quest obviously involves the New Testament documents in ways and for purposes quite alien to the apparent intent of their authors. Indeed, Samuel Sandmel has recently asserted "that the Gospels are not telling about the man that scholarship seeks, but about the human career of a divine being," and he maintains that "to search the Gospels for the man" represents "a distortion of what is in the Gospels."[55] This is not a problem unique to the study of Christian origins, however; historians must frequently use documents in ways and for purposes that their writers never intended, and they must inevitably utilize documents that tell not who a person really was, but rather who the author thinks he was.

In the second place, the historian must at the very outset resolve certain basic questions regarding presuppositions and methodology; perhaps foremost among these is the question whether history is to be regarded as "a closed continuum of effects in which individual events are connected by the succession of cause and

---

54. See, e.g., Fosdick, *The Man from Nazareth as His Contemporaries Saw Him*; Goodspeed, *A Life of Jesus*; Enslin, *Prophet from Nazareth*; and McCasland, *Pioneer of Our Faith*. In a somewhat different way, the following would also fit into this company: Goguel, *Life of Jesus*; and Guignebert, *Jesus*.

55. Sandmel, *We Jews and Jesus*, 108.

effect" or whether this "continuum of historical happenings" can "be rent by the interference of supernatural, transcendent powers."[56] My own view is that the historian, as historian, can reckon with *the historical phenomenon of faith in such supernatural acts*, but not with *the alleged supernatural acts themselves*; the historian must look for all "causes" within history itself.

In the third place, the historian must recognize the impossibility of the "positivistic" view of history as "telling exactly what happened." Historians can encounter the monuments of the past and question these monuments, but they have no direct access to past events. They must acknowledge that all human thinking, their own included, is historically conditioned, and that the work of historians is to posit certain hypotheses about the past, examine these hypotheses on the basis of the available evidence, and ultimately accept, reject, or modify the hypotheses in terms of their comprehensiveness, inner consistency, and cogency in light of the evidence. Historiography, in other words, is as much an "art" as it is a "science," and it never produces certainty.

In the fourth place, the historian (and the theologian) must accept the fact that the results of the quest may or may not be directly relevant and useful for Christian faith. It may well be that much of the current skepticism regarding the possibility of a quest for the historical Jesus is actually rooted in the fear that Schweitzer was right: "either thoroughgoing skepticism or thoroughgoing eschatology," or, as it was recently paraphrased: "the real Jesus was either a raving wild-eyed prophet or else a figure irrevocably buried in history."[57] Most Christians, of course, would prefer that he be "irrevocably buried in history" than that he be "a raving wild-eyed prophet." The historian, however, must prefer to find him, even if this should mean finding a "raving wild-eyed prophet."

In the fifth place, the historian must be willing to re-open the question of sources. This means not only a reassessment of the

---

56. Bultmann, "Is Exegesis without Presuppositions Possible?" 291, 292.

57. Woodward and Schumacher, "Easter 1966—A Quest for the True Jesus," 72.

literary relationships among the Synoptic Gospels but also a re-investigation of the value of the Fourth Gospel as a historical source. It may be that, in some respects at least, the Fourth Gospel preserves a more primitive picture of the historical Jesus than do the Synoptics.

In the sixth place, and finally, it must be conceded that the results of such a quest will be far from satisfying to one who demands certainty regarding the authenticity or inauthenticity of each particular pericope, but these results will be much more adequate for the historian who is attempting to understand the origins of Christianity, and they may be of greater use to the theologian — particularly if the quest proceeds on the basis of the kind of imaginative ingenuity that characterized, for example, the work of Albert Schweitzer.

V

Much difficult work remains to be done, of course, before such a quest can be carried out successfully, but, at the very outset, three tests for the validity of any proposed reconstruction of the historical Jesus can be suggested. As Dahl puts it, the fixed starting point of all our knowledge about Jesus is "that he is the crucified One whom the community, originating in his band of disciples, believed to be the risen Messiah," and "we also know that Jesus worked in Israel and that he himself was born and grew up as a Jew."[58] In other words, we know three things about the historical Jesus with a fair degree of certainty: he was a first-century Palestinian Jew, he was put to death by the Roman authorities, and he was the focus of the faith of the primitive Christian community. Any adequate picture of the historical Jesus, therefore, must satisfy three basic criteria. *In the first place*, it must set Jesus convincingly within the context of first-century Palestinian Judaism; quite apart from any particular view about the "nature" of Jesus, it must be obvious that the historical antecedents, influences, and environment surrounding him were Jewish. *In the second place*, it must show why his life ended in execution at the

---

58. Dahl, "Problem of the Historical Jesus," 154.

hands of the Roman authorities; as Dahl points out, "an obvious weakness of many descriptions of Jesus as a very pious and very humane, but somewhat harmless teacher lies in the fact that it is not understood why high priests and Romans had any kind of interest in the execution of this man."[59] *In the third place*, it must account for, or at least illumine, the birth of the Christian community; as Sir Edwyn Hoskyns insisted a generation ago, "any historical reconstruction which leaves an unbridgeable gap between the faith of the primitive church and the historical Jesus must be both inadequate and uncritical: inadequate, because it leaves the origin of the church unexplained; and uncritical, because a critical sifting of the evidence of the New Testament points towards the life and death of Jesus as the ground of primitive Christian faith, and points in no other direction."[60]

None of these criteria can easily be satisfied. *First*, there is still much work to be done before any comprehensive picture of first-century Judaism can be formed, and this work must include further examination of the Dead Sea Scrolls. *Secondly*, "a historical description of the death of Jesus is still a most difficult and complicated task" because of the significant gaps in present knowledge regarding the times and practices.[61] *Thirdly*, there is still great disagreement among scholars regarding the exact nature of the earliest Christian faith, and, moreover, the creative influence of the reported post-resurrection "appearances" of Jesus and of the "coming of the Holy Spirit"—that is, of various kinds of "ecstatic experiences"—must be taken into account in any attempt to speak meaningfully about the birth of the Christian community. These difficulties, however, are no different in kind from those that face all historical scholarship and should not immediately lead to the conclusion that the task is impossible.

This proposal does not, of course, assume the invalidity of what I have called the "atomistic" or "inductive" approach to the quest for the historical Jesus; rather, it suggests that the two

---

59. Dahl, "Problem of the Historical Jesus," 159.
60. Hoskyns and Davey, *Riddle of the New Testament*, 170.
61. Dahl, "Problem of the Historical Jesus," 158.

kinds of methodology be used jointly to supplement and correct each other. The "atomistic" or "inductive" approach attempts to authenticate particular motifs and bits of tradition, while the "holistic" or "deductive" approach attempts to form a more or less comprehensive picture of the historical Jesus. At those points where the results of the two approaches coincide or approximate one another, historians can be relatively certain that they are on solid historical ground.[62]

---

62. It should be noted that the three criteria proposed above are stated in a somewhat different way by T. W. Manson in "Quest of the Historical Jesus—Continued," 11. It should also be recognized that much of the argument in this paper was anticipated a generation ago by Goguel in *Life of Jesus,* 204–15.

Chapter 2

The Kingdom of
the Son of Man
and the Kingdom
of the Father
in Matthew

An Exercise in *Redaktionsgeschichte*[1]

I

Modern study of the Synoptic Gospels has convinced most scholars that the proclamation of God's coming Kingdom stood at the very heart of the message of the historical Jesus.[2] It is not entirely clear, however, just what Jesus himself understood to be the nature of this Kingdom or the time and manner of its arrival. Indeed, there is even some question about how the various writers of the Synoptic Gospels conceived this Kingdom. In particular, the presence of certain terminological peculiarities in the Gospel of Matthew suggests a number of perplexing problems.

"The Kingdom of the Son of Man and the Kingdom of the Father in Matthew: An Exercise in *Redaktionsgeschichte*," *CBQ* 30,4 (October 1968) 573–79. Copyright © 1968 Catholic Biblical Association of America. Reprinted with permission.

1. Norman Perrin ("Wredestrasse Becomes the Hauptstrasse," 296–300) observes that the movement in New Testament scholarship "which is today sweeping all before it" is "somewhat inappropriately called *Redaktionsgeschichte*." It involves a study of the ways in which the various Evangelists selected, reinterpreted, adapted, revised, and composed traditions to serve their own particular theological and practical purposes. One of the pioneering works in this field is the brilliant essay by Bornkamm, "End-Expectation and Church in Matthew," which originally appeared as "Enderwartung und Kirche im Matthäusevangelium."

2. See, e.g., Perrin, *Kingdom of God in the Teaching of Jesus*.

It has long been noted, of course, that, while Matthew[3] occasionally refers to the "Kingdom of God," which is the characteristic term in Mark and Luke,[4] he much more frequently speaks of the
"Kingdom of Heaven" or, literally, "Kingdom of the Heavens," a
phrase that is totally absent from Mark and Luke.[5] Because of this,
some exegetes and theologians have insisted that Matthew makes
a distinction between the Kingdom of Heaven and the Kingdom
of God. For example, the type of Protestant theological conserva-
tism known as "Dispensationalism" asserts that the Kingdom of
Heaven, or the rule of the heavens over the earth through the messianic reign of Christ, is the organic, earthly, and temporal manifestation of the eternal and spiritual Kingdom of God. The object
of the former is the establishment of the latter, and ultimately, it
is believed, the Kingdom of Heaven will merge into the Kingdom
of God.[6] This distinction between the Kingdom of Heaven and the
Kingdom of God is further supported by an appeal to other passages in the New Testament that appear to speak of two stages in
the realization of God's sovereignty over the created order.[7]

Most critical scholars today, however, are of the opinion that
the terms "Kingdom of God" and "Kingdom of Heaven" function as virtual synonyms and that the difference in expression is
to be accounted for primarily in terms of the Jewish practice of
employing substitutes for the divine name whenever possible.[8]
Thus, Matthew's preference for "Kingdom of Heaven" is taken
simply as an indication of his "Jewishness" as contrasted with
Mark's and Luke's "non-Jewishness." Or, occasionally, it is sug-

---

3. The names "Matthew," "Mark," and "Luke" are here used to refer
to the anonymous authors of the respective Synoptic Gospels.

4. Matthew refers to the "Kingdom of God" in 12:28; 19:24; 21:31b;
and 21:43. He also speaks of "his kingdom" (6:33), "your kingdom"
(6:10), "my Father's kingdom" (26:29), and "the kingdom of their Father"
(13:43).

5. Matt 3:2; 4:17; 5:3, 10, 19 (*bis*), 20; 7:21; 8:11; 10:7; 11:11, 12; 13:11, 24,
31, 33, 44, 45, 47, 52; 16:19; 18:1, 3, 4, 23; 19:12, 14, 23; 20:1; 22:2; 23:13; 25:1.

6. See, e.g., the notes in Scofield, *The Holy Bible*, on Matt 3:2 and 6:33.

7. See, e.g., 1 Cor 15:22–28, which speaks of a Kingdom of Christ or
Kingdom of the Son to be succeeded by the Kingdom of the Father.

8. See, e.g., BAG 134.

gested that Matthew preserves the Semitic idiom likely employed by Jesus himself, but that this idiom would have been meaningless or at least misleading to the Greek ear and was consequently changed within the Hellenistic Church, a change that is reflected in the usage of Mark and Luke.[9] In either case, it is assumed that "Kingdom of God" and "Kingdom of Heaven" refer to the same reality, and the two-stage doctrine of the Kingdom described above is rejected.

At the same time, however, many critical scholars today believe that the Gospel of Matthew does make a distinction between the "Kingdom of the Son of Man," on the one hand, and the "Kingdom of the Father," on the other, identifying the former with the existing Christian Church and the latter with the eschatological state after the Final Judgment.[10] The following statement is typical:

> In addition to the general terms "kingdom" and "kingdom of heaven" (= kingdom of God), Matthew speaks of the "kingdom of the Son of Man" and the "kingdom of the Father." The former refers to the Church in the present Age in its mixed form, including good and bad. The kingdom of the Father is the Age beyond the consummation, when only the faithful are present among the People of God.[11]

This distinction is based primarily on Matthew's allegorical interpretation of the Parable of the Weeds (the Parable is found in Matt 13:24–30 and the interpretation in 13:36–43, with the Parables of the Mustard Seed and the Leaven and a short statement about Jesus' use of parables intervening). Because the distinction cannot be found in the other Synoptic Gospels, it might be viewed simply as Matthew's way of reconciling Jesus' original proclamation of the imminent (or present) Kingdom of God with the subsequent course of actual history, in which nothing visibly new appeared

---

9. See, e.g., Ladd, *Jesus and the Kingdom*, 106 n. 12.

10. See, e.g., Bornkamm, "End-Expectation and Church in Matthew," 44, and other scholars cited in n. 3 there.

11. Kee, Young, and Froehlich, *Understanding the New Testament*, 287.

other than the Christian community, the church. This problem of reconciling Jesus' original eschatological message with the subsequent course of history was, of course, a vexing one for many of the New Testament writers and has continued to trouble exegetes and theologians down to the present. It would appear, then, that Matthew distinguished two successive stages in the coming of the Kingdom: the Kingdom of the Son of Man (the church in the present age) and the Kingdom of the Father (the future consummation); this, at least, is what many scholars maintain.

The real question, however, is whether Matthew does, in fact, make a distinction between the Kingdom of the Son of Man and the Kingdom of the Father and, if so, whether he identifies the former with the church in the present age and the latter with the eschatological state after the Final Judgment.

II

There is no denying the fact that Matthew's allegorical explanation of the Parable of the Weeds (13:37–43), which is almost certainly secondary and appears to reflect the distinctive concerns of the Evangelist himself,[12] *could* be interpreted as suggesting a distinction between the Kingdom of the Son of Man and the Kingdom of the Father:

> *The Son of man* will send his angels, and they will gather out of *his kingdom* all causes of sin and all evil-doers, and throw them into the furnace of fire; there men will weep and gnash their teeth. Then the righteous will shine like the sun in *the kingdom of their Father*. (Matt 13:41–43a; emphasis mine)

It must be pointed out, however, that two other passages in Matthew also speak of the Kingdom of the Son of Man or the Kingdom of Jesus (which, for the Evangelist, would surely be identical with the Kingdom of the Son of Man) and that neither of these passages unequivocally identifies the Kingdom of the Son of Man with the church in the present age. Matt 16:28 reads: "Truly,

---

12. Jeremias, *Parables of Jesus*, 84–85.

I say to you, there are some standing here who will not taste death before they see the Son of man coming in his kingdom." The parallels in Mark 9:1 (which speaks of the Kingdom of God coming "with power") and in Luke 9:27 (which speaks simply of the Kingdom of God) do not mention the future coming of the Son of Man, and it appears that the Matthean version of this saying is a modification representing the distinctive theology of the Evangelist himself.[13] The implication clearly is that the Kingdom of the Son of Man is expected to come in the future. But does "future" here mean future from the standpoint of the Evangelist (in which case the Kingdom of the Son of Man could not possibly be identical with the church in the present age) or simply future from the standpoint of the historical Jesus (in which case the coming of the Kingdom of the Son of Man might be identified with the birth of the church)? The same ambiguity appears in the other relevant passage, Matt 20:21, which speaks of "your" (= Jesus') kingdom. The parallel in Mark 10:35–37, which reads "your glory" rather than "your kingdom," suggests again the presence of a peculiarly Matthean concept of the Kingdom. And, again, the implication clearly is that this Kingdom of Jesus (= Kingdom of the Son of Man) is expected to come in the future, but it is not clear whether this "future" from the standpoint of Jesus' ministry is also regarded as future from the standpoint of the Evangelist. Thus, neither Matt 16:28 nor Matt 20:21 can be used to support the distinction between the Kingdom of the Son of Man (= the church in the present age) and the future Kingdom of the Father.

It is highly significant, moreover, that Matt 16:28 speaks of the Son of Man "coming in (or with) his kingdom," thus apparently equating the coming of the Son of Man with the coming of the Kingdom of the Son of Man. And it is quite clear elsewhere that Matthew regards the coming of the Son of Man as an eschatological event in the future; see, e.g., Matt 16:27; 24:29–31; and 26:64 (all of which have parallels in both Mark and Luke); Matt 24:26–27, 37–41, 42–44 (all of which have parallels in Luke); and particularly

---

13. See Perrin, *Rediscovering the Teaching of Jesus*, 16–17.

Matt 10:23; 24:3; and 25:31–46 (which have no parallels in either Mark or Luke).

Even more significant is the fact that there are two passages in Matthew (both of them unique to Matthew) that unequivocally refer to the rule of the Son of Man (or of Jesus) in an eschatological sense, though the first of these does not use the terms "Kingdom" or "King." Matt 19:28 has Jesus saying to the disciples, "Truly, I say to you, in the new world, when the Son of man shall sit on his glorious throne, you who have followed me will also sit on twelve thrones, judging the twelve tribes of Israel" (see the similar statement in Luke 22:29–30: "As my Father appointed a kingdom for me, so do I appoint for you that you may eat and drink at my table in my kingdom, and sit on thrones judging the twelve tribes of Israel"). The well-known passage, Matt 25:31–46, also speaks of a time at the end "when the Son of man comes in his glory" and sits on his glorious throne to separate the sheep from the goats at the Last Judgment.

This brief survey of relevant passages in Matthew suggests, therefore, that the Evangelist apparently regards the coming of the Kingdom of the Son of Man as still future, not already present in the form of the Christian church, and that he relates the coming of this Kingdom very closely to the Final Judgment. This is also true, of course, of his treatment of the Kingdom of Heaven/Kingdom of God, and it would be very difficult to deduce from these passages that Matthew makes any distinction between the Kingdom of the Son of Man and the Kingdom of Heaven/Kingdom of God. How, then, shall we understand Matt 13:37–43 (Matthew's allegorical interpretation of the Parable of the Weeds), which apparently does distinguish between the Kingdom of the Son of Man and the Kingdom of the Father?

First, it should be noted that, although most scholars do identify the Kingdom of the Son of Man here with the church in the present age, Rudolf Bultmann rejects this identification and interprets the statement that "they will gather out of his kingdom all causes of sin and all evil-doers" to mean "out of the kingdom which will appear *then*," thus seeing even here a reference to the future coming of the Kingdom of the Son of Man, which would be identical with the Kingdom of the Father.[14] Such an interpretation is surely intrinsically possible, and, in light of the passages considered above, it must be regarded as most likely correct.

Furthermore, most commentators have simply assumed that the phrase, "the kingdom of their Father," is equivalent to "the kingdom of God." Nothing more than a look at Mark 11:10a ("Blessed is the kingdom of our father David that is coming!"), however, is needed to recognize the possibility of another interpretation. The "Father" here might represent some messianic figure and thus be virtually equivalent to "the Son of Man," not "God."[15] Indeed, it is doubtful whether the idea of a "Kingdom of God" plays any real part in the theology of Matthew. The phrase occurs only four times, and, in each case, it apparently was a part of the pre-Matthean tradition that was simply taken over without change by the Evangelist.[16] Normally, however, Matthew changes

---

14. Bultmann, *History of the Synoptic Tradition*, 187 n. 3.

15. Lindars (*New Testament Apologetic*, 171) argues that the terminology in Mark 11:10a agrees with the religious usage of Ps 118:25 "in late Judaism as a prayer for the restoration of the Davidic kingdom (now thought to be imminent)" and concludes that the statement is likely original. Kümmel (*Promise and Fulfilment*, 116), however, asserts that "David is practically nowhere else called 'our Father', and there is nowhere at all any mention of the 'coming' of the kingdom of David"; his conclusion is that Mark 11:10a is "presumably a secondary construction"; cf. also Fuller, *Foundations of New Testament Christology*, 112, who accepts Kümmel's view. Whether the statement in Mark 11:10a is original or secondary, and whether it can be paralleled in pre-Christian Jewish literature, is completely irrelevant to our argument, however. Mark 11:10a demonstrates that it was possible within the early church to speak of "the kingdom of our father David that is coming," and nothing more is needed at this point.

Matt 26:29, which has Jesus speaking of "my Father's kingdom," does not necessarily invalidate the argument, for here, as in Matt 13:43, the "Father" is not explicitly identified as God; it is true that the parallels in Mark 14:25 and Luke 22:18 do refer to "the kingdom of God," but the question must be raised as to why Matthew has changed "the kingdom of God" to "my Father's kingdom" (assuming, of course, that it was Matthew who made the change, not Mark and Luke).

16. Matt 12:28 ("But if it is by the Spirit of God that I cast out demons, then the kingdom of God has come upon you") is paralleled in Luke 11:20 ("But if it is by the finger of God that I cast out demons, then the

the terminology to "Kingdom of Heaven" or simply "Kingdom," not because as a pious Jew he shrinks from using the divine name, and not necessarily because this usage more accurately reflects the Semitic idiom of the historical Jesus,[17] but rather because "Kingdom of Heaven" fits better with his theology of the Son of Man coming in his Kingdom. But even if Matthew does in this passage equate "Father" with "God," as he certainly does elsewhere in the Gospel, this does not necessarily imply that he is thereby distinguishing between two Kingdoms, or even two successive stages of the same Kingdom. As Bultmann has observed, the New Testament is full of "naïve pronouncements" that virtually equate Jesus and God, *so far as Jesus' function is concerned*.[18] Thus, Matthew might easily speak of one and the same Kingdom

---

kingdom of God has come upon you"), and the authenticity of the Lukan version has been vigorously defended; see, e.g., Perrin, *Rediscovering the Teaching of Jesus*, 63–65. Matt 19:24 ("Again, I tell you, it is easier for a camel to go through the eye of a needle than for a rich man to enter the kingdom of God") is found almost verbatim in Mark 10:25 and Luke 18:25 and thus is almost certainly not original with Matthew; furthermore, it should be noted that Matthew himself uses the term "Kingdom of Heaven" in the preceding verse, where the Markan and Lukan parallels both read "Kingdom of God." Matt 21:31b ("Jesus said to them, 'Truly, I say to you, the tax collectors and the harlots go into the kingdom of God before you'"), though it is not paralleled in the other Synoptic Gospels, appears to be the original conclusion of the Parable of the Two Sons and thus is clearly pre-Matthean; see Jeremias, *Parables of Jesus*, 80. And Matt 21:43 ("Therefore I tell you, the kingdom of God will be taken away from you and given to a nation producing the fruits of it") also appears to be pre-Matthean; see Perrin, *Rediscovering the Teaching of Jesus*, 37–38. Three other passages refer either to "his (= God's) kingdom" (Matt 6:33), "your (= God's) kingdom" (Matt 6:10), or "my Father's kingdom" (Matt 26:29), but, in each case, the saying is paralleled in one or both of the other Synoptics and thus appears to be pre-Matthean.

17. It is true that "Kingdom of the Heavens" is much more frequent in the Jewish Rabbinic literature than "Kingdom of God"; see Kuhn, "Βασιλεύς, Βασιλεία, Βασίλισσα, Βασιλεύω, συμβασιλεύω, Βασίλειος, Βασιλικός, C: מלכות שמים in Rabbinic Literature," 571. It is not altogether clear which of the two expressions would most likely have been used by the historical Jesus; see K. L. Schmidt, "Βασιλεύς, Βασιλεία, Βασίλισσα, Βασιλεύω, συμβασιλεύω, Βασίλειος, Βασιλικός, E," 582.

18. Bultmann, "Christological Confession of the World Council of Churches," 281–84.

as both the "Kingdom of the Son of Man" (= Jesus) and the "Kingdom of the Father" (= God). Indeed, in the final analysis, his theology would require that the Kingdom of the Son of Man be also regarded as the Kingdom of the Father.

III

In light of the overall evidence, therefore, it appears that the distinction between the Kingdom of the Son of Man and the Kingdom of the Father and the identification of the former with the Christian church in the present age simply cannot be substantiated. Matthew speaks of *one* Kingdom, which he regards as still future (though imminent); he normally designates this Kingdom as "the Kingdom of Heaven" (literally, "the Kingdom of the Heavens") or simply "the Kingdom," and the key figure in his view of the Kingdom is not God, but the coming Son of Man.

Chapter 3

A Method for Identifying Redactional Passages in Matthew on Functional and Linguistic Grounds

The Purpose of the Paper

The purpose of this paper[1] is threefold: *first* and primarily, to propose a method for identifying on functional grounds, confirmed where possible by linguistic grounds, those passages in the Gospel of Matthew that can, with a reasonable degree of certainty, be regarded as redactional rather than traditional; *second*, to propose criteria for distinguishing the work of the final redactor from that of possible earlier redactors in the gospel; and *third*, to suggest some ways in which a careful application of the proposed method might contribute toward both the reconstruction of the redactional history of the gospel and the solution of the Synoptic Problem.

"A Method for Identifying Redactional Passages in Matthew on Functional and Linguistic Grounds." *CBQ* 39,1 (January 1977) 76–93. Copyright © 1977 Catholic Biblical Association of America. Reprinted with permission.

1. This paper has grown out of discussions, covering a period of more than a year, carried on within the Southwest Seminar on Gospel Studies, which meets periodically at Perkins School of Theology, Southern Methodist University, Dallas, Texas. Other members of the Seminar who have participated significantly in these discussions include William R. Farmer, Joseph B. Tyson, Philip L. Shuler, Dennis Tevis, and David B. Peabody, and they have contributed greatly to the development of the method to be proposed. Members of the Seminar cannot, of course, be held responsible for the final form of this paper.

Five points in this statement of purpose call for brief comment: (1) Matthew has been chosen quite arbitrarily as the object of study, but it is anticipated that the method to be developed here will also apply, *mutatis mutandis*, to Mark and Luke (and probably also to John).[2] (2) The term "redactional" refers to the more or less conscious and intentional activity of the person(s) directly involved in the overall process of collecting, selecting, adapting, revising, interpreting, arranging, linking, and perhaps expanding the primitive traditions about Jesus—a process that reached its culmination in the final composition of the gospels; redactional material, therefore, is material that derived from the hand of a redactor, editor, composer, or author and, as such, is to be distinguished from traditional material.[3] (3) This paper deals with the identification of *passages* (i.e., entire paragraphs, sentences, or, in some cases, clauses) that are redactional rather than traditional, not with the identification of redactional *elements* (e.g., single words, phrases, or clauses) within passages that are primarily traditional.[4] (4) It is important that functional categories (i.e.,

---

2. As will be discussed below, this paper does not presuppose any particular view regarding the chronological and literary relationships among the Synoptic Gospels, and, in the absence of such presupposition, the method for identifying redactional passages must be essentially the same for each of the gospels. Peabody, a graduate student at Southern Methodist University, has begun the task of applying the method proposed in this paper to the Gospel of Mark.

3. In one sense, of course, it could be said that the traditions about Jesus were redactional from the very beginning; that is, any relating of a tradition, whether oral or written, would necessarily have involved some elements of selection, interpretation, and arrangement and perhaps a significant degree of elimination, addition, and revision. Indeed, Rudolf Bultmann suggests that the work of the final redactor involved nothing new in principle, but only carried forward and completed what had already begun in the earliest period of oral transmission; see his *History of the Synoptic Tradition*, 321; cf. 6, 48, 88, 322. This paper, however, is not concerned with the more or less natural and spontaneous development of primitive traditions, particularly in their oral stage, but rather with the more intentional activity of a redactor or redactors who consciously worked with the traditional materials according to his/their own concerns and purposes.

4. These latter, no doubt, occur at many points in the gospel, and their identification is a quite legitimate and necessary undertaking if a study of

how a particular passage functions within the gospel as a whole or within a given section of the gospel) form the initial basis for identifying passages as redactional rather than traditional;[5] once a passage has been identified as redactional on functional grounds, it is then proper to examine that passage for the presence of verbal, syntactical, and ideational features that, if found elsewhere in the gospel, may suggest the hand of the redactor also at these other points. (5) Although it is conceivable that all redactional materials in Matthew are the work of a single redactor, allowance must be made for at least the possibility of more than one stratum of redactional material; if there was such earlier redactional work, it might have included redaction of separate sources later used by the final redactor or possibly even earlier redaction of most if not all of the gospel as it now stands.

Basic Presuppositions of the Paper

Any method for identifying redactional passages in a gospel is inevitably governed by certain basic presuppositions, and it is important that these presuppositions be made clear, at least insofar as they are conscious. *The first presupposition* of this paper is that, while some literary relationship, direct and/or indirect, almost certainly exists between Matthew and the other synoptic gospels, the exact nature and extent of this relationship are not clear. The Synoptic Problem, in other words, is yet to be solved. Thus, a satisfactory method for identifying redactional passages in Matthew cannot, at least for the present, be based upon any

---

all redactional materials in Matthew is the object, but the identification of redactional *passages* must come first and must, at least in large measure, form the basis for the later identification of redactional elements in passages that are primarily traditional.

5. One might even speak here simply of "common sense considerations," as has been done by William R. Farmer in an unpublished paper entitled, "Proposed Methodology for Redaction Criticism," 2: "Where are the passages in the Gospel being studied which most likely have been composed by the evangelist? That is, where, on the basis of common sense considerations, would we expect that the evangelist most probably has created transitions uniting materials that he has utilized in the composition of his Gospel?"

particular hypothesis regarding the origin of the gospel and its
literary and chronological relationships to Mark and Luke.[6]

The second presupposition is that, despite frequent and sometimes serious disagreements regarding details and implications,
the general insights of form criticism are valid. Specifically,
it is agreed that: (1) with the possible exception of the Passion
Narrative, the primitive traditions about Jesus originally circulated orally, primarily in the form of separate and distinct units
(pericopes) rather than as parts of a connected narrative; (2) most,
at least, of these pericopes can be classified according to more or
less easily recognizable categories or "forms" in the literature of
antiquity contemporaneous with the gospels; and (3) these pericopes, either in their original separate state or as combined in
earlier collections, form most of the basic source material for the
gospels.

The third presupposition is that, however difficult it may in actual practice be to separate them, there is, at least in principle, a

---

6. Most scholars, presupposing the priority of Mark and the validity
of the "Q" hypothesis, have assumed that redaction criticism of Matthew
and Luke is, at least in principle, relatively simple and that it is Mark
that poses the serious problem for the redaction critic; see, e.g., Stein,
"Methodology for Ascertaining a Markan Redaction History," 181–82;
Strecker, "Passion- and Resurrection Predictions in Mark's Gospel," 422;
and Perrin, *What Is Redaction Criticism?* 57. It is believed by such scholars
that redactional materials in both Matthew and Luke can most easily be
identified by noting, first, that which is unique to the particular gospel
under study and, second, the ways in which the author has deleted from,
added to, revised, or rearranged his alleged Markan and "Q" sources.
Only occasionally is it suggested that the redaction history of Matthew
be studied without dependence upon the Two-Source Hypotheses; see,
e.g., Thompson, "Composition of Mt 8:1–9:34," 366: "What is needed is
to study Matthew in terms of Matthew, as we tend to study John in terms
of John." It is clear, however, that Thompson does, in fact, presuppose
and, at times, depend upon the Two-Source Hypothesis in his analysis
of Matthew; in addition to other statements in the article referred to, cf.
his *Matthew's Advice to a Divided Community* and "Historical Perspective
in the Gospel of Matthew." Jack Dean Kingsbury appears to be moving
increasingly away from an uncritical dependence upon the Two-Source
Hypothesis in his studies of Matthew, and the results have been suggestive and exciting; he continues, however, to presuppose, from time
to time, the validity of the hypothesis; see, most recently, his *Matthew:
Structure, Christology, Kingdom.*

very real distinction between traditional and redactional materials in Matthew.[7] This does not necessarily imply, however, that the redactor was a mere "scissors-and-paste" craftsman who composed redactional passages simply to provide a framework for his source material, nor does it suggest that tradition and redaction in Matthew are easily separable.[8] Nevertheless, the distinction between tradition and redaction is not a meaningless distinction, nor is the attempt to separate the two foredoomed to failure.

The fourth presupposition is that, in the present study, the "burden of proof" must be assigned to the claim that particular passages are redactional rather than traditional or, stated differently, that the "benefit of the doubt" is to be given to the claim that particular passages are traditional.[9]

A Method for Identifying Redactional Passages

As has already been noted, a method for identifying redactional passages in Matthew must be developed without dependence upon any particular hypothesis regarding the chronological and

---

7. This would be true, even if the author of the gospel were an eyewitness and his source material consisted solely of his own recollections. His memories would then be the "tradition," and the "redaction" would be his particular presentation of those memories. Despite the undeniable fact that memory is always to some extent also interpretation, there remains, at least in principle, a distinction between the two, however tenuous the dividing line might be.

8. See, e.g., Thompson, "Historical Perspective in the Gospel of Matthew," 244 n. 2: "My basic methodological presupposition is that Matthew's editorial activity—whether it be called redaction or composition—was so thorough-going and proceeded out of such a unique vision that it transformed all that he touched." It is quite possible that, at times, tradition and redaction are so interwoven as to be practically inseparable. This does not appear to be case at all points in the gospel, however.

9. This would not be the case, of course, in a form critical study, where the purpose of the study would be to eliminate all *redactional* material in an attempt to work back through the *tradition* (perhaps in "quest of the historical Jesus"); there, the safer procedure would clearly be to treat all questionable materials as likely redactional or, in other words, to identify redactional materials on a *maximal* basis. Here, however, the purpose is the exact opposite: to eliminate all traditional materials in an attempt to identify that which is almost certainly redactional, and the safer procedure, therefore, is to treat all questionable materials as likely traditional and thus to identify the redactional materials on a *minimal* basis.

literary relationships among the gospels. This means that the use of Mark and "Q" as sources by the author of Matthew cannot be presupposed, and the problem at hand is, therefore, essentially the same as that confronting scholars who presuppose the two-source hypothesis when they attempt a study of the redaction history of Mark. Thus, it would appear that methodological principles that have been developed for the redactional study of Mark should now be applicable, *mutatis mutandis*, to Matthew. Georg Strecker observed almost a decade ago, however, that "the methodological problem of redaction criticism [of Mark] has not been worked out in a clear presentation and remains a matter of urgent importance,"[10] and, unfortunately, this observation is still in large measure true. A few scholars have attempted to provide criteria for distinguishing between tradition and redaction in Mark,[11] but, for the most part, these attempts are weakened by their presupposition of Markan priority and, most significantly, by their failure to establish any "control" as a starting point for a redactional study of the gospel. There must be some body of material, however small, that can be regarded with reasonable certainty

---

10. Strecker, "Passion- and Resurrection Predictions in Mark's Gospel," 423 n. 5.

11. Willi Marxsen, who, in 1956, produced his epochal work on Markan redaction criticism, articulated no comprehensive and consistent set of methodological principles for identifying redactional materials in the gospel; see his *Mark the Evangelist*. The first significant contribution came from Johannes Schreiber, who, in 1961, proposed four principles for determining the theology of Mark; see his "Die Christologie des Markusevangeliums," 154–55; cf. Schreiber, *Theologie des Vertrauens*, 1–21. For a somewhat similar set of principles, see Quesnell, *The Mind of Mark*, 46–57; and, for a summary of Quesnell's principles, see Weeden, *Mark — Traditions in Conflict*, 10 n. 5. For critical analyses and evaluations of Schreiber's principles, see, e.g., J. M. Robinson, "Problem of History in Mark, Reconsidered," 134–35; and, especially, Weeden, *Mark — Traditions in Conflict*, 5–11. Weeden's own methodological approach is set forth on pp. 11–19 of his book. More recently, Robert H. Stein has proposed a number of criteria for identifying the theological emphases of Mark; see his "Methodology for Ascertaining a Markan Redaction History," 181–98. He has also suggested certain questions that should be posed in determining whether a particular passage is redactional or traditional; see his "'Redaktionsgeschichtliche' Investigation."

as redactional rather than traditional, in which the characteristic vocabulary, style, themes, etc., of the redactor can initially be recognized. Otherwise, there is serious danger of circular argumentation, in which certain passages are regarded as redactional because they exhibit redactional features, but the features are regarded as redactional because they occur in redactional passages. The first task of redaction criticism, therefore, is the development of a method for identifying a "hard core" of redactional passages in the gospel under study; once this is done, the identification of additional passages as redactional can proceed in an "organic" manner.

The method here proposed for identifying redactional passages in Matthew involves a series of stages. *The first stage* is to isolate, on the basis of "common sense considerations," those passages (i.e., paragraphs, sentences, or, in some cases, clauses) in Matthew that, on "functional" grounds, can, with a reasonable degree of plausibility, be regarded as redactional, or at least potentially redactional, rather than traditional. Certain types of passages in the synoptic gospels are almost universally regarded as redactional by modern critical scholarship because of their function within a gospel as a whole or within some section of a gospel. Such passages include: (1) passages whose primary function appears to be that of explaining, interpreting, or otherwise commenting upon the accompanying material;[12] (2) passages whose primary function appears to be that of providing condensed summaries, not of specific or particular episodes or activities in the life of Jesus, but rather of some general feature of his preaching, teaching, healing, or fame;[13] (3) passages whose primary function appears to be that of foreshadowing or anticipating events that

---

12. A good example of this type of passage in Matthew would be the so-called "formula quotations" (Matt 1:22–23; 2:15b, 17–18, 23b; 4:14–16; 8:17; 12:17–21; 13:35; 21:4–5; 27:9–10), whose function clearly is that of explaining, interpreting, or commenting upon the narrative by relating it to certain passages in the Jewish scriptures.

13. Examples of such summaries are Matt 4:23–25; 9:35; 11:1b; and 15:30–31. It may be that such passages provide clues for understanding how the general framework of the gospel has been constructed.

are to be related later in the gospel;[14] (4) passages whose primary function appears to be that of introducing collections of narrative or sayings material, of providing transitions between such materials, or of providing generalizing conclusions to such materials;[15] and perhaps (5) passages whose primary function appears to be that of providing brief indications of time, place, or circumstances that are not intrinsic to the accompanying material.[16] At this first stage, no rigorously articulated criteria for identifying passages as redactional are applied, and different scholars will undoubtedly develop somewhat different lists of passages. There should, however, be a significant degree of agreement among the various lists, and, without too much difficulty, it should be possible to achieve a consensus regarding most passages. This list of passages, as finally compiled, may be termed a "Maximal List" or a list of potentially redactional passages.[17]

---

14. The so-called "passion predictions" (Matt 16:21; 17:22–23; 20:17–19; 26:1–2) can be regarded as an example of this type of passage. It may well be that this third type of passage, together with the second, provides a kind of "programmatic" framework for the entire gospel; see, e.g., Kingsbury, *Matthew: Structure, Christology, Kingdom*, 1–39.

15. Such passages have been designated as "seams" or "sutures"; see, respectively, Stein, "Methodology for Ascertaining a Markan Redaction History," 183–84, and his "'Redaktionsgeschichliche' Investigation"; and Farmer, "Proposed Methodology for Redaction Criticism," 2. On the importance of such passages for redaction criticism, see also, e.g., Best, *Temptation and Passion*, 23.

16. Rudolf Bultmann refers to such passages as "situation-indicators" and maintains that most are editorial constructions; see, e.g., his "Study of the Synoptic Gospels," 25–27. He suggests that such a situation indicator be regarded as a part of the tradition only if it is "necessarily presupposed by the subsequent story"; see Bultmann, *History of the Synoptic Tradition*, 338.

17. During the spring of 1974, Tyson and I compiled such a Maximal List. It contained the following passages: Matt 1:1, 17, 18a, 22–23; 2:1a, 5b–6, 15b, 17–18, 23b; 3:1–2, 3, 5–6, 7a, 13; 4:1, 11, 12–13, 14–16, 17, 18a, 21a, 23–25; 5:1–2; 7:28–29; 8:1, 5a, 14a, 16, 17, 18, 23, 27, 28a; 9:1, 8, 9a, 10–11, 14, 18a, 26, 27a, 28a, 30b, 31, 32a, 33b, 35, 36; 10:1–2a, 5a; 11:1, 2–3, 7a, 10, 20, 25a; 12:1–2, 9, 10, 14–16, 17–21, 25a, 38, 46; 13:1–3a, 10, 14–15, 18, 24a, 31a, 33a, 34–36, 45a, 47a, 51, 53–54a, 54b–56; 14:1, 13–14, 15, 22–23, 33, 34–36; 15:1–2, 7b–9, 10a, 12, 15, 21, 29, 30–31, 32a, 39; 16:1a, 1b, 4b, 5a, 12, 13a, 20, 21; 17:1, 5a, 9a, 13, 14a, 19, 22–23, 24a, 25b; 18:1a, 1b, 21; 19:1–2,

The second stage in identifying redactional passages in Matthew is to narrow the Maximal List on the basis of a rigorous application of the criterion that the burden of proof must be assigned to the claim that any given passage is redactional and thus to produce a "Minimal List" including only those passages that, on functional grounds, are regarded as *almost certainly* redactional rather than traditional. This means the elimination of all passages that even conceivably might be traditional including all sayings on the lips of Jesus or any other character,[18] as well as most, if not

---

3a, 3b, 13a, 13b, 23a; 20:17–19, 20a, 20b, 29; 21:1a, 4–5, 12a, 14, 16b, 17, 18, 23a, 23b, 45–46; 22:1, 15, 16–17, 22, 23a, 23b–28, 33, 34, 35–36, 41, 43–44, 46; 23:1; 24:1, 3a, 15b; 26:1–2, 3–5, 6, 16, 17a, 20, 26a, 30, 31b, 36a, 47a, 55a, 56a, 56b, 57–58; 27:1–2, 8, 9–10, 15–16, 18, 57a, 62a; 28:1a, 11a, 16b, 16–17. We were unable to reach agreement regarding 9:30b; I regarded it as redactional and attached it to 9:31; Tyson, however, saw it as an integral part of the preceding pericope, 9:27–30. In addition, Tyson had originally listed 2:22–23a; 8:28b; 14:3–5; 17:1b; 21:1b, 43–44 as redactional, and I had listed 15:10b; 19:24a; 21:33a, but all of these were removed after discussion between the two of us. One of the principal criteria employed by us was that materials not forming an integral part of the various "forms" identified by form criticism should be regarded as very likely redactional. Subsequent discussion with Farmer, however, suggested that a number of passages that we had included in our Maximal List as potentially redactional were, in fact, parts of the often overlooked form known as a *chreia* and thus should not be included in the list. Passages thus to be eliminated from the Maximal List are Matt 9:10–11, 14; 11:2–3; 12:1–2, 10, 38, 46; 13:10, 36, 54b–56; 14:1, 15; 15:1–2, 12, 15; 16:1; 17:19; 18:1, 21; 19:3, 13, 23a; 20:20; 21:18, 23b; 22:16–17, 23–28, 35–36, 41; 24:1; 27:15–16; 28:16–17. On the *chreia*, see, e.g., Farmer, *The Synoptic Problem: A Critical Analysis*, 266–70 and the literature there cited.

18. Some sayings passages in Matthew are almost certainly redactional (cf., e.g., the Fourth Gospel, where it is clear that many such passages are redactional). Nevertheless, the Minimal List must contain only those passages whose *primary functions* are *clearly* redactional, and such cannot, with certainty, be maintained regarding the sayings, because Jesus or some other character may have been reported in the tradition as saying something that served an explanatory, interpretive, anticipatory, etc., function. It is assumed that some of the sayings passages in the Maximal List may be returned to an expanded list at a later stage on linguistic grounds.

Of particular interest are the so-called "passion predictions" (Matt 16:21; 17:22–23; 20:17–19; 26:1–2), which are widely regarded as redac-

all, of the brief indications of time, place, or circumstances.[19] It is by no means claimed that the Minimal List thus produced will include *all* of the redactional passages in Matthew, nor is it claimed that all passages on the list will necessarily be the work of the same redactor. Nevertheless, the list will provide a hard core of almost certainly redactional passages.[20]

The third stage in identifying redactional passages in Matthew is to compile a list, in order of decreasing frequency, of all significant linguistic phenomena[21] that occur twice or more in the passages on the Minimal List, noting the specific passages in which

---

tional. All except the first of these, however, occur as sayings of Jesus and thus cannot, with a rigid application of the burden of proof criterion, be identified, on functional grounds alone, as certainly redactional. The first is in the form of indirect, not direct, discourse, and its form implies that it represents a summary of something that was to occur repeatedly; nevertheless, it cannot be established with certainty on functional grounds alone that 16:21 is redactional, particularly in light of the fact that it clearly forms an integral part of the larger pericope, 16:21–23.

19. Here, the question as to whether such "situation indicators" are "necessarily presupposed by the subsequent story" is relevant (see n. 16 above), Nevertheless, Bultmann's proposed criterion is not entirely satisfactory for at least two reasons: first, the criterion enables one to identify only material that is *potentially* redactional, not *certainly* so, because it claims to point only to the certainly traditional material; and, second, the criterion is not really trustworthy even for identifying the certainly traditional material, because it is quite possible that a redactor might have created a "situation indicator" precisely for the purpose of making more intelligible an otherwise more or less obscure tradition. Cf., e.g., Stein, "'Redaktionsgeschichtliche' Investigation," 77–78. Thus, in compiling a Minimal List, it is safer to omit all such "situation indicators." As in the case of sayings materials, however, it is quite possible that some such material may be returned, on linguistic grounds, to a later expanded list.

20. After discussion within the Southwest Seminar on Gospel Studies in 1974, I produced a Minimal List, containing the following passages: Matt 1:1, 17, 22–23; 2:15b, 17–18, 23b; 3:3; 4:14–16, 23–25; 5:1–2; 7:28–8:1; 8:17; 9:35; 10:1, 5a; 11:1; 12:17–21; 13:1–3a, 24a, 31a, 33a, 34–35, 53; 15:30–31; 19:1–2; 21:4–5; 22:1; 24:15b; 26:1; 27:8, 9–10; 28:15b.

21. Linguistic phenomena include individual words, phrases, and syntactical constructions. Judgments will obviously differ regarding what constitutes a *significant* linguistic phenomenon. "Significant" means something other than what is necessary, inevitable, ordinary, or commonplace. In some cases, a phenomenon may not appear to be "significant" until its recurrence in another passage is noted. Thus, the definition of "significant" must remain subject to continual revision.

each phenomenon occurs.[22] It is not necessarily the case that all such phenomena are redactional in origin, because a redactor might, either intentionally or unintentionally, reproduce in his own composition linguistic phenomena occurring in one or more of his sources. It can be claimed, however, that linguistic phenomena that occur in almost certainly redactional passages are more or less characteristic of the redactor.[23]

The fourth stage in identifying redactional passages in Matthew is to examine the passages that were on the Maximal List but were omitted from the Minimal List for the presence of the significant linguistic phenomena found twice or more in the passages on the Minimal List. Because the passages on the Maximal List have already been identified, on functional grounds, as at least potentially redactional, the presence in certain of these passages of significant linguistic phenomena from passages on the Minimal List (passages that, on functional grounds, have been identified as almost certainly redactional) suggests very strongly that the additional passages containing such phenomena are, in fact, also redactional.[24] Thus, while functional considerations must be regarded as primary in the identification of redactional passages,

---

22. The requirement that a phenomenon occur "twice or more" is somewhat arbitrary, to be sure. On the one hand, it could perhaps be argued that *all* significant linguistic phenomena occurring in the Minimal List be included, but this would raise the question as to precisely what constitutes a "linguistic phenomenon." On the other hand, it might be argued that two occurrences are not a sufficiently significant degree of recurrence. Any figure other than two, however, would be equally arbitrary. In general, one might argue as follows: The shorter the phrase or construction, the greater the number of occurrences required to constitute significant recurrence, and the longer the phrase or construction, the fewer the number of occurrences required to constitute significant recurrence. It is my judgment, however, that two occurrences are sufficient for the purposes of this paper.

23. Tevis, a graduate student at Southern Methodist University, has compiled a list of eleven significant linguistic phenomena occurring twice or more in the passages on the Minimal List. It should be noted, however, that his list includes only phrases or clauses, not single words or syntactical constructions. Thus, much more work needs to be done at this stage and at succeeding stages of the investigation.

24. If such a passage on the Maximal List contains more than one of the significant linguistic phenomena found in passages on the Minimal List,

linguistic considerations provide confirmatory evidence in some cases where functional considerations alone are not conclusive, and the greatest degree of certainty can be had when functional and linguistic considerations coincide.[25] At this fourth stage, then, a third or "Expanded List" is produced, consisting of those passages on the Minimal List plus those additional passages on the Maximal List that exhibit significant linguistic phenomena found twice or more in passages on the Minimal List.[26]

The fifth stage in identifying redactional passages in Matthew is to compile a list, in order of decreasing frequency, of all significant linguistic phenomena that occur twice or more in the passages on the new Expanded List, noting the specific passages in which each phenomenon occurs. This new list of phenomena, of course, will be cumulative, including the significant linguistic phenomena found at least twice in the passages on the Minimal List, but

---

this obviously increases still further the probability that the passage is, indeed, redactional. If a particular linguistic phenomenon is found only or primarily in passages that, on functional grounds, are regarded as almost certainly redactional (Minimal List) or as potentially redactional (Maximal List), this increases the probability both that the passages containing such phenomena are, in fact, redactional and that the phenomena themselves are redactional. One question, however, that must be answered satisfactorily if this stage, as well as other stages of the process, is to produce meaningful results is whether linguistic phenomena must be identical or merely similar and, if merely similar, just how similar.

25. Linguistic identity alone might be accounted for by mere coincidence or by assuming that the redactor intentionally or unconsciously reproduced linguistic phenomena that he found in a source.

26. Tevis has suggested that the following passages from the Maximal List be included in the Expanded List on the grounds that each contains one or more of the significant linguistic phenomena occurring twice or more in passages on the Minimal List: Matt 12:15; 13:54a; 21:14; 26:56a; and perhaps 14:13. It should again be noted, however, that Tevis' work is based solely upon recurring phrases and clauses, not single words or syntactical constructions, and that further study will undoubtedly disclose additional significant linguistic phenomena occurring twice or more in passages on the Minimal List and thus lead to additional passages on the Maximal List that should be included in the Expanded List. It is also possible that phenomena occurring only once in passages on the Minimal List but recurring twice or more in other passages on the Maximal List might be regarded as confirmatory evidence of redactional activity.

also including such phenomena that occur only once in the passages on the Minimal List but that now appear more than once in passages on the Expanded List, as well as some phenomena that did not occur at all in passages on the Minimal List but that now appear at least twice in other passages on the Expanded List.[27]

The sixth stage in identifying redactional passages in Matthew is to examine the remaining passages that were on the Maximal List but were omitted from the Minimal List and were not restored to the Expanded List for the presence of the significant linguistic phenomena found twice or more in the passages on the Expanded List. In this way, a fourth or "Further Expanded List" is produced, consisting of those passages on the Expanded List plus those additional passages on the Maximal List that exhibit significant linguistic phenomena found twice or more in passages on the Expanded List.

The seventh stage in identifying redactional passages in Matthew is to continue the process described in stages three through six as long as it produces results. The final list of passages thus produced (the "Final Expanded List") will contains passages that, on functional grounds confirmed where necessary by linguistic grounds, are regarded as almost certainly redactional rather than traditional, and the final list of significant linguistic phenomena thus produced will contain phenomena that are regarded as almost certainly characteristic of a redactor.[28]

---

27. Tevis found no additional significant linguistic phenomena occurring twice or more on the Expanded List, and thus stages five, six, and seven produced no results for him. The fragmentary character of his work has already been noted, however, and it is expected that further study will produce additional results.

28. Methodologically, the procedure thus far summarized is safer and more certain than if one were simply to begin with noting significant linguistic phenomena occurring twice or more in the passages on the Maximal List and assuming that passages containing such phenomena were redactional. The mere recurrence of significant linguistic phenomena is no guarantee that the passages containing the phenomena are redactional, even if, on functional grounds, the passages are regarded as *potentially* redactional. Such recurrence might be based upon mere coincidence, dependence upon a common source, or conscious or unconscious copying. When significant linguistic phenomena occurring twice

At the completion of the seven stages just proposed, the question must be raised as to whether it is now possible to move from the passages on the Final Expanded List and, on the basis of the recurring significant linguistic phenomena in these passages, to discover redactional materials in parts of Matthew not included in the Maximal List and perhaps to confirm the redactional character of passages on the Maximal List but not on the Final Expanded List. Specifically, can it legitimately be assumed that any passage in Matthew containing one or more of the significant linguistic phenomena found twice or more in passages on the Final Expanded List is redactional, and can recurring significant linguistic phenomena in such passages, in turn, become the basis for the identification of an increasingly larger body of redactional material throughout the gospel? It has already been argued that the mere recurrence of significant linguistic phenomena, even in passages that are identified on functional grounds as potentially redactional, is no guarantee that passages containing the phenomena are, in fact, redactional, unless the phenomena themselves have previously appeared in passages regarded as almost certainly redactional. Furthermore, it must be insisted that the occurrence of significant linguistic phenomena in passages that are

---

or more in passages that are almost certainly redactional (Minimal List) also appear in passages that, on functional grounds, are potentially redactional, however, the double evidence of function and linguistic phenomena justifies the conclusion that the latter passages are also almost certainly redactional. Thus, it is necessary to work from a "hard core" of almost certainly redactional passages (Minimal List) and progressively to enlarge the core on the basis of recurring linguistic phenomena until as many passages as possible have been included. Throughout the procedure, functional considerations remain primary, but, where functional considerations are not conclusive, then linguistic considerations provide confirmatory evidence. It is for this reason that the crucial distinction between Maximal List, on the one hand, and Minimal and Expanded Lists, on the other hand, must be maintained throughout. Unless a passage that, on functional grounds, is only *potentially* redactional (Maximal List) can be related linguistically to at least two passages that, on functional grounds supported at times by linguistic grounds, are almost *certainly* redactional (Minimal and Expanded Lists), it is not legitimate to claim that the *potentially* redactional passage is, in fact, almost *certainly* redactional.

not, on functional grounds, regarded as potentially redactional is not necessarily evidence that these passages are redactional, because occurrence of such phenomena might be based upon mere coincidence, dependence upon a common source, or conscious or unconscious copying from the tradition on the part of the redactor. Nevertheless, it might be possible to appeal to linguistic considerations in such a way as a basis for identifying a body of potentially redactional material outside the Maximal List (also perhaps including some passages on the Maximal List but not in the Final Expanded List)[29] and then to develop additional criteria for confirming the redactional character of some or all of this material.[30] It would be necessary to work with extreme caution,

---

29. Such an identification of potentially redactional material might include the following stages: (1) Search the remainder of the gospel, including any passages on the Maximal List that were omitted from the Minimal List and not restored on the Final Expanded List, for the presence of any significant linguistic phenomena found twice or more in passages on the Final Expanded List, and compile a composite list, consisting of all passages on the Final Expanded List plus those additional passages elsewhere in Matthew that exhibit significant linguistic phenomena found twice or more in passages on the Final Expanded List. (2) Compile a list, in order of decreasing frequency, of all significant linguistic phenomena occurring twice or more in passages on the list produced in stage 1, noting the specific passages in which each phenomenon occurs. (3) Continue the process described in stages 1 and 2 as long as it produces results. Working along these lines, Tevis has suggested the presence of significant linguistic phenomena from the Final Expanded List in the following passages outside the Maximal List: Matt 11:23; 12:22; and 17:27. He was not able to produce any results in stages 2 and 3 above, but, again, the fragmentary character of his work should be noted.

30. William R. Farmer has suggested three criteria for identifying significant words, phrases, and syntactical constructions that can, with a reasonable degree of certainty, be regarded as redactional, and these criteria should be useful in confirming the redactional character of linguistic phenomena that have been identified as potentially redactional. He labels the criteria, respectively, "recurrence," "distribution," and "interlacing." Combining the three criteria, it might be argued: The greater the number of occurrences of a particular linguistic phenomenon in Matthew, the greater the distribution of that phenomenon in different sections and in different types of sections of Matthew, and the more frequently a significant linguistic phenomenon is found in the same immediate context as another significant linguistic phenomenon that has been identified as

however, and the degree of certainty to be achieved would surely be considerably less than in those cases where functional considerations alone are decisive or where functional considerations are confirmed by linguistic considerations. Furthermore, the materials thus identified as redactional would, in many instances, probably consist of redactional elements within essentially or primarily traditional passages rather than of passages that themselves are essentially or primarily redactional. For these reasons, this paper will not attempt to extend its proposed method to passages outside the Maximal List.

It is not claimed that the method, as now proposed, will identify all of the redactional passages in Matthew, but, if employed carefully and imaginatively, it should produce a rather considerable list of passages that, on functional and linguistic grounds, can be regarded as almost certainly redactional rather than traditional.[31]

Distinguishing Final Redaction from Earlier Redaction

While all of the passages on the Final Expanded List can be regarded as almost certainly redactional, it can by no means be assumed that all of them are the work of the final redactor of the gospel; indeed, this cannot even be assumed for the passages on

---

either almost certainly redactional or potentially redactional, the greater the probability that the phenomenon in question is redactional. No doubt, different scholars will disagree regarding the exact requirements for satisfying these three criteria and regarding whether it is necessary that a particular phenomenon satisfy all three criteria. It might be argued, for example, that an abundance of interlacing would outweigh a paucity of distribution, and *vice versa*, but that a significant degree of recurrence would be essential in either case. On the criteria, see Farmer, "Proposed Methodology for Redaction Criticism," 1–2, 3; for a somewhat different use of the criteria, see below in this paper.

31. This is not to say, of course, that a redactional passage might not contain some traditional elements, but only that the passage, as it now stands, is essentially the composition of a redactor, whatever sources he may have used.

the Minimal List.[32] It may well be the case that there are multiple "strata" of redactional materials in Matthew and that these strata are at times juxtaposed in a given passage[33] or that a later redactor has reworked material from an earlier redactor so that the resulting passage combines redactional characteristics of both.[34] If, however, the method proposed above is to contribute significantly to the reconstruction of the redactional history of the gospel and/or to the solution of the Synoptic Problem, it is important that, if possible, criteria be developed for distinguishing among the various possible strata of redaction and determining which comes from the hand of the final redactor.

As has already been noted, William R. Farmer has proposed three linguistic criteria for identifying the work of the final redactor: recurrence, distribution, and interlacing.[35] These three criteria can be paraphrased as follows: (1) The more frequently a significant linguistic phenomenon recurs in a particular gospel, the more likely it is that the phenomenon comes from the hand of the final redactor, and this likelihood is increased as the extent of the similarity increases. (2) The more widely distributed a significant linguistic phenomenon is throughout a particular gospel, especially if it is found in different sections and in different types of sections of the gospel, the more likely it is that the phenomenon comes from the hand of the final redactor. (3) The more frequently two or more significant linguistic phenomena are found in the same immediate context, the more likely it is that the phenomena come from the hand of the final redactor.

---

32. The so-called "formula quotations," for example, which are included in the Minimal List, are regarded by some scholars as deriving from a source used by the final redactor; see, e.g., Kilpatrick, *Origins of the Gospel according to St. Matthew*, 57.

33. It is possible, for example, that Matt 4:23 derives from a different redactor than does 4:24–25 (it is even possible that 4:24 and 4:25 come from two different redactors).

34. This latter has almost certainly occurred, e.g., in the case of obviously redactional passages in one gospel that are paralleled by obviously redactional passages in another gospel; cf., e.g., Matt 4:23; Mark 1:39; Luke 4:44.

35. See n. 30 above.

These linguistic criteria are obviously helpful, but they are not conclusive in identifying the work of the final redactor for the following reasons: (1) It is quite possible that the final redactor may have employed one or more sources, each with its own redactional characteristics, which he distributed widely throughout his gospel[36] or that large sections of Matthew or even the bulk of the present gospel may have undergone redaction at the hands of one or more earlier redactors; in such case, a linguistic phenomenon might very well satisfy the criteria of recurrence and distribution without having come from the hand of the final redactor. (2) The criterion of interlacing, while it may be helpful in identifying two or more passages from the same redactional hand, cannot serve as a basis for determining whether this hand is that of the final redactor. (3) As has already been pointed out, it is quite possible that different redactional strata may be juxtaposed or interwoven within a single passage or in adjoining passages; in such cases, the criterion of interlacing becomes highly problematic.[37] (4) It is pos-

---

36. As an example, if it were the case that Mark served as a source for Matthew, then one would normally expect to find Markan redactional phenomena distributed widely throughout many sections of Matthew. Similarly, if Matthew were a source for Mark, Matthean redactional phenomena might well be distributed throughout Mark.

37. Of particular interest is Matt 4:23–25, although certain other passages, such as 7:28–8:1 and 19:1–2 present similar problems. If 4:23–25 is treated as a *single* redactional unit, it contains five of the eleven significant linguistic phenomena identified by Dennis Tevis as occurring twice or more in the passages on the Minimal List, and, through interlacing, it can be related directly to perhaps as many as eight other passages on the Minimal List (4:15; 8:1; 9:35; 10:1; 15:30; 19:1–2; and perhaps 11:1; 13:2). If, however, each of the three verses of Matt 4:23–25 is treated as a *separate* redactional unit, then the following picture emerges: v. 23 contains two of the phenomena and can be related to two or perhaps three other passages on the Minimal List (9:35; 10:1; and perhaps 11:1); v. 24 contains one of the phenomena and can be related to two other passages on the Minimal List (15:30; 19:2); and v. 25 contains two of the phenomena and can be related to three or perhaps as many as five other passages on the Minimal List (4:15; 8:1; 19:1–2; and perhaps 13:2; 15:30). Vv. 24 and 25 can, through interlacing, be related to each other, because both are also related to 19:2 and perhaps 15:30.

sible that a very high degree of interlacing between two passages may indicate not the presence of the same redactional hand, but rather that a later redactor has copied from an earlier redactor.[38] (5) If Farmer's linguistic criteria are to be used fruitfully, meaningful decisions must be made regarding the degree and extent of similarity that are necessary between linguistic phenomena in order to constitute "recurrence,"[39] how many instances of interlacing are necessary in order to guarantee with a reasonable degree of probability that two passages come from the same redactor,[40] and exactly what is meant by "the same immediate context."[41]

In light of these problems and limitations related to the linguistic criteria, it now becomes necessary to propose a fourth criterion for distinguishing the work of the final redactor from that of possible earlier redactors—the criterion of function. Here

---

38. Matt 4:23 and 9:35, for example, read almost *verbatim* the same. On the face of it, it would appear that the two passages come from the same hand. It is possible, however, that a later redactor has copied from an earlier redactor, introducing minor changes to suit his own purposes or to reflect his own style.

39. Cf., e.g., Matt 4:25; 8:1; 19:2; 15:30; also Matt 27:8; 28:15.

40. Tevis has suggested that when a pair of significant linguistic phenomena is interlaced in at least two different redactional passages, this should be adequate to show that the phenomena come from the same redactor and, presumably, that the passages containing the interlaced phenomena also come from the same redactor. By this criterion, for example, Matt 4:25 and 19:1–2 (assuming the redactional unity of 19:1–2) come from the same redactor, because they share two significant linguistic phenomena. If, on the one hand, 4:24–25 is regarded as a redactional unit, then it also shares with 19:1–2 an additional phenomenon. If, on the other hand, neither 4:24–25 nor 19:1–2 is regarded as a redactional unit and each verse is treated as a separate unit, then there is no double interlacing to relate the passages.

41. Tevis points out that, in some cases, the Greek sentence appears to work quite well as the basic unit but that, in other cases, the Greek sentence may include material that has not been identified as (even potentially) redactional (e.g., Matt 5:1–3; 13:24, 31, 33). At times, moreover, "the same immediate context" appears clearly to include more than one sentence. My own proposal would be that as much of the immediate context be used as has previously been identified as redactional; this might be as little as a single clause or as much as an entire paragraph

again, as in the case of the initial identification of potentially redactional passages in the gospel, functional considerations are to
be regarded as primary, with the linguistic considerations providing confirmatory evidence in cases where functional considerations are inconclusive and the greatest degree of certainty being
reached when functional and linguistic considerations coincide.
This criterion of function can be stated as follows: Where it can be
shown that a passage already identified as redactional somehow
provides a key to the literary structure of the gospel as a whole,
then it can be assumed that this passage, at least in its present
form, is potentially the work of the final redactor. A judgment regarding literary structure, however, requires a careful study of the
entire gospel as a literary unit, and, if experience to date is any indicator, scholarly opinions will continue to differ rather widely.[42]
Furthermore, it is possible that the final redactor may, in some
cases, have used passages that had been composed by an earlier
redactor to indicate major divisions of his gospel. For these reasons, the three linguistic criteria proposed by Farmer should now
be used both to test and, hopefully, to confirm the results achieved
on the basis of functional considerations and, once a reasonable
degree of certainty has been reached here, to discover additional
passages in the gospel that can be attributed to the final redactor.

In short, the criteria for distinguishing the work of the final redactor from that of possible earlier redactors can be combined and
stated as follows: When it can be shown that a passage already
identified as redactional somehow provides a key to the literary
structure of the gospel as a whole, then it can be assumed that this
passage, at least in its present form, is potentially the work of the
final redactor; when such a passage contains significant linguistic
phenomena that recur and are widely distributed throughout the
gospel and that are mutually interlaced, then it can be assumed
that this passage, at least in its present form, is almost certainly
the work of the final redactor; and, on the basis of the criteria of
recurrence, distribution, and interlacing of these significant lin-

---

42. See, e.g., Kingsbury, *Matthew: Structure, Christology, Kingdom*, 1–7,
and the literature there cited.

guistic phenomena, additional passages composed by the final redactor can then be sought throughout the gospel.[43]

Use of the Method
for Further Study

Once a significant number of almost certainly redactional passages has been identified in the gospel and a decision has been made regarding which of these passages come from the hand of the final redactor, it should then be possible—on the basis of recurrence, distribution, and interlacing of significant linguistic phenomena in the remaining passages identified as redactional, as well as distribution and function of the passages themselves—to distinguish other distinct strata of redaction (if, indeed, such other strata exist) and perhaps even to reach some judgment as to the relative ages of these strata and/or the portions of the gospel related to each stratum. A careful study of the linguistic and ideational characteristics of each stratum would, of course, constitute a most valuable contribution toward reconstructing the redactional history of the gospel under consideration and the development of early Christianity as a whole.[44]

It is also anticipated that the method proposed for identifying redactional passages in Matthew will aid in solving the Synoptic Problem. Once the method has been applied, in turn, to each of the synoptic gospels (or perhaps initially only to Matthew and Mark, as it is almost unanimously agreed that one or the other of these two is the earliest of the synoptics), and both passages and significant linguistic phenomena from the hand of the final redactor of each gospel have been identified, it should then be possible to make some judgment regarding the literary dependency of one gospel upon another on the basis of the following principle: The

---

43. It may even be possible thus to discover additional materials from the final redactor that were not included in the Final Expanded List or even in the Maximal List (i.e., passages that, on functional grounds, were not identified as even potentially redactional).

44. As has been pointed out, it is assumed that the method proposed in this paper is also applicable to the other gospels, and, indeed, Peabody has begun the task of applying the method to the Gospel of Mark.

appearance in one gospel of significant linguistic phenomena that are characteristic of the final redactor of another gospel suggests that the latter gospel may have served as a source for the former, provided that the phenomena either are in some way foreign to or inconsistent with the recognizable linguistic characteristics of the former gospel, they appear to be somehow "out of place" in the former gospel, or they appear in the former gospel in more or less distorted form.[45]

If, for some reason, it should prove impossible to distinguish final redaction from possible earlier redaction as suggested above, it is, nevertheless, still possible that some progress can be made toward solving the Synoptic Problem, although only in a somewhat negative manner. The problem can be illustrated as follows: If, on the one hand, significant redactional linguistic phenomena that are characteristic of *the final redactor* of Gospel A appear in Gospel B in a manner that is judged to be foreign, inconsistent, out of place, or distorted, then two possibilities emerge: either (1) Gospel B used Gospel A as a source or (2) Gospel B used a source that, either directly or indirectly, used Gospel A as a source. In either case, however, it is clear that there is literary dependency, either directly or indirectly, of Gospel B upon Gospel A. If, on the other hand, significant redactional linguistic phenomena that are characteristic of *an earlier redactor* of Gospel A (or of parts of Gospel A) appear in Gospel B in a manner that is judged to be foreign, inconsistent, out of place, or distorted, then three possibilities emerge: either (1) Gospel B used Gospel A as a source; (2) Gospel B used a source that, either directly or indirectly, used Gospel A as a source; or (3) Gospel A and Gospel B both used, either directly or indirectly, a common source. Here, is clear that Gospel A is *not* literarily dependent upon Gospel B, but it is not necessarily the case that Gospel B *is* literarily dependent, either directly or indirectly, upon Gospel A, because Gospel A and Gospel B may have both been dependent, either directly or indirectly, upon a common source. Thus, unless material in Gospel A can be identified

---

45. Cf., e.g., Farmer, "Proposed Methodology for Redaction Criticism," 4; and Cope, "Synoptic Problem in the Light of Redaction Criticism," 1.

as deriving from the hand of *the final redactor* of that gospel, such material cannot be used to show that Gospel B is dependent, either directly or indirectly, upon Gospel A. Nevertheless, it should be possible to show that Gospel A is *not* dependent, either directly or indirectly, upon Gospel B, and such a demonstration would represent highly significant progress toward the solution of the Synoptic Problem.

It may very well be the case that apparently contradictory evidence will emerge from an examination of particular passages or sections of the gospels; thus, it must be emphasized that any decision regarding literary dependency must be made only after and upon the basis of a thorough application of the method proposed in this paper to each of the gospels as a whole and a careful and complete comparison of the results.

Chapter 4

The Lukan
Nativity Story
and Isaiah 7:14

Some Additional Evidence for Intertextuality

The influence of Isa 7:14 on the Matthean portrayal of Mary as a
"virgin" (παρθένος) prior to the conception and birth of Jesus is
unmistakable.[1] In Matt 1:21, the angel announces to Joseph that
Mary "will bear a son and you will call his name Jesus" (τέξεται
... υἱὸν καὶ καλέσεις τὸ ὄνομα αὐτοῦ Ἰησοῦς), and the wording
of this announcement is almost identical to that of the latter part
of Isa 7:14 (LXX): "Behold, the virgin will conceive and will bear
a son, and you will call his name Emmanuel" (ἰδοὺ ἡ παρθένος
ἐν γαστρὶ ἕξει καὶ τέξεται υἱὸν καὶ καλέσεις τὸ ὄνομα αὐτοῦ

---

1. Robert J. Miller (*Born Divine*, 191–92) suggests that the author of
Matthew probably understood παρθένος in Isa 7:14b to mean "young
woman" rather than "virgin" (see the entire discussion, pp. 189–206).
Matt 1:18 specifies, however, that Mary became pregnant *before* she and
Joseph "came together" (πρὶν ἢ συνελθεῖν αὐτούς). In addition, v. 16
identifies Joseph not as the father of Jesus but rather as "the husband of
Mary, of whom Jesus was born, who is called Christ" (τὸν ἄνδρα Μαρίας
ἐξ ἧς ἐγεννήθη Ἰησοῦς ὁ λεγόμενος χριστός). Finally, v. 19 indicates
that Joseph was concerned lest Mary "be made an example of" (μὴ θέλων
αὐτὴν δειγματίσαι)—i.e., that she be "exposed" or "disgraced" or perhaps even stoned to death for engaging in illicit sex. All of this indicates
that the author of Matthew did not regard Joseph as the father of Jesus.
Thus, the only alternative to a virginal conception would be illegitimacy,
but the author would appear to rule this out by stating in both v. 18 and
v. 20 that Mary became pregnant "of the Holy Spirit" (ἐκ πνεύματος
ἁγίου).

Ἐμμανουήλ).² Then, vv. 22–23 state explicitly that Jesus' conception and approaching birth constitute a fulfillment of "what the Lord has spoken through the prophet" and quote Isa 7:14b almost *verbatim*: "Behold, the virgin will conceive and will bear a son and they will call his name Emmanuel" (ἰδοὺ ἡ παρθένος ἐν γαστρὶ ἕξει καὶ τέξεται υἱὸν καὶ καλέσουσιν τὸ ὄνομα αὐτοῦ Ἐμμανουήλ).³ Thus, it is clear that at least one early Christian writer saw a connection between Isa 7:14 and the conception and birth of Jesus.

The Lukan Nativity Story also portrays Mary as a "virgin" (παρθένος) prior to the conception and birth of Jesus,⁴ but it makes no explicit reference to Isa 7:14. Nevertheless, some scholars have insisted that the Lukan narrative was also influenced by the wording of Isa 7:14 and its immediate context.⁵ Discussion has focused primarily on the Annunciation (Luke 1:26–38) with attention to the striking verbal parallels between Luke 1:31 and the LXX version of Isa 7:14b. The former reads: "And behold, you will conceive and you will bear a son and you will call his name Jesus" (καὶ ἰδοὺ συλλήμψῃ ἐν γαστρὶ καὶ τέξῃ υἱὸν καὶ καλέσεις

---

2. The only differences between Isa 7:14b and Matt 1:21 are: (1) the subject is "the virgin" (ἡ παρθένος) in Isa 7:14b and "Mary" (Μαρίας) in Matt 1:21, (2) Matt 7:21 omits the ἰδοὺ … ἐν γαστρὶ ἕξει that appears in Isa 7:14b, (3) Isa 7:14b has καὶ τέξεται while Matt 1:21 has τέξεται δέ, (4) Isa 7:14b has Ἐμμανουήλ while Matt 1:21 has Ἰησοῦν, and (5) Matt 1:21 adds the words, αὐτὸς γὰρ σώσει τὸν λαὸν αὐτοῦ ἀπὸ τῶν ἁμαρτιῶν αὐτῶν.

3. The only difference is that Isa 7:14b has καλέσεις while Matt 1:23 has καλέσουσιν. A few witnesses, including D, read καλέσεις at Matt 1:23, but this is clearly an assimilation to the reading in Isaiah. It is also true, of course, that Matthew adds, ὅ ἐστιν μεθερμηνευόμενον μεθ᾽ ἡμῶν ὁ Θεός.

4. Luke 1:27; cf. also vv. 34–35.

5. Speaking specifically of Luke 2:1–20 but in words that would be equally applicable to the Lukan Nativity Story as a whole, Charles H. Giblin ("Reflections on the Sign of the Manger," 89) observes that "Luke's citations [of Old Testament texts] are not explicit, but are in the nature of contacts, reminiscences." According to Giblin, such contacts are to be established primarily by looking for "key terms" that are shared by a Lukan and an Old Testament text.

τὸ ὄνομα αὐτοῦ ᾽Ιησοῦν). The latter reads: "Behold, the virgin will conceive and will bear a son and you will call his name Emmanuel" (ἰδοὺ ἡ παρθένος ἐν γαστρὶ ἕξει καὶ τέξεται υἱὸν καὶ καλέσεις τὸ ὄνομα αὐτοῦ ᾽Εμμανουήλ). As the bold type indicates, ten of Luke's fourteen and Isaiah's fifteen words are identical, and an eleventh is simply a different form of the same verb.[6] Moreover, these eleven words appear in exactly the same sequence in Isa 7:14b and Luke 1:31. Other parallels between the Lukan Annunciation Story and the LXX version of Isa 7:14 and its immediate context are: (1) in Luke 1:27, Mary is twice called a "virgin" (παρθένος), and Isa 7:14 speaks of a "virgin" (παρθένος); (2) in Luke 1:27, Joseph is described as "of the house of David" (ἐξ οἴκου Δαυίδ), and Isa 7.13 addresses the "house of David" (οἶκος Δαυίδ); (3) in Luke 1:28, the angel speaks of "the Lord" (ὁ κύριος), and Isa 7:10–11 refers twice to "Lord" (κύριος and κυρίου); and (4) both Luke 1:33 and Isa 7:17 have the phrase, "over the house" (ἐπὶ τὸν οἶκον). For many scholars, these parallels provide clear evidence that the wording of the Lukan Annunciation was influenced by that of Isa 7:14 and its immediate context.[7]

Joseph A. Fitzmyer observes, however, that "each one of [the parallel] phrases occurs elsewhere in the OT … and sometimes with great frequency."[8] In addition, he suggests that "the description of Mary in [Luke] 1:27 is far closer to Deut 22:23 than to Isa 7:14." It is Fitymyer's judgment, therefore, that, "[a]side from superficial parallels in the Greek wording of Lk 1:26–38 and the LXX of Is 7:10–17, there is not a shred of evidence that Luke has fashioned his annunciation in dependence on Isaiah."[9] Similarly,

---

6. τέξῃ in Luke and τέξεται in Isaiah (both from τίκτειν).

7. E.g., Voss, *Christologie der lukanischen Schriften in Grundzügen*, 65–81; Schürmann, *Das Lukasevangelium*, 58–63; Vögtle, *Das Evangelium und die Evangelien*, 46; Schneider, *Das Evangelium nach Lukas*, 1:49.

8. Indeed, Luke 1:31 in its entirety is strikingly similar to the LXX version of Gen 16:11 (identical words, phrases, and clauses appear in bold type): ἰδοὺ σὺ ἐν γαστρὶ ἔχεις καὶ τέξῃ υἱὸν καὶ καλέσεις τὸ ὄνομα αὐτοῦ ᾽Ισμαήλ; see also, e.g., Gen 17:19; Judg 13:3, 5, 7.

9. Fitzmyer, *Gospel according to Luke (I–IX)*, 336, 568 n. 89.

Frans Neirynck denies that the Annunciation Story reflects Isa 7:14 and its immediate context.[10] Thus, Raymond E. Brown concludes that "it is not clear to what extent, if at all, Isa 7:14 entered into Luke's description of the virginal conception."[11]

The influence of Isa 7:14 and its immediate context is also occasionally seen in Luke 2:34. Here, Simeon refers to the infant Jesus as "a sign that is spoken against" (σημεῖον ἀντιλεγόμενον). The parallels are (a) that both Luke 2:34 and Isa 7:14 refer to a "sign" (σημεῖον), (b) that both associate the "sign" (σημεῖον) with an infant (newborn in Luke and shortly to be born in Isaiah), and (c) that both in Luke 2:34 and in the material immediately following Isa 7:14 "the sign has more of a negative than a positive result."[12] As Brown observes, however, it is at least possible that Luke's use of σημεῖον echoes not Hebrew *'ot*, which appears in Isa 7:14 and elsewhere, but rather *nēs*, which means "standard" or "banner" and is also translated in the LXX as σημεῖον.[13] Moreover, Isa 8:18 also refers to children as "signs" (σημεῖα).[14] Thus, it is unclear whether Simeon's reference to the infant Jesus as σημεῖον ἀντιλεγόμενον reflects the influence of Isa 7:14 and its immediate context.

In short, although my own judgment is that both the Lukan Annunciation and Simeon's reference to Jesus as a "sign that is spoken against" (σημεῖον ἀντιλεγόμενον) most likely *do* reflect the influence of Isa 7:14 and its immediate context, there is no scholarly consensus to this effect. Moreover, it is by no means my intention to enter directly into the debate regarding either of these Lukan passages. Rather, I propose to point out evidence for the influence of Isa 7:14 and its immediate context *elsewhere* in the Lukan Nativity Story—namely, in the angelic proclamation

---

10. Neirynck, *L'Évangile de Noël selon S. Luc*, 30.

11. Brown, *Birth of the Messiah*, 149 n. 50.

12. Brown, *Birth of the Messiah*, 461.

13. Brown, *Birth of the Messiah*, 461 n. 49; see, e.g., Isa 11:10–12.

14. Note, however, that (a) the reference is to *children* in the plural, (b) there is no specific mention of their *birth*, and (c) they are called "signs and wonders" (σημεῖα καὶ τέρατα), not simply "signs" (σημεῖα).

to the shepherds (Luke 2:10–12).[15] If such evidence is convincing, this may, in turn, strengthen the case for similar influence in the Lukan Annunciation and Simeon's reference to the infant Jesus as σημεῖον.

Because the Third Evangelist makes no *explicit* reference to Isa 7:14 and its immediate context, it is impossible to *prove* that the angelic proclamation to the shepherds (Luke 2:10–12) was influenced by the material in Isaiah. Nevertheless, there is in my judgment sufficient evidence to make this highly probable. The evidence consists of a number of specific parallels—formal, substantive, and verbal—between the two passages. In addition, it is at least possible that two verbal parallels between Luke 2:14 (the angelic chorus immediately following the proclamation) and Isa 7:11, 13 are relevant in terms of demonstrating such influence. Of particular significance is the fact that some of the parallels to be noted appear to link Luke 2:10–12 to Isa 7:14 and its immediate context *but not to any other passage in the LXX.*

Formal Parallels between
Luke 2:10–12 and
Isaiah 7:13–14

There are three formal parallels between Luke 2:10–12 and Isa 7:13–14:

> 1. The speaker in Isa 7:13–14 is presumably "the Lord"[16] and in Luke 2:10–12 it is "a messenger of the Lord."[17] Thus, in terms of literary genre, both passages can be termed "a message or oracle from the Lord."

---

15. Various scholars have suggested that Luke 2:10–12 was influenced by such passages as Exod 3:12; 1 Sam 2:34; 10:1b; 14:10; 2 Kgs 19:29; 20:9; Isa 37:30; 38:7; and Jer 44 [LXX 51]:29. So far as I can ascertain, however, no one has noted the possible influence of Isa 7:14.

16. Cf. κύριος in v. 10. It is conceivable that the speaker is simply the prophet, but if so he clearly is speaking in the name of and on behalf of the Lord.

17. Ἄγγελος κυρίου (v. 9); cf. ὁ ἄγγελος in v. 10 and τῷ ἀγγέλῳ in v. 13.

2. Isa 7:14 announces the imminent birth of a son (υἱός)
and Luke 2:10–12 announces the recent birth of a child
(βρέφος). Thus, both passages are "birth announcements
from the Lord."

3. Unlike other such "birth announcements" in the LXX,
all of which are addressed either to the father or to the
mother of the child,[18] Isa 7:14 is addressed to people *other*
than the parents—namely, the "house of David"[19]—and
Luke 2:10–12 is addressed to people *other* than the parents
of the child—namely, the shepherds. In this respect, therefore, Luke 2:10–12 is akin to Isa 7:14 but differs from all
other such "birth announcements" in the LXX.

In short, the first and second formal parallels between Luke 2:10–
12 and Isa 7:13–14 link the former passage to the latter, and the
third formal parallel links the former passage *uniquely* to the latter.

Substantive Parallel between
Luke 2:10–12 and Isaiah 7:14

Both Isa 7:14 and Luke 2:10–12 associate the birth of a child—either imminent or recent—with a "sign" (σημεῖον).[20] To be sure,

---

18. The closest parallels to Isa 7:14b are Gen 16:11 (ἰδοὺ σὺ ἐν γαστρὶ
ἔχεις καὶ τέξῃ υἱὸν καὶ καλέσεις τὸ ὄνομα αὐτοῦ Ἰσμαήλ) and Gen
17:19 (ἰδοὺ Σάρρα ἡ γυνή σου τέξεταί σοι υἱὸν καὶ καλέσεις τὸ ὄνομα
αὐτοῦ Ἰσαάκ). The former is addressed to Hagar (the mother) and the
latter to Abraham (the father). Cf. also Judg 13:3, 5, 7.

19. Isa 7:10–11 is addressed to Ahab the King, and it is Ahab who responds in v. 12. V. 13, however, is addressed to "house of David" (οἶκος
Δαυίδ), and both the pronoun (ὑμῖν) and the verb (παρέχετε) are plural.
V. 14 is somewhat confusing because the pronoun (ὑμῖν) is plural but the
verb (καλέσεις) is singular.

20. Although σημεῖον appears nine times elsewhere in the Third
Gospel (Luke 11:16, 29 (*tris*), 30; 21:7, 11, 25; 23:8), only in 2:12 and in
2:34—both of which are part of the Nativity Story—is it associated with
the infant Jesus or with Jesus at all. Moreover, as has already been noted,
Simeon's reference to Jesus (called παιδίον in v. 27) as "a sign that is spoken against" (σημεῖον ἀτιλεγόμενον) is sometimes seen as reflecting
σημεῖον in Isa 7:14 and material in the verses that follow.

Charles H. Giblin insists that the "sign" in Luke 2:12 is not the *birth* of the child *per se* but rather *the circumstances in which the shepherds will find the child*: i.e., ἐσπαργανωμένον καὶ κείμενον ἐν φάτνῃ.[21] If so, then Luke 2:12 might appear to differ from Isa 7:14 in this respect. One might argue, however, that the "sign" in Isa 7:14 is not the *birth* of the child *per se* but rather *the fact that the child is to be called "Emmanuel."* If so, then the two passages agree in identifying the "sign" with something other than the actual *birth* of the child. In any event, however, both Isa 7:14 and Luke 2:10–12 associate the "sign," either directly or indirectly, with the birth of a child. This, however, is *not* the case elsewhere in the LXX.[22] Thus, the association of "sign" and "birth" links Luke 2:10–12 to Isa 7:14 *and to no other passage in the LXX.*

Verbal Parallels
between Luke 2:10–12
and Isaiah 7:13–14

There are six verbal parallels between Luke 2:10–12 and Isa 7:13–14:

1. The vocabulary of Luke 2:10–12 is remarkably similar to that of Isa 7:13–14—more similar, in fact, than to that of any other passage in the LXX. Luke 2:10–12 contains a total of forty-two words. Of these forty-two words, seventeen (i.e., 40 percent) also appear in Isa 7:13–14,[23] and two others are closely approximated.[24] This comes to a total of nineteen of the forty-two words in Luke 2:10–12 (i.e., 45 percent) that can be linked to the vocabulary of Isa

---

21. Giblin, "Reflections on the Sign of the Manger," 95–97.

22. The closest parallel is Isa 8:18, where the prophet speaks of his children as "signs and wonders" (σημεῖα καὶ τέρατα). As indicated above, however (n. 14), the reference here is to *children* in the plural, there is no specific mention of their *birth*, and they are called "signs and wonders" (σημεῖα καὶ τέρατα), not simply "signs" (σημεῖα).

23. Καί (three times in Luke), εἶπεν, μή, ἰδού, ὑμῖν (three times in Luke), τίκτειν, κύριος, ἐν (twice in Luke), Δαυίδ, and σημεῖον.

24. Γάρ (cf. διὰ τοῦτο in Isa 7:14) and ὅτι (cf. διὰ τοῦτο in Isa 7:14).

7:13–14.[25] These nineteen words are here indicated in bold type: **καὶ εἶπεν** αὐτοῖς ὁ ἄγγελος, **μὴ** φοβεῖσθε, **ἰδοὺ** γὰρ εὐαγγελίζομαι **ὑμῖν** χαρὰν μεγάλην ἥτις ἔσται παντὶ τῷ λαῷ, **ὅτι ἐτέχθη ὑμῖν** σήμερον σωτὴρ ὅς ἐστιν χριστὸς **κύριος** ἐν πόλει **Δαυίδ. καὶ τοῦτο ὑμῖν τὸ σημεῖον**, εὑρήσετε βρέφος ἐσπαργανωμένον **καὶ** κείμενον **ἐν** φάτνῃ.

To be sure, three of the words in Luke 2:10–12 appear more than once;[26] thus, there are only thirty-seven *different* words in the passage. Of these thirty-seven, however, twelve (i.e., 32 percent) also appear in Isa 7:13–14,[27] and two others are closely approximated.[28] This comes to a total of fourteen of the thirty-seven *different* words in Luke 2:10–12 (i.e., 38 percent) that can be linked to the vocabulary of Isa 7:13–14.[29] The fact that almost one-half of *all* the words and almost two-fifths of the *different* words in Luke 2:10–12 can be linked to the vocabulary of Isa 7:13–14 suggests the strong probability of a connection between the two texts.

2. Although κύριος refers to God in Isa 7:14 and to Jesus in Luke 2:11, it is anarthrous in both passages. This may or may not be significant, but it is worthy of note.

3. The appearance of two particular words—τίκτειν and σημεῖον—both in Luke 2:10–12 and Isa 7:13–14 is of particular interest. Although τίκτειν appears not only elsewhere in the Gospel of Luke[30] but also in other birth

---

25. Conversely, sixteen of the thirty-nine words in Isa 7:13–14 (i.e., 44 percent) can be linked to the vocabulary of Luke 2:10–12: καί (four times in Isaiah), εἶπεν, Δαυίδ, μή, ὑμῖν (twice in Isaiah), τοῦτο, κύριος, σημεῖον, ἰδού, ἐν, τίκτειν, and τό.

26. Καί (three times), ὑμῖν (three times), and ἐν (twice).

27. Καί (three times), εἶπεν, Δαυίδ, μή, ὑμῖν (twice), κύριος, ἐν (twice), and σημεῖον.

28. Διὰ τοῦτο (cf. γάρ in Luke 2:10) and διὰ τοῦτο (cf. ὅτι in Luke 2:11).

29. Conversely, twelve of the thirty-four *different* words in Isa 7:13–14 (i.e. 38 percent) can be linked to the vocabulary of Luke 2:10–12: καί, εἶπεν, Δαυίδ, μή, ὑμῖν, κύριος, τοῦτο, σημεῖον ἰδού, ἐν, τίκτειν, and τό.

30. Luke 1:31, 57; 2:6, 7, 11.

announcements in the LXX,[31] Luke uses the verb *only* with reference to the births of John and Jesus—i.e., *only* in the Nativity Story.[32] Similarly, although σημεῖον appears elsewhere in the Gospel of Luke[33] and frequently in the LXX,[34] only in Isa 7:14 and in Luke 2:11–12 is it juxtaposed with τίκτειν in such a way as to associate a "sign" (σημεῖον) with the birth (τίκτειν) of a child.

4. Both Luke 2:10–12 and Isa 7:13–14 introduce the birth announcement with the words καὶ εἶπεν. The phrase itself is quite common, of course,[35] but, given the other parallels between Luke 2:10–12 and Isa 7:13–14, the appearance of the same phrase at the beginning of both announcements may be significant.

5. Both Luke 2:10–12 and Isa 7:13–14 specify that the "sign" (σημεῖον) is a sign "to you" or "for you" in the *plural* (ὑμῖν).[36] There are other places in the LXX where a "sign" (σημεῖον) is said to be "to you" or "for you,"[37] but, with only one exception, the "you" is always *singular* (σοι).[38]

6. Both Luke 2:10–12 and Isa 7:13–14 include—in the same sequence—the words τοῦτο, ὑμῖν, and σημεῖον. It is true

---

31. τέξῃ: Gen. 16:11; Judg 13:3, 5, 7; τέξεται: Gen 17:19.

32. John the Baptist: Luke 1:57. Jesus: Luke 1:31; 2:6, 7, 11. Similarly, τίκτειν appears in Matthew *only* with reference to the birth of Jesus (1:21, 23, 25; 2:2)—i.e., *only* in the Nativity Story. Elsewhere in the New Testament, τίκτειν appears only nine times (John 16:21; Gal 4:27; Heb 6:7; Jas 1:15; Rev 12:2, 4 [*bis*], 5, 13), and five of these occurrences (those in Revelation) may also refer, at some level of interpretation, to the birth of Jesus. Thus, it would appear that τίκτειν was, in early Christianity, associated particularly with the birth of Jesus, and this may reflect the influence of Isa 7:14.

33. Luke 11:16, 29 (*tris*), 30; 21:7, 11, 25; 23:8.

34. E.g., Gen 1:14; 4:15; 9:12, 13, 17; Exod 4:8; Deut 7:19; Num 17:25; Josh 2:18; Isa 33:23; Jer 28 (LXX 51):12; Jer 31 (48):9.

35. E.g., Isa 7:12 also begins with καὶ εἶπεν.

36. Luke: τοῦτο ὑμῖν τὸ σημεῖον; Isaiah: δώσει κύριος αὐτὸς ὑμῖν σημεῖον.

37. Exod 3:12; 13:9; 1 Kgdms 2:34; 10:1b; 4 Kgdms 19:29; Isa 37:30; 38:7; Jer 51:29.

38. The exception is Jer 51:29. In 1 Kgdms 14:10, the "sign" is "to us" or "for us" in the plural (ἡμῖν).

that the syntactical function of τοῦτο is different in the two passages[39] and that the Lukan phrasing, τοῦτο ὑμῖν τὸ σημεῖον, is either the same as or similar to a formula that appears several places other than Isa 7:14 in the LXX.[40] For these reasons, the appearance—in the same sequence—of the same three words both in Luke 2:12 and in Isa 7:14 might appear to have no significance so far as any possible connection between the two passages is concerned. Nevertheless, along with other parallels, it is worthy of note. Moreover, it is entirely possible that the τοῦτο ὑμῖν ... σημεῖον of Isa 7:14 called to mind the formulary τοῦτο ὑμῖν τὸ σημεῖον (or, most often, τοῦτο σοι τὸ σημεῖον) elsewhere in the LXX and prompted the Lukan author to include this formula in the angelic announcement to the shepherds.

In short, the verbal parallels between Luke 2:10–12 and Isa 7:13–14 strongly suggest the influence of the latter passage on the former.

Verbal Parallels between Luke 2:14 and Isaiah 7:11, 13

There are at least three possible parallels between the immediate context of Luke 2:10–12 and that of Isa 7:14.

1. Three verses prior to Isa 7:14, in v. 11, King Ahab is invited to request a "sign" (σημεῖον) from God εἰς βάθος ἢ εἰς ὕψος ("unto depth or unto height"). The appearance here of the noun ὕψος ("height") might easily have called to mind the phrase ἐν [τοῖς] ὑψίστοις ("in the highest"), which appears several times in the LXX with reference

---

39. In Isaiah, τοῦτο is the object of the preposition διά and presumably refers back to the entire preceding verse (or verses). In Luke, however, τοῦτο is the subject of the sentence with τὸ σημεῖον as the predicate nominative.

40. Τοῦτο ὑμῖν τὸ σημεῖον (Jer 51:29); τοῦτο ὑμῖν τὸ σημεῖον (Exod 3:12; 13:9; 1 Kgdms 2:34; 10:1b; 4 Kgdms 19:29; Isa 37:30; 38:7).

to God's place of abode[41] and twice—in Ps 148:1 and *Pss. Sol.* 18:10—in expressions of praise to God.[42] This, in turn, might well have inspired the Third Evangelist to include the phrase ἐν ὑψίστοις in the angelic chorus praising God (Luke 2:14), which immediately follows the announcement to the shepherds.

2. It is further possible that Θεῷ and δόξα in Luke 2:14 derive from ὁ Θεός and ἔνδοξος in *Pss. Sol.* 18:10, which, because of its inclusion of the phrase ἐν ὑψίστοις, had been suggested by the ὕψος in Isa 7:11.[43]

3. It is also at least possible that the appearance of ἀνθρώποις in both the LXX version of Isa 7:13 and Luke 2:14 and that of κυρίῳ in Isa 7:13 and Θεῷ in Luke 2:14 are significant. Isa 7:13 speaks of "causing a struggle" (ἀγῶνα παρέχειν) for humans (ἀνθρώποις) and for the Lord (κυρίῳ). This may have suggested the appropriateness, in the angelic chorus, of juxtaposing Θεῷ (i.e., δόξα Θεῷ) and ἀνθρώποις (i.e., εἰρήνη ἐν ἀνθρώποις). Indeed, δόξα and εἰρήνη might be seen as the Lukan way of expressing the very *opposite* of ἀγών: the prophet accuses the house of David of "causing a struggle" (ἀγῶνα παρέχειν) for humans (ἀνθρώποις) and for the Lord (κυρίῳ), but the angels announce "glory to God" (δόξα ... Θεῷ) and "peace among humans" (εἰρήνη ἐν ἀνθρώποις).

---

41. Ps 148:1; Job 16:19; Sir 26:16; 43:9; *Pss. Sol.* 18:10.

42. Ps 148:1 is an exhortation "to praise the Lord from the heavens, praise him in the highest" (αἰνεῖτε τὸν κύριον ἐκ τῶν οὐρανῶν, αἰνεῖτε αὐτὸν ἐν **τοῖς ὑψίστοις**), and *Pss. Sol.* 18:10 extols the greatness and glory of God, who "dwells in the highest" (μέγας ἡμῶν ὁ Θεὸς καὶ ἔνδοξος ἐν **ὑψίστοις** κατοικῶν).

43. As Fityzmyer (*Gospel according to Luke (I–IX)*, 410) notes: "[The hymnic formula δόξα ἐν ὑψίστοις Θεῷ] is not found as such in the Old Testament, but it is based on phrases about 'giving glory' (*doxan didonai*) to God, i.e. honoring him, in such passages as Bar 2:17–18; 1 Esdr 9:8; 4 Macc 1:12."

Conclusion

Considered separately, each of the parallels between the angelic announcement to the shepherds and Isaiah 7 might be explained on
grounds other than the influence of the latter on the former. It
appears highly unlikely, however, that *all* of the parallels noted—
formal, substantive, and verbal—would be present in the absence
of such influence. Moreover, *five* of the parallels are, in my judgment, particularly compelling. Three of them distinguish Luke
2:10–12 and Isa 7:13–14 from *all* other birth announcements: (1)
the third formal parallel—both Isa 7:14 and Luke 2:10–12 are birth
announcements *to people other than the parents,* (2) the substantive
parallel—both Isa 7:14 and Luke 2:10–12 *associate the birth of a child
with a "sign,"* and (3) the third verbal parallel—both Isa 7:14 and
Luke 2:11–12 juxtapose the specific words τίκτειν ("birth") and
σημεῖον ("sign") to indicate this association. The other two parallels suggest a link between Luke 2:10–12 and Isa 7:13–14 that is
stronger than possible links between Luke 2:10–12 and any other
LXX passage or combination of passages: (4) the first verbal parallel—the remarkable *similarity of the vocabulary* of Luke 2:10–12 to
that of Isa 7:13–14, and (5) the fifth verbal parallel—only Luke 2:12
and Isa 7:14 specify that the "sign" (σημεῖον) is a sign *"to you"*
or "for you" in the plural (ὑμῖν). In short, the evidence appears to
indicate that the angelic announcement to the shepherds (Luke
2:10–12) was influenced by Isa 7:13–14 and its immediate context.

If this is, in fact, the case, it may provide further support for
the view that the Lukan Annunciation (Luke 1:26–38) and the reference in Luke 2:34 to the infant Jesus as "a sign that is spoken
against" (σημεῖον ἀντιλεγόμενον) were also influenced by the
Isaiah passage. At the very least, this would be consistent with the
evidence regarding Luke 2:10–12.

Epilogue

The virginal conception of Jesus appears at *only two places* in
the entire New Testament: the Matthean Nativity Story and the
Lukan Nativity Story. Moreover, if the conclusion of the present
study is valid, Jesus' virginal conception is associated *in both places*

with Isa 7:14. According to most versions of the still-dominant Two-Source Hypothesis regarding Synoptic relationships,[44] this would mean that both the virginal conception and its association with Isa 7:14 can be traced to *two independent sources*: the Matthean Nativity Story and the Lukan Nativity Story. If, however, either the Neo-Griesbach/Two-Gospel Hypothesis or the Farrar-Goulder-Goodacre Hypothesis regarding Synoptic relationships is correct,[45] it could mean that both the association of the virginal conception with Isa 7:14 and the virginal conception itself are to be traced to *only one source*: the Matthean Nativity Story.[46] Robert H. Gundry has offered what I regard as a most interesting third alternative—namely, that the Matthean Nativity Story was based in part on "the traditions that later went into Luke 1–2 [i.e., into the Lukan Nativity Story]."[47] If Gundry is correct, it could mean, as in the case of the Neo-Griesbach/Two-Gospel Hypothesis or the Farrar-Goulder-Goodacre Hypothesis, that both the association of the virginal conception with Isa 7:14 and the virginal conception itself are to be traced to *only one source*: in this case, the traditions that later went into the Lukan Nativity Story.[48]

---

44. This hypothesis holds that Mark served as a source for both Matthew and Luke and that Matthew and Luke also used a second common source labeled "Q" by scholars. Most versions of the hypothesis also hold that the authors of Matthew and Luke were unfamiliar with one another's work.

45. The Neo-Griesbach/Two-Gospel Hypothesis holds that Matthew came first and served as a source for Luke, while Mark came last and used both Matthew and Luke. The Farrar-Goulder-Goodacre Hypothesis holds that Mark came first and served as a source for both Matthew and Luke, while Luke also used Matthew. In either case, there is no need for the hypothetical source "Q."

46. Many would argue, of course, that the Lukan Nativity Story derives not from Matthew but rather either from special Lukan material (i.e., "L") or from the author's own composition. If this is the case, then both Jesus' virginal conception and its association with Isa 7:14 would derive from *two independent sources*.

47. Gundry, *Matthew*, 20.

48. It would be possible, of course, that parts of the Matthean Nativity story, including the notion of Jesus' virginal conception and its association with Isa 7:14, derived not from materials that later went into the Lukan Nativity Story but rather from a special Matthean source ("M")

Regardless, however, of which hypothesis regarding Synoptic relationships is assumed, and regardless of whether Jesus' virginal conception and its association with Isa 7:14 are to be traced to two sources or to a single source, a crucial questions remains: Did the idea of the virginal conception originally *derive from* a "midrashic"-like exegesis of Isa 7:14 or did it originally exist *independently of Isa 7:14* and only secondarily come to be associated with this text? Although it is impossible to be certain, my own judgment is that the very idea of Jesus' virginal conception did, in fact, most likely derive from a "midrashic"-like exegesis of Isa 7:14. I base this judgment largely upon the fact that, if the conclusion of the present study is valid, the virginal conception appears nowhere in the NT *except* in association with Isa 7:14.

In answer to the further question, "What led early Christians to Isa 7:14 in the first place?" I would suggest that it was the word *Emmanuel* ("God with us"). Once Christians became convinced that Jesus had been and/or was in some sense "God with us," they would inevitably have gone to Isa 7:14 and there would have found the idea of a virginal conception.[49]

---

or from the author's own composition. In this case, both the notion of virginal conception and its association with Isa 7:14 would derive from *two independent sources*.

49. It may or may not be coincidental that in the Gospel according to Matthew, which contains one of the two Nativity Stories in the New Testament and thus one of the two references in the New Testament to Jesus' virginal conception, Jesus promises to *be with* the disciples in the future; see Matt 18:20 ("For where two or three are gathered in my name, there am I in the midst of them") and Matt 28:20b ("and lo, I am with you always, to the close of the age").

Chapter 5

Demythologizing and Christology

Bultmann's Proposal for Demythologizing the New Testament

The German scholar Rudolf Bultmann's (1884–1976) controversial proposal for "demythologizing" and "existentialist" interpretation of the New Testament became well known in American theological circles in the 1950s and 1960s and, for that matter, among many people who would hardly claim for themselves the title of "theologian" or "New Testament scholar." Although the controversy has long since subsided, the term "demythologizing" remains a part of the current theological lexicon, even for those who know little about its history.[1] Bultmann argued that both the language and the conceptual framework of the New Testament are essentially "mythological"—that is, they reflect a world view that characteristically attributes the origin and goal of the cosmos as well as certain unusual or astonishing happenings within the cosmos to the activity of non-natural or supernatural causes, forces,

---

An earlier version of this paper appeared in *RL* 35,1 (Winter 1965–66) 67–80. Copyright © 1966 Abingdon Press. A slightly revised version appeared in *TUSR* 8 (1964–67) 65–80; a further revised version under the title, "Authentic Existence: The Debate over Demythologizing," in *The Fourth R* 27,2 (March–April 2014) 5–8, 17–20; and the present version in *Forum* Third Series 3,2 (Fall 2014) 31–44. Reprinted with permission.

1. The following summary of Bultmann's position is based largely on his initial essay on the subject, which appeared in German in 1941 and eventually was translated into English as "New Testament and Mythology: The Mythological Element in the Message of the New Testament and the Problem of its Re-interpretation."

or personages. These supernatural causes, forces, or personages are objectified and represented in terms of space, time, causality, and substance and thus are treated as but another part of the physical world. They are, therefore, at least in principle, subject to the same empirical methods of knowledge as any other objects.

For Bultmann, such a mythology was problematic for at least two reasons: (1) Most modern people no longer accept a mythological worldview; rather, they hold a scientific worldview that refuses to reckon with the possibility of any intervention in this world by transcendent or supernatural powers. Thus, for such people, most of the New Testament has become unintelligible, unbelievable, and irrelevant. (2) What is even more important is that the mythological statements of the New Testament are inappropriate to Christian faith itself, for they do violence to the true meaning of God's transcendence by objectifying and purporting to provide empirical information regarding God and divine activity and thus reducing God's hiddenness to a this-worldly immanence that can be observed and evaluated objectively.

According to Bultmann, the true intent of New Testament mythology, like that of mythology in general, is not to provide information regarding a Supreme Being and divine activity but rather to present a particular possibility for understanding human existence. Thus, the message of the New Testament must be released from its traditional mythological framework and reformulated in terms that are not only intelligible, believable, and relevant for modern people but also express the true intent of the Christian kerygma,[2] which is to confront people with the radical possibility and challenge of a new self-understanding. The pressing question, in seeking to interpret the message of the New Testament, is this: What does this message say to me about my own existence? For Bultmann, the most appropriate categories for reformulating the New Testament mythology — ones that would show

---

2. The Greek word *kerygma* means "proclamation," and it refers here to the *content* of the Christian proclamation, namely, the good news that God has acted finally and decisively in Christ for the salvation of humankind.

how the mythological concepts of the Bible actually correspond to the realities in the life of modern people—were those provided by existentialist philosophy, particularly as articulated by the German philosopher Martin Heidegger (1889–1976), with his phenomenological analysis of the formal structure of human existence. When the Christian proclamation is demythologized and reformulated in existentialist (*existential*) terms, its understanding of human existence becomes clear and can challenge people to genuine existential (*existentiell*) decision regarding their own self-understanding.[3]

The question that immediately arises, however, is whether such a demythologizing and existentialist interpretation can be carried out consistently and thoroughly without distorting or perverting the essential thrust of the New Testament message. Is the mythological element in the Christian faith really dispensable? Bultmann insisted that it was, because the understanding of human existence set forth in the New Testament can be restated in strictly existentialist (that is, philosophical) terms. He himself summarized this understanding as one of radical freedom from the past and openness to the future. In other words, authentic existence, which is the concern of the New Testament, is the abandonment of all human or worldly security and the readiness to find security where none can be discerned, namely, in the unseen and unknown possibilities of every future moment. According to Bultmann, authentic existence means understanding oneself no longer in terms of one's past but solely in terms of one's future, which continually presents itself in the form of a gift.

Assuming that Bultmann was right, that the New Testament message can and must be demythologized and reformulated in

---

3. Bultmann drew a distinction between *existential* (translated as "existentialist") and *existentiell* (translated as "existential"). The former refers to the *ontological* (i.e., theoretical) categories of human existence *per se* as articulated philosophically, while the latter refers to the *ontic* (i.e., actual) situation of an individual human being confronted by the demand to choose the direction of his or her own existence and the specific character of that person's individual experience as formed by this decision.

existentialist terms, another crucial question is posed: What place does Jesus or the Christ-event[4] occupy in this proposed reconstruction? Or, to put it differently, is it possible to speak meaningfully of the significance of Christ in non-mythological, existentialist terms? If the New Testament understanding of existence can be articulated without reference to Christ, as Bultmann appeared to maintain, would it not also be possible, indeed necessary, to have a "Christianity without Christ," because Christian faith is nothing more and nothing less than an authentic understanding of one's own being as a person? Bultmann's answer was that, although the nature of authentic existence can be *discovered and articulated* apart from Christ, it cannot be *realized* apart from Christ. The issue is the proper understanding of humankind as "fallen." The New Testament insists that humans, in and of themselves, are totally incapable of releasing themselves from their "fallenness," their inauthentic existence. Every attempt to do so represents an act of self-assertion of the old person to establish his or her own security. It can only result in plunging people further into their "fallen" estate. Authentic existence, the abandonment of all attempts to establish one's own security and the commitment of one's self to the unknown future, can be realized only as response to a proclamation, to a word of deliverance from beyond humankind. Unless this word is rooted in actual history, however, it remains only a piece of wishful thinking and thus a subtle form of self-assertion. The New Testament therefore speaks of an act of God, the event of Christ, and asserts that it is only through response to the proclamation of this event that people become capable of authentic existence; they become able to understand themselves as crucified and dead to their own past and alive to the unknown future. Such response cannot take place once-for-all but can only occur from

---

4. "The Christ-event," when spoken of by Bultmann (and others), refers to the historical event, Jesus of Nazareth, understood not simply as *an* event among other events in human history but rather as *the* event in human history in and through which God has acted finally and decisively for the salvation of humankind.

time to time when the proclamation is actually heard as a word of deliverance. Thus, faith can never be a permanent possession.

Christian faith, then, is humankind's original possibility of authentic existence. It is a possibility *in principle* (i.e., an *ontological* possibility) for all people everywhere and at all times, but it is a possibility *in fact* (i.e., an *ontic* possibility) only in consequence of a particular historical event, the event of Jesus the Christ, God's act of redemption. If this event is mythological, however, then demythologizing and existentialist interpretation must halt at this crucial point.

Clearly, the New Testament portrayal of Jesus is essentially mythological. Statements about his pre-existence, divine sonship, virginal conception, contacts with angelic and demonic forces, supernatural powers, sacrificial death, resurrection, ascension, second coming, and the like are appropriate to the first-century mythological worldviews of Jewish apocalypticism and Hellenistic Gnosticism but not to a contemporary scientific worldview. Can the Christ event, then, be spoken of meaningfully in non-mythological, existentialist terms, or is the mythology essential to New Testament christology?

Bultmann pointed out that the person about whom this mythological language revolves is an actual historical figure, but that various details in the portrayal of this figure are often mutually contradictory. This suggests that the real intention of the myths cannot lie in their objective content or in any factual information that they appear to impart. The purpose of the New Testament's christological mythology is to express the existential significance of the historical figure of Jesus of Nazareth as God's act of salvation, to point to this event as the salvation occurrence that alone makes possible an authentic self-understanding. The event is not mythological because it is not miraculous or supernatural; it does not represent an invasion of this world from beyond. The event is historical, wrought out in space and time, fully explicable and intelligible within the context of world history. Nevertheless, when the event is proclaimed by the Church, it confronts the hearer with the possibility of authentic existence. Thus it is, paradoxically, understood by faith alone as God's act of salvation. Thus, according to Bultmann, it is possible to speak of God's redemptive activity, of his unique eschatological[5] act in Jesus the Christ, in strictly existentialist terms and to avoid the objectifying view of mythology.

Left-Wing Critiques of Bultmann's Proposal

Not surprisingly, Bultmann's proposal was vigorously assailed by many as an implicit denial of the essentials of Christian faith, as a reduction of the gospel to an existentialist philosophy. By others, most of whom had only a casual acquaintance with Bultmann's writings, it was ridiculed as a passing fad or the purely academic concern of an "ivory-tower" university professor. More surprisingly, Bultmann came under attack by so-called "liberal" or "left-wing" theologians for what they saw as his unwillingness to carry his program of demythologizing and existentialist interpretation consistently and thoroughly to its logical conclusion, namely a complete non-mythological reformulation of the New Testament message. It is at the point of Bultmann's christology that most of these criticisms were directed.

American theologian Schubert M. Ogden (1928–), for example, objected to what he called the structural inconsistency in Bultmann's argument, which, he asserted, can be reduced to two mutually incompatible propositions:

1. Christian faith is to be interpreted exhaustively and without remainder as man's[6] original possibility of authentic historical (*geschichtlich*) existence as this is more or less adequately clarified and conceptualized by an appropriate philosophical analysis.

---

5. "Eschatological" refers to that which is last, final, or ultimate. Here, it means that, in Jesus the Christ, God's plan for the salvation of humankind is fulfilled, brought to fruition; there is nothing further that God needs to do.

6. In quotations, I have retained the non-inconclusive language that was still prevalent in the 1950s and 1960s.

    2. Christian faith is actually realizable, or is a "possibility in fact," only because of the particular historical (*historisch*) event Jesus of Nazareth, which is the originative event of the church and its distinctive word and sacraments.[7]

According to Ogden, the two propositions are self-contradictory: If, on the one hand, as the first proposition affirms, Christian faith is to be interpreted solely in existential terms as man's original possibility of authentic self-understanding, then it demonstrably follows that it must be independent of any particular historical occurrence. On the other hand, if the second proposition is true and Christian faith has a necessary connection with a particular historical event, then clearly it may not be interpreted without remainder as man's original possibility of authentic historicity.

    In short, what is involved when these two propositions are affirmed conjointly is the self-contradictory assertion that Christian existence is a historical (*geschichtlich*) possibility open to man as such and yet first *becomes* possible for him because of a particular historical (*historisch*) event.[8]

    In an attempt to overcome this alleged structural inconsistency, Ogden proposed two theses of his own:

    1. Christian faith is to be interpreted exhaustively and without remainder as man's original possibility of authentic existence as this is clarified and conceptualized by an appropriate philosophical analysis.

    2. Christian faith is always a "possibility in fact" because of the unconditioned gift and demand of God's love, which is the ever-present ground and end of all created things; the decisive manifestation of this divine love, however, is the event Jesus of Nazareth, which fulfills and corrects all other manifestations and is the originative event of the church and its distinctive word and sacraments.[9]

---

7. Ogden, *Christ without Myth*, 112, cf. esp. 111–26.

8. Ogden, *Christ without Myth*, 117.

9. Ogden, *Christ without Myth*, 146, 153; for the entire argument, see 146–64.

Bultmann responded to Ogden's criticisms by asserting that what the latter called a structural inconsistency is not necessarily inconsistent at all, for there is a legitimate distinction between a possibility in *principle* and a possibility in *fact*, or, as Bultmann preferred to put it, between an *ontological* possibility and an *ontic* possibility. Because authentic existence is not actually *realized* in a philosophical understanding of human existence but only as an event of human decision in a concrete historical situation, it always stands before people as a future event, not as a permanent possession or quality. What is always an *ontological* possibility in principle, therefore, can become an *ontic* possibility in fact only in the moment of genuine existential decision. Furthermore, authentic existence, understood as existence in freedom and responsibility, cannot be achieved by people in and of themselves, for they are always determined by their own past, and thus every attempt to become free is doomed to relative failure. Radical freedom, or freedom from one's past, is possible only as a gift, and Christian faith contends that this is the gift of God's grace, not as an idea but as an act of God, as a historical event, the event of Jesus the Christ. Bultmann admitted that "this assertion cannot be proved by philosophy; indeed, it is a stumbling block, a *scandalon* for rational thinking," and he asked whether the inconsistency that Ogden saw "is not rather the legitimate and necessary character of what the New Testament calls the stumbling block."[10]

In my opinion, Bultmann was correct in insisting that there is a legitimate distinction between a possibility *in principle* (i.e., an *ontological* possibility) and a possibility *in fact* (i.e., an *ontic* possibility) and that authentic existence can occur only as existential response in an actual historical situation. Bultmann appeared to miss the real thrust of Ogden's objection, however, which was his contention that to make the actual possibility of authenticity contingent on the prior occurrence of *one particular* historical event is not only to deny a person's essential freedom and responsibility but also to involve oneself in the very mythology that Bultmann

---

10. Rudolf Bultmann, rev. of Ogden, *Christ without Myth*, 226.

wanted to escape. The claim that an existential decision in favor of authenticity is possible only as response to the proclamation of *this one event* implies that this event is somehow objectively different in principle as well as in fact from all other events and thus constitutes an invasion into the normal course of history; thus, it is to view this event mythologically rather than existentially. As Ogden put it, "so far as [Bultmann's] argument goes, all that is required is *some* event in which God's grace becomes a concrete occurrence and is received by a decision of faith."[11]

Thus, the real difference between Ogden and Bultmann was not that Ogden saw authentic existence as a general possibility that one can at any time or under any circumstances grasp simply because one is human or because God is God while Bultmann insisted that authentic existence occurs only as existential response to the event of God's grace. The real difference was that Bultmann tied God's grace inseparably to the event of Jesus, or rather to the event of the proclamation of Jesus as the Christ, whereas Ogden refused to limit the event of God's grace to any one particular historical occurrence.

Thus, Ogden asserted that authentic existence, which is what the Christian faith is all about, can be achieved apart from faith in Jesus or faith in the specific proclamation of the church. For the word spoken in Jesus is nothing else than what is spoken everywhere in the actual events of nature and history, and particularly in the Old Testament scriptures. Ogden went on to insist, however, that the word spoken in Jesus is the *normative* expression that makes all other expressions relatively fragmentary, or even false. The event of Jesus is *par excellence* the event that, when proclaimed in its significance, confronts a person with the possibility of a new and authentic existential self-understanding, for in this event the final truth about human existence ceases to be an idea and becomes a living reality. In this way Ogden claimed to have overcome Bultmann's structural inconsistency and to have arrived at a valid interpretation of Christ without myth. The event

---

11. Ogden, *Christ without Myth,* 123.

of Jesus is not *necessary* for authentic existence, but it is the *decisive* and *normative* expression of such existence.

Much of Ogden's argument is persuasive. If Christian faith is to be presented in non-mythological, existentialist terms, it cannot be regarded as necessarily dependent on any one particular historical event. Bultmann himself, however, pointed out an inconsistency in Ogden's position, and, ironically enough, it is essentially the same inconsistency that Ogden attributed to Bultmann:

> I fail to understand how he can say, on the one hand, that the "possibility of Christian existence is an original possibility of man before God" ... and, on the other hand, that "the deepest conviction of Christian faith is that God's saving action has been decisively disclosed in the event Jesus of Nazareth". ... How is it possible to characterize the Christ-event as decisive and ultimate and yet deny that authentic existence becomes reality only as a result of the particular historical occurrence?[12]

By way of summary, one might say that while Ogden correctly called attention to a structural inconsistency in the proposals of Bultmann, his own positive formulations constituted no real improvement, for they shared essentially the same inconsistency. Neither Bultmann nor Ogden was able to reconcile the original demand for a demythologizing and existentialist interpretation with the insistence upon the centrality of Jesus to Christian faith. The one seems necessarily to cancel out the other.

Before the appearance of any of Ogden's writing, a more consistent though much more radical position had been proposed by the Swiss theologian Fritz Buri (1907–1995), who, like Ogden, saw a basic inconsistency in Bultmann's argument.[13] According to Buri, Bultmann demanded a thorough demythologizing and existentialist interpretation of the New Testament but limited this de-

---

12. Bultmann, rev. of Ogden, *Christ without Myth*, 226.
13. Fritz Buri's most important work on this subject is "Entmythologisierung oder Entkerygmatisierung der Theologie."

mand by appealing to a unique historical event that he regarded as God's saving act, the significance of which cannot be expressed in exclusively existentialist terms. In Buri's view, such an appeal constituted a falling back into mythology. The reason for this inconsistency, Buri thought, was that Bultmann was motivated by two mutually incompatible concerns: (1) He wanted to make the Christian message intelligible and relevant to modern people by freeing it from its mythological framework and interpreting it existentialistically. (2) He wanted to retain, rather than eliminate, the unique character of the Christian proclamation as kerygma, that is, as the announcement of the good news that God has acted for humankind's salvation in Christ.

Buri agreed with Bultmann that the Christian message must be demythologized and interpreted in existentialist terms; otherwise it will be incompatible with modern people's understanding of themselves and their world. He argued, however, that such a demythologizing and existentialist interpretation cannot be combined with the retention of the kerygma as kerygma, that is, as the proclamation of a unique act of God. The claim that authentic existence is possible only in consequence of God's act in Jesus the Christ is sheer arrogance, Buri insisted, as is the assertion that God's grace is decisively tied to this particular event. Buri maintained that grace is a possibility, though not a permanent quality or possession of human existence; it is the promise of authentic existence that is given to inauthentic humankind everywhere and at all times. Grace is the experience of one's own life as a gift, and it is not contingent on any one particular historical event. Thus, Buri concluded, an adequate and relevant interpretation of the New Testament today requires not only demythologizing but also "dekerygmatizing," a term that he acknowledged to be a "fighting word" and perhaps misleading. He wanted the kerygma—the proclamation of the Christ event—itself to be demythologized in order to allow its existential significance to become clear. Demythologizing must not be arbitrarily halted, leaving a mythological remainder at the heart of Christian faith. As the Scottish theologian John Macquarrie (1919–2007) summarized Buri's position:

The New Testament teaching will be set free from its mythical
and kerygmatic setting so that we can recognize it as simply
the expression of a concept of authentic existence which is
not restricted to either the New Testament or the Church, but
is to be found elsewhere as well. Salvation has nothing to do
with a once-for-all event, and the value of the New Testament
does not lie in the fact that it speaks of such an event, but in
the fact that it gives expression in mythical terms to authentic
existence.[14]

In the New Testament, Jesus is proclaimed as God's unique eschatological act of salvation. But the fact that the expected Second
Coming (*parousia*) of Jesus never occurred should make it clear
that such a claim is untenable today, and Jesus must now be regarded by modern people as a *symbol* of possible authentic existence, not as the historical *basis* of such existence.

Buri did believe, however, that the mythological form of the
New Testament has value as a symbol of authenticity, a symbol
that can move people to a new self-understanding far more pow-
erfully than any abstract philosophical statement about the nature
of existence. For Buri, the distinctiveness of Christian faith lay in
its treasury of myth and symbol, and the task of theology was to
explicate these Christian symbols, to make clear their existential
significance, to show how they point to authentic existence. The
myths are not, of course, to be understood as giving information
about a higher world or a saving history, but rather as symbolic
expressions of ancient people's awareness of being confronted by
transcendence, expressions that have significance for people today insofar as they offer the possibility of a similar encounter in
the present, calling into question people's self-understanding and
challenging them to see themselves in a new light. According to
Buri, the Christian symbols, as opposed to other sets of symbols,
are most appropriate for Western people, because people cannot
separate themselves from their tradition. They are who they are
because of their history, and a significant part of Western people's

---

14. Macquarrie, *Scope of Demythologizing*, 136.

history is the Christian tradition. Theology is an interpretation of the tradition in which one stands. In Buri's view, it is the Christian faith from which Western people derive their most meaningful symbols of authenticity, recognizing all the while that other people, whose roots are in other traditions, draw their symbols from other sources.[15]

The problem can now be summarized. Bultmann called for the demythologizing of the New Testament and its reinterpretation in existentialist terms. Demythologizing to him meant the rejection of all statements that speak of God and divine activity in objectifying terms, that is, apart from their existential significance for human existence. This, however, does not include the elimination of references to God's unique eschatological act of salvation in the historical event of Jesus the Christ, which alone, according to Bultmann, makes authentic existence an *actual* possibility. Ogden, going further, argued that such demythologizing necessarily involves the rejection of *any one particular* historical event as a prerequisite for authentic existence, but he also asserted that Christian faith can legitimately regard the event of Jesus as the *decisive* manifestation of authenticity and the proclamation of this event as the *decisive* or *normative* call to authenticity. Buri insisted that the kerygma itself must be demythologized and interpreted as neither *necessary* nor necessarily *decisive* for authentic existence, but rather as a symbol of the possibility of such existence. He considered this the logical implication of Bultmann's original demand for a demythologizing and existentialist interpretation, and any less radical conclusion, even though it be drawn by Bultmann himself, a failure to carry the program through consistently.

---

15. As Robert J. Miller has noted (e-mail correspondence to me dated April 10, 2013), Buri erroneously suggested that "the Western people are uniformly from a Christian tradition," thus implying that Jews, for example, are not Western people; moreover, Buri's claim that "it is the Christian faith from which Western people derive their most meaningful symbols of authenticity," while it may have been more-or-less true when Buri wrote more than half a century ago, ignores the "profound secularization" that Western culture has undergone since then and "is (at least) doubtful today."

A Way Forward

As was pointed out earlier, Ogden reduced Bultmann's proposals to two fundamental propositions, accepted the first, but, recognizing that it is inconsistent with the second, reformulated the second. The inconsistency was still not eliminated, however, and, in my judgment, a consistent statement must proceed along the lines suggested by Buri.

A meaningful and relevant interpretation of the New Testament today, then, will presuppose two theses. The first is that suggested by Ogden in his summary of Bultmann's position and followed in his own positive reformulation. It involves the recognition that any theological statement that cannot be interpreted as a statement about humans and their possibilities is meaningless. Only insofar as Christian faith deals with the actualities of human existence as modern people are aware of them can it have any contemporary relevance and meaning. Christian faith does not point to a "real" world somewhere beyond this world in which we live; it speaks of life in the here and now. The New Testament message, therefore, must be demythologized and interpreted in terms of its existential significance for the life of humankind.

Not only does this kind of interpretation make sense to people today; it also discloses more adequately than any other the real intention of the New Testament writers. Christian faith, in essence, means receiving one's life from moment to moment as a gift, as grace; it means giving up every attempt to base the security of one's life on any kind of tangible or objective reality; it means living by faith and not by sight. This alone is authentic existence. To first-century people, with their mythological world view, this could most meaningfully be articulated in mythological terms. For most modern people, other forms of expression must be found—forms that are appropriate to their understanding of themselves and their world. And the church, if it is not to become completely irrelevant, must continually seek such forms of expression.

Furthermore, this first thesis also involves the recognition that an essentially "Christian" understanding of existence can and often has been articulated by persons outside the church and without recourse to what would normally be called theological, Christian, or even religious terminology. When such an understanding is found in other religious traditions, philosophy, psychology, psychiatry, sociology, literature, or elsewhere, the church must accept it as a valid statement of the nature and possibility of authentic existence, whether it makes use of the church's vocabulary and thought forms or chooses its own.

The second thesis is suggested by Ogden's second thesis, but represents an attempt to overcome the inconsistency in his position: Authentic existence is always a possibility not just in *principle* but in *fact*, because every event and every encounter of people's lives confront them with the opportunity and, indeed, the demand for an existential decision regarding their own self-understanding—whether they will understand themselves in terms of their past and thus be bound to the past or whether they will understand themselves in terms of their future and thus be open to the future, receiving the concrete situation as a gift, as an opportunity for authentic response to its promise and claim.

The Christian gospel is the proclamation that such faith, such genuine response, is called for and is indeed a possibility precisely amid the conditions of human existence as we know them. The proclamation of this possibility is, therefore, continually the originative event of the church—the community of faith—and its word and sacraments. The Christian gospel, in other words, is the proclamation to people that they must and can live their lives, if at all, in the here-and-now of their own historical situation. They cannot shift the responsibility for their lives to another person, not even to God, nor to another time and place, not even to heaven. The responsibility is theirs—here and now, and this responsibility is also a promise. The primary significance of the incarnation, as proclaimed by the church, is that it points not to some other world of transcendent being, but to the actualities of human life and experience as the arena where God encounters people, where judgment and grace are at work, that is, where people are confronted by the absolute claims and promises that alone make authentic existence possible. God is to be found, if at all, not somewhere else but here. Authentic existence is not a permanent possession; it can only occur as an event, as a genuine response to the "givenness" of a specific moment. And this means that authentic existence is not an achievement of which a person can boast, a "work" in Pauline terms. Authenticity is never the prior reality but always the response to the gift of the moment, the response to the grace that the situation at hand offers. What constitutes the Christian message as "gospel" ("good news"), then, is precisely its insistence that the authentic existence of which it speaks is always and everywhere an actual possibility, because every given moment offers the possibility of a positive response. It is, therefore, the mission of the church to call people into an awareness of the possibility of living authentically.

Postscript

Bultmann's initial proposal to demythologize the message of the New Testament was written and circulated in 1941, in wartime Germany. Only after the close of World War II did it become generally known throughout Germany, more widely in Western Europe, and eventually in the English-speaking world. It provoked a storm of controversy, particularly during the late 1940s, the 1950s, and the early 1960s.[16] Indeed, the original version of this article, "Demythologizing and Christology," was written at the height of the debate, in 1965.

Today, it is difficult to recall the heat of the demythologizing debate, because, already in the 1950s, New Testament scholars were increasingly focusing their attention on other issues.[17] Within a few years, therefore, "demythologizing" had, for most New Testament scholars, become simply a chapter in the past history of the discipline. Nevertheless, it is my own judgment that Bultmann's demythologizing proposal made some important and

---

16. The most important source for tracing the development of the debate is Hans-Werner Bartsch, ed., *Kerygma und Mythos*. Some of the selections from these volumes are available in English in Bartsch, ed., *Kerygma and Myth*.

17. In Germany, the first of these was "The New Quest for the Historical Jesus," which was initiated by one of Bultmann's own students; see Käsemann, "Problem of the Historical Jesus."

lasting contributions both to New Testament scholarship and to the faith and life of the Christian church. I regard four of these contributions as particularly significant, and each of the four stems from a major influence in Bultmann's thinking and scholarship:[18]

First, as a child of the Enlightenment (also known as Rationalism or the Age of Reason) and in agreement with much of the "liberal" scholarship of the nineteenth and early twentieth centuries, Bultmann recognized that ideas and beliefs grounded in tradition and faith must be subjected to the scrutiny of the scientific method and human reason. This meant that thinking people simply could no longer accept the supernatural features or, as he preferred to call them, the mythological features of the New Testament because these features had become unintelligible, unbelievable, and/or irrelevant. On this point, I think Bultmann was absolutely correct: For the church to insist upon a literal acceptance of the mythological elements of the New Testament results in either (a) a wholesale rejection of the Christian faith, (b) a kind of "schizophrenia" or "bifurcation" whereby people base part of their lives upon a scientific worldview and part upon a mythological worldview, and/or (c) outright hypocrisy, in which people claim to accept the mythology but actually, at the deepest level of their consciousness, realize that it is not credible.

Second, as a product of the History-of-Religions School,[19] and in distinction from at least some "liberal" scholarship, Bultmann recognized that the New Testament could not be understood except within the context of its wider Jewish and Hellenistic religious-philosophical milieu. This involved a recognition that both the

---

18. For much of what follows, I am indebted to Konrad Hammann, *Rudolf Bultmann: A Biography*.

19. The History-of-Religions School was a movement in nineteenth-century Germany that sought to study religion systematically as a socio-political-economic-cultural phenomenon—that is to say, as both influenced by and influencing the particular culture in which it lives. It also involved an examination of similarities and differences among various religions and thus the possible influence of one upon another.

language and the conceptual framework of the New Testament are so inextricably bound up with a mythological worldview that a thoroughgoing elimination of the mythology would mean a total rejection of the New Testament message. Thus, Bultmann insisted that the mythology of the New Testament should be *interpreted* rather than simply *eliminated*, as many of the "liberal" theologians had done. Here, too, I think Bultmann was correct: Both the New Testament scholar and the Christian church must somehow come to terms with the *entire* New Testament, including its mythological features, not just with those portions of it that are easily incorporated into their own worldviews.

Third, as a Christian theologian, Bultmann was concerned with the task of articulating the New Testament message in terms that would be intelligible, credible, and relevant for people holding a scientific worldview. Moreover, he was convinced that this task could be successfully carried out. For him, such articulation meant translating the mythological categories of the New Testament into the existentialist categories set forth by Martin Heidegger. This, however, was only a *tactical* move for Bultmann. His *strategy* was the larger endeavor to translate the New Testament into *whatever* categories would be most effective in communicating its essential message of "good news." This, I submit, remains the essential task of Christian theologians, and it depends upon the contributions of New Testament scholars—particularly those who in some sense or other see their work as being in the service of the church.

Fourth, as one of the founders of New Testament Form Criticism,[20] Bultmann had concluded, two decades before his proposal for demythologizing the New Testament appeared, that the New Testament gospels represent the end-product of a period of oral tradition in which the various passages (pericopes) underwent

---

20. Form Criticism of the New Testament gospels, as practiced by Bultmann and others, classified individual passages (pericopes) by their literary form (parable, miracle story, wisdom saying, etc.), attempted to locate each form in the life and work of the early church (preaching, teaching, debate, etc.), and sought to show how the pericopes were expanded, otherwise adapted, and at times created for such use by the church.

significant alteration, and in some cases were created *de novo*, for use in the preaching, teaching, worship, discipline, and other activities of the early church. This meant that the nature of the available source materials made any "quest for the historical Jesus" simply impossible. This conclusion was completely consistent, however, both with Bultmann's demythologizing and with his existentialist interpretation of the New Testament. The former signaled the end of a literal interpretation of much of the material in the gospels, thus reinforcing the idea that the "quest" was historically impossible; the latter insisted that the "quest" was theologically illegitimate because it sought to provide a secure basis for Christian faith in the historical events involving Jesus of Nazareth. For Bultmann, the desire for such security negated the very essence of faith, which was an openness to each moment as an opportunity for authentic response and thus for authentic existence and a willingness to live with radical uncertainty and insecurity. My own judgment is that Bultmann was essentially correct on both points: the quest for the historical Jesus is impossible if it expects to reconstruct anything remotely resembling a "life of Jesus," and it is theologically illegitimate to the extent that it promises to provide a secure basis for Christian faith. This, I think, is another of the lasting contributions of Bultmann's proposal for a demythologizing and existentialist interpretation of the New Testament.

PART TWO

Relationships among the Canonical Gospels

Chapter 6

An Unexamined Presupposition in Studies of the Synoptic Problem

Until recently, the consensus of critical New Testament scholarship held, with only an occasional dissent, that the Synoptic Problem had, in essence, been solved. The solution, of course, involved some form or other of the Two-Source Hypothesis, with its view of Markan priority and the hypothetical source "Q." Now, however, this consensus has become more or less "destabilized" (to use Albert C. Outler's metaphor adapted from the world of politics),[1] and advocates of Matthean and even Lukan priority are promoting their own rival solutions to the problem, as are those who propose more complex reconstructions of the relationships among the gospels.[2]

In the heat of the debate regarding priority, however, another question has been posed from time to time—a question that is logically antecedent to that about priority.[3] This is the question of whether the Synoptic Problem is, in fact, soluble at all. Some have

---

"An Unexamined Presupposition in Studies of the Synoptic Problem." *RL* 48, 1 (Spring 1979) 41–52. Copyright © 1979 The United Methodist Publishing House. Reprinted with permission.

1. Outler, "'Gospel Studies' in Transition," 23.

2. For a brief survey, see Buchanan, "Current Synoptic Studies."

3. It is also logically antecedent to the question of whether the correct solution to the Synoptic Problem is a strictly literary solution; on this, see, e.g., Walker, "Introduction," 9–10.

suggested that it is not. Joseph A. Fitzmyer, for example, said in 1970:

> The history of Synoptic research reveals that the problem is *practically insoluble*. As I see the matter, we cannot hope for a definitive and certain solution to it, since the data for its solution are scarcely adequate or available to us. Such a solution would imply a judgment about the historical genesis and literary relationship of the first three gospels, whereas the data for a historical and literary judgment of this nature are so meagre and of such a character as to preclude certitude.[4]

More recently, Outler has expressed essentially the same viewpoint:

> I regard this whole problem as *formally* insoluble. Methodologically, I do not share the optimism ... that it is not solved now but could be. I know how many of my colleagues live by the faith that one of these days we'll get the hang of this and we'll get it done right. I do not myself know how it could so be done.[5]

Similarly, Reginald H. Fuller observes that solving the Synoptic Problem, "at the present juncture, seems both impossible and unnecessary," suggesting that "a universally acceptable solution ... will not be found and that a pluralism of viewpoints is perfectly respectable in this as in many other matters and indeed is the only viable possibility for today."[6] John J. O'Rourke expressed it most bluntly in a paper presented at the 1975 annual meeting of the Society of Biblical Literature when he reiterated his earlier characterization of the Synoptic Problem as "a can of worms" and as-

---

4. Fitzmyer, "Priority of Mark," 132. Fitzmyer does qualify his opinion by acknowledging (p. 163 n. 4) that "there may be some as yet undreamed-of application of data processing by computers to the problem, i.e., some method not tied to the usual sort of literary judgments which have marked the history of Synoptic research so far."

5. Quoted in Walker, "Introduction," 12.

6. Fuller, "Classics and the Gospels," 176, 192.

serted: "I know that it remains such, and I am as certain as one can possibly be in literary studies concerning ancient literatures that it will remain such."[7]

I do not wish at this time to deal in any comprehensive way with the general question of whether the Synoptic Problem is soluble, although I must confess that my basic sympathies at the moment lie with the position articulated by Fitzmyer, Outler, Fuller, O'Rourke, and others. Rather, I wish to isolate one particular aspect of the question and to suggest that, unless and until this one aspect is resolved satisfactorily, the Synoptic Problem as a whole must necessarily remain unsolved, even if all other aspects of the problem should be cleared up fully and adequately. The particular aspect of the question that I have in mind relates to the present state of the extant texts of the three Synoptic Gospels.

Most discussion of the Synoptic Problem tacitly presuppose that the earliest surviving manuscripts of Matthew, Mark, and Luke are similar enough to the autographs of these three gospels (or at least to the texts of the three that are presumed to have originally stood in some sort of literary relationship to one other) that these surviving manuscripts can legitimately be used as the basis of establishing critical texts, which, in turn, can be compared for purposes of determining matters of chronological priority, literary relationship, and the like—in short, for solving the Synoptic Problem.[8] This is the "unexamined presupposition" referred to in the title of this article. I maintain, however, that there are very strong grounds for questioning this presupposition—that, as Leander E. Keck suggests, "Any strictly literary solution to the

---

7. O'Rourke, "The Synoptic Problem Is a 'Can of Worms.'" At the same meeting, Joseph B. Tyson presented the opposing view under the title, "The Synoptic Problem Should Be Solvable."

8. Cf., e.g., Kilpatrick, "Some Thoughts on Modern Textual Criticism and the Synoptic Gospels," 290: "So far we have recognized that the Synoptic Problem has been reopened to discussion, but those who have taken part in the discussion have, for the most part, assumed certain things. They have assumed that for each Gospel there was an original text, an author's copy or something very like it, from which our manuscripts are descended."

Synoptic Problem is frustrated by the fact that we do not have texts for any of the gospels that are so nearly identical with the autographs as to justify adducing variations in wording as clear evidence of dependence."[9] My reasons follow.

I

As Bruce M. Metzger points out, textual criticism is both a "science" and an "art." As an art, it "refers to the application of reasoned considerations in choosing among variant readings." Thus:

> To teach another how to become a textual critic is like teaching another how to become a poet. The fundamental principles and criteria can be set forth and certain processes can be described, but the appropriate application of these in individual cases rests upon the student's own sagacity and insight.[10]

In other words, the state of the extant manuscript evidence is such that the textual critic is often forced to rely upon more or less subjective considerations in choosing among variant readings. This means that thoroughly reliable critical texts have not been and apparently cannot be established for the various New Testament documents. Metzger summarizes the situation as follows:

> All known witnesses of the New Testament are to a greater or less extent mixed texts, and even the earliest manuscripts are not free from egregious errors. Although in very many cases the textual critic is able to ascertain without residual doubt which reading must have stood in the original there are not a few other cases where he can come only to a tentative decision based on an equivocal balancing of probabilities. Occasionally none of the variant readings will recommend itself as original, and he will be compelled either to choose the reading which he judges to be least unsatisfactory or to indulge in conjectural emendation. In textual criticism, as in other areas of historical research, one must seek not only to

---

9. Keck, "Oral Traditional Literature and the Gospels," 121.
10. Metzger, *Text of the New Testament*, v, 211–12.

learn what can be known, but also to become aware of what, because of conflicting witnesses, cannot be known.[11]

This apparent impossibility of establishing reliable critical texts is particularly unfortunate in studies of the Synoptic Problem, for, as Charles Wolfe points out, these studies require "a more careful and exhaustive establishment of the text than is required in many other fields of study because the conclusions depend upon such minute points of comparison and contrast." Wolfe examines two instances in which Burnett Hillman Streeter and B. C. Butler argued for opposing solutions to the Synoptic Problem on the basis of different variants in the same passages, and he observes that "there are an additional sixty-five instances in which Streeter's argument depends upon a choice of variants." It is surely true, as Wolfe insists, that an "argument constructed upon the text can be no sounder than the condition of the text itself."[12] It is also surely true that the present condition of the text is not such as to warrant any high degree of confidence in the use of this text as the basis for determining matters of chronological priority and literary relationship among the Synoptic Gospels.

II

All of the above is well known, of course, but another factor in the situation is often overlooked. Apart from fragments, no extant manuscript of any of the Synoptic Gospels can be dated with assurance any earlier than the end of the third century, roughly two centuries after the original composition of these gospels by most reckonings,[13] and serious attempts to reconstruct the textual history of the gospels reach back no further than the end of the

---

11. Metzger, *Text of the New Testament*, 246.

12. Wolfe, "Use and Abuse of Textual Criticism."

13. Some authorities would date $\mathfrak{P}^{75}$ near the *beginning* of the third century (e.g., Metzger, *Text of the New Testament*, 41, 255), while others date it around the *end* of the third century (e.g., Kümmel, *Introduction to the New Testament*, 519). This papyrus, however, contains only portions of Luke. P[45] (early third century) contains seven leaves of Luke, six of Mark, and only two fragmentary leaves of Matthew.

second century at best.[14] This compels us to raise the question: How much and in what ways were the texts altered during the two centuries between their original composition and the date of the earliest now extant manuscripts?

A partial answer to this question can perhaps be extrapolated from what is known about the history of the texts *after* the appearance of the earliest extant manuscripts, that is, after the end of the third century. Here, there is abundant evidence of textual alteration. Such alteration was apparently "the result both of scribal error and of editorial emendation."[15] It is the latter, editorial emendation, that appears to be of greatest significance in the present discussion for, as M. M. Parvis points out, such editorial emendation would at times have been regarded as a religious duty:

> It is because the books of the NT are religious books, sacred books, canonical books, that they were changed to conform to what the copyist believed to be the true reading. His interest was not in the "original reading" but in the "true reading." This is precisely the attitude toward the NT which prevailed from the earliest times to the Renaissance, the Reformation, and the invention of printing.[16]

Indeed, "Irenaeus, Clement of Alexandria, Tertullian, Eusebius, and many other Church Fathers accused the heretics of corrupting the Scriptures in order to have support for their special views," and even "within the pale of the Church one party often accused another of altering the text of Scriptures."[17]

Metzger discusses seven types of "intentional changes" in the texts,[18] and it should be noted that one of the more common types of change is "harmonistic corruptions" or "assimilations" of the text of one gospel to that of another. Streeter appealed to

---

14. See, e.g., Kümmel, *Introduction to the New Testament*, 519.
15. Clark, "Transmission of the New Testament," 618.
16. Parvis, "Text, NT," 595.
17. Metzger, *Text of the New Testament*, 201.
18. Metzger, *Text of the New Testament*, 195–96.

this phenomenon to account for certain of the so-called "minor agreements" of Matthew and Luke against Mark,[19] and Keck suggests that this "phenomenon of textual assimilation frustrates any strictly literary solution" to the Synoptic Problem.[20] It should also be noted at this point that there is perhaps some textual evidence that entire pericopes, such as John 7:53–8:11, for example, may have been transferred from one gospel to another.[21]

The point of all this is that such abundant evidence of textual alteration *after* the appearance of the earliest now extant manuscripts creates a very strong *a priori* presumption that *at least* as much alteration also occurred *before* the appearance of these manuscripts. It is generally agreed that the traditions about Jesus probably underwent greater alteration during the period of their oral transmission than after they were put into written form. Analogously, it can be argued that the written documents underwent greater alteration before their "canonization" than after (as will be discussed below, all extant manuscripts of the Synoptic Gospels date from a time after the effective canonization of the writings had already occurred). Indeed, G. D. Kilpatrick asserts that "the great majority of deliberate changes in the texts were made at a time when our knowledge of the history of the text is slight or non-existent, namely in the latter part of the first century and in the second century,"[22] and George A. Kennedy believes that we "must . . . allow for the possibility that the text of the gospels was somewhat fluid into the second century, that the gospels continued to exercise an influence on one another, and

---

19. Streeter, *The Four Gospels*, 5th ed., 307–25.

20. Keck, "Oral Traditional Literature and the Gospels," 121.

21. John 7:53–8:11 is omitted by most early authorities, but it can be found variously at the end of the Fourth Gospel, after John 7:36, after John 7:44, *and after Luke 21:36.* Barrett (*Gospel according to St John,* 491) suggests that "it closely resembles in form and style the synoptic narratives (especially the style of Luke)." Note, too, that Matt 11:25–27/Luke 10:21–22 is so similar in style and tone to many parts of the Fourth Gospel that it is sometimes referred to as "the Johannine interpolation."

22. Kilpatrick, "Some Thoughts on Modern Textual Criticism and the Synoptic Gospels," 276.

that passages were adapted to reflect historical developments and liturgical uses."[23]

The probability of such textual fluidity at least into the second century is increased with the observation that in many parts of the New Testament there is, in fact, some evidence of textual alteration that occurred prior to the appearance of any of the surviving manuscripts and thus cannot be demonstrated on the basis of textual variants. It is widely held, for example that chapter 21 of the Fourth Gospel was not originally a part of this Gospel, even though it is found in all of the surviving manuscripts.[24] Similarly, it is believed by many that the Pauline corpus as a whole, as well as individual letters within this corpus, did not achieve its present form until some time after Paul's death and that the letters contain editorial interpolations, glosses, omissions, and perhaps rearrangements within the material.[25]

All of this suggests that the original texts of the Synoptic Gospels may have been significantly different from any of the surviving manuscripts. If this is true, then the chronological and literary relationships among the originals may now be impossible to determine.

III

Much more is involved here, however, than merely a matter of textual criticism, even though such criticism itself raises serious questions regarding the possibility of solving the Synoptic Problem. A third factor in the situation must be explored. There is a growing body of evidence that each of the Synoptic Gospels circulated at one time in a version or versions significantly different from the versions that survive, and the differences now envisioned pertain not just to textual variations within particular pericopes but rather to the overall contents and form of the respective gospels. This poses almost insurmountable problems for

---

23. Kennedy, "Classical and Christian Source Criticism," 154.

24. See, e.g., Kee, *Jesus in History*, 254.

25. See, e.g., Knox, *Chapters in a Life of Paul*, 18, for a general statement on the subject.

any attempt to determine the *original* contents and form of any of these gospels.

It is not completely clear, for example, whether Marcion in the second century altered an earlier form of the Gospel of Luke, as his critics charged, whether the version eventually canonized was an altered form of Marcion's Luke, or whether the truth of the matter involves come combination of these alternatives. Most modern scholars have accepted the view of Irenaeus and Tertullian that Marcion's gospel was an abridged or "mutilated" form of the Gospel of Luke in essentially its present form.[26] John Knox has argued, however, that Marcion made use of a kind of "early Luke" or "proto-Luke," which only later was revised and combined with other materials to form a work whose purpose was, at least in part, anti-Marcionite and which is now known as Luke-Acts.[27] Morton Scott Enslin, among others, believes that "Knox's arguments are not lightly to be dismissed and merit more attention than they have apparently received."[28] What is clear is that at least two versions of Luke existed in the second century, that only one of these versions survived, and that there is no certain way of determining which of the two, if either, approximates the original. The question, then, is: Which of the versions should properly be compared with Matthew and Mark for purposes of determining matters of chronological priority and literary relationship? If Marcion's version was significantly different from the version that survived, as it apparently was, and if his version was in significant respects closer to the original, which we cannot now know with any assurance, then the Synoptic Problem is probably insoluble, at least so far as Luke's place in the problem if concerned.

The case is not too different with regard to the Gospel of Mark. Morton Smith has recently cited strong evidence for the existence

---

26. Irenaeus, *Adversus Haereses* 3.11.7; Tertullian, *Adversus Marcionem* 4.2. See, e.g., von Campenhausen, *Formation of the Christian Bible*, 160–61.

27. Knox, *Marcion and the New Testament*; cf. his "Acts and the Pauline Letter Corpus," 287 n. 8. Knox's views are developed further by West, "A Primitive Version of Luke in the Composition of Matthew." For an opposing view, see, e.g., Talbert, *Luke and the Gnostics*, 108–9.

28. Enslin, "Marcion, Gospel of," 163.

of at least two rather different forms of this gospel in the second
century, the so-called "Secret Gospel of Mark" and the version
that survived,[29] and Olof Linton has argued that the extant texts
of Mark reflect at least two revisions of the gospel, one of these
revisions dating from the second century.[30] Thus, it cannot simply
be assumed that the now extant manuscripts of Mark are substantially identical with the original. Helmut Koester points out
some of the implications of this for advocates of the Two-Source
Hypothesis, and much of what he says applies equally to all theories of Synoptic relationships:

> I have no doubt ... that the two-source hypothesis is essen-
> tially correct. Both Matthew and Luke have used Mark. But
> which "Mark"? And what shall we call Matthew and Luke in
> relation to Mark? What other evidence is there about "early"
> Gospels?
>
> "Ur-Markus" hypotheses are not popular. But is it pos-
> sible to assume that the Markan text which is transmitted in
> most of our New Testament manuscripts, i.e., the "canonical
> Mark," was the text used by Matthew and Luke? (Leaving
> aside for the moment the fact that we do not even know the
> earliest and most reliable text of "canonical Mark," not even
> its original ending.) The well-known common omissions of
> Matthew and Luke (e.g., Mk. 4:26–29; 8:22–26), but also such
> details as "Is not this the carpenter, the son of Mary?" in Mk.
> 6:3 as compared to Mt.'s and Luke's "Is not this the son of the
> carpenter (Joseph)" are significant indicators of the problem.
> Furthermore, does Luke's omission of Mk. 6:45–7:26 indicate
> that his "Mark" was different from, and more original than
> Matthew's? This would lead us to assume that there were
> at least two different copies of Mark in existence in the first

---

29. Morton Smith, *Clement of Alexandria and a Secret Gospel of Mark* and
The Secret Gospel. For a penetrating analysis and discussion of Smith's
views, see, e.g., Fuller et al., *Longer Mark*, which includes a response by
Smith and by other scholars.

30. Linton, "Evidence of a Second-Century Revised Edition of St.
Mark's Gospel."

century A.D. But also "canonical Mark" may be based on an older copy which existed in the first century, and Matthew and Luke could be considered as Markan "revisions," albeit rather substantial revisions of Mark.[31]

George A. Kennedy has recently suggested that the Gospel of Mark came into its final form in two distinct stages,[32] and this appears to be supported by Clement of Alexandria's Letter to Theodore, recently discovered by Smith.[33] If this is correct, then it is by no means clear that the earlier version would simply have disappeared when the later version made its appearance, and it is certain that the relationship between the earlier version and the other Synoptics would not be the same as the relationship between the later version and the other Synoptics. For example, it is conceivable that the earlier version might have been a source for Matthew and/or Luke, while one or both of these Gospels in turn might have formed part of the source material for the later version of Mark. Indeed, Kennedy proposes the following:

> It is ... not impossible both that Matthew could have influenced Mark and that Mark could have influenced our text of Matthew. Their authors could have used each other's notes, the second to write a systematic gospel could have had knowledge of the first, and the Greek translation of Matthew, if the Gospel was composed in Aramaic as the external tradition says, could have utilized significant portions of the text of Mark. Luke could have used the notes of Matthew or Mark, the Aramaic text of Matthew, the Greek text of Mark, or the Greek text of Matthew, if a translation was then available, but notes or oral tradition used by Luke could also have been used by Matthew and Mark, and the Greek translation of Matthew, if later than Luke, could have been influenced by Luke.[34]

---

31. Koester, "Response," 29.
32. G. A. Kennedy, "Classical and Christian Source Criticism," 147–51.
33. See, e.g., Meeks, "Hypomnēmata from an Untamed Sceptic," 167.
34. G. A. Kennedy, "Classical and Christian Source Criticism," 153–54.

Even the Gospel of Matthew may very well have existed in more than one form. Papias' problematic statement that "Matthew composed the oracles (logia) in the Hebrew language and each one interpreted (or translated) them as best he could," if taken at face value, suggests the existence of more than one form of this Gospel (one in Hebrew or Aramaic and more than one in another language or languages).[35] Moreover, various of the no longer extant non-canonical gospels, such as the Gospel of the Ebionites, the Gospel according to the Hebrews, and the Gospel of the Nazarenes, are often regarded as differing versions of the Gospel of Matthew.[36] Thus, it is impossible to be certain that the surviving Gospel of Matthew is substantially identical with the original gospel.

In the case of all three Synoptic Gospels, therefore, there are strong indications that differing versions existed in the second century, that the different versions appealed to different Christian groups, that these groups often held conflicting theological and ecclesiastical views, and that only one version of each gospel eventually survived. It is not clear, however, that the surviving version was necessarily the original version or even a close approximation of the original. Koester summarizes the situation as follows:

> A consideration of only those Gospels which are included in
> the canon of the New Testament already indicates that there
> must have been a great variety of copies and/or editions
> of Gospels, some of these slightly altered editions of their
> *Vorlage*, others extensive revisions. During the period from
> ca. A.D. 50 to the end of the second century, there was also no
> protection against alteration for any of this literature. What
> finally came to be the canonical version may not have been
> the original at all. It is very probable that this was not the case

---

35. Eusebius, *Historia Ecclesiastica* 3.39.16. Kennedy has argued that the Papias reference should be taken seriously; see his "Classical and Christian Source Criticism," 150, 154.

36. For a full discussion of the problem, see, e.g., Vielhauer, "Jewish-Christian Gospels"; cf. also Schoeps, *Jewish Christianity*, 14.

with respect to Mark and John. Gospels or editions of the four New Testament Gospels which, to us, look very "apocryphal" may have been in existence together with and even prior to the canonical forms of the Gospels.[37]

The inevitable question, then, is this: Which version of each gospel should be compared with which version of each other gospel for purposes of determining matters of chronological priority and literary relationship? The question is rendered academic, however, by the fact that only one version of each gospel has survived.

IV

The fourth and final factor to be considered has to do with the fact, already mentioned, that no extant manuscript of any of the Synoptic Gospels can confidently be dated any earlier than the end of the third century. From this time on, however, increasing numbers of manuscripts are available, and despite what was said earlier about the problematic condition of these texts, it must be noted that all of them reflect *more or less* the same form, a form that can be called the "canonical" form. Here, a very serious question appears: Why do we have no manuscripts dating from earlier than the late third century? What became of the earlier manuscripts? It is possible, of course, that they were simply worn out from constant use or that they perished during Roman persecutions of the period,[38] but the question takes on an intriguing new aspect when it is recalled that the third century (the line of demarcation between the extant manuscripts and those that did not survive) marked both real triumph of "catholic" (or "proto-catholic") Christianity over the various "gnostic," "Jewish," and other varieties and the effective establishment of what was to become the "orthodox" canon of Scripture. It is surely not unreasonable to suggest that the people who defined "orthodox" Christianity

---

37. Koester, "Response," 30; cf. also Shepherd, "Response," 51–52.
38. See, e.g., Metzger, *Text of the New Testament*, 201 n. 1.

and established the limits of the canon may also have had something to say about the particular form and text of the writings thus canonized. It is also at least possible that these same people were responsible, either directly or indirectly, for the intentional suppression and even destruction of variant forms of the gospels that they regarded as less useful and, indeed, even dangerous to "catholic" Christianity. Note that it was *Marcion's* version of Luke that disappeared, the version of Mark used by the *Carpocratians*, and the versions of Matthew used by various groups of *Jewish* Christians!

There is ample evidence that early church leaders often felt no scruples against revising and suppressing documents that they regarded as deficient, defective, or destructive in terms of promoting the full truth of the Christian faith. It is widely held, for example, that the Greek text of Josephus was "edited" by Christian hands in order to provide a non-Christian testimony to the messiahship and resurrection of Jesus;[39] indeed, it has even been suggested that Eusebius may have been the "editor" in question.[40] It is also clear that copies of Tatian's *Diatessaron* were sought out and destroyed by Syrian church leaders in the fifth and sixth centuries, after Tatian had been adjudged heretical.[41] Finally, the disappearance of much of the non-canonical gospel material (some of which, at least, was used by groups outside the bounds of what was to become "orthodox" or "catholic" Christianity) supports the view that "heterodox" literature was suppressed by the emerging "catholic" consensus. It is likely that variant forms of the gospels dating from the second century, manuscripts of the gospels dating from before the end of the third century, and gospels not canonized all met the same fate: they were suppressed and perhaps even destroyed by church leaders.[42]

---

39. For a judicious review of the evidence, see, e.g., Thackeray, *Josephus*, 125–53.

40. The suggestion comes from Shlomo Pines and David Flusser; see, e.g., Anonymous, "Josephus and Jesus," 55.

41. See, e.g., Vööbus, "Syriac Versions," 851.

42. For a summary of the evidence, see Morton Smith, *Jesus the Magician*, 1–2.

If versions of one or more gospels existed that were significantly different from what became the canonical versions (and it is certain that such versions did exist in the second century and perhaps later), it would be precisely these different versions that "catholic" Christianity would have been concerned to suppress. Thus, we must conclude that we now possess only the *canonical* versions of the three Synoptic Gospels (that is, the versions that were acceptable to the "orthodox" leadership), and we cannot (or at least do not now) know the exact relationship between these versions and the originals.

Conclusion

The four factors discussed above point to a strong possibility and even probability that all of the surviving texts of the Synoptic Gospels are substantially different from the original texts and thus cannot legitimately be used as a basis for determining matters of chronological and literary relationship among the gospels. Thus, the Synoptic Problem may very well be finally insoluble. Further investigation of the matter must include studies in textual criticism, as well as in the development of "catholic" Christianity during the late second and the third centuries.[43]

---

43. The basic idea for this paper developed as a result of an extended telephone conversation on April 12, 1976, with Albert C. Outler. Outler should not in any way be held responsible for the paper, but he should be given credit for suggesting some of its content.

Chapter 7

"Nazareth"

A Clue to Synoptic Relationships?

The Gospel of Luke places Jesus' rejection at Nazareth immediately after his temptations by the devil, that is, at the very beginning of his public ministry (Luke 4:16–20); the Gospels of Matthew and Mark, however, place it considerably later in the narrative—Mark after the raising of Jairus' daughter (Mark 6:1–6a) and Matthew still later, after a series of parables (Matt 13:53–58).[1] Furthermore, Matthew and Mark have essentially the same account of the episode, but Luke's account is significantly different. Because of these differences in placement and content, a few scholars have assumed that Jesus was rejected twice in Nazareth and that Luke reports the earlier rejection and Matthew and Mark the later one.[2]

"'Nazareth': A Clue to Synoptic Relationships?" Pp. 105–18 in *Jesus, the Gospels, and the Church: Essays in Honor of William R. Farmer*. Ed. E. P. Sanders. Macon, GA: Mercer University Press, 1987. © Mercer University Press, 1987. Reprinted with permission.

1. An interesting and important question—not, however, to be explored in this paper—is why Matthew and Mark have the episode at different points in their respective narratives, particularly in light of the fact that neither of them is in agreement with Luke.

2. See, e.g., Lane, *Gospel according to Mark*, 201 n. 2: "An examination of a synopsis ... indicates that the parallel between Mk. 6:1–6a and Lk. 4:16–30 is extremely slight. The key point of parallelism is the traditional word (in different formulations) that 'a prophet is not accepted in his own country.' This is merely a traditional aphorism that can exist without context (as in the Oxyrhynchus Papyrus 1 No. 6=the Coptic Gospel of Thomas, Logion 31) or in a different context (as John 4:44). The conclusion seems probable that Mk. 6:1–6a and Lk. 4:16–30 describe two distinct visits to Nazareth. They do not narrate the same visit from merely different points of view." The chief difficulty with such a judgment, of course, is what would appear to be the inherent improbability that two such

Others, without necessarily assuming two rejections, have argued for a distinctive source or sources, reflecting a variant version of the rejection episode, underlying the Lukan account.[3] Most recent commentators, however, maintain that Matthew and Mark reflect the earlier tradition and that Luke[4] has himself altered both the sequence and the content for theological and/or literary reasons, perhaps making use of distinctive source material for certain of the details of his version. The view of Joseph A. Fitzmyer is typical:

> From v. 23 it is clear that Luke was aware of a period of Jesus' ministry in Capernaum prior to this visit to Nazareth. He is, then, consciously making this episode the first of the ministry, know that it was not really such. ... Here Luke has transposed the account of Jesus' visit to his hometown from later on in the gospel tradition (see Mark 6:1–6a; Matt 13:53–58), where it is recounted shortly before the end of the Galilean ministry. ... Though there is little similarity in the details or in

---

similar episodes should occur. For another example of the same type of problem, compare Matthew's and Mark's accounts of the anointing at Bethany (Matt 26:6–13; Mark 14:3–9; cf. John 12:1–8) with Luke's earlier account of an anointing in an unnamed city (Luke 7:36–50). It may be, indeed, that the modern scholar should refrain from asking such historical questions as whether there were one or two rejections at Nazareth and simply explore the literary relations among the accounts and the literary/theological interests of the respective authors.

3. See, e.g., Streeter, *The Four Gospels*, rev. ed., 209–10; Schmid, *Das Evangelium nach Lukas*, 110; Schürmann, "Zur Traditionsgeschichte der Nazareth-Perikope." Hans Conzelmann (*Theology of St. Luke*, 32) notes the difficulty of determining whether such a passage as Luke 4:16–30 is "derived from a special source" or represents "a free adaptation by Luke" of a source such as Mark (or perhaps Matthew): "If the latter could be proved, we should possess not only a striking illustration of his own theological outlook, but also of the degree to which he has modified his sources. But we are in a vicious circle, for the requisite proof presupposes a knowledge of these very factors, i.e., of Luke's own views and of the degree to which he has adapted the sources."

4. For the sake of convenience, I refer to the authors of the four gospels as "Matthew," "Mark," "Luke," and "John." This by no means, however, implies acceptance of the traditional views regarding actual authorship.

the wording of the Lucan and Marcan form of the account of this visit, the substance of the two stories is the same. ... The Lucan form of the story of the Nazareth visit owes its inspiration to Mark 6:1–6a. ... It is better to regard the Lucan story as a reworking of the Marcan source ... a reworking with the sources suggested ... by Bultmann.[5]

Occasionally, however, it has been suggested that Matthew (but not Mark), while placing his own rejection story later in the narrative, nevertheless reflects a tradition that also (like Luke) placed Jesus' rejection at Nazareth immediately after his temptation[6] (indeed, it has even been suggested that this order might be closer to the actual historical facts than that followed by Matthew and Mark[7]). The purpose of the present paper is to argue that Matthew does, in fact, reflect such a tradition and that the relation between Luke's rejection story (including the two verses immediately preceding and the two immediately following: Luke

---

5. Fitzmyer, *Gospel according to Luke (I–IX)*, 526–27; cf. 71: "Jesus' visit to Nazareth (Mark 6:1–6) is transferred by Luke to the beginning of Jesus' Galilean ministry (4:16–30) to serve a programmatic purpose: it presents in capsule form the theme of fulfillment and symbolizes the rejection that will mark the ministry as a whole." In agreement with most scholars, Fitzmyer presupposes that Luke's primary source, at this point as well as elsewhere, is Mark (advocates of the Griesbach Hypothesis, of course, would assume that Luke has departed from Matthew in essentially the same ways as advocates of the Two-Source Hypothesis see him departing from Mark). The "sources suggested ... by Bultmann" relate to Luke 4:23, 25–27; see Bultmann, *History of the Synoptic Tradition*, 32: "Vv. 25–27 clearly came to Luke from the tradition (originally Aramaic? cp. Wellhausen). ... In order to fit vv. 25–27 in, Luke has, as I suppose, constructed a scene on the pattern of Mk. 6¹⁻⁶, and at the same time in v. 23 used the παραβολή which has been handed down in another context."

6. See, e.g., Schweizer, *Good News according to Matthew*, 67, and *Good News according to Luke*, 86; Gundry, *Matthew*, 59–60.

7. According to Schweizer (*Good News according to Matthew*, 67), "such a rejection might explain why Jesus moved to Capernaum with his family (John 2:12), so that only his (married) sisters stayed in Nazareth (Mark 6:3)"; cf. Gundry, *Matthew*, 59–60. In addition, it might be expected that, immediately after his baptism and temptations, Jesus would return to Nazareth to begin his public ministry.

4:14–32) and Matthean material at the same point in the narrative (Matt 4:12–17) is such as to suggest that Matthew and Luke are, at this point in the narrative, making use of common (or, at least, similar) source material—perhaps what modern scholarship has called "Q." It appears, too, that Luke is here following the source material more closely than is Matthew.

A careful examination of the two passages reveals at least seven clues pointing to such a relation between Matthew and Luke. These clues appear most clearly when the two passages are printed in parallel columns as follows:

Matt 4:12–17	Luke 4:14–32
And having heard that John had been arrested,	(Cf. Luke 3:19–20: But Herod the tetrarch, being reproved by him concerning Herodias the wife of his brother and concerning all the evil things that Herod had done, added also this to them all, that he shut up John in prison).
he withdrew into Galilee;	And Jesus returned in the power of the Spirit into Galilee, and a report concerning him went out through all the surrounding country. And he was teaching in their synagogues, being glorified by all. And he came into Nazareth, where he had been brought up, and he entered the synagogue, as was his custom, on the Sabbath day, and he stood up to read, and the book of the prophet Isaiah was given to him, and having opened the book he found the place where it was written, "The Spirit of the Lord is upon me, because he has anointed me to preach good news to the poor. He has sent me to proclaim release to the captives and recovering of sight to the blind, to set at liberty those who are oppressed, to proclaim the acceptable year of the Lord." And he closed the book, and gave it back to

the attendant, and sat down; and the
eyes of all in the synagogue were fixed
on him. And he began to say to them,
"Today this scripture has been fulfilled
in your hearing." And all spoke well
of him, and wondered at the gra-
cious words which proceeded out of
his mouth; and they said, "Is not this
Joseph's son?" And he said to them,
"Doubtless you will quote to me this
proverb, 'Physician, heal yourself; what
we have heard you did at Capernaum,
do here also in your own country.'"
And he said, "Truly, I say to you, no
prophet is acceptable in his own country. But in truth, I tell you, there were
many widows in Israel in the days of
Elijah, when the heaven was shut up
three years and six months, when there
came a great famine over all the land;
and Elijah was sent to none of them
but only to Zarephath, in the land of
Sidon, to a woman who was a widow.
And there were many lepers in Israel
in the time of the prophet Elisha; and
none of them was cleansed, but only
Naaman the Syrian." When they heard
this, all in the synagogue were filled
with wrath. And they rose up and put
him out of the city, and led him to the
brow of the hill on which their city was
built, that they might throw him down
headlong. But he, passing through their
midst, was going [away].

and having left Nazareth,
having come, he dwelt in
Capernaum, which is by the
sea in the region
of Zebulun and Naphtali;
in order that what was spoken by the prophet Isaiah
might be fulfilled: "The land
of Zebulun and the land of

And he went down to Capernaum,
a city of Galilee;

Naphtali, toward the sea across
the Jordan, Galilee of the
Gentiles—the people who sat
in darkness have seen a great
light, and for those who sat
in the region and shadow of
death light has dawned."
From that time Jesus began to   and he was teaching them
preach, saying, "Repent, for
the kingdom of heaven is at
hand."

       on the Sabbath;

(Cf. Matt 7:28–29: And when
Jesus had finished these words,
the crowds were astonished at   and they were astonished at his
his teaching,   teaching,
for he was teaching them as   for his word was with authority.
one having authority,
and not as their scribes.)

The first clue that Matthew and Luke may be using common (or similar) source material appears in Matthew's reference to Jesus leaving Nazareth (Matt 4:13). Matthew has not previously indicated that Jesus went to Nazareth after his temptations (he only has him going into "Galilee"), but here Jesus leaves Nazareth. Commentators have attempted in various and sometimes interesting ways to smooth over the difficulty,[8] but the problem re-

---

8. See, e.g., Bruce, "Synoptic Gospels," 91: "Jesus naturally went to Nazareth first, but He did not tarry there"; cf. Lenski, *Interpretation of St. Matthew's Gospel*, 163: "John 2:12 reports that Jesus transferred his home from Nazareth to Capernaum shortly after he first returned to Galilee from the Jordan. When Matthew writes, 'and having left Nazareth, having come, he dwelt in Capernaum,' these aorists merely mark facts without particular reference to the exact past moment in time. We are simply to know that, when the Baptist was imprisoned, Jesus no longer lived in Nazareth but in Capernaum." Perhaps the most interesting suggestion is that of Kingsbury (*Matthew: Structure, Christology, Kingdom*, 16) that Matt 4:13 "is directly associated both formally and materially with 2:23": "We can observe how flawlessly the one passage picks up on the other: '… *and*

mains. Furthermore, the participial construction in Greek appears
to suggest a merely passing or incidental reference to something
presumably already known to the readers. It would appear, therefore, according to Matthew, that Jesus did, in fact, go to Nazareth
after his temptations (as in Luke), but nothing is said in Matthew
about anything that happened while he was there—there is only
the bare mention of his leaving. The Greek root of the participle
referring to his leaving, however, is a compound root, carrying the idea of "leaving behind," "abandoning," "forsaking,"
or "deserting."[9] Thus, there may well be more than meets the

---

he came and dwelled in a city which is called Nazareth, in order that what was
spoken by the prophets might be fulfilled …' (2:23); '… *and he left Nazareth
and came and dwelled in Capernaum beside the sea,* in the regions of Zebulun
and Naphtali, in order that what was spoken by Isaiah the prophet might
be fulfilled …' (4:13–14). From this we learn that the 'divinely ordained'
travels of Jesus, which began in ch. 2, do not, as Matthew tells it, come to
an end until Jesus settles in Galilee, which is the region in which God has
decreed he should embark upon his public ministry to Israel. To signal
the termination of these travels and to ready Jesus for the beginning of
his public ministry is the dual purpose of 4:12–16." The most obvious
problem with this interpretation is, of course, the fact that, between Matt
2:23 and Matt 4:13, it is clear that Jesus has been away from Nazareth
(see Matt 3:13: "Then Jesus came from Galilee to the Jordan to John, to
be baptized by him"; 4:1: "Then Jesus was led up by the Spirit into the
wilderness to be tempted by the devil"; 4:12: "Now when he heard that
John had been arrested, he withdrew into Galilee." A further difficulty is
the fact that the spelling of "Nazareth" is different in the two passages
(on this, see the "second clue" below). It is true that the crucial words
in Matt 2:23 and Matt 4:13 are parallel (Matt 2:23: "And having gone, he
dwelt in a city called Nazareth, in order that what was spoken by the
prophets might be fulfilled"; Matt 4:13: "And … having gone, he dwelt
in Capernaum … in order that what was spoken by Isaiah the prophet
might be fulfilled"). Such parallelism clearly reflects the editorial hand
of Matthew (or perhaps of Matthew's source material), but it does not
eliminate the problem in Matthew's reference to Jesus leaving Nazareth.

9. The verb is καταλείπειν. See, e.g., Matt 19:5: "a man shall *leave*
his father and mother and be joined to his wife." In only two other passages does Matthew use the verb: 16:4b (after refusing to give any sign
to "an evil and adulterous generation … except the sign of Jonah"): "So
he *left* them and departed"; and 21:17 (after being rebuked by the chief
priests and scribes for allowing children to cry out, "Hosanna to the Son

eye in Matthew's apparently passing reference to Jesus leaving Nazareth. The root suggests some strong reason for leaving—perhaps a reason such as rejection by the people of Nazareth (as is spelled out at this point in the Lukan narrative). It is important to observe, too, that Luke (unlike both Matthew and Mark in their later accounts of the rejection) makes specific reference to Jesus leaving Nazareth after his rejection (Luke 4:30).

It is possible, of course, that Luke, using Matthew as a source and noting Matthew's obscure reference to Jesus leaving Nazareth, has seized the occasion to introduce a rejection story at this point and then has omitted Matthew's later (somewhat different) account. This possibility, however, leaves unexplained Matthew's reference to Jesus leaving Nazareth. More likely, Matthew, using a source that (like Luke) included a rejection story at this point, has eliminated the rejection story (perhaps because he chooses to include a somewhat different rejection story later in the narrative), retaining only an obscure allusion to it. It is possible that the source used by Matthew is the Gospel of Luke itself. This appears unlikely, however, in light of general arguments that have been advanced against Matthew's use of Luke as a source.[10]

---

of David!"): "And *leaving* them, he went out of the city to Bethany and lodged there." See Beare, *Gospel according to Matthew*, 114: "Matthew alone tells us of a definitive move from Nazareth, from the home of Jesus' childhood and youth where his mother and his brothers and his sisters were still living (Mt. 13:55), to Capernaum. To our evangelist, this change of abode is not an incidental item of topographical interest. It is a fulfillment of prophecy, and it establishes Jesus in a region where a mission to Israel can be carried on in an environment which includes Gentiles. It is a foreshadowing of the great Gentile mission that is to come. There is perhaps also a suggestion of the breaking of family ties. Not merely is the time of tutelage over, and the security of the family circle removed, but the service of the kingdom of God takes precedence over the closest bonds of affection."

10. Even Robert L. Lindsey, who argues that Luke was the earliest gospel, does not believe that Matthew made *direct* use of Luke; rather, in his view, Matthew and Luke used some of the same source material (i.e., Q and a so-called Proto-Narrative or "PN"), and Matthew also used Mark, who, in turn, had used Luke. See Lindsey's "Modified Two-Document Theory," his *New Approach to the Synoptic Gospels*, and his *Hebrew*

Apparently, then, Matthew and Luke are here using either different sources, both of which include a rejection story at this point, or the same source. Although certainty is by no means possible, the application of "Ockham's Razor" (*Entia non sunt multiplicanda praeter necessitatem*), if nothing else, would favor the latter hypothesis: Matthew and Luke are here using the same source material. In any case, some type of relation between Matthew and Luke appears clear at this point—a relation in which Luke reflects a primary and Matthew a secondary version of the tradition.

A second clue that Matthew and Luke may be using common (or, at least, similar) source material appears in the spelling of the place name, "Nazareth." The name occurs three times in the Gospel of Matthew. Twice, the best textual evidence points to a spelling of either Ναζαρέτ (Matt 2:23) or Ναζαρέθ (Matt 21:11), which are by far the more common spellings in the New Testament as a whole.[11] At Matt 4:13 (the text now under consideration), however, the spelling is the unusual Ναζαρά.[12] In light of the fact that Matthew elsewhere uses the more common spelling,

---

Translation of the Gospel of Mark, 44–45. Cf. Kümmel, *Introduction to the New Testament*, 64: "The dependence of Mt on Lk is no longer defended today and can drop from consideration."

11. The name occurs twelve times in the gospels and Acts and nowhere in the remainder of the New Testament. The references are: Ναζαρέτ (Matt 2:23; Mark 1:9; John 1:45, 46); Ναζαρέθ (Matt 12:11; Luke 1:26; 2:4, 39, 51; Acts 10:38); and Ναζαρά (Matt 4:13; Luke 4:16). It should be noted that none of the gospel passages mentioning "Nazareth" is parallel to any other passage containing the name—at least not explicitly so.

12. To be sure, there is significant manuscript evidence for Ναζαρέθ at Matt 4:13, including the original reading of Codex Sinaiticus. The correction of Sinaiticus and the original of Codex Vaticanus read Ναζαρά, however, and, in light of the fact that the spelling elsewhere in the New Testament, except for Luke 4:16, is consistently Ναζαρέτ or Ναζαρέθ, it must be assumed that Vaticanus is correct and that Sinaiticus initially reflects an assimilating tendency (that also appears in the majority of later manuscripts) but was then corrected to conform to Vaticanus or some other manuscript with the same reading. Unless Ναζαρά is original, it is difficult to understand why Sinaiticus would have been changed from the much more common Ναζαρέθ to the much rarer Ναζαρά. On variations in the Greek spelling generally, see BAGD, 532; Brown, *Birth of the Messiah*, 207–8; Fitzmyer, *Gospel according to Luke (I–IX)*, 530.

it is unlikely that he has himself introduced the unusual spelling at this point;[13] more likely, use of a source is reflected. This likelihood is strengthened by the observation that the only other occurrence in the New Testament of the unusual spelling, Ναζαρά, is precisely in Luke's account of Jesus' rejection at Nazareth (Luke 4:16). Initially, this might suggest that the source being followed by Matthew at this point is, in fact, the Gospel of Luke. In light of the fact that Luke elsewhere is completely consistent in his use of the spelling, Ναζαρέθ, however, it appears that Luke, too, is here using a Greek source with the spelling, Ναζαρά.[14] Again, it is possible that Luke is here using Matthew as a source, but this would imply that Matthew, in turn, is also using a source containing the unusual spelling. For reasons already suggested in connection with the first clue, however, it is unlikely that Luke is using Matthew. It is also unlikely, for reasons cited above, that Matthew is using Luke as a source. Thus, as in the case of the first clue, the evidence appears to indicate that Matthew and Luke are here using either different sources, both of which contain the unusual spelling of "Nazareth," or the same source, with the latter being the more likely possibility.

A third clue that Matthew and Luke may be using common (or similar) source material appears in Matthew's reference to the arrest of John the Baptist (Matt 4:12). Matthew has not previously mentioned John's arrest (he reports it later at Matt 14:1–2—interestingly enough, immediately after his account of Jesus' rejection at Nazareth;[15] cf. also Mark 6:14–29, where it is separated from the rejection story by the report of Jesus sending out the Twelve); Luke, however, has mentioned it (Luke 3:19–20, just prior to the

---

13. It is possible, of course, but not probable, that Matthew's more usual spelling elsewhere reflects use of source material and that Ναζαρά is his own preferred spelling.

14. See Luke 1:26; 2:4, 39, 51; Acts 10:38. It is unlikely that Ναζαρά reflects an older Semitic form of the name, as has been argued by some; see Brown, *Birth of the Messiah*, 207–8.

15. At this later point, Matthew reports not only the arrest but also the death of John (as does Mark). At 4:12, however, he mentions only the arrest, even as only the arrest is reported in Luke 3:19–20.

story of Jesus' baptism, as the conclusion to the John-the-Baptist material). At 4:12, however, Matthew mentions the arrest—again, as in the case of his reference to Jesus leaving Nazareth, almost in passing,[16] as though it would already be known to the readers.[17] It is barely possible that Luke, seeing Matthew's obscure allusion at this point, would introduce an account of John's arrest earlier in his own narrative, thus making Matthew's reference intelligible; this would imply, however, that Luke then eliminated the reference to John's arrest at the point where Matthew has it, thus, in fact, removing the need for introducing his own account of the arrest earlier in the narrative. More likely, Matthew (like Luke) is here using a source that reports the arrest of John before it reports the beginning of Jesus' public ministry. If so, as in the case of the rejection story, Matthew has eliminated the account of John's arrest (perhaps because he chooses to include a somewhat different and more expanded account later in the narrative), retaining only an obscure allusion to it. Again, the source used by Matthew could be the Gospel of Luke, but, for reasons already cited, this appears unlikely. Apparently, then, Matthew and Luke are using the same (or similar) source material at this point.

A *fourth clue* that Matthew and Luke may be using common (or similar) source material appears in their common reference to Jesus going to Capernaum upon leaving Nazareth (Matt 4:13; Luke 4:31) and in the fact that both Matthew and Luke (unlike Mark) append some further characterization of Capernaum—Matthew with the words, "which is by the sea in the region of Zebulun and Naphtali," followed by a fulfillment-of-prophecy formula, and Luke simply with the words, "a city of Galilee." It should be noted, at this point, that while Matthew (like Luke)

---

16. Ἀκούσας δὲ ὅτι Ἰωάννης παρεδόθη.

17. Mark 1:14 also refers at this point to the arrest of John without having previously mentioned it, but his reference (μετὰ δὲ τὸ παραδοθῆναι τὸν Ἰωάννην) is perhaps a bit more direct and categorical than is Matthew's (ἀκούσας δὲ ὅτι Ἰωάννης παρεδόθη). Clearly, Matthew and Mark are related at this point, either directly or indirectly, but the nature of the relation is not immediately apparent.

has Jesus proceeding immediately to Capernaum after leaving Nazareth, Mark (who, of course, has no reference to Jesus being in or leaving Nazareth) interjects the call of the four disciples (Mark 1:16) before indicating that Jesus went to Capernaum (Mark 1:21); Matthew, on the other hand, has the call of the disciples after the move to Capernaum (Matt 4:18–22; Luke, of course, has a somewhat similar call story later in the narrative, at Luke 5:1–11).

A fifth clue that Matthew and Luke may be using common (or similar) source material appears in the fact that each has two references to "Galilee"—the first at the beginning of the pericope (Matt 4:12; Luke 4:14) and the second in connection with the reference to Capernaum (Matt 4:15; Luke 4:31)—and that the two references in each are parallel as regards content. In Luke, of course, the two references are separated by the account of Jesus' rejection at Nazareth. Mark, it should be noted, has only the former reference to "Galilee" (Mark 1:14).

A sixth clue that Matthew and Luke may be using common (or similar) source material appears in the fact that each includes a fulfillment-of-prophecy formula and each appeals to a passage (different passages, to be sure) from Isaiah (Matt 4:14–16; Luke 4:17–21). (Mark has no such fulfillment-of-prophecy formula or scriptural reference.) It is true that, while Luke has the appeal to prophecy as a part of the rejection story, Matthew associates it with the move to Capernaum. If Matthew is familiar with an account similar to Luke's, however, but has chosen to eliminate the actual rejection story at this point, he may well have decided, nevertheless, to preserve an appeal to prophecy (indeed, to the prophet Isaiah) but to choose a different passage in light of his omission of the rejection story.

A seventh clue that Matthew and Luke may be using common (or similar) source material appears in the fact that each concludes his account with a reference to Jesus preaching (Matt 4:17) or teaching (Luke 4:31b–32). The difference between "preaching" and "teaching" may be insignificant, indicating only the literary and/or theological preferences of the two writers. It may well be, however, that Matthew has, at this point in his narrative, turned to a different source: as already noted his next pericope is the call of the four disciples (Matt 4:18–22; cf. Mark 1:16–22), which does not appear in Luke, where, instead, there is the account of the miraculous catch of fish and call of three disciples (Luke 5:1–11).

On the basis of these seven clues, it is possible to build a very strong case that Matthew and Luke are using common (or similar) source material for the parallel passages under consideration and, indeed, that Luke reflects the source material more closely than does Matthew. Specifically, it appears that Matthew was familiar with a rejection story similar to or identical with that included by Luke and that, in Matthew's source material, this rejection story appeared at the same point in the narrative as it now appears in Luke. This raises a question about the possibility of a similar relation between Matthew and Luke at others points in the two gospels where such a relation has not generally been recognized. It is beyond the scope of this paper to explore the matter in detail, but an examination of the two narratives about John the Baptist (Matt 3:1–17; Luke 3:1–22) does reveal phenomena that are strikingly similar to those that have been observed in Matt 4:12–17 and Luke 4:14–32.

One such phenomenon occurs at the beginning of the two John-the-Baptist reports. Matthew begins with the words, "In those days," with no indication as to just *which* "days" are intended (clearly, however, the reference cannot be to the immediately preceding passage, which speaks of Joseph, Mary, and the young Jesus settling in Nazareth). Robert H. Gundry, among others, suggests that Matthew has brought the words forward from Mark 1:9 in order to "weld together John's ministry and Jesus' baptism in a single episode."[18] On the face of it, however, it appears more likely that Mark would have moved the words to a later point in the narrative—a point where they are, indeed, more intelligible—than that Matthew would have moved them forward in such a way as to leave them without any clear reference. So far as possible links between Matthew and Luke are concerned, however, it is important to note that the parallel passage in Luke begins

---

18. Gundry, *Matthew*, 41.

with the words, "In the fifteenth year of the reign of Tiberius Caesar, Pontius Pilate being governor of Judea, and Herod being tetrarch of Galilee, and his brother Philip tetrarch of the region of Iturea snd Trachonitis, and Lysanias tetrarch of Abilene, in the high-priesthood of Annas and Caiaphas ..." In other words, Luke supplies a possible reference for Matthew's "In those days." It is possible, of course, that Luke, using Matthew as a source and noting the latter's obscure "In those days," has decided to amplify and clarify the reference; it is also possible that Matthew has simply abbreviated Luke's reference. It is at least equally possible, however, that both Matthew and Luke are here using a source that begins the narrative about John's preaching with some indication of the date. If so, Matthew has apparently shortened the reference in such a way as to make it virtually meaningless, and it may be that Luke has expanded or otherwise revised the reference. In any case, this represents yet another instance in which Matthew has some type of obscure reference that becomes intelligible only in light of parallel material in Luke,

Further examination of the Matthean and Lukan materials on John the Baptist, particularly when compared with the parallel Markan material (Mark 1:2–11), discloses other possible links between Matthew and Luke—links involving both sequence and content. The following are noteworthy: (1) As already noted, both Matthew (3:1) and Luke (3:1–2), but not Mark (1:1), begin the narrative with a chronological reference. (2) Both Matthew (3:1) and Luke (3:2–3) proceed immediately to a direct statement about John and his preaching, while Mark (1:2–3) begins with a quotation from Mal 3:1 and Isa 40:3. (3) Both Matthew (3:3) and Luke (3:4–6) then introduce the quotation from Isaiah (Luke in an expanded form), and both omit the quotation from Malachi. (4) Both Matthew (3:7–10) and Luke (3:7–9) include John's "brood of vipers" message, but Mark does not.[19] To be sure, there are also indications of links between Matthew and Mark and between

---

19. For a convenient outline that illustrates these data, see Lord, "Gospels as Oral Traditional Literature," 60–61.

Luke and Mark, but it is clear that, for much of the material, Matthew and Luke are related to each other, either directly or indirectly, quite independently of the relation of each to Mark. This, of course, has long been noted by commentators and has been explained on the basis of the various source theories held by the respective commentators (e.g., both Matthew and Luke are here dependent upon the hypothetical source, Q; Luke is here dependent upon Matthew; or Matthew is here dependent upon Luke). Sometimes, it is argued that sheer coincidence is the explanation. On the basis of the earlier examination of Matt 4:12–17 and Luke 4:14–32, however, it appears likely that Matthew and Luke are here using common (or similar) source material (perhaps Q) and, indeed, that Luke follows this source material more closely than does Matthew.

Standing between the narratives about John the Baptist and Luke's account of the rejection at Nazareth (and Matthew's obscure reference to Jesus leaving Nazareth), in both Matthew and Luke, is the story of Jesus' temptations by the devil (Matt 4:1–11; Luke 4:1–13). Despite the significant differences between the two accounts, virtually all scholars agree that the accounts are related, either directly or indirectly.[20] Again, the specific explanation depends upon the particular source theory held by the commentator, but, as in the case of the materials about John the Baptist, it appears most likely that Matthew and Luke are here using common (or similar) source material.

Preceding the narratives about John the Baptist, in both Matthew and Luke, are the birth and infancy narratives (Matt 1:18–2:23; Luke 1:5–2:52). Virtually all modern scholars have agreed that Matthew and Luke here reflect different source materials.[21] Gundry, however, has recently made a much more persuasive argument than most scholars would have thought possible that, in his birth and infancy narratives, "Matthew used haggadic

---

20. See Schnackenburg, "Der Sinn der Versuchung Jesu bei den Synoptikern."

21. For a discussion of sources, see Brown, *Birth of the Messiah*, 104–19, 244–50.

and midrashic techniques on the very tradition later appearing in the early chapters of Luke,"[22] and, indeed, that Q should be expanded to include "not only the material usually designated as Q, but also the nativity story and some of the material peculiar to Matthew (M) and Luke (L)." His argument is that "Q included much more than is usually thought ... but at times Matthew redacted it so freely that his drawing on Q has gone unrecognized and separate traditions have wrongly been posited."[23] Although much further study of the birth and infancy narratives is needed, the conclusions drawn in the present paper tend to suggest that Gundry may be correct. If so, then it would appear that Matthew and Luke are drawing on common (or similar)) source material from the beginning of their gospels (except, perhaps, for the John-the-Baptist material in Luke 1) at least as far as Luke's account of Jesus' rejection at Nazareth and his move to Capernaum. It would also appear that, at least for much of the material, Luke follows the source more closely than does Matthew.

Whether the same is true in later sections of the two gospels requires considerable additional investigation. I have suggested elsewhere, for example, that all of the Synoptic "Son of Man" sayings, even those that are unique to Matthew and to Luke, are to be traced to the Q source material used by both Matthew and Luke.[24]

> Whether this Q was written or oral, whether Matthew and Luke made independent use of it or one of the two also knew the other, and whether Matthew and/or Luke also used other sources, perhaps even one or more sources common to both, are not important for our purposes.[25]

What is important is an apparently growing body of evidence indicating that the source material common to Matthew and Luke was more extensive than is generally supposed. Specifically, so far as the reports of the preaching of John and the early preaching

---

22. Gundry, *Matthew*, xi.
23. Gundry, *Matthew*, 4–5.
24. Walker, "Son of Man Question," chap. 12 in this volume.
25. Walker, "Son of Man Question," chap. 12, p. 236 in this volume.

of Jesus are concerned it now appears likely that Matthew and Luke had access to some common (or similar) non-Markan source material beyond what is usually included under the heading of Q. Additional study may well uncover additional evidence supporting such a hypothesis, and, if so, the generally accepted solutions to the Synoptic Problem will require re-examination.

Chapter 8

Martha and Mary in the Third and Fourth Gospels

An Exercise in Source Criticism

Introduction

The sisters, Martha and Mary, appear at two points in the Fourth Gospel: first, in the report of Jesus raising their brother Lazarus from the dead (John 11:1–44) and then fourteen verses later, in the account of Mary anointing Jesus' feet (John 12:1–8).[1] Elsewhere in the New Testament, Martha and Mary appear only once—at Luke 10:38–42. Recent literature regarding the two sisters has been voluminous. Focusing in large part on the question of the status and role of women in the Jesus movement and/or in the early church, this literature exhibits widely divergent understandings and assessments of the portrayals of the two women in the Johannine and Lukan pericopes.[2]

"Martha and Mary in the Third and Fourth Gospels: An Exercise in Source Criticism." Pp. 123–35 in *Resourcing New Testament Studies: Literary, Historical, and Theological Essays in Honor of David L. Dungan*. Ed. Allan J. McNicol, David P. Peabody, and J. Samuel Subramanian. New York and London: T & T Clark International, 2009. Copyright © 2009 Allan J. McNicol, David B. Peabody, and J. Samuel Subramanian. Reprinted with permission.

1. The two incidents are separated only by John 11:45–57, which reports various reactions to the resurrection of Lazarus.

2. On Luke 10:38–42, see, e.g., Schüssler Fiorenza, *But She Said*, 51–76; and Levine with Blickenstaff, *Feminist Companion to Luke*, 161–96, 197–213, 214–31, 232–45. Noting that interpretations of Luke 10:38–42 "vary according to the methods, experiences, and textual priorities each

It is not the purpose of the present study, however, to explore issues related to the status and role of women. Rather, I propose simply to point out some significant parallels between two of the pericopes in question—Luke 10:38–42 and John 12:1–8—and to suggest that the latter pericope is based in part on the former. If this suggestion is correct, it will, of course, shed some light on the larger question of the relationship between the Third and Fourth Gospels.

John 12:1–8 and Matt 26:6–13/Mark 14:3–9

John 12:1–8 reports a meal (δεῖπνον) that is served for Jesus in Bethany—in the home of Lazarus[3]—shortly before the Passover.[4] Martha does the "serving" (διακονεῖν), and Lazarus is among those sharing the meal (εἷς ... ἐκ τῶν ἀνακειμένων σὺν αὐτῷ). Apparently during the meal, Mary anoints Jesus' feet with expensive ointment (μύρον νάρδου πιστικῆς) and wipes them with her hair. This provokes Judas Iscariot to complain that the ointment should have been sold and the proceeds given to the poor, whereupon Jesus responds with words that include a reference to his impending death and the statement, "For the poor you always have with you, but me you do not always have" (τοὺς πτωχοὺς γὰρ πάντοτε ἔχετε μεθ᾽ ἑαυτῶν, ἐμὲ δὲ οὐ πάντοτε ἔχετε).

This pericope is reminiscent of Matt 26:6–13/Mark 14:3–9,[5] where, also in Bethany, shortly before the Passover,[6] a meal is served in the house of "Simon the leper," and Jesus is present. During the meal, an unnamed woman anoints Jesus' head with ex-

---

author brings to the study," Levine ("Introduction," 15) observes that "no consensus has been, or likely will be, reached on this pericope." On the Johannine pericopes, see, e.g., Levine with Blickenstaff, *Feminist Companion to John*, 1:36–40, 143–58, 186–87; 2:23–24, 86–92, 108–12.

3. Presumably also the home of Martha and Mary.

4. "Six days before the Passover."

5. Matt 26:6–13 and Mark 14:3–9 are essentially identical in their basic features, but, as is often the case, the Markan account is somewhat more detailed than the Matthean. The pericope is absent from the Third Gospel, although a similar episode appears at Luke 7:36–50.

6. Apparently two days before the Passover (Matt 26:2/Mark 14:1).

pensive ointment (μύρον βαρυτίμου in Matthew; μύρου νάρδου πιστικῆς πολυτελοῦς in Mark). This draws the complaint that the ointment should have been sold and the proceeds given to the poor,[7] whereupon Jesus responds with words that include the statement, "For the poor you always have with you, but me you do not always have,"[8] and a reference to his impending death.

To be sure, there are significant differences between John 12:1–8 and Matt 26:6–13/Mark 14:3–9: (1) neither Lazarus, Martha, nor Mary is mentioned in Matthew/Mark, but all three are present in John; (2) the location of the episode in Matthew/Mark is in the home of Simon the leper, but Simon is not mentioned in John and the event occurs in the home of Lazarus; (3) the woman who anoints Jesus is unnamed in Matthew/Mark, but she is identified as Mary in John; (4) in Matthew/Mark it is Jesus' head that is anointed, but in John it is his feet; and (5) in Matthew/Mark it is simply "some" (Mark) or "the disciples" (Matthew) who object to the woman's action, but in John it is Judas Iscariot.

Nevertheless, the basic framework of John 12:1–8 is essentially the same as that of Matt 26:6–13/Mark 14:3–9: (1) the timing shortly before Passover, (2) the setting in Bethany, (3) the meal, (4) the woman, (5) the expensive ointment, (6) the anointing, (7) the objection that the ointment should have been sold and the proceeds given to the poor, and (8) Jesus' response, including a reference to his impending death and the statement about the poor.

---

7. The complaint is made by "the disciples" in Matt 26:8 but simply by "some" in Mark 14:4.

8. Πάντοτε γὰρ τοὺς πτωχοὺς ἔχετε μεθ᾽ ἑαυτῶν, ἐμὲ δὲ οὐ πάντοτε ἔχετε in Matt 26: 11; πάντοτε γὰρ τοὺς πτωχοὺς ἔχετε μεθ᾽ ἑαυτῶν, καὶ ὅταν θέλητε δύναοθε αὐτοῖς εὖ ποιῆσαι, ἐμὲ δὲ οὐ πάντοτε ἔχετε in Mark 14:7. Except for the word order (πάντοτε ... τοὺς πτωχοὺς in Matthew and τοὺς πτωχοὺς ... πάντοτε in John) the Matthean and Johannine versions are identical. The Markan version differs from the Matthean in that it has καὶ ὅταν θέλητε δύναοθε αὐτοῖς εὖ ποιῆσαι between πάντοτε γὰρ τοὺς πτωχοὺς ἔχετε μεθ᾽ ἑαυτῶν and ἐμὲ δὲ οὐ πάντοτε ἔχετε. David B. Peabody regards what he terms the "broken parallelism" in Mark as an indication that Mark was written later than Matthew (conversation on August 4, 2005).

Moreover, much of the actual wording of John 12:1–8 is identical or similar to that of Matt 26:6–13/Mark 14:3–9:

1. ὁ οὖν Ἰησοῦς ... ἦλθεν εἰς Βηθανίαν (John 12:1; cf. τοῦ δὲ Ἰησοῦ γενομένου ἐν Βηθανίᾳ in Matt 26:6 and καὶ ὄντος αὐτοῦ ἐν Βηθανίᾳ in Mark 14:3)

2. εἷς ... ἐκ τῶν ἀνακειμένων σὺν αὐτῷ (John 12:2; cf. αὐτοῦ ἀνακειμένου in Matt 26:7 and κατακειμένου αὐτοῦ in Mark 14:3)

3. μύρου νάρδου (John 12:3; cf. μύρου νάρδου in Matt 26:7 and μύρου in Mark 14:3)

4. πολυτίμου (John 12:3; cf. βαρυτίμου in Matt 26:7 and πολυτελοῦς in Mark 14:3)

5. Ἰούδας ὁ Ἰσκαριώτης εἷς ἐκ τῶν μαθητῶν αὐτοῦ (John 12:4; cf. οἱ μαθηταί in Matt 26:8 and τινες in Mark 14:4)

6. διὰ τί τοῦτο τὸ μύρον οὐκ ἐπράθη τριακοσίων δηναρίων καὶ ἐδόθη πτωχοῖς; (John 12:5; cf. ἐδύνατο γὰρ τοῦτο πραθῆναι πολλοῦ καὶ δοθῆναι πτωχοῖς in Matt 26:9 and ἠδύνατο γὰρ τοῦτο τὸ μύρον πραθῆναι ἐπάνω δηναρίων τριακοσίων καὶ δοθῆναι τοῖς πτωχοῖς in Mark 14:5)

7. εἶπεν οὖν ὁ Ἰησοῦς (John 12:7; cf. γνοὺς δὲ ὁ Ἰησοῦς εἶπεν αὐτοῖς in Matt 26:10 and ὁ δὲ Ἰησοῦς εἶπεν in Mark 14:6)

8. ἄφες αὐτήν (John 12:7; cf. ἄφετε αὐτήν in Mark 14:6)

9. ἵνα εἰς τὴν ἡμέραν τοῦ ἐνταφιασμοῦ μου τηρήσῃ αὐτό (John 12:7; cf. πρὸς τὸ ἐνταφιάσαι με ἐποίησεν in Matt 26:12 and εἰς τὸν ἐνταφιασμόν in Mark 14:8)

10. τοὺς πτωχοὺς γὰρ πάντοτε ἔχετε μεθ' ἑαυτῶν, ἐμὲ δὲ οὐ πάντοτε ἔχετε (John 12:8; cf. πάντοτε γὰρ τοὺς πτωχοὺς ἔχετε μεθ' ἑαυτῶν, ἐμὲ δὲ οὐ πάντοτε ἔχετε in Matt 26:11 and πάντοτε γὰρ τοὺς πτωχοὺς ἔχετε μεθ' ἑαυτῶν ... , ἐμὲ δὲ οὐ πάντοτε ἔχετε in Mark 14:7).

Thus, despite the differences between Matt 26:6–13/Mark 14:3–9 and John 12:1–8, "no one really doubts" that the Johannine pericope is "describing the same scene" as that portrayed in the Synoptic passages.[9] Moreover, the parallels—both substantive and verbal—are such as to make it virtually certain that the Fourth Evangelist is here dependent either upon Matthew and/or Mark or upon some common or similar source.[10]

John 12:1–8 and Luke 7:36–50

John 12:1–8 is also reminiscent, however, of Luke 7:36–50. Here, during a meal in the house of a Pharisee named Simon,[11] an unnamed "sinner" woman[12] anoints Jesus' feet with ointment, where-

---

9. Brown, *Gospel according to John (i–xii)*, 449. In the Fourth Gospel, the episode comes immediately before the Triumphal Entry into Jerusalem; in Matthew and Mark, however, it is somewhat later in the sequence of events—after the Entry and shortly before the Last Supper.

10. Brown (*Gospel according to John (i–xii)*, 450–52) opts for the latter, suggesting further that John may, at some points, reflect an earlier version of the account than do Matthew and Mark. C. K. Barrett (*Gospel according to St John*, 409), however, suggests that "there is no more economical hypothesis than that the tradition reached [John] by way of Mark." Another possibility, of course, is that the tradition reached John by way of Matthew.

11. Note that Matt 26:6/Mark 14:3 places the anointing in the home of "Simon the leper." According to Joseph A. Fitzmyer (*Gospel according to Luke (I–IX)*, 689), it is "strange" that the name "Simon" is not introduced until v. 40 of the Lukan narrative and may suggest the influence of Mark 14:3 at this point.

12. The Greek reads, γυνὴ ἥτις ἦν ἐν τῇ πόλει ἁμαρτωλός (v. 37, see also v. 39, where the Pharisee describes her as a "sinner" [ἁμαρτωλός] and v. 47, where Jesus refers to "her many sins" [αἱ ἁμαρτίαι αἱ πολλαί]. Fitzmyer (*Gospel according to Luke (I–IX)*, 683) translates γυνὴ ἥτις ἦν ἐν τῇ πόλει ἁμαρτωλός as "a certain woman in the town known to be a sinner," but equally possible would be "a certain woman known in the town to be a sinner" (note, however, that the word "known" does not appear in the Greek). The nature of her "sinfulness" is not disclosed, but Simon's statement, "If this man were a prophet, he would have known who and what sort of woman this is who is touching him, for she is a sinner," may suggest that she was a prostitute. As Fitzmyer (*Gospel according to Luke (I–IX)*, 689) notes, however, this "is at most implied, not being said openly in the text." Barbara E. Reed ("'Do You See This Woman?'" 113) argues, on the basis of the imperfect tense of ἦν (v. 37) and the perfect tense of ἀφέωνται (vv. 47 and 48), that the woman had *formerly* been a sinner but no longer was.

upon Simon criticizes not the woman but Jesus, and Jesus responds. Many of the details of Like 7:36–50 parallel those of Matt 26:6–13/Mark 14:3–9: (1) the host named Simon, (2) the meal, (3) the woman, (4) the ointment, (5) the anointing, (6) an objection, and (7) a response from Jesus. A principal difference, of course, is that Matthew and Mark have the woman anointing Jesus' head, while it is his feet that she anoints in Luke.

Scholars have debated the relation between the episode narrated in Luke 7:36–50 and that reported in Matt 26:6–13/Mark 14:3–9. Some believe them to be the same, but Brown argues that they reflect two separate incidents. In his view, Matt 26:6–13 and Mark 14:3–9 "represent an almost pure form of the second incident," which occurred shortly before Jesus' death, while Luke 7:36–50 "presents us with a story of the first incident," which occurred earlier during Jesus' Galilean ministry, "but with much admixture of detail from the second incident."[13] It is not the purpose of the present study, however, to unravel the relations between Matt 26:6–13/Mark 14:3–9 and Luke 7:36–50 but rather to relate both Matt 26:6–13/Mark 14:3–9 and Luke 7:36–50 to John 12:1–8.

As regards the anointing of Jesus' feet rather than his head, John 12:1–8 is in agreement with Luke 7:36–50 as over against Matt 26:6–13/Mark 14:3–9. In addition, John 12:1–8 reflects some of the distinctive wording of Luke 7:36–50: (1) τοὺς πόδας τοῦ Ἰησοῦ (John 12:3; cf. τοὺς πόδας αὐτοῦ in Luke 7:38); and (2) ἐξέμαξεν ταῖς θριξὶν αὐτῆς τοὺς πόδας αὐτοῦ (John 12:3; cf. ταῖς θριξὶν τῆς κεφαλῆς αὐτῆς ἐξέμασσεν καὶ κατεφίλει τοὺς πόδας αὐτοῦ in Luke 7:38).[14] Thus, Brown observes that, while John 12:1–8 fol-

---

13. Brown, *Gospel according to John (i–xii)*, 450–51.

14. Noting the repetition of τοὺς πόδας and the fact that a few witnesses have τοὺς πόδας αὐτοῦ before rather than after ταῖς θριξὶν αὐτῆς in John 12:3, Frederick C. Grant ("Was the Author of John Dependent upon the Gospel of Luke?" 290), argued that τοὺς πόδας αὐτοῦ is "certainly a gloss" and καὶ ἐξέμαξεν ταῖς θριξὶν αὐτῆς is "probably a gloss," inserted under the influence of Luke 7:38; see also, more cautiously, Bultmann, *Gospel of John*, 415 n. 1. According to John Amedee Bailey (*Traditions Common to the Gospels of Luke and John*, 3), however, "the fact that all of the manuscripts of any importance at all offer these words

lows the basic framework of Matt 26:6–13/Mark 14:3–9, certain of
its details are closer to those of Luke 7:36–50.[15] Brown concludes,
therefore, that John 12:1–8 "represents a form of the second [i.e.,
the Matthean/Markan] incident into which have been incorporated details from *the Lucan form* of the first incident."[16] In short,
John 12:1–8 appears to be based in large part upon Matt 26:6–13/
Mark 14:3–9 or a common or similar source, but also in part upon
Luke 7:36–50 or a common or similar source.

John 12:1–8 and
Luke 10:38–42

Certain of the details of John 12:1–8, however, cannot be accounted for by reference either to Matt 26:6–13/Mark 14:3–9 or to
Luke 7:36–50. Most significant in this regard are: (a) the presence
of Lazarus, (b) the presence of Martha and her role in "serving,"
and (c) the identification of the woman who anointed Jesus as
Mary. It is my suggestion that these details derive from the narrative found in Luke 10:38–42, which, as has already been noted,
is, except for John 11:1–44 (the raising of Lazarus), the only other
reference to Martha and Mary in the entire New Testament.

To be sure, the story-line in Luke 10:38–42 bears little apparent
resemblance to the Johannine anointing episode, and, at first
glance, it is difficult to relate the two pericopes. A closer look,
however, reveals a number of significant parallels: (1) in both
passages, Martha and Mary are mentioned by name;[17] (2) in both

---

excludes this as a possibility." Moreover, the somewhat awkward repetition of τοὺς πόδας in John 12:3 (τοὺς πόδας τοῦ Ἰησοῦ and τοὺς πόδας
αὐτοῦ) may well reflect the fact that τοὺς πόδας αὐτοῦ appears not just
twice but three times in Luke 7:38.

15. Brown, *Gospel according to John (i–xii)*, 449. For a table showing the
parallels, see p. 450. Barrett (*Gospel according to St John*, 409) suggests that
John likely knew Luke at this point. For a detailed discussion that arrives
at the same conclusion, see Bailey, *Traditions Common to the Gospels of Luke
and John*, 1–8.

16. Brown, *Gospel according to John (i–xii)*, 451.

17. As already noted, they appear elsewhere in the New Testament
only in John 11:1–46.

passages, Martha and Mary are described as "sisters";[18] (3) in both passages, Martha is mentioned first and then Mary;[19] (4) both passages apparently involve the serving of a meal;[20] (5) in both passages, Martha, not Mary, is the one doing the "serving";[21] (6) the same Greek root is used for the "serving" in both passages;[22] (7) in both passages, Mary is doing something other than "serving"; (8) in both passages, what Mary is doing might well have been seen as unconventional;[23] (9) in both passages, Mary's

---

18. This is stated both in Luke 10:39, 40 and, shortly before John 12:1–8, in John 11:1, 3, 5, 28. Warren Carter ("Getting Martha Out of the Kitchen," 218), among others, has suggested that "sister" (ἀδελφή) may "point beyond a relation of kinship ... to denote ... joint participation in the community of the disciples of Jesus." See also, e.g., D'Angelo, "Reconstructing the 'Real' Women from Gospel Literature," 217: "in the case of Martha and Mary, sisterhood may represent but a shared commitment to the mission, rather than blood relationship." Be that as it may, the same term (ἀδελφή) is used in both Luke and John to describe the relationship between Martha and Mary.

19. Cf. John 11:1, where Mary appears first and then Martha.

20. This is stated in John 12:2 and probably implied in Luke 10:38–42. Schüssler Fiorenza (*But She Said*, 51–76) argues that διακονία/διακονεῖν in Luke 10:38–42 refers not specifically to the serving of a meal but rather in a more general sense to carrying out the "womanly" responsibilities of a household. This, however, would certainly include the serving of meals. Indeed, the very fact that Martha "received" Jesus (ὑπεδέξατο αὐτόν; note: many MSS, including important ones, add "into her house") suggests that providing a meal would be a part of the hospitality. Carter ("Getting Martha Out of the Kitchen," 223), among others, argues that διακονία/διακονεῖν in Luke-Acts refers not to the preparation and serving of food at all but rather to "responsibilities of leadership and ministry on behalf of the church." I regard this as unlikely, however, in Luke 10:40.

21. See, e.g., Barrett, *Gospel according to St John*, 411: "This feature, and the contrasted notice of Mary, suggest strongly that John was aware of Luke."

22. Διακονία/διακονεῖν in Luke 10:40; διακονεῖν in John 12:2.

23. On Mary "sitting at Jesus' feet" (Luke 10:39), see, e.g., Alexander, "Sisters in Adversity," 211: "her behavior overturns accepted norms for a woman." Others, however, have argued that "sitting at Jesus' feet" could represent either the traditional silent wife, sitting at the feet of her husband at the table, or the student sitting at the feet of the rabbi; see, e.g., Schüssler Fiorenza, "A Feminist Critical Interpretation for Liberation," 26–28.

activity places her in close physical proximity to Jesus; (10) in both passages, it is specifically Jesus' "feet" that are associated with Mary's location;[24] (11) in both passages, an objection is raised against Mary's behavior;[25] (12) in both passages, Jesus responds to the objection in such a way as to defend Mary's behavior; (13) in both passages, Mary's behavior is apparently seen as preferable to or more significant than that of Martha;[26] and (14) the rather uncommon word μέλειν ("to be a source of care" or "concern") appears in both passages.[27]

Both the number and the nature of these parallels almost inevitably suggest a literary relationship between Luke 10:38–42 and John 12:1–8 — indeed, that the Fourth Evangelist must have known and been influenced by the Martha/Mary story in essentially its Lukan form. Particularly significant in this regard are the presence of Martha in the Johannine narrative and the fact that her role is that of "serving." As John Amedee Bailey notes, the seemingly incidental reference to Martha "is completely extrinsic" to the story-line, "occurring in a story otherwise concerned only with Mary." In his view, it almost certainly derives from Luke 10:38–42.[28] Indeed, apart from Luke 10:38–42, there would appear to be no reason for John 12:1–8 to mention Martha at all and particularly to portray her role as that of "serving."

---

24. In Luke 10:39, she is "sitting at the feet of the Lord"; in John 12:3, she "anointed Jesus' feet and wiped his feet with her hair."

25. In Luke 10:40, Martha objects that Mary is not helping her with the serving; in John 12:4–5, Judas Iscariot objects that the ointment should have been sold and the proceeds given to the poor.

26. This is clearly stated in Luke 10:41–42. In John 12:1–8, Mary's behavior is explicitly defended (vv. 7–8) but nothing is said regarding Martha's activity except simply that she "was serving"; clearly, however, it is Mary's actions that are being highlighted in the narrative and not Martha's.

27. Used by Martha with reference to Jesus in Luke 10:40; used by the narrator with reference to Judas in John 12:6. Elsewhere in Luke-Acts, the word appears only at Acts 18:17; elsewhere in the Fourth Gospel, only at John 10:13; elsewhere in the New Testament only at Matt 22:16/Mark 12:14; Mark 4:38; 1 Cor 7:21; 9:9; 1 Pet 5:7.

28. Bailey, *Traditions Common to the Gospels of Luke and John*, 5.

Luke 10:38–42 and Matt 26:6–13/Mark 14:3–9/Luke 7:36–50

What is not immediately apparent, however, is why the Fourth Evangelist would associate the Martha/Mary story in Luke 10:38–42 with the anointing stories in Matt 26:6–13/Mark 14:3–9 and Luke 7:36–50 in such a way as to produce John 12:1–8. My suggestion is that there are two rather obvious links.

The first link is to be found in the geographical location of the anointing episode. Luke 7:36–50 is silent regarding the location, but Matt 26:6/Mark 14:3 has it in Bethany. For the Fourth Evangelist, however, Bethany is significant specifically because it is the home of Lazarus, Martha, and Mary.[29] Further, according to John, these three siblings enjoy a very close relationship with Jesus.[30] If Jesus was being entertained in Bethany, therefore, then surely Lazarus, Martha, and Mary would be present![31] Indeed, they would most likely be the hosts.[32] Thus, it is the Matthean/Markan location of the anointing in Bethany that brings Lazarus, Martha, and Mary into the Johannine narrative. The presence of Martha and Mary, however, immediately calls attention to Luke 10:38–42, where Jesus has a meal in the presence—apparently in the home—of Martha and Mary. Once this association is made,

---

29. This is made clear in John 11:1 and is reiterated at the very beginning of the anointing narrative (12:1), where Bethany is referred to specifically as the place "where Lazarus was." Indeed, this "Bethany" is mentioned in the Fourth Gospel (11:1, 18; 12:1) *only* in connection with Lazarus, Martha, and Mary (John 1:28 refers to a different "Bethany" that was "beyond the Jordan," not "near Jerusalem" as in 11:18).

30. John 11:3, 5, 11, 35–36.

31. Noting that "Lazarus plays no part in the story, and is not mentioned again till v. 9," Barrett (*Gospel according to St John*, 411) suggests "that John had no independent narrative here, but simply identified the characters of the Marcan story, which was placed at Bethany, with the family he had already mentioned as resident there."

32. E.g., Barrett, *Gospel according to St John*, 411: "the most probable view is that Lazarus, Mary, and Martha should be thought of as providing the meal."

Luke 10:38–42 becomes available to provide details regarding the respective roles for Martha and Mary in John's version of the anointing episode:[33] Martha "serves" (as in Luke 10:38–42), and the woman who is engaged in a very different activity—one that places her in close physical proximity to Jesus' feet and subjects her to criticism (as in Luke 10:38–42)—is now identified as Mary. Thus, the place name "Bethany"—the home of Lazarus, Martha, and Mary in the Fourth Gospel—provides the initial link between the anointing stories in Matt 26:6–13/Mark 14:3–9 and Luke 7:36–50 and the Martha/Mary story in Luke 10:38–42.[34]

The second likely link between the Martha/Mary story (Luke 10:38–42) and the anointing stories (Matt 26:6–13/Mark 14:3–9 and Luke 7:36–50) is to be found in a striking verbal similarity between Luke 7:38 and Luke 10:39. In Luke 10:39, Mary is "sitting at the Lord's feet" (παρακαθεσθεῖσα πρὸς τοὺς πόδας τοῦ κυρίου) listening to his words. Matt 26:6–13/Mark 14:3–9 makes no reference to Jesus' feet, but the unnamed woman in Luke 7:38 is "standing behind [Jesus] at his feet" (στᾶσα ὀπίσω παρὰ τοὺς πόδας αὐτοῦ) when she wets his feet with her tears, wipes them with her hair, kisses them, and anoints them with ointment. The verbal parallel almost inevitably suggests that the woman "standing behind [Jesus] at his feet" in Luke 7:38 might also be the one "sitting at the Lord's feet" in Luke 10:39, and the latter is unambiguously identified as Mary the sister of Martha. Indeed, it may even be the case that the Fourth Evangelist sees positioning herself "at Jesus' feet" as a characteristic behavior of Mary, because it is also she who "fell at [Jesus'] feet" (ἔπεσεν αὐτοῦ πρὸς τοὺς πόδας) in

---

33. Lazarus is not mentioned in Luke 10:38–42 and thus has no role in John 12:1–8 other than simply to be present.

34. It is even possible that Luke 10:38–42 might be seen as simply a variant version of the anointing incident. Luke 7:38 reports that the woman stood behind Jesus "at his feet" (παρὰ τοὺς πόδας αὐτοῦ), wet his feet with her tears, wiped them with the hair of her head, kissed them, and anointed them with ointment. Thus, the statement in Luke 10:39 that Mary was sitting "at the Lord's feet" (πρὸς τοὺς πόδας τοῦ κυρίου) might serve as an abbreviated depiction of the same incident.

John 11:32. In any case, a woman in close physical proximity to Jesus' feet provides a likely link between the Martha/Mary story in Luke 7:38–42 and the anointing story in Luke 7:36–50, which has already been associated with the rather similar anointing story in Matt 26:6–13/Mark 14:3–9. Thus, Martha appears in John 12:2 as the one who "serves" (as in Luke 10:40) and the unnamed woman who anoints Jesus' feet (Luke 7:38) is identified in John 12:3 as Mary the sister of Martha.

Luke 10:38–42 would also appear to explain why the Fourth Evangelist chooses to follow Luke 7:38 in having the woman anoint Jesus' feet rather than his head as in Matt 26:7/Mark 14:3.[35] Brown suggests that John sees Mary's action as constituting "an anointing of Jesus' body for burial" (John 12:7) and observes that "one might anoint the feet of a corpse as part of the ritual of preparing the whole body for burial."[36] This may well be correct, but under such circumstances not only the feet but also other parts of the corpse would presumably be anointed. Why, then, specifically the *feet*? Various suggestions have been offered.[37] Gail R. O'Day may be at least partially correct in her view that Mary's act of anointing and wiping Jesus' feet "is essential to the Johannine

---

35. Brown (*Gospel according to John (i–xii)*, 450–51) observes that anointing someone's feet "seems pointless" and "is really unparalleled"; he suggests, therefore, that, despite Luke 7:38, no such anointing actually occurred; rather, the penitent woman weeps, her tears fall on Jesus' feet, "and she hastily wipes them away with her hair." Brown then says with regard to John 12:3: "If Luke's anointing of the feet is anomalous, the woman's action becomes even more extraordinary in John when she proceeds to wipe off the perfume she has just applied! Luke's description of the wiping away of tears makes sense, but since the Johannine account does not mention tears, the action of wiping has now been transferred to the perfume."

36. Brown, *Gospel according to John (i–xii)*, 454.

37. According to Barrett (*Gospel according to St John*, 412), "John may have abandoned the anointing of Jesus' head, as recounted in Mark, because it suggested too crudely the anointing of a messianic king of a kind inconsistent with his understanding of Jesus, and adopted a suggestion provided by his other source, Luke."

account" because it "prefigures" Jesus' own act of washing and wiping the disciples' feet at the farewell meal (John 13:4–5).[38] The simplest explanation, however, is the following: Matt 26:7/ Mark 14:3 has the woman anoint Jesus' *head*, but Luke 10:39 has her anoint his *feet*, and the Fourth Evangelist must therefore decide which to follow. The scales are tipped, however, by the fact that the author has already identified the woman in question as Mary, and Luke 10:39 has Mary sitting specifically at Jesus' *feet*, not at his head. In short, once Luke 10:38–42 has been linked to the anointing episode, it becomes almost inevitable that the anointing of Jesus' *feet* (as in Luke 10:39), not his head (as in Matt 26:7/Mark 14:3), would be adopted by the Fourth Evangelist.

Two additional details in John 12:1–8 remain to be explained. The first is the apparently inexplicable fact that Mary anoints Jesus' feet with expensive ointment and then immediately proceeds to wipe it off. In Luke 7:38, the unnamed "sinner" woman wets Jesus' feet with her tears, and it is the tears that she wipes off before applying the ointment. Presumably, the reason for her weeping is either "repentance for her sins" or "joy at the realization of the forgiveness of her sins by God that she has already experienced."[39] In either case, her weeping is related to the fact that she is (or has been) a "sinner" (ἁμαρτωλός). All of this makes perfectly good sense. Once the woman in question has been identified by the Fourth Evangelist as Mary of Bethany, the sister of Martha and Lazarus, however, she can no longer be portrayed as a "sinner";[40] thus, there is no reason for her to weep and therefore

---

38. O'Day, "Gospel of John," 701; see also, e.g., Kysar, *John*, 187. O'Day notes that the word for "wiping" in Luke 7:38 and John 11:2; 12:3 (ἐκμάσσειν) is the same word used in John 13:5.

39. Fitzmyer, *Gospel according to Luke (I–IX)*, 689.

40. Except in John 4:7–30 (the Samaritan woman at the well), Jesus does not associate with "sinners" at all in the Fourth Gospel (John 7:53–8:11 is almost certainly a later interpolation), and even here the emphasis is not on her "sinfulness" as much as on the fact that she is a woman and a Samaritan. Indeed, the term "sinner" (ἁμαρτωλός) is applied only to Jesus himself in the Fourth Gospel (John 9:16, 24, 25, 31).

no tears on Jesus' feet to be wiped away. Nevertheless, the act of wiping Jesus' feet is retained, presumably simply because it appears in Luke 7:38. The result, however, is the apparent nullification of the anointing itself.

The second as yet unexplained detail is the fact that, just as the unnamed woman in Luke 7:38 has her hair unbound, the same is apparently true of Mary in John 12:3.[41] Most scholars have assumed that the unbinding of a woman's hair in public would have violated the Palestinian-Jewish custom of the time.[42] Thus, while it might not be particularly surprising in Luke 7:38, where the woman in question is characterized as a "sinner," it would clearly be "out of character for the virtuous Mary of Bethany."[43] If this is the case, then it would appear that the Fourth Evangelist has simply retained this detail from the Lukan narrative without recognizing its inappropriateness in the new context. J. F. Coakley and others, however, have argued that flowing hair was not necessarily frowned on in the case of *unmarried* women.[44] Thus, on the assumption that Mary was herself unmarried, her unbound hair would not necessarily be problematic. In either case, however, retention of the wiping of Jesus' feet in the Johannine narrative would almost inevitably necessitate retention also of the unbound hair. Both the unbound hair and the wiping of Jesus' feet in John 12:3, therefore, appear to reflect the influence of Luke 7:38.[45]

In short, certain apparent anomalies in the Johannine narrative are best explained by assuming that the Fourth Evangelist

---

41. Fitzmyer (*Gospel according to Luke (I–IX)*), 689) says regarding the woman in Luke 7:38 that, "having loosened her headdress, she unbound her hair," thus suggesting that her hair was originally bound. This, however, is not in the text. Her hair may have been unbound from the beginning of the narrative.

42. See, e.g., the literature cited in Keener, *Gospel of John*, 2:863 n. 249.

43. Brown, *Gospel according to John (i–xii)*, 451.

44. Coakley, "Anointing at Bethany and the Priority of John."

45. It is possible, of course, that references to Jesus' "feet" reflect the Semitic euphemism in which "feet" really means "genitals." See, e.g., Exod 4:25; Judg 3:24; Ruth 3:4, 7, 8; 1 Sam 24:3; Isa 6:2; 7:20.

has associated the Martha/Mary story in Luke 10:38–42 with the anointing stories in Matt 26:6–13/Mark 14:3–9 and Luke 7:36–50 in such a way as to produce John 12:1–8.

Summary

The basic framework of John 12:1–8 comes either from Matt 26:6–13/Mark 14:3–9 or from a common or similar source, with certain of the details added from Luke 7:36–50 or a common or similar source. Although Lazarus, Martha, and Mary are mentioned in none of the Synoptic anointing stories, they appear in John 12:1–8 because they are regarded by John as friends of Jesus and the meal is being served in their hometown, Bethany—likely in their own home. Details regarding the respective roles of Lazarus, Martha, and Mary, however, come essentially from the Martha/Mary story in Luke 10:38–42. Aside from his mere presence, Lazarus has no role in the Johannine narrative because he is not mentioned at all in Luke 10:38–42. Because it is Martha alone who does the "serving" in Luke 10:40, she alone is assigned the same role in John 12:2, even though neither Matt 26:6–13/Mark 14:3–9 nor Luke 7:36–50 makes reference to anyone "serving."[46] Because Mary is not involved in the "serving" in Luke 10:39 but rather is engaged in the unconventional activity of sitting at Jesus' feet and listening to his words, she is identified in John 12:3–8 as the one who engages in the even more unconventional activity of anointing and wiping Jesus' feet and who, in turn, is first criticized and then defended. In short, it is essentially the Martha/Mary story in Luke 10:38–42 that provides the details regarding the respective roles of Martha and Mary in John 12:1–8. Moreover, some of the specific vocabulary in John 12:1–8 apparently comes from Luke 10:38–42 (i.e., the διακον- root and μέλειν).

---

46. Brown (*Gospel according to John (i–xii)*, 453) suggests that "the picture of Martha serving at table may represent the influence of the similar picture of Martha in Luke x 40."

Implications for the Relation between
the Third and Fourth Gospels

Parallels between the Fourth Gospel and the Synoptic Gospels have long been noted and have led some scholars to conclude that the Fourth Evangelist must have known and used one or more of the Synoptics.[47] As D. Moody Smith notes, however, "the problem of the relationship between John and Luke" constitutes "a special field of study" because of the nature of the "agreements or points of contact" between the two gospels. According to Smith, these include some agreements of wording or order, "shared perspective, knowledge, or information," "common silence or suppression of information, or departures from what we find in the other Gospels," appearance of "some of the same personages," and "marked similarities unique to Luke and John in the passion narrative."[48] According to many scholars, such parallels most likely result simply from use of common or similar source materials by the Third and Fourth Evangelists.[49] Indeed, Raymond E. Brown suggests that "during the oral formation of the Johannine stories and discourses ... , there very probably was some cross-influence from the emerging Lucan Gospel tradition."[50] Some scholars, however, while maintaining the independence of the basic Johannine tradition from the Synoptic Gospels, argue that the final redaction of the Fourth Gospel reflects knowledge both of

---

47. For discussion, see, e.g., Neirynck, "John and the Synoptics"; D. M. Smith, *John among the Gospels*. According to Kysar ("John, the Gospel of," 921), "the issue remains at a stalemate."

48. D. M. Smith, *John among the Gospels*, 86–87; see the discussion, pp. 85–110, 159–69.

49. E.g., Schniewind, *Die Parallelperikopen bei Lukas und Johannes*; F. C. Grant, "Was the Author of John Dependent upon the Gospel of Luke?" 285–307; Parker, "Luke and the Fourth Evangelist"; Maddox, *Purpose of Luke-Acts*, 158–79. For a similar view but with the added feature that John consistently has the more original form of the material shared by Luke and John, see Cribbs, "St. Luke and the Johannine Tradition"; his "Study of the Contacts that Exist between St. Luke and St. John"; and his "Agreements that Exist between Luke and John."

50. Brown, *Gospel according to John (i–xii)*, xlvii.

Lukan tradition and of the Gospel of Luke in its final or canonical form.[51] Going further, Bailey maintained more than four decades ago that the Fourth Evangelist knew the Gospel of Luke.[52]

If my own reconstruction of the relationship between John 12:1–8 and Luke 10:38–42 is correct, it would appear that the Fourth Evangelist knew the Lukan Martha/Mary story in essentially its canonical form. Otherwise, it is difficult to account for the specific points of contact between the two pericopes.[53]

Addendum: Why Judas Iscariot as the Critic of Mary?

Neither Matt 26:6–13/Mark 14:3–9, Luke 7:36–50, nor Luke 10:38–42 accounts for the fact that it is specifically Judas Iscariot who raises the objection to Mary's action in John 12:4–6. In the other anointing stories, the identity of the objector(s) becomes increasingly specific as one moves from Mark to Matthew to Luke: in Mark 14:4, it is simply "some"; in Matt 26:8, "the disciples"; and in Luke 7:39, a single individual, the Pharisee named Simon. Following the lead of this progression, the Fourth Evangelist may well have decided not only to have a single objector but also to provide a name.[54] It could not be Luke's Simon the Pharisee, however, because Simon is not mentioned in John 12:1–8. According to Matt 26:8, it should be one of Jesus' disciples, and John 12:4 identifies

---

51. E.g., Dauer, *Johannes und Lukas*; Heekerens, *Die Zeichen-Quelle der johanneischen Redaktion.*

52. Bailey, *Traditions Common to the Gospels of Luke and John.* For Bailey's list of other scholars holding the same view, see pp. 4–5, n. 2.

53. See above under "John 12:1–8 and Luke 10:38–42."

54. Clearly, the dramatic impact of the narrative becomes greater with a single named objector. According to Bultmann (*Gospel of John*, 415, n. 6) the naming of a single individual "corresponds to the tendency of the tradition to name anonymous persons": see also Bultmann, *History of the Synoptic Tradition*, 67–68, 241, 310). E. P. Sanders (*Tendencies of the Synoptic Tradition*, 185), however, notes the somewhat surprising fact that, while "there seems to be a clear tendency in the post-canonical material to substitute proper names for nouns or pronouns," "there are no clear differences among our Gospels at this point"; see the entire discussion, pp. 88–189.

Judas as "one of his disciples." But why specifically Judas Iscariot rather than one of the other disciples? Brown suggests two possible reasons. The first is "that the Johannine identification of the disgruntled disciple at Bethany as Judas was [simply] part of the popular tendency to present Judas in a hostile light." The second is that Judas may in fact have been the one who was responsible for the common funds and that, precisely for this reason, it was he who objected to what he regarded as a waste of the expensive ointment.[55]

If John was familiar with the Gospels of Matthew and/or Mark, however, another possibility emerges. Both Matthew and Mark place Judas' agreement to betray Jesus immediately after their accounts of the anointing (Matt 26:14–16; Mark 14:10–11).[56] This may suggest that the anointing episode was regarded, at least in part, as the provocation that led Judas to enter into the agreement. This, in turn, might well imply that it would have been Judas Iscariot who raised the objection to the anointing. Three features of John 12:4–6 would appear to support this likelihood: (1) Just as Matt 26:14/Mark 14:10 identifies Judas as "one of the twelve,"[57] John 12:4 identifies him as "one of his disciples."[58] (2) Just as Matt 26:15–16/Mark 14:10–11 reports Judas' actual agreement to "betray" (παραδιδόναι) Jesus, John 12:4 describes him as "he who was to betray" Jesus (ὁ μέλλων αὐτὸν παραδιδόναι), using the same word (παραδιδόναι) for "betrayal." (3) Just as Matt 26:14–

---

55. Brown, *Gospel according to John (i–xii)*, 453.

56. Although Luke's anointing episode is much earlier (7:36–50), Judas's agreement to betray Jesus comes at essentially the same point in the overall Lukan narrative as in Matthew and Mark (i.e., shortly before the Last Supper). The Fourth Gospel has no report of such an agreement, stating only that the devil "put it into the heart of Judas Iscariot" to betray Jesus (John 13:2).

57. Matthew: εἷς τῶν δώδεκα ὁ λεγόμενος Ἰούδας Ἰσκαριώτης; Mark: Ἰούδας Ἰσκαριὼθ ὁ εἷς τῶν δώδεκα.

58. Εἷς τῶν μαθητῶν αὐτοῦ. The followers of Jesus are frequently referred to in the Fourth Gospel as "the disciples" but only at John 6:67, 70, 71; 20:24 are they characterized as "the Twelve"; this apparent preference for "the disciples" may explain why "the Twelve" in Matt 26:14/Mark 14:10 becomes "the disciples" in John 12:4.

16/Mark 14:10–11 states that money was involved in Judas' agreement to betray Jesus,[59] John 12:6 characterizes him as a "thief" who "had the money box" and "used to take what was put into it." In short, the Fourth Gospel's identification of Judas as one of Jesus' "disciples" (12:4), its reference to his impending "betrayal" of Jesus (12:4), and its depiction of him as a "thief" (12:6) could all have been suggested by Matt 26:14–16/ Mark 14:10–11, which immediately follows the Matthean/Markan account of the anointing. This might well make Judas the most likely candidate for the role of objecting to Mary's anointing of Jesus feet.

---

59. Indeed, Matt 26:15a reports that Judas, taking the initiative, asked the chief priests, "What will you give me if I deliver him to you?"

Chapter 9

The Lord's Prayer in Matthew and in John

Similarities have occasionally been noted between the so-called "High Priestly Prayer" of Jesus in the Fourth Gospel[1] and the "Lord's Prayer"[2] as found in Luke and, more particularly, in Matthew and the Didache.[3] Raymond E. Brown, for example, says of the High Priestly Prayer:

"The Lord's Prayer in Matthew and in John." *NTS* 28, 2 (April 1982) 237–56. Copyright © Cambridge University Press 1982. Reprinted with permission.

1. John 17. On the designation of this prayer as a "High Priestly Prayer," see, e.g., Brown, *Gospel according to John (xiii–xxi)*, 747: "But if Jesus is a high priest here, it is not primarily in the sense of one about to offer sacrifice, but more along the lines of the high priest described in Hebrews and in Rom viii 34—one who stands before the throne of God making intercession for us."

2. The title, "Lord's Prayer," does not, of course, occur in any of the earliest Christian writings. It is possible that early Christians referred to the prayer by the double term, "Abba! Father!" (Rom 8:25; Gal 4:6); see, e.g., C. W. F. Smith, "Lord's Prayer," 154; Kittel, "ἀββᾶ," 6; but cf. also, e.g., Schrenk and Quell, "πατήρ, πατρῷος, πατριά, ἀπάτωρ, πατρικός," 1006.

3. Luke 11:2–4; Matt 6:9–13; Didache 8:2. The shorter version, found in Luke, is widely (though not universally) regarded as the more primitive, while the longer version, found in Matthew and, with only slight variations, in the Didache, is often understood as a liturgical expansion of the original. For a survey and evaluation of various arguments regarding the original form of the prayer, see, e.g., Harner, *Understanding the Lord's Prayer*, 11–17. Joachim Jeremias ("Lord's Prayer in the Light of Recent Research," 91) summarizes as follows: "The common substance of both texts, which is identical with its Lucan form, is the oldest text. The Gentile-Christian church [represented by Luke] has handed down the Lord's Prayer without change, whereas the Jewish-Christian church

There are definite parallels to the petitions of the Lord's
Prayer: compare the petition "May your name be glorified
[hallowed]" to the themes of glorification of the Father and
the use of the divine name in xvii 1, 11–12; the petition "May
your will be done" to the theme of completing the work that
the Father gave Jesus to do in xvii 4; the petition "Deliver us
from the Evil One" to the theme expressed almost in the same
words in xvii 15.[4]

Such parallels almost inevitably suggest the possibility of some
type of literary relationship, either direct or indirect, between the
two prayers. Thus, Graham Smith, for example, maintaining that
early Christians would have felt free to incorporate materials
from one prayer that was attributed to Jesus into another such
prayer, particularly if the two prayers shared a common context
in Christian worship, argues that two of the three Matthean "additions" to Luke's version of the Lord's Prayer may have been
prompted by petitions in the High Priestly Prayer and in Jesus'
Gethsemane prayer, since all three prayers were regarded as "authentic words and prayers of the Lord Himself, addressed to the
Father," and the three shared a common context in early Christian
worship, namely, "corporate prayer in the Name of Jesus and the
eucharistic/paschal commemoration."[5]

[represented by Matthew], which lived in a world of rich liturgical tradition and used a variety of prayer forms, has enriched the Lord's Prayer
liturgically. Because the form transmitted by Matthew was the more
richly elaborated one, it soon permeated the whole church." It should
be noted, however, that Jeremias regards the Matthean wording as at
some points closer to the original than the Lukan (pp. 91–93), and thus
he concludes (p. 93) that "the Lucan version has preserved the oldest
form with respect to *length*, but the Matthean text is more original with
regard to *wording*." It should also be noted that Luke's version contains
important textual variants, for the most part apparently assimilations to
the Matthean text.

  4. Brown, *Gospel according to John (xiii–xxi)*, 747; cf. e.g., Dodd,
Historical Tradition in the Fourth Gospel, 333–34.

  5. Graham Smith, "Matthaean 'Additions' to the Lord's Prayer," 54–
55. Smith traces γενηθήτω τὸ θέλημά σου (Matt 6:10) to μὴ τὸ θέλημά

Smith's hypothesis is interesting, but it obviously presupposes that both the High Priestly Prayer and the Gethsemane prayer *in its Lukan form*[6] antedate Matthew's version of the Lord's Prayer, and this is hardly likely, particularly in the case of the High Priestly Prayer, since it is widely recognized that this prayer is the composition, if not of the Fourth Evangelist himself, at least of the author of one of his primary sources,[7] and there is no reason to believe

---

μου ἀλλὰ τὸ σὸν γινέσθω in Jesus' Gethsemane prayer (Luke 22:42) and ἀλλὰ ῥῦσαι ἡμᾶς ἀπὸ τοῦ πονηροῦ (Matt 6:13) to ἀλλὰ ἵνα τηρήσῃς αὐτοὺς ἐκ τοῦ πονηροῦ in the High Priestly Prayer (John 17:15).

6. Only the Lukan form (μὴ τὸ θέλημά μου ἀλλὰ τὸ σὸν γινέσθω) has striking verbal similarities to the third petition of the Lord's Prayer in Matthew (γενηθήτω τὸ θέλημά σου). Matthew (26:39) has οὐχ ὡς ἐγὼ θέλω ἀλλ᾽ ὡς σύ, while Mark (14:36) has οὐ τί ἐγὼ θέλω ἀλλὰ τί σύ. To be sure, Matthew reports a second occurrence of the Gethsemane prayer (26:42) in words identical to the third petition of his version of the Lord's Prayer (γενηθήτω τὸ θέλημά σου), but, if Matthew has incorporated the petition from his own version of the Gethsemane prayer into the Lord's Prayer, the question remains regarding the source of his version of the Gethsemane prayer. It is more likely that he has expanded the Gethsemane narrative by including the petition from the Lord's Prayer (note that Luke does not report a repetition of the Gethsemane prayer, and Mark [14:39] says simply, "And again he went away and prayed, saying the same words").

7. See, e.g., Barrett, *Gospel according to St John*, 417: "The present prayer is a summary of Johannine theology relative to the work of Christ. ... The effect of putting this summary into the form of a prayer is to consummate the movement of Christ to God which is the theme of the last discourses, and anticipates his lifting up on the cross." Cf. also, e.g., Käsemann, *Testament of Jesus*, 3: "it is unmistakable that this chapter is a summary of the Johannine discourses and in this respect is a counterpart to the prologue." Käsemann explicitly asserts (p. 5) that the prayer "was composed [by the Evangelist] in the form of a prayer" and points out (p. 4): "In the composition of chapter 17, the Evangelist undoubtedly used a literary device which is common in world literature and employed by Judaism as well as by New Testament writers. It is the device of the farewell speech of a dying man." On the question of possible sources used by the Fourth Evangelist, see, e.g., Kümmel, *Introduction to the New Testament*, 200–217. Rudolf Bultmann (*Gospel of John*, esp. 486–522) assigns most of the High Priestly Prayer to the "Discourse Source" or *Offenbarungsreden*. On Bultmann's source theory, see, e.g., D. M. Smith, *Composition and Order of the Fourth Gospel*. Hereafter, the author of the High Priestly Prayer will be referred to simply as "John" or "the (Fourth) Evangelist," with no in-

that the author of Matthew knew the Fourth Gospel.[8] Indeed, it is generally assumed that the direction of influence, if any, ran in the opposite direction— that is, that the Fourth Evangelist knew one or more of the Synoptic Gospels or, at least some of the same traditions, or the same types of traditions, drawn upon by the other Evangelists.[9] Moreover, it is intrinsically probable that a short prayer intended to serve as a model for the disciples, such as the Lord's Prayer, would have been much more firmly imbedded in the primitive tradition of the church than would the lengthy and rather complicated discourse-in-the-form-of-a-prayer that constitutes the High Priestly Prayer.[10] Thus, Smith's hypothesis must be rejected.

Proceeding in the opposite direction, however, Brown suggests that, since various parts of the High Priestly Prayer "have Synoptic parallels," the Prayer was probably constructed "by elaborating upon traditional sayings of Jesus."[11] More specifically, C. H. Dodd points out that "there are places where the Fourth Gospel appears to echo the language of the Lord's Prayer," citing two such places in the High Priestly Prayer. He then comments that "it is difficult to believe" that "these coincidences are purely fortuitous" and suggests that "such passages seem to presuppose

---

tention of thereby resolving either the question of sources or that of the authorship of the Fourth Gospel.

8. Indeed, the generally accepted dating of the two gospels, if nothing else, would make this highly unlikely; see, e.g., Kümmel, *Introduction to the New Testament*, 119–20, 246.

9. Even if the Fourth Evangelist knew Mark and/or Luke, however, most scholars regard it as less likely that he also knew Matthew; see, e.g., Kümmel, *Introduction to the New Testament*, 201–4; cf. Tyson, *Study of Early Christianity*, 215: "The use of Matthew [by John] is not seriously entertained."

10. Käsemann, *Testament of Jesus*, 5: "This is not a supplication, but a proclamation directed to the Father in such manner that his disciples can hear it also. The speaker is not a needy petitioner but the divine redeemer and therefore the prayer moves over into being an address, admonition, consolation and prophecy. Its content shows that this chapter, just like the rest of the farewell discourse, is part of the instruction of the disciples."

11. Brown, *Gospel according to John (xiii–xxi)*, 745.

a homiletical treatment of the several petitions of the [Lord's] prayer."[12]

Building upon the suggestions of Brown and Dodd, and assuming, first, that the High Priestly Prayer is the composition of the Fourth Evangelist or of the author of one of his sources,[13] second, that it would be normal procedure for the author of a prayer to be attributed to Jesus to use one or more other prayers also attributed to Jesus as a model, and, third, that knowledge and use of the Lord's Prayer were widespread in the early church,[14] I now propose that the basic content, to a somewhat lesser degree the overall structure, and occasionally at significant points the actual language of the High Priestly Prayer can best be understood as a re-working and expansion of the basic themes of the Lord's Prayer in terms of the specifically Johannine theology—or,

---

12. Dodd, *Historical Tradition in the Fourth Gospel*, 333–34; cf. his *Interpretation of the Fourth Gospel*, 417 n. 4. Dodd cites John 17:11: πάτερ ἅγιε τήρησον αὐτοὺς ἐν τῷ ὀνόματί σου (cf. Matt 6:9: πάτερ … ἁγιασθήτω τὸ ὄνομά σου) and 17:15: ἵνα τηρῇς αὐτοὺς ἐκ τοῦ πονηροῦ (cf. Matt 6:13: ῥῦσαι ἡμᾶς ἀπὸ τοῦ πονηροῦ). Dodd also refers to John 6:33 (ὁ πατήρ μου δίδωσιν ὑμῖν τὸν ἄρτον ἐκ τοῦ οὐρανοῦ τὸν ἀληθινόν; cf. Matt 6:11: τὸν ἄρτον ἡμῶν τὸν ἐπιούσιον δὸς ἡμῖν σήμερον), which, of course, is not a part of the High Priestly Prayer. Dodd's summary of the "homiletical treatment" of the passages from the Lord's Prayer (p. 334) is as follows: "in the sanctity of the name of the Father is the strong protection of believers; the Father in heaven to whom they pray for ἄρτος ἐπιούσιος answers the prayer by the gift of ἄρτος ἀληθινός, and while they are by his appointment still in the world, with all its perils and trials, he answers the prayer for deliverance from the evil that is in the world." Dodd does not believe, however, "that John needed to learn his Paternoster out of the Gospel according to Matthew," since "the prayer must have belonged to the liturgical tradition of the church from the earliest period, and it is from that source that both Matthew and John (as well as Luke) have drawn."

13. See n. 7 above.

14. Jeremias ("Lord's Prayer in the Light of Recent Research," 82–85), among others, has argued that use of this prayer was widespread in the ancient church, particularly as a part of the eucharistic and baptismal liturgies, but that the privilege of using the prayer was restricted to "those who were full members of the church"; cf. also, e.g., Dodd, *Historical Tradition in the Fourth Gospel*, 334.

in short, that the High Priestly Prayer represents a type of "midrash" on the Matthean version of the Lord's Prayer.[15] Specifically, I shall attempt to show that every element in Matthew's version of the Lord's Prayer receives some sort of treatment in the High Priestly Prayer and that every element in the High Priestly Prayer can plausibly be regarded as based upon or related to something in Matthew's version of the Lord's Prayer.[16]

The discussion of the two prayers will follow the order of the Matthean version of the Lord's Prayer, using the commonly ac-

---

15. On the term "midrash," see, e.g., Townsend, "Rabbinic Sources," 41: "the word *midrash* comes from the Hebrew verb *darash*, which in post-biblical times meant 'expound' or 'interpret'. Thus, a midrash is a work that expounds or interprets Scripture." The aim of midrash "was to elucidate the meaning of the text of the Holy Writ, to penetrate into its inner significance, to deduce from it new laws and principles, and to establish by reference to it authentic religious and ethical doctrines" (Epstein, "Midrash," 376). Samuel Sandmel (*Hebrew Scriptures*, 344) observes that, while the "root meaning" of "midrash" could be translated as "inquiry," that is, "inquiry into what a Scriptural verse means or implies," the term has a derivative meaning that might be rendered as "embellishment"; he continues: "Midrash, as embellishment, takes on the connotation of the romantic, or the fanciful, or the bizarre, for imagination was often creative and unrestrained. The ancient rabbis were gifted at midrash, as was Paul; the various accounts of Jesus in the New Testament Gospels and in those gospels that were not included in the New Testament reveal a comparable Christian gift for midrash. In the post-biblical period, then, midrash had a rich and robust existence." For a full treatment, see, e.g., M. P. Miller, "Midrash," 593–97; cf. also Le Déaut, "Apropos a Definition of Midrash." To be sure, the meaning of the term "midrash" is somewhat "stretched" in the present discussion, since the subject of the "midrash" is not Holy Writ but rather words attributed to Jesus. Nevertheless, the dominical sayings must have been regarded in the early church as on a level at least approaching that of Scripture, and there is ample evidence that they were subject to various types of interpretive and applicational techniques. For a provocative study of Paul's use of dominical sayings, see Dungan, *Sayings of Jesus in the Churches of Paul.* For a highly controversial argument that Matthew is a midrashic adaptation and expansion of Mark, see Goulder, *Midrash and Lection in Matthew.*

16. Hereafter, unless otherwise specified, references to "Matthew's version of the Lord's Prayer" or "the Matthean version" will include the version of the prayer found in the Didache, since this version is so similar to the Matthean version.

cepted division of the prayer into the address, the three "thou" petitions, and the three "we" petitions.[17]

The Address

Matthew begins the Lord's Prayer with πάτερ ἡμῶν ὁ ἐν τοῖς οὐρανοῖς ("Our father who is in the heavens"),[18] while John begins the High Priestly Prayer simply with πάτερ ("Father"), which is repeated in vv. 5, 11, 21, 24, and 25, once (v. 11) as πάτερ ἅγιε ("Holy Father") and once (v. 25) as πατήρ δίκαιε ("Righteous Father").[19] Of course, John's use of πάτερ ("Father") as the address, in and of itself, is by no means an indication that he knows and is here following the Lord's Prayer.[20] Moreover, if he is using the Lord's Prayer as a model, the simple πάτερ would tend to sug-

---

17. See, e.g., Harner, *Understanding the Lord's Prayer*.

18. On this title, see, e.g., Schrenk and Quell, "πατήρ, πατρῷος, πατριά, ἀπάτωρ, πατρικός," 979–81, 985–87. Note that the Didache has the singular τῷ οὐρανῷ ("the heaven") rather than the plural τοῖς οὐρανοῖς ("the heavens"), perhaps reflecting non-Jewish influence.

19. The first three *occurrences* (vv. 1, 5, and 11) are in the vocative case, while the last three (vv. 21, 24, and 25) are nominative in form (note, however, that in v. 25 the nominative form, πατήρ, is combined with an adjective in the vocative case, δίκαιε). There is, of course a tendency in Hellenistic Greek "for the nominative to usurp the place of the vocative" (BDF 81–82), As to why John uses the vocative form the first three times and the nominative the last three, it can only be surmised that, toward the end of the prayer, he in effect forgets that he is composing a prayer and lapses into "discourse" style (see, e.g. Brown, *Gospel according to John (xiii–xxi)*, 748: "Because there is an audience, the prayer is just as much revelation as it is intercession. The 'you' addressed is God, but Jesus is speaking to the disciples as much here as in the rest of the Discourse"); or, since this does not explain the use of the vocative case δίκαιε with the nominative πατήρ in v. 25, perhaps the πατήρ in v. 21 is "a real nominative" (Barrett, *Gospel according to St John*, 429), which then influences the forms in vv. 24 and 25. On πάτερ ἅγιε ("Holy Father"), see, e.g., Didache 10:2, where the same form of address occurs in the eucharistic prayer, which is in some respects similar to the High Priestly Prayer, as is also the also the first eucharistic prayer in Didache 9:2–4.

20. See, e.g., Barrett, *Gospel according to St John*, 418: "This name for God is very frequent in John and the most natural for use in a prayer ascribed to Jesus." Cf. further, Jeremias, "Abba"; his "Lord's Prayer in the Light of Recent Research," 95–98; and Kittel, "ἄββα," 5–6.

gest that it is the Lukan rather than the Matthean version of the prayer that he has in mind.[21] It is possible, however, that John's reference to Jesus "having lifted up his eyes to heaven" (ἐπάρας τοὺς ὀφθαλμοὺς αὐτοῦ εἰς τὸν οὐρανόν) at the beginning of the High Priestly Prayer (v. 1) is an allusion to Matthew's phrase, "who is in the heavens" (ὁ ἐν τοῖς οὐρανοῖς).[22] Furthermore, there are plausible reasons for John to have shortened the Matthean form of the address if he did know it. It would have been necessary for him to eliminate the word ἡμῶν ("our"), because he presents the prayer not as a model for the disciples but rather as an actual prayer of Jesus. Having thus eliminated the first word after πάτερ ("Father"), he might very well have also eliminated the remainder of the phrase,[23] particularly in light of the fact that there apparently was a tendency in the Hellenistic church to avoid such a phrase as "Father in the heavens."[24] In addition, the Evangelist

---

21. Matthew's version begins with πάτερ ἡμῶν ὁ ἐν τοῖς οὐρανοῖς, while Luke's begins simply with πάτερ. A number of manuscripts, some of them ancient, read πάτερ ἡμῶν ὁ ἐν τοῖς οὐρανοῖς ("Our Father who is in the heavens") at Luke 11:2, but this is almost certainly an assimilation to the Matthean text; see, e.g., C. W. F. Smith, "Lord's Prayer," 154.

22. It is perhaps significant that, in a similar context in 11:41, John reads ἦρεν τοὺς ὀφθαλμοὺς ἄνω ("he lifted up his eyes") rather than ἐπάρας τοὺς ὀφθαλμοὺς αὐτοῦ εἰς τὸν οὐρανόν ("having lifted up his eyes to heaven"), and it is therefore possible that the εἰς τὸν οὐρανόν ("to heaven") in 17:1 reflects the influence of the Matthean version of the Lord's Prayer. Note that John has the singular τὸν οὐρανόν ("the heaven"), while Matthew has the plural τοῖς οὐρανοῖς ("the heavens"); Didache also has the singular τῷ οὐρανῷ ("the heaven"), however, this being one of the very few differences between Matthew's and Didache's versions of the Lord's Prayer.

23. The author could, of course, have used something such as πάτερ μου ("My Father"), perhaps followed by something such as ὁ ἐν τοῖς οὐρανοῖς ("who is in the heavens"); indeed, John does frequently have Jesus refer to God as ὁ πατήρ μου ("my Father") but this never occurs in a context of prayer, where the customary Johannine address is simply πάτερ ("Father").

24. The phrase never occurs in the Fourth Gospel. Schrenk and Quell ("πατήρ, πατρῷος, πατριά, ἀπάτωρ, πατρικός," 985–86) suggest that Luke, writing for the Greek world, characteristically changes the Jewish expression, "Father in the heavens," whenever he finds it in the tradition, and John, also writing for a Hellenistic audience, may well have done the same.

may have felt it inappropriate to have the Son address the Father so specifically as being "in the heavens," thus implying a "spatial" distance between the two, since, in the High Priestly Prayer, "Jesus already assumes the role of heavenly intercessor that 1 John ii 1 ascribes to him after the resurrection."[25]

At this point, I have not, of course, demonstrated that John knew the beginning of the Lord's Prayer in either Matthew's or Luke's version, nor have I demonstrated that, if he knew either version, it was Matthew's. What I have suggested is that the evidence thus far is compatible with the thesis that John was familiar with the Lord's Prayer and, indeed, in its Matthean version. I shall show later that there are portions of the High Priestly Prayer that have parallels in the Matthean, but not the Lukan, version of the Lord's Prayer and that, for this reason, could not have been derived from Luke's version. Thus, the cumulative weight of the evidence should, in retrospect, indicate that in the address, as elsewhere, John is using Matthew's version of the Lord's Prayer.[26]

The First "Thou" Petition

The first "thou" petition, in both Matthew and Luke, reads, ἁγιασθήτω τὸ ὄνομά σου ("Hallowed be your name").[27] John does not have the petition in precisely this form, but there are four features of the High Priestly Prayer that appear to echo the petition.[28]

---

25. Brown, *Gospel according to John (xiii–xxii)*, 747.

26. It is possible, of course, that John knew both the Matthean and the Lukan versions of the Lord's Prayer, following sometimes the one and sometimes the other. Since all of the Lukan version is included within the Matthean, however, with only minor verbal differences, it would be virtually impossible to demonstrate that John knew Luke's version, unless, at the points of minor verbal difference between Matthew and Luke, John agreed with Luke against Matthew.

27. Marcion's text of Luke apparently had ἐλθέτω τὸ πνεῦμά σου τὸ ἅγιον ἐφ᾽ ἡμᾶς καὶ καθαρισάτω ἡμᾶς ("Your Holy Spirit come upon us and cleanse us") as the first petition; see, e.g., Jeremias, "Lord's Prayer in the Light of Recent Research," 83–94.

28. Cf., e.g., Brown, *Gospel according to John (xiii–xxii)*, 747: "compare the petition 'May your name be glorified [hallowed]' to the themes of glorification of the Father and the use of the divine name in xvii 1, 11–12"; also Dodd, *Historical Tradition in the Fourth Gospel*, 333.

In the first place, there are the repeated references to the
"name" (ὄνομα) of God and the suggestion that the mission of
Jesus on earth was that of revealing the name of God, which had
been given to him by the Father,[29] and of keeping the disciples
"in" his name.[30]

> I have manifested your name to the people whom you gave
> me out of the world (v. 6a). ... Holy Father, keep them in your
> name, which you have given me, that they may be one, even
> as we are one. While I was with them, I kept them in your
> name, which you have given me (vv. 11b–12a). ... I made
> known to them your name, and I will make it known, that the
> love with which you have loved me may be in them, and I in
> them (v. 26).[31]

---

29. Brown, *Gospel according to John (xiii–xxii)*, 754: "Verse 2 mentioned
the men that God had given to Jesus; vs. 4 said that Jesus had glorified
God on earth by completing the work that God had given him to do.
Verses 6–8 bring these two themes together: the work of Jesus that glorified God was his revelation of God to those whom God had given him. In
6 the task of revelation is phrased in terms of making God's name known.
(This chapter is the only place in John where Jesus is explicitly said to
have revealed God's name to men.)" See the entire discussion, pp. 754–56.
Since it is only in the High Priestly Prayer that Jesus' revelation of God is
characterized as the revelation of the divine "name," it is quite possible
that John is here influenced by the petition in the Lord's Prayer about the
"hallowing" of God's name.

30. Brown, *Gospel according to John (xiii–xxii)*, 759: "The 'in' is both local
and instrumental: they are to be both marked with and protected by the
divine name that has been given to Jesus."

31. There is a textual problem regarding the antecedent of the relative
pronoun "which" in vv. 11b–12a. Brown (*Gospel according to John (xiii–
xxii)*, 759) summarizes the evidence and the most likely solution: "The
best witnesses, including P[66], have the dative neuter singular relative,
and this means that 'your name' is the antecedent. A large number of
later and less reliable textual witnesses have a masculine plural relative,
the antecedent of which must be 'them', namely, the disciples. We have
accepted the first reading, while SB and NEB accept the second (RSV is
ambiguous). The second reading probably represents a scribal harmo-
nization with vv. 2, 6, and 9, which speak of men being given by God to
Jesus. The reading we have followed makes 11 and 12 the only instances
where God is said to have given the (divine) name to Jesus."

In the second place, there is the emphasis upon "glorification," which may reflect the "hallowing" of the divine name in the
Lord's Prayer. To be sure, the meaning of "to glorify" (δοξάζειν)
is not identical with that of "to hallow" (ἁγιάζειν), but, in this
context of prayer, the difference is not great.[32] It is never specifically stated, of course, that it is the "name" of God that is to be
glorified, but frequently in Jewish literature "the name of God is
used as a synonym for God himself,"[33] and Philip B. Harner suggests that this is the case in the Lord's Prayer, where reference to
the name of God "is a way of referring to God in his innermost
nature, especially as he reveals himself to men and acts on their
behalf."[34] It is also true that the glorification in the High Priestly
Prayer is a mutual glorification of the Son by the Father and of
the Father by the Son that extends even to the disciples, but this
difference from the Lord's Prayer can readily be accounted for in
light of the Johannine christology[35] and the Fourth Gospel's somewhat "mystical" view of the relationship between the Father, the
Son, and the disciples.[36] Thus, the following statements in the
High Priestly Prayer about "glorification" and "glory" can quite

---

32. Harner (*Understanding the Lord's Prayer*, 60–67) suggests that
"Hallowed be your name" is "a petition that God himself might act by
manifesting his holiness" (p. 66). Cf. also Brown, *Gospel according to John
(xiii–xxii)*, 747, where "glorified" in the High Priestly Prayer and "hallowed" in the Lord's Prayer are apparently equated.

33. Harner, *Understanding the Lord's Prayer*, 61.

34. Harner, *Understanding the Lord's Prayer*, 63.

35. On Johannine christology, see, e.g., Sidebottom, *Christ of the Fourth
Gospel in the Light of First-Century Thought*. The Johannine christology is
clearly significantly different from ("higher" than) that of the Synoptic
Gospels, not to mention that of the historical Jesus; thus, it is understandable that not only the Father but also the Son should be "glorified."

36. See, e.g., Dodd, *Interpretation of the Fourth Gospel*, 195–96: "At ev-
ery point the unity of the Father and Son is reproduced in the unity of
Christ and believers. As the love of the Father for the Son, returned to
Him by obedience, establishes a community of life between Father and
Son, which exhibits itself in that He speaks the Father's word and does
His works, so the disciples are loved by Christ and return His love in
obedience; in doing so, they share His life, which manifests itself in do-
ing His works; it is really He who does them (just as the works of Christ

plausibly be regarded as part of the Johannine midrash on the first "thou" petition of the Lord's Prayer:

> Glorify your Son that the Son may glorify you (v. 1b). ... I glorified you on earth, having accomplished the work that you gave me to do; and now, Father, glorify me in your own presence with the glory that I had with you before the world was made (vv. 4–5). ... All mine are yours, and yours are mine, and I am glorified in them (v. 10). ... The glory that you have given me I have given to them, that they may be one even as we are one (v. 22). ... Father, I desire that they also, whom you have given me, may be with me where I am, to behold my glory that you have given to me in your love for me before the foundation of the world (v. 24).

In the third place, there is in the High Priestly Prayer at least the very strong implication that the manifestation of the divine name is, in fact, the glorification of the Father and perhaps even that the "name of God" and the "glory of God" are identical.[37] Thus, the glorification of the Father and the manifestation of the Father's name are both expressions of the petition, "Hallowed be your name":

---

are done by the Father), and by the doing of them the Father is glorified in the Son. This is what is meant by the expression, 'I in you and you in me.'" Cf. the entire discussion, pp. 187–200.

37. See, e.g., Brown, *Gospel according to John (xiii–xxi)*, 754: "The work of Jesus that glorified God was his revelation of God to those whom God had given him. In 6 the task of revelation is phrased in terms of making God's name known." Note that both the divine name and the glory are given by the Father to the Son and by the Son to the disciples (vv. 11–12 and 22). On the relationship between "name" of God and "glory" of God, see, e.g., Bietenhard, "ὄνομα, ὀνομάζω, ἐπονομάζω, ψευδώνυμος," 272: "The name of God belongs to His manward side, the side of revelation. In this respect—especially in Jn.—it is linked with δόξα. ὄνομα thus expresses the concrete connection between God and man, the personal relationship which declares itself in a specific approach of God and which demands a specific approach from man. When Jesus prays: 'Father, glorify your name', and God answers: 'I have glorified it, and will glorify it again,' Jn. 12.28 (note 12.23), the three words ... πατήρ, δοξάζω ... and ὄνομα are so closely connected with one another that they have to be expounded together."

I glorified you on earth, having accomplished the work that you gave me to do (v. 4). ... I have manifested your name to the people whom you gave me out of the world (v. 6a). ... I made known to them your name, and I will make it known, that the love with which you have loved me may be in them, and I in them (v. 26).

In the fourth place, particularly since, outside the High Priestly Prayer, John rarely uses the adjective ἅγιος ("holy") or the cognate verb ἁγιάζειν ("to hallow") and never any other word from the same root,[38] it is quite possible that the πάτερ ἅγιε ("Holy Father") in v. 11 and perhaps also the references to the "sanctification," "consecration," or "hallowing" (ἁγιάζειν) of both the disciples and Jesus in vv. 17 and 19 are reminiscent of the "Hallowed be your name" (ἁγιασθήτω τὸ ὄνομά σου) in the Lord's Prayer.

Finally, it can plausibly be argued that the persistent rabbinic theme of the "sanctification" or "hallowing of the name" (*kiddush ha-shem*) by the noble deeds and, ultimately, by the martyrdom of the righteous[39] is reflected in the High Priestly Prayer's references to Jesus' faithfulness to his divine mission and its allusion to his crucifixion.[40]

---

38. Except in association with πνεῦμα ("Spirit"), i.e., as the "Holy Spirit" (1:33; 14:26; 20:22), the adjective ἅγιος ("holy") occurs only at 6:69 and there as part of the title ὁ ἅγιος τοῦ θεοῦ ("The Holy One of God"); the verb ἁγιάζω (to hallow") occurs only at 10:36, where the reference is to the one (i.e., Jesus) whom "the Father hallowed and sent into the world" (ὃν ὁ πατὴρ ἡγίασεν καὶ ἀπέστειλεν εἰς τὸν κόσμον).

39. See, e.g., Jastrow, *Dictionary of the Targumim, the Talmud Babli and Yerushalmi, and the Midrashic Literature*, 2:1319; Montefiore and Loewe, *Rabbinic Anthology*, e.g., lxxxix–xci, 86–87, 117, 232–71, 305, and 326.

40. The allusions to the crucifixion are to be seen in the references to Jesus leaving the world and coming to the Father (vv. 11, 13, etc.) and perhaps even the references to the glorification of the Son (e.g., vv. 1, 5; cf. such passages as 3:14 and 12:32, where the "lifting up" of the Son apparently refers both to his crucifixion and to his exaltation). It is understandable that the allusions to the crucifixion are nothing more than allusions, since, as the Evangelist constructs the scene, the crucifixion is still in the future; the statements in the High Priestly Prayer, however, presuppose the crucifixion as an accomplished fact.

Thus, the first "thou" petition of the Lord's Prayer appears to be reflected in the High Priestly Prayer in (a) the references to the divine name, (b) the statements about the glorification of the Father, the Son, and the disciples, (c) the use of the terms ἅγιος ("holy") and ἁγιάζειν ("to hallow"), and (d) the references and allusions to Jesus' faithfulness and martyrdom.

The Second "Thou" Petition

The second "thou" petition, in both Matthew and Luke, reads, ἐλθάτω ἡ βασιλεία σου ("Your kingdom come").[41] Again, John does not have the petition in precisely this form, but this is easily understandable in light of the almost complete absence of "Kingdom of God" or "Kingdom of Heaven" terminology in the Fourth Gospel.[42] There are, however, various elements in the High Priestly Prayer that appear to echo the petition.

In the first place, the initial declaration in the High Priestly Prayer, ἐλήλυθεν ἡ ὥρα ("the hour has come") most likely rep-

---

41. Didache has ἐλθέτω rather than ἐλθάτω, as do a number of manuscripts, some of them ancient, in Luke, but the meaning is the same. On a more significant variant, see, e.g., C. W. F. Smith, "Lord's Prayer," 156: "A few witnesses testify to the substitution for this petition in Luke the words ἐλθάτω τὸ ἅγιον πνεῦμά σου ἐφ᾽ ἡμᾶς καὶ καθαρισάτω ἡμᾶς, 'May your Holy Spirit come upon us and cleanse us' (162, 700, Gregory of Nyssa, Maximus). It appears to be a Christian variant rather than an original reading, although it fits Luke's emphasis on the Holy Spirit. It may possibly have been a form connected with Christian initiation." Cf. e.g., Jeremias, "Lord's Prayer in the Light of Recent Research," 83–84. According to Tertullian, Marcion had it as a substitute for the first petition (see n. 27 above).

42. "Kingdom of Heaven" never occurs in the Fourth Gospel, and "Kingdom of God" is found only at 3:3, 5, leading Raymond E. Brown (*Gospel according to John (i–xii)*, 130, cf. 135–36) to suggest the possibility "that there is traditional material in the Nicodemus discourse." Note, however, Evans, "Kingdom of God, of Heaven," 25: "The word 'king' is used of Jesus frequently in the Fourth Gospel (1.49; 6.15; 12.13, 15; 18.33, 37, 39; 19.3, 12, 14–15, 19, 21), and in 18.36 Jesus himself speaks of his 'kingship' (ERV-ASV 'kingdom'; the Greek is βασιλεία), which 'is not of this world'. This usage implies the idea of a spiritual sovereignty which Jesus is already exercising as Messiah." Apparently, then, in the Fourth Gospel, Jesus is the king, not God.

resents a reinterpretation of the petition ἐλθάτω ἡ βασιλεία σου ("Your kingdom come") in light of the Johannine "realized eschatology."[43] The same verb is used, but with a highly significant shift from the aorist imperative to the perfect indicative, and the basic structure of the sentence is the same. Most important, of course, is the change from ἡ βασιλεία σου ("your kingdom") to ἡ ὥρα ("the hour"), but this latter is a "technical Johannine term referring to the period of the passion, death, resurrection, and ascension,"[44] and, in light of John's realized eschatological outlook, it functions in the Fourth Gospel in much the same way as does "Kingdom of God" or "Kingdom of Heaven" in the Synoptic Gospels.

In the second place, it is widely recognized that the Synoptic concept of the Kingdom of God has been reinterpreted in the Fourth Gospel as "eternal life" or simply "life,"[45] and the High Priestly Prayer quite early on, in vv. 2 and 3, refers to the eternal life (ζωὴ αἰώνιος or αἰώνιος ζωή) that Jesus gives to his disciples.[46] This eternal life is further identified as "knowing the

---

43. See, e.g., Schüssler Fiorenza, "Eschatology of the NT," 275–76: "This evangelist views eschatological salvation as realized in the present. Believers already possess eternal life and no longer come under judgment (5.24). It is debated whether the so-called future, apocalyptic statements (5.28; 6.27; 12.25; 14:2–3; 17.24) are a genuine element of the evangelist's theology or whether they are added by an ecclesiastical redactor (Bultmann). Even if these statements did originally belong to the gospel text, they are outnumbered, and the basic mood of the gospel reflects realized eschatology."

44. Brown, *Gospel according to John (xiii–xxi)*, 99; cf. the fuller discussion, 517–18.

45. See, e.g., Evans, "Kingdom of God, of Heaven," 25: "In general, however, this evangelist has reinterpreted the teaching of Jesus, so that instead of speaking of the kingdom of God he speaks of eternal life, or LIFE." Cf. e.g., Howard, "Gospel according to St. John," 743: "Eternal life (vs. 3), the *summum bonum* in this Gospel, as the kingdom of God is in the Synoptics, consists in the knowledge of God."

46. V. 2 is translated in the Revised Standard Version, "since thou hast given him power over all flesh, to give eternal life to all whom thou hast given him." Since the Greek here translated as "to all whom" is the neuter singular, πᾶν ὅ (literally "everything which") in either the nominative or the accusative case, and since there is an indirect object in the dative plural later in the sentence (αὐτοῖς), a better translation might be, "since

only true God and Jesus Christ, who has been sent by God" (ἵνα γινώσκωσιν σὲ τὸν μόνον ἀληθινὸν Θεὸν καὶ ὃν ἀπέστειλας Ἰησοῦν Χριστόν). Thus, Jesus' gift of eternal life is the Johannine equivalent of the coming of the Kingdom.

In the third place, the High Priestly Prayer speaks, in v. 2, of the "authority over all flesh" that has been given to the Son (καθὼς ἔδωκας αὐτῷ ἐξουσίαν πάσης σαρκός), surely suggesting a kind of kingly authority, particularly since the reference comes shortly after the assertion that "the hour has come" (ἐλήλυθεν ἡ ὥρα) and immediately before the mention of "eternal life"[47] and, similarly, speaks of the "glory" given to the Son by the Father and the people of God given to the Son.

Thus, the second "thou" petition of the Lord's Prayer appears to be reflected in the High Priestly Prayer in the references to (a) "the hour" having come, (b) eternal life, and (c) the "authority over all flesh," the glory, and the people who have been given to the Son.

The Third "Thou" Petition

The third "thou" petition in Matthew reads, γενηθήτω τὸ θέλημά σου, ὡς ἐν οὐρανῷ καὶ ἐπὶ γῆς ("Your will be done, as in heaven also on earth").[48] As with the other "thou" petitions, John does not have the petition in precisely this form, but it appears to be echoed in at least two ways in the High Priestly Prayer.

In the first place, Jesus speaks in v. 4 of "having accomplished the work that you gave me to do" (τὸ ἔργον τελειώσας ὃν δέδωκάς μοι ἵνα ποιήσω). Elsewhere in the Fourth Gospel (4:34), "accomplishing the work" of God (ἵνα … τελειώσω αὐτοῦ τὸ ἔργον) is more specifically identified with "doing the will" of

---

thou hast given him power over all flesh, to give to them everything which thou has given him, namely, eternal life." (A similar construction occurs in v. 3: ὃν ἀπέστειλας Ἰησοῦν Χριστόν.)

47. Note that it is the Son, not the Father, who is king in the Fourth Gospels (see n. 42 above), and this kingship is present, not future (see n. 43 above).

48. A number of manuscripts, some of them ancient, include this petition in Luke, but this is apparently an assimilation to Matthew's text.

God (ἵνα ποιῶ τὸ θέλημα τοῦ πέμψαντός με),[49] and Jesus speaks of having "come down from heaven, not to do my own will, but the will of him who sent me" (καταβέβηκα ἀπὸ οὐρανοῦ οὐχ ἵνα ποιῶ τὸ θέλημα τὸ ἐμὸν ἀλλὰ τὸ θέλημα τοῦ πέμψαντός με), and "the will of him who sent me" is specified as follows (6:38–40):

> And this is the will of him who sent me, that I should lose nothing of all that he has given me, but raise it up at the last day. For this is the will of my Father, that every one who sees the Son and believes in him should have eternal life, and I will raise him up at the last day.

This, in turn, leads back to the High Priestly Prayer, where Jesus says (v. 12), "While I was with them, I kept them in your name, which you have given me; I have guarded them, and none of them is lost except the son of perdition, that the scripture might be fulfilled." Thus, "accomplishing the work" of God is apparently equated with "doing the will" of God on earth, and the will of God includes guarding those who have been given to the Son by the Father, as well as giving eternal life to those who see and believe.[50] Thus, Jesus has done the will of the Father.

Perhaps more striking, however, than this somewhat indirect reference to the will of God is the specification, immediately preceding the statement about "accomplishing the work that you gave me to do," that it was "on earth" (ἐπὶ τῆς γῆς) that the Son glorified the Father. This is almost certainly an "echo" of "on earth" (ἐπὶ γῆς) in the third petition of the Lord's Prayer, since the idiom

---

49. Cf. also John 5:30; 6:38–40.

50. Cf., e.g., Brown, *Gospel according to John (xiii–xxi)*, 747: "compare … the petition 'May your will be done' to the theme of completing the work that the Father gave Jesus to do in xvii 4." If John did, in fact, know the Lord's Prayer, it is highly probable that traces of its influence would appear in parts of the Fourth Gospel other than the High Priestly Prayer. Dodd, for example, (*Historical Tradition in the Fourth Gospel*, 333) finds an "echo" of the Lord's Prayer in John 6:33, and it is possible now to suggest similar "echoes" in 4:34; 5:30; and 6:38–40.

is characteristically non-Johannine,[51] the phrase is superfluous at this point in the High Priestly Prayer, and the contrast between "on earth" (ἐπὶ τῆς γῆς) and "with yourself" (παρὰ σεαυτῷ) in v. 5 parallels the contrast between "in heaven" (ἐν οὐρανῷ) and "on earth" (ἐπὶ γῆς) in the Lord's Prayer.

Thus, the third "thou" petition in the Lord's Prayer appears to be reflected in the High Priestly Prayer in (a) the reference to Jesus "having accomplished the work" given to him by the Father and (b) the specification that it was "on earth" that the Son glorified the Father.

The Three "Thou" Petitions: Summary

The examination of John's treatment of each of the three "thou" petitions in the Lord's Prayer having now been completed, it appears that the Fourth Evangelist makes no clear and consistent distinction among the meanings of the three petitions, but rather weaves them together, echoing first one and then another as he articulates his own theology of the work of Christ. In so doing, however, he is not unfaithful to the actual meaning of the Lord's Prayer, where the three "thou" petitions apparently "express different aspects of essentially the same idea," namely, "God's work of bringing in his new time of salvation."[52] It is true that, for the

---

51. Apart from this verse, the word γῆ ("earth") appears only eight times in the Fourth Gospel (3:22, 31; 6:21; 12:24, 32; 21:8, 9, 11) always preceded by a preposition (εἰς, ἐκ, ἀπό, or ἐπί). In only two other instances (3:31; 12:32), however, does it mean "earth" as opposed to "heaven" (cf. ὁ ὢν ἐκ τῆς γῆς and ὁ ἐκ τοῦ οὐρανοῦ in 3:31), and the only other instance of ἐπὶ τῆς γῆς (6:21) clearly means "at the land" (with reference to the landing of a boat).

52. Harner, *Understanding the Lord's Prayer*, 60, 81. Scholars have debated at length whether the three "thou" petitions "express different aspects of essentially the same idea" or "quite different ideas." Harner concludes quite cogently (pp. 80–81): "We have seen that they all refer to God's work of bringing his new time of salvation. In this sense they all express essentially the same idea . ... The petitions differ in the sense that they depict different aspects of the idea that God is bringing his salvation. God's 'name' signifies his essential nature and personal identity. The petition that God may sanctify his name stands first, because God's work

most part, the petitions of the Lord's Prayer are transformed in the High Priestly Prayer into assertions of accomplished fact and the implied future references[53] into past tenses, but, as already suggested, such a transformation is understandable and even inevitable in light of the realized eschatological outlook of the Fourth Evangelist. Thus, it appears that the three "thou" petitions of the Matthean version of the Lord's Prayer do, in fact, receive a type of midrashic treatment in the High Priestly Prayer. "Hallowed be your name; your kingdom come, your will be done on earth as [it is] in heaven" becomes: "I have manifested your name; I have glorified you on earth; The hour has come; You have given him power over all flesh, to give eternal life to all whom you have given him; [I have] accomplished the work that you gave me to do; I am coming to you."

The First "We" Petition

In the Lord's Prayer, there is a quite clear distinction between the three "thou" petitions, which make up the first half of the prayer, and the three "we" petitions, which form the second half. As Philip B. Harner states it:

> In the "thou" petitions the disciples ask God to complete the work of salvation that he has initiated through the ministry of Jesus. Then in the "we" petitions they ask God to satisfy their own needs as they live within the new time of salvation and look forward to its completion.[54]

---

of salvation originates within his innermost being. God's 'kingdom' is the expression of his nature in his effective reign over the world, and his 'will' is the work that he performs in his role as king. These two petitions refer more specifically to God's external relationship to his world."

53. It is generally agreed that the "thou" petitions in the Lord's Prayer are eschatological in their reference, but it is debated whether this eschatology should be understood as purely "futuristic" or as what some have called "inaugurated"; see, e.g., Harner, *Understanding the Lord's Prayer*, 81, cf. 139 n. 17.

54. There are also stylistic differences between the "thou" petitions and the "we" petitions; see, e.g., Harner, *Understanding the Lord's Prayer*, 83. Jeremias ("Lord's Prayer in the Light of Recent Research," 100) sug-

In the High Priestly Prayer, on the other hand, the distinction is much less clear, and the two types of petitions are, to some extent, interwoven in the prayer. Nevertheless, there is one point at which the Fourth Evangelist makes it explicit that the emphasis in the prayer shifts from the Father and the Son to the disciples. In vv. 9 and 10, Jesus says, "I am praying for them; I am not praying for the world but for those you have given me, for they are yours; all mine are yours, and yours are mine, and I am glorified in them."[55] Thus, it is not surprising that traces of the three "we" petitions of the Lord's Prayer can also be found in the High Priestly Prayer and that these traces occur primarily in those parts of the prayer where Jesus is specifically praying for the disciples.

The first "we" petition in Matthew reads τὸν ἄρτον ἡμῶν τὸν ἐπιούσιον δὸς ἡμῖν σήμερον ("Give us this day our daily bread" or perhaps "our bread for tomorrow").[56] Once again, the petition is not found in precisely this form in the High Priestly Prayer. Indeed, at first glance, it appears not to be reflected at all, and this would perhaps not be too surprising, since the exact meaning of the petition has always been a matter of debate,[57] and it is con-

---

gests that the "thou" petitions recall the Jewish *Kaddish* prayer (see pp. 98–99) and that, in the Lord's Prayer, "the accent lies completely on the new material which Jesus has added, that is, on the two 'We-petitions',", which thus "form the real heart of the Lord's Prayer, to which the two 'Thou-petitions' lead up" (note that Jeremias is working not from the Matthean but rather from the Lukan form of the prayer, which has only *two* "thou" petitions and *two* "we" petitions).

55. Cf. also v. 20: "I do not pray for these only, but also for those who believe in me through their word."

56. Luke has τὸν ἄρτον ἡμῶν τὸν ἐπιούσιον δίδου ἡμῖν τὸ καθ᾽ ἡμέραν ("Give us each day our daily bread" or perhaps "our bread for the morrow"), but Matthew's wording is likely closer to the original; see, e.g., Jeremias, "Lord's Prayer in the light of Recent Research," 91–92; Harner, *Understanding the Lord's Prayer*, 84–85.

57. Debate centers around the meaning of ἐπιούσιος in the phrase τὸν ἄρτον ἡμῶν τὸν ἐπιούσιον. See, e.g., Harner, *Understanding the Lord's Prayer*, 85–86: "In general, according to the derivation that we assume, there are four major possibilities for the meaning of *epiousios*. It could mean (1) 'necessary for existence,' (2) 'for today,' (3) 'for the coming day,' or (4) 'for the future.'" Agreement has not been reached; see, e.g., the

ceivable that the Fourth Evangelist would simply have ignored it, because he, too, was uncertain of its meaning. A closer look at the High Priestly Prayer, however, suggests that the first "we" petition is, in fact, echoed, although in a rather indirect fashion, particularly in the references to the "eternal life" that is given by the Son, to the "oneness" of the disciples in their union with the Father and the Son, and to the "words" given the disciples by the Son.

The High Priestly Prayer speaks of the Son as having given to the disciples the words (ῥήματα) given to him by the Father (v. 8; cf. v. 14), the divine name given to the Son by the Father (vv. 6 and 26), the glory given to the Son by the Father (v. 22), knowledge of the Father and the Son (v. 3), the oneness shared by the Father and the Son (vv. 11, 21, and 23), or, in short, eternal life (vv. 2 and perhaps 24). Elsewhere in the Fourth Gospel (especially in ch. 6), it is made clear that Jesus himself is "the bread of life" (ὁ ἄρτος τῆς ζωῆς) or "the living bread that came down from heaven" (ὁ ἄρτος ὁ ζῶν ὁ ἐκ τοῦ οὐρανοῦ καταβάς), and it is claimed that "he who eats this bread will live forever" (ὁ τρώγων τοῦτον τὸν ἄρτον ζήσει εἰς τὸν αἰῶνα) or, more specifically, that "He who eats my flesh and drinks my blood abides in me, and I in him" (ὁ τρώγων μου τὴν σάρκα καὶ πίνων μου τὸ αἷμα ἐν ἐμοὶ μένει κἀγὼ ἐν αὐτῷ), and "he who eats me will live because of me" (ὁ τρώγων με κἀκεῖνος ζήσει δι᾽ ἐμέ). Clearly, the language here is eucharistic language,[58] the idea being that it is in the Eucharist that the oneness of the disciple with the Son and thus, by implication, with other disciples is realized and, along with this oneness, eternal life.[59] It is these themes of eucharistic oneness and eternal

---

discussion in Harner, 85–99; and Jeremias, "Lord's Prayer in the Light of Recent Research," 100–101.

58. So, e.g., Brown, *Gospel according to John (i–xii)*, 268–94, who, however, makes a distinction between vv. 35–50, where the eucharistic theme is "only secondary," and vv. 51–58, where it "comes to the fore and becomes the exclusive theme" (p. 284).

59. Note the eucharistic prayer in Didache 9:4: "As this broken bread (τοῦτο τὸ κλάσμα) was scattered upon the mountains, but was brought together and became one, so let thy Church be gathered together from

life that are then picked up and developed in the High Priestly Prayer, when Jesus prays to the Father "that they all may be one; even as you, Father, are in me, and I in you, that they also may be one in us" (v. 21; cf. vv. 11, 22–23, and 26) and speaks of giving eternal life to all those whom the Father has given him (vv. 2 and 3).[60] Having already, earlier in his Gospel (6:32–58), had Jesus explain that he is the "bread of life" and that "he who eats my flesh and drinks my blood abides in me, and I in him" and thus "has eternal life," John need now only have Jesus refer in the High Priestly Prayer to "eternal life" (vv. 2 and 3) and to the oneness of the disciples in their union with the Father and the Son (vv. 11, 21, 22–23, and 26) to suggest the first "we" petition of the Lord's Prayer, which he apparently interprets in the sense of "Give us this day our eschatological bread."[61] Similarly, the reference in the

---

the ends of the earth into thy kingdom." Note also Ignatius' reference (Eph 20) to "breaking one bread (ἕνα ἄρτον κλῶντες), which is the medicine of immortality, the antidote that we should not die, but live for ever in Jesus Christ."

60. Note that the High Priestly Prayer's setting in the Fourth Gospel is the last gathering of Jesus with the disciples on the evening before his death, which, in the Synoptic Gospels, is the occasion of the inauguration of the Eucharist. Jeremias ("Lord's Prayer in the Light of Recent Research," 82–85) argues that, throughout the ancient church, "the Lord's Prayer was a constituent part of the celebration of the Lord's Supper" (p. 83), and many interpreters have also associated the High Priestly Prayer with the ancient Eucharist, citing particularly the parallels with the eucharistic prayers found in Didache 9–10; for a summary of the evidence, see, e.g., Brown, *Gospel according to John (xiii–xxi)*, 745–47; note, however, that Brown regards the association as only "possible."

61. Note that Dodd (*Historical Tradition in the Fourth Gospel*, 333) associates this petition of the Lord's Prayer with the reference to "the true bread from heaven" (τὸν ἄρτον ἐκ τοῦ οὐρανοῦ τὸν ἀληθινόν) in John 6:32. Harner (*Understanding the Lord's Prayer*, 97–98) suggests that the petition should be translated, "Give us this day our bread for the future"; he continues: "In this sense the followers of Jesus would be praying that they may receive, here and now, some of the benefits of the future time of salvation. The phrase 'this day' refers to the present aspect of the kingdom, and 'bread for the future' symbolizes the future aspect of the kingdom." Such an interpretation of the petition is not far removed from the realized eschatology of the Fourth Gospels.

High Priestly Prayer to the "words" (ῥήματα) given by the Father to the Son and by the Son to the disciples (v. 8; cf. v. 14) points to the "bread of life," for Jesus has already said that his words are "spirit and life" (6:63), and Simon Peter has confessed (6:68) that Jesus has "the words of eternal life" (ῥήματα ζωῆς αἰωνίου).

The Second "We" Petition

The second "we" petition in the Lord's Prayer reads καὶ ἄφες ἡμῖν τὰ ὀφειλήματα ἡμῶν, ὡς καὶ ἡμεῖς ἀφήκαμεν τοῖς ὀφειλέταις ἡμῶν ("And forgive us our debts, as we also have forgiven our debtors").[62] Again, the petition does not appear in this form in the High Priestly Prayer; indeed, of all the petitions in the Lord's Prayer, this is probably the most difficult to find reflected in the High Priestly Prayer, since the idea of "forgiveness," both divine and human, is totally absent from the prayer, as it is, with one notable exception, from the Fourth Gospel as a whole.[63] Rudolf Bultmann, however, suggests that the Fourth Evangelist expresses a similar thought in such terms as ἁγιάζειν ("to sanctify") and καθαρίζειν ("to purify" or "cleanse").[64] The presence of ἁγιάζειν ("to sanctify") has already been noted in vv. 17 and 19 of the High Priestly Prayer, where Jesus prays that the Father will "sanctify" the disciples "in the truth" (ἁγίασον αὐτοὺς ἐν τῇ

---

62. Didache has καὶ ἄφες ἡμῖν τὴν ὀφειλὴν ἡμῶν, ὡς καὶ ἀφίεμεν τοῖς ὀφειλέταις ἡμῶν ("And forgive us our debt, as we also forgive out debtors"), while Luke has καὶ ἄφες ἡμῖν τὰς ἁμαρτίας ἡμῶν, καὶ γὰρ αὐτοὶ ἀφίομεν παντὶ ὀφείλοντι ἡμῖν ("And forgive us our sins, for we ourselves also forgive every one who is indebted to us"). The wording of the Matthean version is likely closer to the Aramaic original; see, e.g., Jeremias, "Lord's Prayer in the Light of Recent Research," 92.

63. The "notable exception" is John 20:23, which reads, "If you forgive the sins of any, they are forgiven (ἄν τινων ἀφῆτε τὰς ἁμαρτίας ἀφέωνται αὐτοῖς); if you retain the sins of any, they are retained." This is surely based upon pre-Johannine tradition; see Matt 16:19; 18:18. Otherwise, neither the verb ἀφιέναι in the sense, "to forgive," nor the noun ἄφεσις ("forgiveness") occurs anywhere in the Fourth Gospel. Note that "forgiveness" terminology is also rare in the latters of Paul; see, e.g., Knox, *Chapters in a Life of Paul*, 142–45.

64. Bultmann, "ἀφίημι, ἄφεσις, παρίημι, πάρεσις," 512.

ἀληθείᾳ and ἵνα ὦσιν καὶ αὐτοὶ ἡγιασμένοι ἐν ἀληθείᾳ).[65] The verb καθαρίζειν ("to purify" or "cleanse") does not occur in the Fourth Gospel,[66] but the adjective καθαρός ("pure" or "clean") occurs three times, all in the context of Jesus' final gathering with his disciples. In 13:10-11, there may be a reference to baptismal "cleansing,"[67] but, in 15:3, Jesus makes it clear that it is "the word that I have spoken to you" that cleanses the disciples (ἤδη ὑμεῖς καθαροί ἐστε διὰ τὸν λόγον ὃν λελάληκα ἡμῖν). Then, in the High Priestly Prayer, Jesus stresses, in v. 14, that he has given God's word to the disciples (ἐγὼ δέδωκα αὐτοῖς τὸν λόγον σου),[68] he asks the Father, in v. 17a, to "sanctify them in the truth" (ἁγίασον αὐτοὺς ἐν τῇ ἀληθείᾳ), and, finally, he makes it explicit, in v. 17b, that it is God's word that is truth (ὁ λόγος ὁ σὸς ἀλήθειά ἐστιν). Thus, the references to the "purification" or "sanctification" of the disciples in the truth (i.e., in God's word spoken by the Son) appear to reflect the first part of the petition in the Lord's Prayer, "And forgive us our debts."[69]

The second part of the petition, "as we also have forgiven our debtors," appears to be reflected in the High Priestly Prayer in at least two ways. First, there is the very interesting transitional statement in the prayer, "I do not pray for these only, but also for

---

65. Clearly, ἁγιάζειν ("to sanctify") cannot here have the same meaning as ἀφιέναι ("to forgive"), since, in the Fourth Gospel, Jesus speaks also of his own "sanctification" or "consecration" (17:19; cf. 10:36). Nevertheless, it appears to represent a Johannine re-interpretation of the Synoptic idea of "forgiveness."

66. The verb does occur twice in 1 John (1:7, 9), in the sense of "cleansing" from sin or unrighteousness. It is by no means certain, however, that the same author wrote both the Fourth Gospel and the First Epistle; thus, the epistle can be used to illuminate the thought of the Fourth Evangelist only with caution; see, e.g., Kümmel, *Introduction to the New Testament*, 442–45.

67. See, e.g., Bultmann, *Gospel of John*, 466–73.

68. Cf. v. 6 and perhaps v. 8.

69. Apparently, according to the Fourth Evangelist, the disciples have already been cleansed by the word that Jesus gave them. Insofar as they remain in that word (also expressed as remaining in the divine name and remaining in the Son), they need no further cleansing.

those who are to believe in me through their word" (v. 20), which has been preceded by the statement, "As you did send me into the world, so I have sent them into the world" (v. 18). This points toward a responsibility that the disciples have toward other people, here, however, not that of forgiveness but rather that of witnessing to the divine love. Further, there is the prayer "that they [all] may be one even as we are one, I in them and you in me, that they may become perfectly one, so that the world may know that you have sent me and have loved them, even as you have loved me" (vv. 22b–23; cf. vv. 11 and 21). Only at this point, in both the Lord's Prayer and the High Priestly Prayer, is there any mention of "interpersonal relations" among the disciples or between the disciples and others. Apparently, the basic thought is that, just as the Father and the Son are one in their mutual love, and the Son and the disciples are one in their mutual love, so now the disciples themselves are to be one in their mutual love for each other, and thus the world will know the reality of this all-embracing oneness.[70] Forgiveness of one another is thereby transformed into witnessing to the divine love, love for one another, and oneness in Christ.

Thus, both parts of the second "we" petition of the Lord's Prayer appear to be reflected in the High Priestly Prayer in terms of the Fourth Evangelist's own theological emphases and interests.

The Third
"We" Petition

The third "we" petition in the Lord's Prayer reads καὶ μὴ εἰσενέγκῃς ἡμᾶς εἰς πειρασμόν, ἀλλὰ ῥῦσαι ἡμᾶς ἀπὸ τοῦ πονηροῦ ("And lead us not into temptation [or testing], but de-

---

70. Cf., e.g., John 13:34–35: "A new commandment I give to you, that you love one another; even as I have loved you, that you also love one another. By this all men will know that you are my disciples, if you have love for one another." It is possible that the prayer for oneness in the church reflects a concern about schism, but see, e.g., Bultmann, *Gospel of John*, 512–18 on vv. 20–23.

liver us from evil [or from the evil one]").[71] Here, the High Priestly
Prayer has a very similar petition, which, at one point, repeats the
language of the Lord's Prayer almost *verbatim*. Indeed, it is at this
point that the Fourth Evangelist's knowledge of the Lord's Prayer
in its Matthean version becomes most evident.[72] The High Priestly
Prayer reads (vv. 11b–15):

> Holy Father, keep them in your name, which you have given
> me, that they may be one, even as we are one. While I was
> with them, I kept them in your name, which you have given
> me; I have guarded them, and none of them is lost but the son
> of perdition, that the scriptures might be fulfilled. But now I
> am coming to you; and these things I speak in the world, that
> they may have my joy fulfilled in themselves. I have given
> them your word; and the world has hated them because they
> are not of the world, even as I am not of the world. I do not
> pray that you should take them out of the world, but that you
> should keep them from the evil one (ἵνα τηρήσῃς αὐτοὺς ἐκ
> τοῦ πονηροῦ).

Joachim Jeremias argues convincingly that the first part of the
Lord's Prayer's third "we" petition is, at least in part, a prayer
for preservation from apostasy in the final great time of testing
(i.e., persecution),[73] and the section of the High Priestly Prayer
just quoted, with its reference to Judas Iscariot ("the son of perdition") as one who was not "kept" in the Father's name, apparently
suggests something of the same meaning: Jesus is praying that the
Father will protect the disciples from falling away in apostasy in
the face of the world's hatred.[74]

---

71. Luke reads only καὶ εἰσενέγκῃς ἡμᾶς εἰς πειρασμόν ("And lead
us not into temptation" or "testing") in the best manuscripts; a number
of witnesses, some of them ancient, include ἀλλὰ ῥῦσαι ἡμᾶς ἀπὸ τοῦ
πονηροῦ ("but deliver us from evil" or "from the evil one"), but this is
most likely an assimilation to the Matthean text.

72. See, e.g., Brown, *Gospel according to John (xiii–xxi)*, 747; Dodd,
Historical Tradition in the Fourth Gospel, 333.

73. Jeremias, "Lord's Prayer in the Light of Recent Research," 105–6.

74. Note that this is apparently not the final eschatological testing, as it
probably is in Matthew's Lord's Prayer, but rather the day-to-day opposi-
tion encountered by the disciples in the world.

More specifically, when Jesus prays that the Father will "keep them from the evil one" (τηρήσης αὐτοὺς ἀπὸ τοῦ πονηροῦ), he clearly echoes the second part of the third "we" petition in the Lord's Prayer, "but deliver us from the evil one" (ἀλλὰ ῥῦσαι ἡμᾶς ἐκ τοῦ πονηροῦ).[75] As Raymond E. Brown says:

> This line is the Johannine parallel to the petition in the Matthean version of the Lord's Prayer: "Free us from the Evil One" (Matt vi 13 — customarily but less accurately rendered as "Deliver us from evil"). The preceding petition in Matthew which deals with the final trial ("temptation") shows that a deliverance at the end of days is envisaged. John's petition is in terms of realized eschatology: it asks for protection while the disciples are in the world.[76]

Thus, perhaps more clearly than at any other point, it appears that, in the case of the third "we" petition, the Fourth Evangelist has composed a type of midrashic expansion and interpretation of Matthew's version of the Lord's Prayer.

The Three "We" Petitions: Summary

As with the "thou" petitions, the Fourth Evangelist has not maintained a clear and consistent distinction among the meanings of the three "we" petitions, drawing rather upon first one and then

---

75. Debate continues regarding the preferable translation of τοῦ πονηροῦ in Matthew; see, e.g., Harner, *Understanding the Lord's Prayer*, 110–13. On τοῦ πονηροῦ in the High Priestly Prayer, see, e.g., Barrett, *Gospel according to St John*, 425: "It is impossible to be certain whether John means ὁ πονηρός or τὸ πονηρόν. The only other uses of πονηρός in the gospel are 3.19; 7.7—both adjectival. But the use in 1 John (2.13f.; 3.12; 5.18f.) suggests strongly that John is thinking of the Evil One, not of evil. The death of Jesus means the judgment of the prince of this world (12.31; 14.30; 16.11), but he is not deprived of the power to harm the disciples, if they are left without divine aid." Despite the parallels in 1 John (and see n. 66 above on using 1 John to illuminate the thought of the Fourth Evangelist), τοῦ πονηροῦ is an idiom that is foreign to the Fourth Gospel, except in the High Priestly Prayer, and its presence here may well be the result of the influence of the Lord's Prayer.

As for John's use of τηρεῖν ("to keep") rather than the ῥύεσθαι of the Lord's Prayer, note that ῥύεσθαι never occurs in the Fourth Gospel.

76. Brown, *Gospel according to John (xiii–xxi)*, 761.

another as he articulates his concerns for the life of the church in
the world: concerns for the life and unity of the church ("Give us
this day our bread for tomorrow"), for the purity and oneness of
the church ("Forgive us out debts, as we also have forgiven our
debtors"), and for the preservation of the church from apostasy
("Lead us not into temptation, but deliver us from the Evil One").

Conclusion

Near the beginning of this paper, it was suggested "that the basic
content, to a somewhat lesser degree the overall structure, and
occasionally at significant points the actual language of the High
Priestly Prayer can best be understood as a re-working and expansion of the basic themes of the Lord's Prayer in terms of the
specifically Johannine theology." Content and language have
been discussed, but a word must now be said regarding structure. It would appear that vv. 1 thorough 8 are, for the most part,
a midrashic expansion of the three "thou" petitions in the Lord's
Prayer, while vv. 9 through 19 relate primarily to the three "we"
petitions. Thus far, the structure of the High Priestly Prayer reflects that of the Lord's Prayer. Vv. 20 through 26, then, are essentially a recapitulation of the themes developed earlier in the
prayer and, as such, include elements from both the "thou" and
the "we" petitions.

Finally, it must be noted that the existence of some type of
literary relationship between the High Priestly Prayer and the
Matthean version of the Lord's Prayer does not, in itself, necessarily imply a literary relationship between the Fourth Gospel and
the Gospel of Matthew (and/or the Didache). It is widely held,
however, that Matthew "was written in Antioch or, more generally, in Syria";[77] many scholars believe that the Didache also originated in Syria;[78] and there are plausible arguments for assuming
that the Fourth Gospel reflects a Syrian milieu.[79] Thus, a literary

---

77. Kümmel, *Introduction to the New Testament*, 119; cf. Farmer, "Post-
Sectarian Character of Matthew."

78. See, e.g., Vielhauer, *Geschichte des urchristlichen Literatur*, 737.

79. See, e.g., Kümmel, *Introduction to the New Testament*, 247.

relationship among two or three of the documents in question is a very real possibility. It is also possible, however, as Dodd suggests, that the Lord's Prayer "belonged to the liturgical tradition of the church from the earliest period"[80] and that the Fourth Evangelist has simply drawn from this tradition. The fact that he uses the Matthean rather than the Lukan version of the prayer, however, may strengthen the case for tracing the Fourth Gospel to a Syrian milieu, but this question requires much further investigation.

---

80. Dodd, *Historical Tradition in the Fourth Gospel*, 334.

PART THREE

The Son of Man

Chapter 10

The Origin of the Son of Man Concept as Applied to Jesus

I

The "Son of Man problem in the Gospels," as Matthew Black so aptly puts it, "is one of the most perplexing and challenging in the whole field of Biblical theology."[1] More than a decade ago, A. J. B. Higgins spoke of the "bewildering mass of material" that had been produced on the subject during the previous quarter of a century,[2] and this "mass" has continued to grow since he wrote.[3] Most of

---

"The Origin of the Son of Man Concept as Applied to Jesus." *JBL* 91,4 (December 1972) 482–90. Copyright © 1972 Society of Biblical Literature. Reprinted with permission in *TUSR* 10 (1970–1973), 67–75. Reprinted in Vincent L. Tollers and John R. Maier, eds., *The Bible in Its Literary Milieu: Contemporary Essays*, 156–65. Reprinted with permission.

1. Black, "Son of Man Problem," 305.

2. Higgins, "Son of Man-*Forschung*," 119.

3. The more important recent books on the Son of Man problem include: Sjöberg, *Der verborgene Menschensohn in den Evangelien*; Tödt, *Son of Man in the Synoptic Tradition*; Higgins, *Jesus and the Son of Man*; Borsch, *Son of Man in Myth and History*; Hooker, *Son of Man in Mark*; and Borsch, *Christian and Gnostic Son of Man*. Other books that contain significant treatments of the subject include: Mowinckel, *He That Cometh*, 346–450; Cullmann, *Christology of the New Testament*, 137–92; Enslin, *Prophet from Nazareth*, 137–48; Hahn, *Titles of Jesus in Christology*, 15–67; Jüngel, *Paulus und Jesus*, 2nd ed., 215–62; Fuller, *Foundations of New Testament Christology*, 34–43, 65, 119–25, 143–54, 229–30, 233–34. Recent articles dealing with the Son of Man are much too numerous to list, but mention should be made of the extremely thorough and important treatment by Carsten Colpe, "ὁ υἱὸς τοῦ νθϱώπου." Some of the other more significant articles will be referred to in the course of this paper.

the recent discussion has revolved around two interrelated questions: (1) the derivation and consequent meaning of the term and
concept, "Son of Man," and (2) the authenticity and interpretation
of the various Son of Man sayings in the New Testament gospels.[4]
As regards the first question, despite some continuing dissent and
disagreement concerning details, there has emerged a significant
consensus among New Testament scholars that "Son of Man" is
intended in the gospels as a kind of "messianic" title[5] and that the
term is derived from the world of Jewish apocalypticism,[6] which,
it is widely assumed, held "the conception of a transcendent, pre-
existent heavenly being, the Son of Man, whose coming to earth
as judge would be a major feature of the drama of the End time."[7]

---

4. For surveys of the discussion, see, e.g., Foakes Jackson and Lake,
Beginnings of Christianity, 345–418; N. Schmidt, "Recent Study of the Term
'Son of Man'"; Peake, "Messiah and the Son of Man"; Riesenfeld, *Jésus
transfiguré*; McCown, "Jesus, Son of Man"; BAG, 842–43; Higgins, "Son
of Man-*Forschung*"; Hodgson, "Son of Man and the Problem of Historical
Knowledge"; Fuller, *New Testament in Current Study*, 37–43; Black, "Son
of Man Problem"; Perrin, *Kingdom of God in the Teaching of Jesus*, 90–129;
Marlow, "*Son of Man* in Recent Journal Literature"; Marshall, "Synoptic
Son of Man Sayings"; Haufe, "Das Menschensohn-Problem"; Higgins,
"Is the Son of Man Problem Insoluble?"

5. Howard M. Teeple ("Origin of the Son of Man Christology") interprets the terms "Messiah" and "messianic" in a very broad sense, insisting that the proper distinction to be drawn is not between "Son of
Man" and "Messiah" but rather between "Son of Man type Messiah" and
other types of "Messiah" (e.g., "Son of David type Messiah"). Norman
Perrin ("Son of Man in Ancient Judaism and Primitive Christianity," 24,
and *Rediscovering the Teaching of Jesus*, 170–71), on the other hand, prefers
"apocalyptic redeemer figures" as the broad category and makes a distinction between "Son of Man" and "Messiah."

6. See, e.g., Tödt, *Son of Man in the Synoptic Tradition*, 22. Numerous
suggestions have been offered as to the possible origin of the Son of Man
image in Jewish apocalypticism, but the present evidence points increasingly to a Canaanite origin; see, e.g., Colpe, "ὁ υἱὸς τοῦ ἀνθρώπου,"
406–20.

7. The quotation is from Perrin (*Rediscovering the Teaching of Jesus*,
164), who, however, does not accept this view (see below). It should be
noted that the weaknesses in this assumption have often been recognized even by scholars who accept it; see, e.g., Tödt, *Son of Man in the
Synoptic Tradition*, 30–31; Colpe, "ὁ υἱὸς τοῦ ἀνθρώπου," 420–30; and the

As regards the second question, some scholars still hold that all or most of the Son of Man sayings are genuine self-references of the historical Jesus,[8] and others find an authentic element primarily in those sayings that allude to the present situation, activity, and authority of the Son of Man,[9] but increasingly the tendency is either, on the one hand, to reject all except certain of the apocalyptic Son of Man sayings and to deny that these are *self*-references of Jesus[10] or, on the other hand, to attribute all of the Son of Man sayings without exception to the early church.[11]

Recently, Norman Perrin has re-opened the Son of Man question in a fresh and exciting way by (1) vigorously challenging the widespread assumption of a Son of Man concept in Jewish apocalypticism, (2) denying the authenticity of all of the Son of Man sayings in the New Testament gospels and attributing the Son of Man

---

comments by Perrin in "Son of Man in Ancient Judaism and Primitive Christianity," 19.

8. E.g., T. W. Manson, *Teaching of Jesus*, 211–34; Taylor, *Names of Jesus*, 33–34; Stauffer, *New Testament Theology*, 109–11; Cullmann, *Christology of the New Testament*, 152–64.

9. Particularly Schweizer, *Erniedrigung und Erhöhung bei Jesus und seinen Nachfolgern*, 88–93; "Der Menschensohn"; *Lordship and Discipleship*, 39–41; "Son of Man"; *Erniedrigung und Erhöhung bei Jesus und seinen Nachfolgern*, 2nd ed., 33–52, 65–71; and his "Son of Man Again." Cf. also J. A. T. Robinson, *Jesus and His Coming*, 37–82.

10. E.g., Knox, *Death of Christ*, esp. 86–102; Bultmann, *Theology of the New Testament*, 1:26–32, and, for individual texts, his *History of the Synoptic Tradition* (both original and revised versions); cf. also Bultmann, "Reich Gottes and Menschensohn"; Bornkamm, *Jesus of Nazareth*, 175–78, 228–31; Hahn, *Titles of Jesus in Christology*, esp. 21–28; Jüngel, *Paulus und Jesus*, 2nd ed., 215–62; Fuller, *Foundations of New Testament Christology*, 119–25; and esp. Tödt, *Son of Man in the Synoptic Tradition*. Higgins (*Jesus and the Son of Man*) agrees on the question of authenticity but maintains that Jesus did identify himself with the coming Son of Man.

11. Esp. Vielhauer, "Gottesreich und Menschensohn in der Verkündigung Jesu," "Jesus und der Menschensohn," and "Ein Weg der neutestamentlichen Theologie?" See also Käsemann, "Sentences of Holy Law in the New Testament," "Beginnings of Christian Theology," and "On the Subject of Primitive Christian Apocalyptic"; Conzelmann, "Present and Future in the Synoptic Tradition," and "Jesus Christus," 630–31. Cf. also Teeple, "Origin of the Son of Man Christology."

christology to an exegetical process at work in the church similar to that which has been detected in the Qumran community, and (3) ascribing to the author of Mark the major role in the creative use of Son of Man traditions in the New Testament period.[12]

On the basis of a critical examination of the use of "Son of Man imagery" in Jewish apocalyptic and midrashic literature, Perrin concludes:

> There is no sufficient relationship between the use of Son of Man in I Enoch and IV Ezra for us to suppose that they are both reflections of a common conception. What we have is the imagery of Dan. 7.13 being used freely and creatively by subsequent seers and scribes. These uses are independent of one another; the common dependence is upon Dan. 7.13 on the one hand and upon the general world of apocalyptic concepts on the other. Similarly, the scribes of the midrashic traditions in their turn use the imagery of Dan. 7.13 in connection with the Messiah. Although they abandon the general world of apocalyptic concepts, none the less they find Dan 7.13 every bit as useful in their presentation of the Messiah as did the seer of IV Ezra in his.[13]

If this is true, and, in my opinion, Perrin's argument is convincing, then Jewish literature and thought provided no unified and consistent Son of Man concept in the first century. What was at hand, rather, was simply the precedent of "the varied use of 'Son of Man imagery,'"[14] and the apocalyptic Son of Man concept that appears in the New Testament gospels must, therefore, have originated either with Jesus himself or with the early Christian community.

---

12. Perrin, "Mark XIV.62"; "Son of Man in Ancient Judaism and Primitive Christianity," 17–28; *Rediscovering the Teaching of Jesus.*, 164–99; "Creative Use of the Son of Man Traditions by Mark"; "Son of Man in the Synoptic Tradition"; and "Literary *Gattung* 'Gospel.'"

13. Perrin, *Rediscovering the Teaching of Jesus*, 172 and cf. 164–73; also his "Son of Man in Ancient Judaism and Primitive Christianity," 25–26. See also Leivestad, "Exit the Apocalyptic Son of Man."

14. Perrin, *Rediscovering the Teaching of Jesus*, 166, and his "Son of Man in Ancient Judaism and Primitive Christianity," 20.

Perrin then maintains that the apocalyptic Son of Man concept originated not with the historical Jesus, but with the primitive church. A careful form-critical and tradition-historical analysis of the Son of Man sayings in the Synoptic Gospels indicates "that Jesus could not have spoken of the coming of the Son of Man, either in reference to himself or in reference to an eschatological figure other than himself," because all of the apocalyptic Son of Man sayings, under close scrutiny, turn out to be the products of an exegetical tradition in the early church.[15] Following Barnabas Lindars in particular,[16] Perrin points out:

> The earliest Christians made most significant use of the OT in their theologizing. They developed major aspects of their belief and expectation from OT texts, interpreting the texts in the light of their experience and their experience in the light of the texts. The Christian practice here paralleled that of the Qumran scribes and, like those scribes, the Christians read the OT texts as strictly relating to themselves and their experiences, and they exercised very considerable freedom in regard to the wording of the texts.[17]

Specifically, Perrin claims that the expectation of the coming of Jesus as apocalyptic Son of Man is a "product" of such an "exegetical process" that was at work in the early church.[18]

Apparently, according to Perrin, "the first Christological step taken by the early church was that of interpreting the resurrection in the light of" the first verse of Psalm 110:

---

15. Perrin, *Rediscovering the Teaching of Jesus*, 198 (for the analysis of the sayings, see 173–99 and his "Son of Man in the Synoptic Tradition"). Perrin does accept the authenticity of certain of the "present" Son of Man sayings (e.g., Luke 7:34=Matt 11:19), but he insists that "Son of Man" here is not a title but "simply an idiomatic self-designation of the speaker in contrast to another person, the idiom known to us from the rabbis" ("Son of Man in the Synoptic Tradition," 14; cf. Vermes, "Appendix E."

16. Lindars, *New Testament Apologetic.*

17. Perrin, *Rediscovering the Teaching of Jesus*, 23.

18. Perrin, "Son of Man in the Synoptic Tradition," 4.

The LORD says to my lord: "Sit at my right hand,
Till I make your enemies your footstool."[19]

The Christian exegesis of this verse produced the *mār* Christology, as well as the particular eschatology expressed in *maranatha* (1 Cor 16:22; Did. 10:6). The beginning of the Son of Man christology, however, can be traced to a secondary "Christian exegetical tradition in which the original interpretation of the resurrection in terms of Ps 110.1 was expanded by the use of Dan 7.13: the resurrection of Jesus is now interpreted as his ascension to God *as Son of Man*."[20] Just as Enoch became Son of Man on the basis of an interpretation of his translation, so Jesus became Son of Man on the basis of an interpretation of his resurrection.[21]

II

I am strongly inclined to accept Perrin's basic reconstruction of the origin of the Son of Man christology, so far as it goes. What he fails to explain, however is precisely why Ps 110:1 first came to be

---

19. Perrin, "Son of Man in the Synoptic Tradition," 4; see his *Rediscovering the Teaching of Jesus,* 175–76. More recently, Perrin ("Recent Trends in Research in the Christology of the New Testament," 222) has apparently accepted the view of Fuller and others that behind the exaltation christology based on Ps 110:1 can be found traces of a still more primitive Christology that held that "Jesus is the one who at his resurrection/ascension was predestined to appear as the Christ at the parousia." This does not, however, necessarily effect his conclusions regarding the origin of the Son of Man Christology.

20. Perrin, *Rediscovering the Teaching of Jesus,* 179; see the full discussion, 175–84.

21. Perrin, "Son of Man in Ancient Judaism and Primitive Christianity," 26, and *Rediscovering the Teaching of Jesus,* 173; cf. his "Son of Man in the Synoptic Tradition," 5 n. 7: "The parallels between the Son of Man in I Enoch and the New Testament are to be explained ... by the fact that two roughly contemporary groups in the same Jewish apocalyptic milieu have done the same kind of thing in the same kind of way. The Enoch saga interprets the translation of Enoch by means of Ezekiel and Dan 7; the Christian traditions understood the fate of Jesus as a translation/assumption and interpreted it by means of Ps 110:1; Zech 12:10ff. and Dan 7:13."

interpreted by the further use of Dan 7:13. What caused the two texts to be combined in the early Christian exegetical tradition? In general terms, of course, it could be pointed out that the two passages have a natural affinity in that they both speak of exaltation to a position of preeminence by God and, indeed, in the presence of God, and this might explain their association. Moreover, some scholars believe that Jewish exegesis had already, as early as the first century, given a "messianic"[22] interpretation of both Psalm 110[23] and Dan 7:13–14,[24] although this is debatable.[25] Apparently, however, it was characteristic of early Christian exegesis, at least in many instances, to combine Old Testament texts not on the basis of mere general affinity, but rather on the basis of specific verbal similarities.[26] Perrin himself suggests a possible precedent in Jewish exegetical practice when he points out that the Similitudes of *1 Enoch* 37–71 interpret the translation of Enoch on the basis of Ezekiel 1 and Daniel 7 and thus identify him as "Son of Man." The term "son of man" is applied to Ezekiel[27] and also occurs in Daniel 7 and thus forms a natural link between the two passages.[28] In the light of this precedent, the apparent absence of such a link

---

22. See n. 5 above.

23. This was frequent in late and rabbinic Judaism; see, e.g., Str-B, 4:452–65.

24. See, e.g., Mowinckel, *He That Cometh*, 335–36; Moore, *Judaism in the First Centuries of the Christian Era*, 2:334–37.

25. Regarding Psalm 110, Borsch (*Son of Man in Myth and History*, 396 n. 2) says: "There is little evidence that Ps 110:1 was employed messianically by Jews in Jesus' lifetime, but its use here [i.e., in Mark 12:35–37] shows that someone could make the connection. If the Church could have done this, there is no reason why someone before them could not have done so also."

26. For example, the phrase "right hand" is apparently the verbal link between Ps 16:8–11 and Ps 110:1 (see, e.g., Acts 2:25–36). See also my argument below for the verbal link between Ps 110:1 and Ps 8:6; cf. Lindars, *New Testament Apologetic*, 50–51. For a parallel to this in the Qumran material, see 4QFlor 10–13, where the verbal link between 2 Sam 7:11–14 and Amos 9:11 is "I will raise up."

27. Ezek 2:1 and frequently thereafter.

28. Perrin, "Son of Man in Ancient Judaism and Primitive Christianity," 21–22, and *Rediscovering the Teaching of Jesus*, 167–68.

between Ps 110:1 and Dan 7:13 in the early Christian exegetical tradition is all the more remarkable.

I suggest, however, that the combination of Ps 110:1 and Dan 7:13 occurred in two stages, that a link between the two texts can be found in Psalm 8, and that the key passage in demonstrating this link are Mark 12:36b and 1 Cor 15:25.

Ps 110:1, which Perrin regards as the starting point for the exegetical tradition that eventually produced the Son of Man christology, reads as follows in the LXX version (LXX 109:1): εἶπεν ὁ κύριος τῷ κυρίῳ μου κάθου ἐκ δεξιῶν μου ἕως θῶ τοὺς ἐκθροὺς σου ὑποπόδιον τῶν ποδῶν σου ("The Lord said to my lord, 'Sit at my right hand, until I make your enemies a footstool for your feet.'"). This is quoted almost *verbatim* in Acts 2:34b–35, the only difference being the absence of the article before κύριος and its application to Jesus. It is also quoted in Mark 12:36b, but this time an apparently insignificant difference appears:[29] in place of ὑποπόδιον ("footstool"), the text reads ὑποκάτω ("under"), resulting in the phrase ὑποκάτω τῶν ποδῶν σου ("under your feet") rather than the ὑποπόδιον τῶν ποδῶν σου ("a footstool of [or for] your feet") of Ps 110:1.[30] Now, the interesting fact is that the phrase ὑποκάτω τῶν ποδῶν also appears in the LXX version of Ps 8:6 (LXX 8:7), which reads: καὶ κατέστησας αὐτὸν ἐπὶ τὰ ἔργα τῶν χειρῶν σου πάντα ὑπέταξας ὑποκάτω τῶν ποδῶν αὐτοῦ ("And you placed him over the works of your hands, you subjected all things under his feet."). It is quite possible, then, that the ὑποπόδιον τῶν ποδῶν σου of Ps 110:1 suggested to the early Christian mind the ὑποκάτω τῶν ποδῶν αὐτοῦ of Ps 8:6 and that Mark 12:36b reflects a conflation of the verses, either conscious and intentional or unconscious and unintentional, in the Christian exegetical tradition.[31] This possibility becomes vir-

---

29. See Lindars (*New Testament Apologetic*, 46–47), who argues, on other grounds, that the quotation of Ps 110:1 in Mark 12:36b reflects a later exegetical development than that in Acts 2:34b–35.

30. Matt 22:44 follows Mark's ὑποκάτω, but Luke 20:43 returns to the ὑποπόδιον of Ps 110:1.

31. The presence in Mark 12:36 and Matt 24:44 of ὑποκάτω rather than ὑποπόδιον has, of course, been noted before, as has the probability of its derivation from Ps 8:6; see, e.g., Krister Stendahl, *School of St. Matthew*, 78.

tually a certainty, however, when it is noted, as Lindars points out, that the two texts are quite regularly combined or associated elsewhere in the New Testament.[32] Thus, for example, 1 Cor 15:25 says that Christ "must reign until he has put all his enemies under his feet" (δεῖ γὰρ αὐτὸν βασιλεύειν ἄχρι οὗ θῇ πάντας τοὺς ἐκθροὺς [αὐτοῦ] ὑπὸ τοὺς πόδας αὐτοῦ), combining the τοὺς ἐκθροὺς of Ps 110:1 with a modified version of the ὑποκάτω τῶν ποδῶν αὐτοῦ of Ps 8:6.

Apparently, then, the early Christians initially used Ps 110:1, particularly the first half of the verse (εἶπεν ὁ κύριος τῷ κυρίῳ μου κάθου ἐκ δεξιῶν μου), to interpret the resurrection of Jesus as an exaltation to the right hand of God as "Lord," but the second half of the verse (ἕως θῶ τοὺς ἐκθρούς σου ὑποπόδιον τῶν ποδῶν σου), which served the purpose of explaining the delay of the *parousia*, subsequently led them to Ps 8:6 with its strikingly similar ending (πάντα ὑπέταξας ὑποκάτω τῶν ποδῶν αὐτοῦ), with the result that Psalm 8 was then also applied to Jesus. Thus far, the exegetical development appears clear and logical, but how does Ps 8:6 then serve as the link between Ps 110:1 and Dan 7:13? The answer is equally clear and logical: Psalm 8 also refers in v. 4 (LXX v. 5) to a "son of man" (υἱὸς ἀνθρώπου), here used, of course, simply as a synonym for "man" (ἄνθρωπος). To the early Christian mind, however, which had already come to regard Psalm 8 as referring to Jesus on the basis of its association with Ps 110:1,[33] this would undoubtedly be understood as an identification of Jesus as "Son of Man," and it would almost inevitably suggest a connection with another reference to the term "son of

---

32. Lindars, *New Testament Apologetic*, 50–51.

33. Perrin (*Rediscovering the Teaching of Jesus*, 181) observes that once the use of a particular text is established, "it would be natural to go on to use other aspects of the passage." C. H. Dodd (*According to the Scriptures* and *Old Testament in the New*) has argued that the early Christians tended to draw material from whole blocs of Old Testament texts (e.g., entire chapters) rather than from individual sentences or phrases and that the context in which a particular word, phrase, or statement originally stood was very much in the mind of the Christian exegete. This may be overstated, but the context would obviously have been in the mind of the exegete and would quite easily have suggested to him further possibilities of interpretation and application.

man," viz., Dan 7:13. I suggest, therefore, that Psalm 8 forms the most probable link between the primitive Christian use of Ps 110:1 to interpret the resurrection of Jesus as his exaltation to the right hand of God as "Lord" and the subsequent use of Dan 7:13 to interpret that exaltation further as the exaltation of Jesus as *"Son of Man."*

Once Ps 110:1 and Dan 7:13 were combined in this way,[34] further exegetical developments followed, as Perrin has shown.[35] Originating, then in a particular Christian exegetical tradition having to do with the exaltation of Jesus, the apocalyptic Son of Man concept was taken up and used in a variety of early Christian forms[36] and, ultimately, was employed more or less systematically by the author of Mark in his attempt to correct what he regarded as a "false christology" in the early church.[37]

III

One problem remains. This use of Ps 8:6 to serve as a link between Ps 110:1 and Dan 7:13 and thereby to create a Son of Man christology for Jesus is possible only on the basis of the *Greek* texts of the passages in question; it cannot be worked out in Hebrew or Aramaic.[38] Thus, if my reconstruction of the origin of the Son of Man christology is valid, we must conclude that it

---

34. The two are used together in Mark 14:62 and parallels and in Acts 7:56. Perrin (*Rediscovering the Teaching of Jesus*, 179) argues that the two usages "cannot be dependent upon one another" and that they, therefore, constitute double testimony for the combination of Ps 110:1 and Dan 7:13 in the Christian exegetical tradition. Cf. also the Ascension story in Acts 1:9, which Perrin regards as dependent ultimately upon the Ps 110:1 tradition but containing "an echo" of Dan 7:13 in the reference to the "cloud."

35. Perrin, *Rediscovering the Teaching of Jesus*, 184.

36. Perrin, "Son of Man in the Synoptic Tradition," 7–10.

37. Perrin, "Creative Use of the Son of Man Traditions by Mark," and "The Literary *Gattung* 'Gospel.'"

38. Ps 110:1 in the Hebrew ends *'ad-'āšît 'ōyᵉbẹ(y kā hᵃdōm lᵉraglẹ(y)kā*. Ps 8:6 (8:7) in the Hebrew ends: *kōl šattāh taḥat-raglā(y)w*. Thus, the similarities are much less striking than in the Greek. Moreover, Ps 8:4 (8:5) uses the Hebrew *bẹn-'ādām* for "son of man," while Dan 7:13 has the Aramaic *bar-''ᵉnāš*.

was the Greek-speaking, not the Aramaic-speaking, church that first understood Jesus in apocalyptic terms as Son of Man. This, however, constitutes no real weakness in or objection to the reconstruction. Ferdinand Hahn has argued, primarily on linguistic grounds, that even the chronologically earlier use of Ps 110:1 to speak of Jesus' exaltation cannot have originated in the Aramaic-speaking Palestinian church,[39] and Howard M. Teeple, among others, has maintained that the Son of Man christology originated in Hellenistic-Jewish Christianity—perhaps with Stephen and the Hellenistic-Jewish Christians in Jerusalem or, more likely, among Hellenistic-Jewish Christians in Syria.[40] The former possibility is particularly intriguing.

It has frequently been noted that one of the very few occurrences of "Son of Man" outside the gospels is Acts 7:56, where it is applied to Jesus by "the radical hellenistic Jewish convert, Stephen."[41] It may be that this is simply an indication "that the author of Acts associated the Son of Man christology with Hellenistic Jewish-Christianity, not with the primitive Jerusalem church,"[42] or it may be that it reflects a correct memory that Stephen and his group actually held a Son of Man christology.[43]

---

39. Hahn, *Titles of Jesus in* Christology, 104–7.

40. Teeple, "Origin of the Son of Man Christology." Teeple also acknowledges (p. 238) that the Son of Man sayings "may have originated in Greek."

41. Teeple, "Origin of the Son of Man Christology," 241; cf., e.g., Tödt, *Son of Man in the Synoptic Tradition*, 303–5; Barrett, "Stephen and the Son of Man," 32–28.

42. Teeple, "Origin of the Son of Man Christology," 248.

43. Schweizer ("Son of Man," 123) says: "This scene of the Son of Man standing upright, as well as the use of this term outside the words of Jesus, is so unusual that the report seems to go back to the very event of the execution of Stephen." Similarly, Cullmann (*Christology of the New Testament*, 181–88) argues that "the little known but very important early Christian group of the Hellenists" was "the circle which fostered the Son of Man Christology" (183); Cullmann also believes, however, that the history of the Son of Man concept can be traced from what he terms "esoteric Judaism" through the teaching of Jesus and the christology of the Hellenists to the Fourth Gospel. On the importance of Stephen and the Hellenists, see Simon, *St. Stephen and the Hellenists*.

Clearly, the conflict between the "Hellenists" and the "Hebrews" in the early Jerusalem church was over more than just the daily distribution of food (Acts 6:1).[44] Teeple points out that "the hellenistic Jewish-Christians were unorthodox enough in Jewish sight to be persecuted, while the original church was traditional enough to be allowed to remain," and he poses the question: "Did the hellenists' unorthodoxy include the belief that Jesus is the Son of Man?"[45] If the Son of Man christology did begin with Stephen and the hellenistic-Jewish Christians in Jerusalem, then "the split between the original Jerusalem church of the disciples and the Hellenistic converts from the diaspora is quite understandable."

> The earlier belief, that Jesus was the Messiah who had been raised from the dead and exalted to heaven, was not theological heresy. Judaism contained traditions that certain human beings (Enoch, Moses, Elijah, Isaiah, and Jeremiah) had been exalted to heaven and that all righteous Jews would be raised from the dead. But the claim that the human Jesus who had lived on earth is the divine, pre-existent Son of Man was a belief that bordered on blasphemy because it was a threat to monotheism. ... The fears of the orthodox were justified, for the Son of Man christology helped to prepare the way for the fuller deification of Jesus later in gentile Christianity.[46]

The apparent absence of a full-blown Son of Man concept in pre-Christian Judaism that has been noted by Perrin calls into question certain details of Teeple's reconstruction, but it may well be, as he suggests, that the Son of Man christology originated with the "Hellenists" in Jerusalem and that the differences between "Hellenists" and "Hebrews" included, among other things, a conflict between a Son of Man christology and a Son of David christology. In any case, I suggest that it was among Greek-speaking, not Aramaic-speaking, Christians that the exegetical tradition produced the Son of Man christology.

---

44. See, e.g., Cullmann, "Dissensions within the Early Church," 85–87.
45. Teeple, "Origin of the Son of Man Christology," 248.
46. Teeple, "Origin of the Son of Man Christology," 249–50.

Chapter 11

The Son of Man

Some Recent Developments

Some years ago, Matthew Black observed that "the Son of Man problem in the Gospels is one of the most perplexing and challenging in the whole field of Biblical theology."[1] Similarly, A. J. B. Higgins has spoken of the "bewildering mass of material" that has been produced on the subject.[2] More recently, Higgins and Morna D. Hooker have discussed in print the question of whether the Son of Man problem is finally insoluble.[3] Indeed, Hooker has even reported that, when Black heard that she was working on the Son of Man problem, his advice consisted of a single word: "Don't!"[4]

Nevertheless, Son of Man research continues,[5] and, in my judgment, there recently have been some highly significant developments in at least one "wing" of this research—developments that, if generally accepted, may well point in the direction of an answer to the question of the origin of the Son of Man christology.

"The Son of Man: Some Recent Developments." *CBQ* 45,4 (October 1983) 584–607. Copyright © 1983 Catholic Biblical Association of America. Reprinted in slightly revised version as first part of "The Son of Man Question and the Synoptic Problem," in *New Synoptic Studies: The Cambridge Gospel Conference and Beyond* (ed. William R. Farmer; Macon, GA: Mercer University Press, 1983) 261–301. Reprinted with permission.

1. Black, "Son of Man Problem," 305.
2. Higgins, "Son of Man-*Forschung*," 119.
3. Higgins, "Is the Son of Man Problem Insoluble?"; Hooker, "Is the Son of Man Problem Really Insoluble?"
4. Hooker, "Is the Son of Man Problem Really Insoluble?" 155.
5. For recent bibliographies, see Casey, *Son of Man*, 241–59: Higgins, *Son of Man in the Teaching of Jesus*, 159–68; and Coppens, *La relève apocalyptique du messianisme royal*, 2–6.

I must stress, however, that, at the moment, these developments have by no means gained the support of New Testament scholarship as a whole; indeed, the recent book on the subject by Higgins either explicitly or implicitly rejects all of them.[6] Despite this fact, I believe that the developments have merit and need further exploration. I propose, therefore, to summarize these recent developments in Son of Man research in terms of six propositions, each of which will be stated and briefly explained. Then, in conclusion, I shall offer a suggestion for further research.

Proposition One

There was no Son of Man title or concept as such in first-century Judaism; therefore, the titular use of the term and the concept associated with it must have originated either with Jesus himself or within the early Christian community.

The term "son of man" was, of course, not unknown in first-century Judaism. In the Hebrew Bible, the singular, *ben 'ādām* ("son of man"), occurs thirteen times in parallelism with either *'îš* ("man") or *'ĕnôš* ("man") as a synonym for "human being."[7] Similarly *ben 'ĕnôš* ("son of man") occurs at Ps 144:3 in parallelism with *'ādām* ("human being").[8] In addition, *ben 'ādām* is found some ninety-three times in Ezekiel[9] and at Dan 8:17 as a form of direct address or quasi-vocative, applied to the prophet himself.[10] Outside the

---

6. Higgins, *Son of Man in the Teaching of Jesus*.

7. Num 23:19; Isa 51:12; 56:2; Jer 49:18, 33; 50:40; 51:43; Ps 8:5; 80:18; 146:3 (in parallelism with *nādîb*); Job 16:21 (in parallelism with *geber*); 25:6; 35:8. It is true that Ps 80:18 may refer to the king; see, e.g., Gelston, "Sidelight on the 'Son of Man.'" Even so, however, "son of man" is not here used as an independent title; moreover, it can plausibly be argued that the reference is not to the king at all but rather to the nation Israel.

8. Note also the many examples of the plural.

9. E.g., Ezek 2:1, 3; 3:1, 3, 4, 10.

10. Some scholars have seen in this usage the background for the Son of Man sayings in the New Testament gospels and thus have emphasized the "prophetic consciousness" allegedly implied by the term; see, e.g., Parker, "Meaning of 'Son of Man'"; Duncan, *Jesus, Son of Man*, esp. 135–205; Campbell, "Son of Man"; and Eichrodt, "Zum Problem des Menschensohns." For a critique of this position, see, e.g., Fuller, *Mission and Achievement of Jesus*, 99–102.

Hebrew Bible, however, the appearance of the Hebrew phrase is rare.[11] It is clear that the term is not used as a title in the extant Hebrew texts, either for an expected messianic or eschatological figure or for anyone else,[12] nor is there any "Son of Man" concept as such in the documents. Furthermore, it appears that the term itself was not used in ordinary day-to-day speech, but rather "only in contexts composed in poetic or solemn diction and style."[13]

In Aramaic, the evidence is more extensive, and it is now clear that "son of man" was in use in Palestine by the first century, both in the generic sense of "human being" and in the indefinite sense of "someone" or "anyone."[14] Moreover, some scholars have argued for a third use, the so-called circumlocutional use, in which it could serve as a substitute for the first-person personal pronoun and mean "I" or "me."[15] This third use has been vigorously disputed, however, by others.[16] The Aramaic term has not been

---

11. For a survey of the data, see Fitzmyer, "New Testament Title 'Son of Man,'" 146–47.

12. The Hebrew expression with the definite article, *ben hā'ādām*, has been found only once, where the article has been added above the line, in 1 QS 11:20; see Fitzmyer, "New Testament Title 'Son of Man,'" 146.

13. Fitzmyer, "New Testament Title 'Son of Man,'" 146.

14. See, e.g., Campbell, "Origin and Meaning of the Term Son of Man"; Bowman, "Background of the Term 'Son of Man'"; Black, "'Son of Man' in the Teaching of Jesus"; Vermes "Appendix E." The phrase appears in various forms: *bar nāš, bar nāšā', bar 'ĕnāš, bar 'ĕnāšā', bar 'ĕnôš,* and *bar 'ĕnôšā'*. According to Fitzmyer, however, it never appears without the initial *aleph* until sometime after the first century; see his review of Black, *Aramaic Approach*.

15. E.g., Meyer, *Jesu Muttersprache*, 92–97; Campbell, "Origin and Meaning of the Term Son of Man," 152–54; Formesyn, "Was There a Pronominal Connection for the 'Bar Nasha' Selfdesignation?" and esp. Vermes, "Appendix E," 310–28.

16. Some scholars maintain that the Aramaic phrase for "son of man" is primarily a generic term and that, while it may at times include the speaker, such usage does not constitute a genuine circumlocution for the first person; see, e.g., Borsch, *Son of Man in Myth and History*, 23 n. 4; Colpe, "ὁ υἱὸς τοῦ ἀνθρώπου," 403–4; Jeremias, "Die älteste Schicht der Menschensohn-Logien," esp. 165 n. 9; Jeremias, *New Testament Theology*, 261 n. 1; Boers, "Where Christology Is Real," 304; Gelston, "Sidelight on the 'Son of Man,'" 189 n. 2. Fitzmyer allows for the possibility of a subdivision of the generic sense of "son of man" into collective and inclusive, and he does recognize the circumlocutional use of "son of man" in the

found, however, as a form of direct address, like the Hebrew *ben 'ādām* used of the prophet Ezekiel, nor is it used as a title.

Nevertheless, at least until recently, there has been a widespread assumption among New Testament scholars that, when the New Testament speaks of "the Son of Man," it refers to an expected messianic or eschatological figure familiar to the first-century world of Jewish apocalyptic thought and literature.[17] According to this view, "there existed in Jewish apocalyptic the conception of a transcendent, pre-existent heavenly being, the Son of Man, whose coming to earth as judge would be a major feature of the drama of the End time."[18] It has been assumed by most that this Son of Man concept stemmed from the reference in Dan 7:13 to "one like a son of man" (*kĕbar 'ēnāš*), that it revealed itself in

---

late phase of Aramaic, insisting, however, that it is not legitimate to infer from this that the usage was current in the first century. For the continuing debate between Fitzmyer and Vermes, see Fitzmyer, review of Black, *Aramaic Approach;* Vermes, *Jesus the Jew,* esp. 163–68, 188–91; Fitzmyer, "Contribution of Qumran Aramaic," 396–97; Vermes, "'Son of Man' Debate"; Vermes, "Present State of the 'Son of Man' Debate"; Fitzmyer, "New Testament Title 'Son of Man'"; Fitzmyer, "Another View of the 'Son of Man' Debate." A recent full-scale study of the Son of Man question (Casey, *Son of Man,* 224–28, esp. 226–27) concludes that "in Aramaic a speaker could use a general statement, in which the expression for 'man' was בר נשא, in order to say something about himself," that such usage was "no more than a particular application of this well-known Aramaic locution," and that the application of such a statement to himself "by an Aramaic speaker is the sort of development of existing usage that could occur on the lips of native speakers of the language at any time." As I shall indicate below, I am not persuaded by Vermes' arguments and thus have no reason to think that there was, either in the first century or later, a genuinely circumlocutional use of "son of man." Regarding the generic and indefinite uses, however, there is no disagreement.

17. See, e.g., Tödt, *Son of Man in the Synoptic Tradition,* 22: "The intimate connexion of the synoptic presentation of the Son of Man with that of Jewish apocalyptic literature can no longer be seriously contested." Numerous suggestions have been offered as to the possible origin of such a Son of Man figure in Jewish apocalyptic, but a Canaanite mythological origin has gained increasing acceptance; see, e.g., Colpe, "ὁ υἱὸς τοῦ ἀνθρώπου," 406–20; M. S. Smith, "'Son of Man' in Ugaritic."

18. The quotation is from Perrin, *Rediscovering the Teaching of Jesus,* 164; Perrin, himself, however, did not finally accept this view (see below).

various ways in the Similitudes of *1 Enoch* 37–71, *4 Ezra*, and perhaps elsewhere, and that it formed the background for the Son of
Man sayings in the New Testament gospels.

Scholars had long recognized, of course, that there were significant differences among the various Jewish writings suppos-
edly reflecting this Son of Man concept, but they had attempted
to reconcile or explain these differences in various ways.[19] In
recent years, however, the very assumption that there ever was
such a title and concept in first-century Judaism has come under
increasingly serious and sustained attack.[20] According to a growing consensus, it is now "embarrassingly obvious that the Son of
Man was not a current title in Judaism at all."[21] Indeed, the entire
concept appears to be nothing more than "a product of modern
scholarship."[22] "Son of Man" is not used as a title in Dan 7:13,
where the reference is simply to a "human-like figure"[23] in contrast to the four beast-like figures of the vision, nor does the term
become a title in *1 Enoch* or *4 Ezra* or elsewhere in Jewish literature.[24] The closest thing to a Son of Man title or concept among

---

19. See, e.g., Tödt, *Son of Man in the Synoptic Tradition*, 30–31; and Colpe,
"ὁ υἱὸς τοῦ ἀνθρώπου," 422–33.

20. See, e.g., Perrin, "Son of Man in Ancient Judaism and Primitive
Christianity"; his *Rediscovering the Teaching of Jesus*, 164–75; Vermes,
"Appendix E"; Vermes, *Jesus the Jew*, 160–91. Leivestad, "Der apokalyp-
tische Menschensohn"; Leivestad, "Exit the Apocalyptic Son of Man";
Casey, *Son of Man*, esp. 7–141,

21. Lindars, "Re-enter the Apocalyptic Son of Man," 52.

22. Casey, *Son of Man*, 139; cf., e.g., Winter, review of Perrin,
Rediscovering the Teaching of Jesus, 784: "If Perrin's interpretation of the
Son of Man sayings in the Synoptic Gospels is correct—and it is supported by Vermes's ... study of the linguistic use of 'bar-nash(a)' in Jewish
Aramaic—then the place of origin of the [Son of Man] myth is not to be
sought in Iran, or in Judea or even in Ugarit, but in the German universi-
ties."

23. Casey (*Son of Man*) consistently uses this term to translate the *kĕbar*
'ĕnāš of Dan 7:13.

24. Regarding the Similitudes of *1 Enoch*, see, e.g., Fitzmyer, "New
Testament Title 'Son of Man,'" 153: "[Son of Man] has been regarded as a
'messianic' title, mainly because of its association with the title Messiah in
Ethiopic Enoch (e.g., 48:2, 10), whereas it in no way suggests an anointed
figure *per se*. But if J. T. Milik's latest theory about the second part of the

first-century Jews was simply the precedent of "the varied use of the 'Son of Man' imagery"[25] from Dan 7:13 by various writers and for different purposes. Thus, a recent full-scale examination of the evidence leads to this conclusion: "The Jews had no Son of man concept, and their use of Dan. 7 did not turn *bar 'ĕnāš* into a title. It follows that the origin of the Gospel term ὁ υἱὸς τοῦ ἀνθρώπου must be sought in developments for which Jesus or his followers were responsible."[26]

Proposition Two

No Son of Man title or concept as such can be detected in the
authentic sayings of the historical Jesus; therefore, the titular
use of the term and the concept associated with it must have
originated within the early Christian community.

On the basis of certain well-known facts regarding the Son of Man sayings in the New Testament gospels, most scholars in the past have assumed that Jesus did, in fact, use the term "Son of Man" as a title, with reference either to himself or to some other figure yet to come. These facts are the following: (1) The title "Son of Man" is almost completely absent from early Christian literature other than the canonical gospels.[27] (2) The title occurs in all four of the

---

Book of Enoch, the so-called Similitudes, were to prove acceptable, then the entire question of the conflated titles of the mysterious figure in that part of the book would have to be scrutinized again and precisely for the roots of this conflation in pre-Christian Palestinian Judaism. For Milik maintains that the Similitudes represent a Christian substitution. It replaced the Book of the Giants which was part of the Book of Enoch at Qumran and which he has now discovered among the published and unpublished material from Qumran." Scholars have long debated whether the Similitudes are pre-Christian in date; see, e.g., Fuller, *Foundations of New Testament Christology*, 37–38.

25. Perrin, "Son of Man in Ancient Judaism and Primitive Christianity," 20, and his *Rediscovering the Teaching of Jesus*, 166.

26. Casey, *Son of Man*, 139. For the argument that Son of Man was never intended or understood as an independent messianic or eschatological title, even in the gospel traditions, see Leivestad, "Exit the Apocalyptic Son of Man." Most scholars, however, agree that, "in the Greek text of the gospels as we have it, ὁ υἱὸς τοῦ ἀνθρώπου is understood as a title" (Jeremias, *New Testament Theology*, 261).

27. On this point, see further under "Proposition Six" below.

canonical gospels, and, indeed, in all of what are commonly taken to be the various strata of the gospel traditions: the triple tradition, the various double traditions, special Matthew, special Luke, and John. (3) With only one exception, and this in the Fourth Gospel,[28] the title is found in the gospels only on the lips of Jesus himself.[29] (4) The references to "Son of Man" on the lips of Jesus are always in the third person, never the first, and, in some cases, a rather clear distinction between Jesus and the Son of Man appears to be implied.[30] The assumption, of course, is that, if the title had originated within the early church, it would likely be found also in Christian literature outside the canonical gospels, it might well be missing from one or more of the gospels themselves (or, at least, from one or more of the strata of tradition lying behind the gospels), it would probably be applied to Jesus by persons other than Jesus himself, and there would be no sayings that even appear to suggest a distinction between Jesus and the Son of Man.

Most discussions of the authenticity of the various Son of Man sayings have disregarded the Fourth Gospel on the grounds that "it makes no positive contribution to the problem of Jesus and the

---

28. John 12:34.

29. Cf., however, Fitzmyer, *Gospel according to Luke (I–IX)*, 579: "An alternative way of interpreting [Luke 5:24 with parallels in Matt 9:6 and Mark 2:10] is to make of it a comment of the evangelist (or of the pre-Marcan compiler), which is addressed to the readers of the Gospel as 'you.' ... This would mean that the Son of Man saying is no longer on the lips of Jesus—a view contrary to a pet thesis of many modern interpreters of the christological titles. ... It seems to me that this is a better solution to the problematic v. 24; it forms a suture joining the pronouncement-story to the second part of the miracle-story. Such comments to the reader are rare, indeed, in the Synoptic tradition, but not wholly unknown (see Mark 13:14b), and more frequent in the Johannine tradition (e.g., 4:2; 17:3; 19:35; 20:30–31)." See also, e.g., Boobyer, "Mark 11, 10a and the Interpretation of the Healing of the Paralytic"; Boobyer, "Secrecy Motif in St. Mark's Gospel"; Ceroke, "Is Mk 2,10 a Saying of Jesus?" 380; Cranfield, *Gospel according to Saint Mark*, 100. Note, too, that at Mark 8:31 (cf. Luke 9:22); Mark 9:9 (cf. Matt 17:9); and Luke 24:7 the discourse attributed to Jesus is indirect rather than direct (in each of these passages the reference is to the impending suffering and/or resurrection of the Son of Man); this could be interpreted as an indication that someone other than Jesus uses the title.

30. E.g., Mark 8:38/Luke 9:26.

Son of Man"[31] but simply reflects a later development of the types of tradition already present in the Synoptic Gospels. Moreover, at least until rather recently, most scholars have accepted the now conventional division of the Synoptic Son of Man sayings into three groups: (1) sayings in which Jesus alludes to the present situation, status, activity, and/or authority of the Son of Man—the so-called "present Son of Man sayings"; (2) sayings in which he refers to the impending betrayal, rejection, suffering, death, and/or resurrection of the Son of Man—the so-called "suffering Son of Man sayings"; and (3) sayings in which he speaks of the exaltation and/or future coming of the Son of Man—the so-called "future Son of Man sayings."[32] Various types of criteria have been proposed for distinguishing between authentic and inauthentic sayings within these groups,[33] but it would not be correct to say that any general consensus has been reached. It has been argued by some that all three types of Son of Man sayings—"future," "suffering," and "present"—include genuine self-references of the historical Jesus.[34] Others have found an authentic element

---

31. Higgins, *Jesus and the Son of Man*, 185. For more positive assessments of the Johannine materials, see, e.g., Borsch, *Son of Man in Myth and History*, 257–313; Smalley, "Johannine Son of Man Sayings"; Lindars, "Son of Man in the Johannine Christology." For other studies, see, e.g., Schulz, *Untersuchungen zu Menschensohn-Christologie im Johannesevangelium*; Schnackenburg, "Der Menschensohn im Johannesevangelium"; Freed, "Son of Man in the Fourth Gospel"; Moloney, *Johannine Son of Man*; Coppens, "Le Fils de l'homme dans l'évangile johannique"; Coppens, *La relève apocalyptique du messianisme royal*, 45–103.

32. This division is most often attributed to Rudolf Bultmann; see, e.g., his *Theology of the New Testament*, 1:30. Actually, it had been suggested earlier in Foakes Jackson and Lake, *Beginnings of Christianity*, 368–84, and it was worked out in Héring, *Le royaume de Dieu et sa venue*, 88–100. More recently, it was reaffirmed in the unpublished Heidelberg dissertation: Iber, "Überlieferungsgeschichtliche Untersuchungen zum Begriff des Menschensohn im Neuen Testament." For opposing views, see n. 45 below.

33. See, e.g., Teeple, "Origin of the Son of Man Christology," 216–23.

34. E.g., T. W. Manson, *Teaching of Jesus*, 211–34; Taylor, *Names of Jesus*, 33–34; Stauffer, *New Testament Theology*, 109–11; and Cullmann, *Christology of the New Testament*, 152–64.

primarily in the "present" and/or "suffering" sayings,[35] and still others have rejected all of the sayings except a few with a "future" reference.[36] In recent years, however, scholars working from two quite different directions have made a strong case that none of the sayings in which "Son of Man" appears as a title is authentic.

Particularly among German scholars, the tendency, until recently, has been: (1) to attribute both the "present" and the "suffering" Son of Man sayings to the early Christian community, with the possible exception of a relatively small number of "present" sayings, where the term is used not as a title but simply in the common Semitic sense of "a human being," "someone," or "anyone," or possibly as a circumlocution for the first-person personal pronoun;[37] and (2) to find an authentic element in certain of the "future" sayings, maintaining, however, that Jesus here speaks not of himself but rather of some other figure yet to come.[38] Philipp Vielhauer and others, however, have worked out detailed argu-

---

35. Eduard Schweizer (*Erniedrigung und Erhöhung bei Jesus und seinen Nachfolgern*, 88–93; "Der Menschensohn"; *Lordship and Discipleship*, 39–41; "Son of Man"; *Erniedrigung und Erhöhung bei Jesus und seinen Nachfolgern*, 2nd ed., 33–52, 65–71; "Son of Man Again"), for example, maintains that the first group has the best claim to authenticity, that the second probably preserves some authentic traditions, and that there may well be a genuine core in the third group. In the first group, the authentic core would be the references to "humility"; in the second group, the references to being "handed over"; and in the third group, the references to "exaltation" (not "coming"). Thus, it is likely, according to Schweizer, that Jesus spoke of himself as the Son of Man who was to be humiliated and rejected by men but then exalted by God. Cf. also, e.g., J. A. T. Robinson, *Jesus and His Coming*, 37–82.

36. See esp. Tödt, *Son of Man in the Synoptic Tradition*; cf. also, e.g., Bultmann, *Theology of the New Testament*, 1:26–32, and, for the individual texts, his *History of the Synoptic Tradition* (rev. ed.); cf. also Bultmann, "Reich Gottes und Menschensohn"; Knox, *Death of Christ*, 86–102; Bornkamm, *Jesus of Nazareth*, 175–78, 228–31; Hahn, *Titles of Jesus in Christology*, 15–67; Jüngel, *Paulus und Jesus*, 2nd ed., 215–62; Fuller, *Foundations of New Testament Christology*, 119–25. Higgins (*Son of Man in the Teaching of Jesus*) agrees on the question of authenticity, but, unlike the others, maintains that Jesus did identify himself with the coming Son of Man.

37. On this last possible use, see nn. 15 and 16 above.

38. See n. 36 above.

ments, based both upon exegesis of the relevant texts and upon studies in the history of religions, against the authenticity even of the "future" sayings.[39] These arguments have not been universally accepted, of course, but even scholars who reject Vielhauer's conclusions have been compelled to acknowledge that his work is "thoughtful and highly significant,"[40] and some have been much more positive, speaking, for example, of "the devastating evidence" produced by Vielhauer and commenting that his "exegetical arguments have been questioned, but not disproved," that "there have been at best protests against" his use of materials from the history of religions, and that his "work thus remains fundamentally unchallenged."[41] The development of the thought of Norman Perrin regarding this matter is, I think, both impressive and perhaps indicative of the shift in opinion: Perrin initially maintained that the only "two viable positions with regard to the Son of man in the synoptic tradition" were that represented by H. E. Tödt ("all except a very small core of apocalyptic sayings must be ascribed to the church") or that maintained by Vielhauer ("all Son of man sayings must be ascribed to the church").[42] Eventually, however, Perrin was led by his own research to embrace the position that *all* Son of Man sayings must be ascribed to the early Christian community.[43]

Proceeding along rather different lines, two scholars in Great Britain, Geza Vermes and Maurice Casey have reached somewhat similar conclusions.[44] Vermes rejects the conventional threefold

---

39. See esp. Vielhauer, "Gottesreich und Menschensohn in der Verkündigung Jesu," "Jesus und der Menschensohn," and "Ein Weg der neutestamentlichen Theologie?" esp. 26–28. Cf. also, e.g., Käsemann, "Sentences of Holy Law in the New Testament," "The Beginnings of Christian Theology," and "On the Subject of Primitive Christian Apocalyptic"; Conzelmann, "Present and Future in the Synoptic Tradition" and *Jesus: The Classic Article*, 43–46; Teeple, "Origin of the Son of Man Christology." Cf. also the works by Perrin cited in n. 57 below.

40. Tödt, *Son of Man*, 329.

41. Boers, "Where Christology Is Real," 308.

42. Perrin, "Son of Man in the Synoptic Tradition," 3.

43. See the works by Norman Perrin cited in n. 57 below.

44. See Vermes, *Jesus the Jew*, esp. 177–86; Casey, *Son of Man*, esp. 157–240.

grouping of the Son of Man sayings,[45] noting that it is based "on purely subjective exegetical criteria," and proposes another method of classification based on criteria "that are objective and formal." His groups are (1) sayings with no reference to Dan 7:13; (2) sayings with an indirect reference to Dan 7:13; and (3) sayings with a direct reference to Dan 7:13.[46] After a careful study, Vermes concludes that none of the sayings directly or indirectly referring to Dan 7:13 can be traced back to the historical Jesus and that the only authentic sayings are those that are independent of Dan 7:13, in which, according to standard Aramaic usage, Jesus uses the term "son of man" not as a title but either in the generic sense of "a human being," in the indefinite sense of "someone" or "anyone," or as a circumlocution for "I" or "me."[47] Similarly, Casey proposes a tentative fourfold division of the Son of Man sayings: (1) sayings that can reasonably be regarded as examples of the Aramaic idiom; (2) sayings that predict the death of the Son of Man; (3) "sayings which were produced by the early Church

---

45. Other scholars have objected that the conventional grouping, although convenient, is also somewhat arbitrary, artificial, and perhaps even misleading; that it is difficult to determine the appropriate category for certain of the sayings (e.g., Matt 20:28/Mark 10:45); that the categories are not applicable to the Son of Man sayings in the Fourth Gospel; and that even the labels assigned to the groups may be misleading. See, e.g., Hooker, *Son of Man in Mark*, 80, and "Is the Son of Man Problem Really Insoluble?" 159–60. Cf. also, e.g., W. Manson, "Son of Man and History," where a twofold grouping is proposed. See, most recently, Tuckett, "Present Son of Man."

46. Vermes, *Jesus the Jew*, 177–78; see p. 179 for a list of passages in each group.

47. Vermes, *Jesus the Jew*, 180–86. Vermes identifies twenty sayings, noting that these sayings "echo a peculiar speech-form that is genuinely Aramaic, and fit so well into the Gospels that, if the interpretations advanced [by me] are accepted, there is no reasonable doubt why Jesus should not have uttered them" (p. 182). The twenty sayings are: Mark 2:10/Matt 9:6/Luke 5:24; Mark 2:28/Matt 12:8/Luke 6:5; Matt 16:13; Mark 8:31; Mark 9:9/Matt 17:9; Mark 9:12/Matt 17:12; Mark 9:31/Matt 17:22/Luke 9:44; Mark 10:33/Matt 22:18/Luke 18:31; Mark 10:45/Matt 20:28; Mark 14:21/Matt 26:24/Luke 22:22; Mark 14:41/Matt 26:45; Luke 6:22; Matt 8:20/Luke 9:58; Matt 11:19/Luke 7:34; Luke 12:10; Matt 12:40/Luke 11:30; Matt 26:2; Luke 19:10; 22:48; 24:7.

under the influence of Dan 7:13"; and (4) "a disparate group" of
other Son of Man sayings.[48] Casey then argues that none of the
sayings influenced by Dan 7:13 has a serious claim to authenticity.[49] His conclusion is that the term *bar 'ēnāš* has its *Sitz im Leben*
in the life of Jesus, but ὁ υἱὸς τοῦ ἀνθρώπου as a title has its *Sitz
im Leben* in the work of the early Church.[50]

Thus, it appears to me that a very strong case has been made
against the authenticity of any of the Son of Man sayings in the
New Testament gospels where "Son of Man" is used as a title.[51] If
this case is valid, then the inevitable implication is that the titular
use of "Son of Man" and the related concept must have originated
within the early Christian community. This conclusion will be further confirmed by the development to be discussed below under
"Proposition Three."

Before moving on to "Proposition Three," however, it is necessary to take account of the possibility, argued by Vermes and
Casey, that Jesus *did* use the term "son of man" not as a title but
rather as a simple circumlocution for the first-person personal
pronoun; that this usage stands behind some of the Son of Man
sayings in the gospels; and that, when seen in the light of Dan 7:13
by early Christians, it formed the basis for the Son of Man title and

---

48. Casey, *Son of Man*, 237; see p. 236 for a list of passages in each
group.

49. Casey, *Son of Man*, 213.

50. Casey, *Son of Man*, 239. Casey (pp. 228–33) identifies twelve sayings
that he believes "may reasonably be held to be derived from this Aramaic
idiom," suggesting "that these sayings go back to twelve authentic sayings of Jesus, and that, with the exception of Mark 9.12, … all other Son
of man sayings in the Gospels are to be attributed to the activities of the
early Church." The twelve sayings are: Mark 2:10/Matt 9:6/Luke 5:24;
Mark 2:28/Matt 12:8/Luke 6:5; Matt 8:20/Luke 9:58; Matt 11:19/Luke 7:34;
Matt 12:32/Luke 12:10; Luke 22:48; Mark 10:45/Matt 20:28; Mark 14:21a/
Matt 26:24a/Luke 22:22; Mark 14:21b/Matt 26:24b/Luke 12:8b; Mark 8:38/
Matt 16:27/Luke 9:26; Mark 8:31/Luke 9:22; Mark 9:31/Matt 17:22/Luke
9:44; Mark 10:33/Matt 20:18/Luke 18:31 (the same authentic saying lies
behind the last three passages on the list).

51. This is not necessarily to say, of course, that Jesus never used the
term "son of man" in the generic, the indefinite, or possibly even the circumlocutional sense; on this, see below.

concept. As has already been noted,[52] the case for the circumlocutional use of "son of man" in Aramaic has been argued in detail by Vermes, who cites a number of alleged examples from extant Aramaic documents, and who has been supported in principle by Casey. Vermes' evidence has been criticized in various ways, however, by such scholars as Frederick H. Borsch, Carsten Colpe, Joachim Jeremias, Hendrikus W. Boers, A. Gelston, and Joseph A. Fitzmyer. The criticism by Fitzmyer relates almost entirely to the question of whether the circumlocutional use had appeared as early as the first century, and thus is countered rather easily by Casey.[53] Other criticisms, however, are more substantive. Boers, for example, asserts:

> the Aramaic expression *bar nasha* without the demonstrative, "this (son of man)," is never a self-designation. ... The only exception is where *bar nasha* is used generically in such a way that it is evident the user claims for himself what is true for every other man. In not a single instance of the new evidence brought forward by Geza Vermes does the speaker claim for himself anything which he does not claim as something which is true for man in general. This is the only sense in which any of the "present" sayings could be considered authentic.[54]

Similarly, Borsch observes:

> Despite Vermes' convictions ... , it does not appear to us that any of his examples provide unambiguous illustrations. The references may still be just to *any man*. Though the speaker may occasionally include himself under this reference, this does not make it into a genuine circumlocution any more than would a comparable usage in English. E.g., "A man can't work miracles. What do you expect of me?"[55]

---

52. See n. 15 above.
53. Casey, *Son of Man*, 227.
54. Boers, "Where Christology Is Real," 307.
55. Borsch, *Son of Man in Myth and History*, 23 n. 4.

My own judgment is that Vermes has not made his case, and that Jeremias is correct when he asserts: "It is not true that *bar 'enāšā* is to be found as a periphrasis for 'I.'"[56] This does not, of course, rule out the possibility that Jesus may have used the term "son of man" in the generic or indefinite sense, but it does mean that such usage could not have formed the basis for the later Christian view that Jesus himself was *the* Son of Man in any titular sense. Thus, my own judgment is that the conclusion stands: the titular use of "Son of Man" and the concept associated with it originated within the early Christian community and not on the basis of any authentic sayings of the historical Jesus.

Proposition Three

> The origin of the Son of Man title and concept can be found within early Christianity as the product of a pesher-type exegetical process similar to that which has been discovered among the sectaries of Qumran.

Although Vielhauer rejected the authenticity even of the eschatological Son of Man sayings in the gospels, he nevertheless accepted the prevailing view that there were an eschatological Son of Man title and concept in first-century Judaism and thus made no attempt to explain how such a title and concept might first have originated within early Christianity. Here, the decisive breakthrough was made by Perrin, who, unlike Vielhauer, rejected the widespread assumption of a Son of Man title and concept in Judaism. In agreement with Vielhauer, he denied, on form-critical and traditio-historical grounds, the authenticity of the eschatological Son of Man sayings, but then, moving beyond Vielhauer, he argued that the expectation of the coming of Jesus as eschatological Son of Man was the product of exegetical developments at work within the early Christian community.[57] This process began,

---

56. Jeremias, *New Testament Theology*, 261 n. 1.

57. See esp. Perrin, "Mark XIV.62," "Son of Man in Ancient Judaism and Primitive Christianity," "Son of Man in the Synoptic Tradition," and *Rediscovering the Teaching of Jesus*, 164–99. On the *pesher* method of interpretation, see, most recently, Horgan, *Pesharim*, esp. 229–59; Brownlee,

according to Perrin, with the interpretation of Jesus' resurrection in the light of Ps 110:1 (LXX 109:1), which reads, "The Lord said to my lord, 'Sit at my right hand, till I make your enemies your footstool'" (εἶπεν ὁ κύριος τῷ κυρίῳ μου κάθου ἐκ δεξιῶν μου, ἕως ἂν θῶ τοὺς ἐχθρούς σου ὑποπόδιον τῶν ποδῶν σου). The Christian exegesis of this verse produced the *mārêh* christology, as well as the particular eschatological expectation expressed in *maranatha*.[58] The origin of the Son of Man christology, however, can be traced to a secondary Christian exegetical tradition, in which the initial interpretation of the resurrection on the basis of Ps 110:1 was expanded by the use of Dan 7:13, with the result that the resurrection was then seen as Jesus' ascension to God *as Son of Man*. Thus, the concept of Jesus as Son of Man originated within the exegetical tradition of the early church, and it represented a secondary, not the primary, Christological development within this tradition.

Perrin's hypothesis appears to me to represent the most likely solution to the problem of the origin of the Son of Man christology within the early church.[59] What Perrin failed to explain, however,

---

Midrash Pesher of Habakkuk, esp. 23–36. For a brief summary, see, e.g., Black, "Christological Use of the Old Testament in the New Testament," 1: "*Pesher* ... describe[s] the free, creative, imaginative, and at times bold, even audacious, exegesis of the Qumran writings, to a very large extent inspired by their apocalyptic character. Its chief characteristics are its assumptions: (*a*) that scripture has a veiled, eschatological meaning; (*b*) that this cryptic meaning may be ascertained, if necessary, by a forced and even abnormal construction of the Biblical text, e.g., by combining texts, by interpreting textual variants, even by rearranging letters; and (c) that the meaning so obtained can then be applied to present events or circumstances in which it is fulfilled."

58. This latter judgment, however, is open to question; see, e.g., Hahn, *Titles of Jesus in Christology*, 73–103; Fuller, *Foundations of New Testament Christology*, 156–58; Black, "Christological Use of the Old Testament in the New Testament," 6–11; Boers, "Where Christology Is Real," 315–17; Fitzmyer, "Semitic Background of the New Testament *Kyrios*-Title."

59. See, e.g., Boers, "Where Christology Is Real," 312: "Once the exegetical traditions suggested by Perrin are recognized, it is not difficult to explain the further development of all the other Son of Man sayings. ..." Note, however, that Casey (*Son of Man*, 181–82) rejects Perrin's hypothesis, arguing that it is "not convincing."

was precisely *why* and *how* Ps 110:1 first came to be interpreted by the further use of Daniel 7, so that Jesus' presence at God's right hand became his presence there *as Son of Man*. What caused the two texts to be combined in the early Christian exegetical tradition? I have attempted elsewhere to demonstrate that the link between Ps 110:1 and Dan 7:13 was Psalm 8,[60] and my argument was subsequently accepted in print by Perrin, who spoke of it as a "refinement" that both strengthened and distinctly improved his own hypothesis.[61] The Septuagint version of Ps 110:1 (LXX 109:1) ends with the words ὑποπόδιον τῶν ποδῶν σου ("a footstool for your feet"). The entire verse is quoted almost *verbatim* in Acts 2:34b–35 and applied to Jesus. It is also quoted in Matt 22:44/Mark 12:36/Luke 20:42b–43, but an apparently insignificant difference appears in the Matthean and perhaps the Markan versions:[62] in place of ὑποπόδιον ("footstool"), the text reads ὑποκάτω ("under"), resulting in the phrase ὑποκάτω τῶν ποδῶν σου ("under your feet") rather than the ὑποπόδιον τῶν ποδῶν σου ("a footstool for your feet") of Ps 110:1. It is to be noted, however, that the phrase ὑποκάτω τῶν ποδῶν σου also appears in Ps 8:6 (LXX 8:7). It appears, then, that the early Christians initially used the first part of Ps 110:1 (εἶπεν ὁ κύριος τῷ κυρίῳ μου κάθου ἐκ δεξιῶν μου) to interpret the resurrection of Jesus as his ascension to the right hand of God, but the second part of the verse (ἕως ἂν θῶ τοὺς ἐχθρούς σου ὑποπόδιον τῶν ποδῶν σου), which served the

---

60. Walker, "Origin of the Son of Man Concept," chap. 10 in this volume.

61. Norman Perrin, "Postscript" to "Mark XIV.62," 19, 21–22; cf. also his "Son of Man," 835, where my argument is incorporated into his own reconstruction of the origin of the Son of Man christology.

62. The textual evidence is rather equally divided for Mark but is clear for Matthew. In my article cited above (n. 60), I failed to note this fact and called attention (p. 188 n. 30) only to the Markan reading, observing that "Matt 22:44 follows Mark's ὑποκάτω, but Luke 20:43 returns to the ὑποπόδιον of Ps 110:1." This not only overlooked the textual problem in Mark but also presupposed the priority of Mark and its use by both Matthew and Luke. For a concise treatment of the textual problem and its implications for the Synoptic Problem, see Fee, "Modern Text Criticism and the Synoptic Problem," 163–64.

purpose of explaining the nature of Jesus' activity at God's right hand and the reason for the delay of the *parousia*, led them to Ps 8:6 with its strikingly similar ending (ὑποκάτω τῶν ποδῶν σου), and the result was that Psalm 8 as a whole was then applied to Jesus.[63] Of decisive significance at this point, however, is the fact that Psalm 8 also refers, two verses earlier, to "son of man" (υἱὸς ἀνθρώπου), here used, of course, simply as a synonym for "human being" (ἄνθρωπος). To the early Christian mind, however, which had already associated Psalm 8 with Jesus on the basis of its link with Ps 110:1, this would almost inevitably have been understood as an identification of Jesus as "Son of Man" and would then have suggested a connection with another passage using the term "son of man," viz., Dan 7:13. Thus, the movement from Ps 110:1 to Ps 8:6 to Ps 8:4 to Dan 7:13 appears clear and logical, and, as Perrin observed, "this kind of movement from one text to another is characteristic of early Christian exegesis."[64]

---

63. Ps 110:1b and Ps 8:6 are also conflated, either explicitly or implicitly, at 1 Cor 15:27; Phil 3:21; Eph 1:22; Heb 2:6–9; 1 Pet 3:22.

64. Perrin, "Postscript," 21–22. Cf. his *Rediscovering the Teaching of Jesus*, 181, for the observation that, once the use of a text has been established, "it would be natural to go on to use other aspects of the passage." Cf. also Dodd, *According to the Scriptures*, and his *Old Testament in the New*, for the argument that the early Christians tended to draw material from whole blocs of Old Testament material (e.g., entire "chapters") rather than just from individual sentences or phrases, and that the context in which a particular word, phrase, or statement originally stood was very much in the mind of the Christian exegete. Cf., however, Fuller, *Foundations of New Testament Christology*, 233, for an opposing judgment: "In view of the atomistic exegesis current at the time (cf. only Isa 53!) it is a hazardous *argumentum e silentio* to infer that Ps. 8:4 was in Paul's mind when he quoted Ps. 8:6." For alternative suggestions that the connecting link between Ps 110:1 and Dan 7:13 might be either Ps 80:17 or Ps 110:2–3, see, respectively, Gelston, "Sidelight on the 'Son of Man,'" and Doeve, *Jewish Hermeneutics in the Synoptic Gospels and Acts*, 152–53. Cf., on the other hand, Casey, *Son of Man*, 181–82, for the argument that it is not necessary "to suppose that there was another OT passage which was used to connect Ps. 110:1 and Dan.7:13 and was subsequently dropped." Note, nevertheless, that Casey does not disagree, in principle, with the notion of such movement from text to text; he simply finds it unnecessary in this particular instance.

This reconstruction of the origin of the Son of Man title and concept within the early Christian exegetical tradition, if valid, greatly strengthens the case, summarized under "Proposition Two" above, against the authenticity of the eschatological Son of Man sayings and thus of the Son of Man title and concept presupposed by these sayings.

Proposition Four

Of the various types of Son of Man sayings preserved in the gospels, those that reflect the influence of Dan 7:13 and thus are eschatological in nature most nearly represent the earliest stage in the development of the Son of Man title and concept; all other types are secondary and derivative.

If "Proposition Three" is valid, then the earliest use of "Son of Man" as a title and the earliest form of the concept associated with it were those based upon a combination of Dan 7:13 and Ps 110:1 (with Psalm 8 as the link between the two verses).[65] Traces

---

65. The possibility cannot be ruled out, of course, that the title and concept originated on the basis of a combination of Ps 8:4 with Ps 110:1, even before 8:4 led the scribes on to Dan 7:13. In a letter to me dated September 10, 1980, Harold W. Attridge offers the following suggestion: "Have you given any thought to the use of Son of Man terminology in Hebrews? 'Son of Man' appears there only in the quotation from Ps. 8:5–7 at Heb. 2:6–8. The term is clearly understood as a reference to Jesus, as the exegetical comments in Heb. 2:8–9 indicate. Ps. 110 plays a conspicuous role in Heb., of course. Note in particular that the catena of scriptural quotations in chap. 1 ends with Ps. 110:1 and that the quotation of Ps. 8 ends with the *hypokatō tōn podōn autou* phrase. I think that you could argue that Heb. gives evidence of precisely the sort of *Stichwort* association of the two texts which you postulate. It is also interesting that Heb. makes virtually no use of Dan. At most there a few allusions to Danielic language, but none of them involve Son of Man imagery. Is it possible that the interpretation of Son of Man from Ps. 8 as a reference to Jesus in Hebrews is independent of the use of Daniel for this purpose? I think in any case that Heb. is independent of the Synoptic tradition. (On the supposed allusion to Gethsemane in Heb. 5:7, the most likely text on which Synoptic dependence might be based, see my little piece in *JBL* 98 [1979] 90–92.) I wonder, then, if Heb. might reflect the earliest phase of the development of the Son of Man tradition." *Note:* The article to which Attridge refers is "'Heard Because of His Reverence' (Heb 5:7)."

of this combination can be found in at least two places in the New Testament: (1) Matt 26:64/Mark 14:62/Luke 22:69 speaks of the Son of Man "sitting (καθήμενον) at the right hand (ἐκ δεξιῶν) of power (τῆς δυνάμεως)" and (in Matthew and Mark) "coming (ἐρχόμενον) on/with (ἐπί/μετά)[66] the clouds of heaven"; and (2) Acts 7:56 has Stephen refer to "the Son of Man standing (ἑστῶτα) at the right hand (ἐκ δεξιῶν) of God."[67] Once the Son of Man title and concept were established on the basis of this combination of Dan 7:13 and Ps 110:1, further developments could occur, sometimes without reference to Ps 110:1. For example, it appears that an apologetic tradition using Zech 12:10–14 to interpret the Passion was brought in to produce the idea that "all the tribes of the earth" will see the Son of Man coming on the clouds of heaven and will mourn (traces of this are present in Matt 24:30/Mark 13:26/Luke 21:17).[68] Eventually, all reference to Ps 110:1 dropped out, as did the connection with Zech 12:10–14 and the Passion apologetic, "as emphasis came to be put more and more upon the expectation of Jesus' 'second coming', as Son of Man, and as this expectation came to exist in its own right, independently of the exegesis which gave it birth."[69] All of these developments,

---

66. Matthew has "on" (in agreement with the LXX); Mark has "with" (in agreement with Theodotion and the Aramaic).

67. Perrin, *Rediscovering the Teaching of Jesus*, 176–80. Perrin argues (pp. 177–79) that the combination of Ps 110:1 and Dan 7:13 found in Matt 26:54/Mark 14:62/Luke 22:69 and the same combination found in the pre-Lukan *Vorlage* of Acts 7:56 cannot be dependent upon one another and thus represent independent evidence of this combination in the early Christian exegetical tradition. He also (p. 179) finds traces of the same combination in the Ascension story in Acts 1:9.

68. Cf. also John 19:37; Rev 1:7.

69. Perrin, *Rediscovering the Teaching of Jesus*, 184, cf. 173–84. According to Perrin, the idea of the *parousia* did not make it appearance until the fusion of Son of Man tradition (Dan 7:13) with passion apologetic (Zech 12:10–14); i.e., the earliest Christian use of Dan 7:13 was an interpretation of the Ascension. Casey (*Son of Man*, 181–82), however, argues that, from the very beginning, Christian exegetes applied Dan 7:13 to the *parousia*. The question, of course, is whether these exegetes interpreted the "coming" of Dan 7:13 as a coming *to* God (i.e., ascension) or a coming *from* God to earth (i.e., *parousia*). Theodotion's version, in agreement with

however, can quite legitimately be designated as, in some sense, eschatological in nature, and they lie behind a number of the Son of Man sayings in the gospels.[70]

Once this eschatological concept of Jesus as Son of Man had developed, additional Son of Man sayings were formulated.[71] One group of sayings spoke of the earthly career of Jesus as the Son of Man (the so-called "present" Son of Man sayings). In some cases, sayings of this type may have been based upon sayings (possibly even authentic sayings of Jesus) already using "son of man" in the generic or the indefinite sense.[72] In others, the title may have been substituted for the first-person personal pronoun in already existing sayings.[73] Elsewhere, altogether new sayings may have been created to express the view that "Son of Man" was an appropriate

---

the Aramaic, clearly refers to a coming *to* God: "and behold, with (μετά) the clouds of heaven one like a son of man was coming (ἐρχόμενος ἦν), and he came (ἔφθασεν) to (ἕως) the Ancient of Days and was presented (προσηνέχθη) before him." The LXX, on the other hand, is ambiguous: "and behold, upon (ἐπί) the clouds of heaven one like a son of man was coming (ἤρχετο), and as an ancient of days he came (παρῆν), and those present (οἱ παρεστηκότες) came with (παρῆσαν) him." In general, the New Testament use of Dan 7:13 appears to reflect the text of Theodotion more closely than it does that of the LXX; see, e.g., Wevers, "Theodotion." My own conclusion is that Perrin, rather than Casey, is likely correct on the matter.

70. In the triple tradition, Matt 16:27/Mark 8:38/Luke 9:26; Matt 24:30/ Mark 13:26/Luke 21:27; Matt 26:64/Mark 14:62/Luke 22:69; in the double tradition: Matt 24:27/Luke 17:24; Matt 24:37/Luke 17:26; Matt 24:39/Luke 17:30; Matt 24:44/Luke 12:40; in Special Matthew: Matt 10:23; 13:41; 16:28; 19:28; 25:31; in Special Luke: Luke 12:8; 18:1; 21:36.

71. Note that Tödt (*Son of Man in the Synoptic Tradition*, 224–31), among others, also regards the eschatological Son of Man sayings as the oldest: first, for him, are the authentic sayings in which Jesus, without reference to Scripture, speaks of the Son of Man as an expected figure other than himself; then come the sayings that refer to the heavenly activity of the Son of Man in terms of Dan 7:13; finally, there are the expanded apocalyptic traditions regarding the activities of the Son of Man. Only subsequently were the earthly ministry sayings and the passion sayings produced.

72. E.g., Matt 8:20/Luke 9:58; Matt 9:6/Mark 2:10/Luke 5:24; Matt 11:19/ Luke 7:34; Matt 12:8/Mark 2:28/Luke 6:5; Matt 12:32/Luke 12:10; Matt 12:40 (cf. Luke 11:30); Matt 26:64/Mark 14:21/Luke 22:22; Luke 22:48.

73. E.g., Luke 6:22 (cf. Matt 5:11); Matt 16:13 (cf. Mark 8:27/Luke 9:18).

title for Jesus during his lifetime on earth. In any case, what is apparently reflected here is the tendency, which can be observed elsewhere, to project back into the lifetime of Jesus the attributes and status originally believed to have become his only after the resurrection (or perhaps not to become his until the *parousia*).[74] Another group of sayings referred to the betrayal, rejection, suffering, death, and/or resurrection of the Son of Man (the so-called "suffering" Son of Man sayings). These apparently reflect a series of developments, in which Passion apologetic and Son of Man tradition interacted.[75] Which of these two groups—"present" Son of Man sayings or "suffering" Son of Man sayings—developed first cannot be determined with any real certainty, but Tödt and others maintain that the "suffering" sayings were later than the "present" sayings.[76] Indeed, it may even be the case that the "suffering" sayings represent simply a further development of the "present" sayings.[77]

---

74. On this, see, e.g., Lindars, *New Testament Apologetic*, 138–39. Cf. also, e.g., Perrin, "Use of *(Para)didonai* in Connection with the Passion," esp. 102: "There was a very definite tendency in early Christianity to reflect on the significance of the ministry of Jesus as the ministry of the Son of Man as can be seen from Matt. 13:37." Just how widespread this tendency may have been in the case of the Son of Man christology must, however, await further consideration below under "Proposition Six."

75. Hahn (*Titles of Jesus in Christology*, 37–42) identified three types of suffering Son of Man sayings: (1) those that predict his suffering without reference to Scripture (Matt 17:22/Mark 9:31/Luke 9:44; Matt 20:18/Mark 10:33/cf. Luke 18:31; Matt 26:45/Mark 14:41); (2) those that do refer to Scripture (Matt 26:64/Mark 14:21/Luke 22:22; Mark 8:31/Luke 9:22/cf. Matt 16:21); and (3) one that appeals to Isaiah 53 for a soteriological interpretation of his death (Matt 20:28/Mark 10:45). Somewhat similarly, Perrin ("Use of *(Para)didonai* in Connection with the Passion") argues that an original development of *(para)didónai* as a technical term to describe the passion interacted with a passion apologetic using certain Old Testament passages and Son of Man traditions and later with the use of Isaiah 53 to interpret the cross.

76. Tödt, *Son of Man in the Synoptic Tradition*, 269–77, cf. 141–219.

77. On, e.g., Matt 20:28/Mark 10:45, see Perrin, "Use of *(Para)didonai* in Connection with the Passion," 102. Cf. also Tuckett, "Present Son of Man," 70, for the argument "that most of the present Son of Man sayings in Q are, as in Mark, not so much about the present authority of Jesus as about rejection and suffering."

It is true, of course, that Vermes and Casey argue for the authenticity of a number of the "present" Son of Man sayings and/
or the "suffering" Son of Man sayings, either in essentially their
present form or in some earlier form.[78] In so doing, however, they
also argue that these sayings, in their original form, did not involve the *titular* use of "Son of Man" or the concept associated
with it. Thus, their arguments support the view that the Son of
Man title and concept, as such, were originally eschatological in
nature, since, even if other types of sayings now involving the
title and concept are earlier in origin, they nevertheless did not
properly become *Son of Man sayings* in the usual sense of the term
until they were associated with an already developed Son of Man
title and concept.

Proposition Five

Relatively speaking, the Son of Man christology developed
rather late within the exegetical tradition of the early church,
and it apparently developed among Greek-speaking, not
Aramaic-speaking, Christians.

It is often assumed that the Son of Man concept was an essential
part of the very earliest christological thinking of the Christian
community,[79] but this assumption must be rejected if "Proposition
Three" and "Proposition Four" are valid. According to Perrin,
the first stage of the exegetical process that led to the Son of Man
christology was the interpretation of Jesus' resurrection in terms
of Ps 110:1, and the use of Dan 7:13, with its "son of man" reference, represented, at best, a second stage. According to my
argument under "Proposition Four," however, which was subse-

---

78. See above under "Proposition Two."

79. This assumption generally presupposes the authenticity of at
least some of the eschatological Son of Man sayings; see, e.g., Fuller,
Foundations of New Testament Christology, 143–44: "Jesus had declared that
his own eschatological word and deed would be vindicated by the Son
of man at the end. Now his word and deed had received preliminary
yet certain vindication by the act of God in the resurrection. The earliest
church expressed this new-born conviction by identifying Jesus with the
Son of man who was to come."

quently accepted by Perrin, the Son of Man concept represented at least a third stage in the process, with the move from Ps 110:1 to Psalm 8 intervening between it and the initial stage. It must now be pointed out, however, that Hendrikus W. Boers, Ferdinand Hahn, and I have independently identified exegetical traditions that, in our judgment, antedated even the use of Ps 110:1 to interpret the resurrection of Jesus. In Boers' view, it was an understanding of Jesus' death resulting from a combination of Psalm 16 and Psalm 18 that prepared his followers for the resurrection "appearances," which then became the real basis for the resurrection faith, which, in turn, was interpreted in light of Ps 110:1 (and other passages, such as Ps 2:7).[80] This view was subsequently accepted by Perrin as a "refinement" that greatly strengthened and improved his own hypothesis.[81] I have called attention to "traces of at least three ... exegetical developments [that] can be detected in the early chapters of Acts" — involving the use of Ps 68:19a (18a in English), Deut 18:15–19, and Ps 16:8–11 — and have suggested that the origin of the resurrection faith in its most primitive form was based, at least in part, upon such exegetical developments.[82] Finally, Hahn and others have argued convincingly that Ps 110:1 itself contains three different elements: that the first element ("Sit at my right hand") played a role in the very early Palestinian tradition but that the second element ("till I make your enemies your footstool"), which, according to my own hypothesis, formed the bridge between Ps 110:1 and Ps 8:6, was not applied to Jesus until somewhat later, when the church found it necessary to explain and clarify the nature of his present activity at the right hand of

---

80. Boers, "Psalm 16 and the Historical Origin of the Christian Faith" and "Where Christology Is Real," 310–12.

81. Perrin, "Postscript," 19–21; cf. also his "Son of Man," 834–35, where Boers' hypothesis is incorporated into his own reconstruction of the origin of the Son of Man christology.

82. Walker, "Christian Origins and Resurrection Faith," chap. 17 in this volume, esp. pp. 340–43. Cf. also, e.g., J. A. T. Robinson, "The Most Primitive Christology of All?" for the suggestion that the most primitive christology was based, at least in large part, upon an interpretation of Deut 18:15–19,

God and to account for the delay in the final coming of God's kingdom.[83] Much more work needs to be done along these lines, but, if such arguments as those advanced by Boers, Hahn, and me have any validity at all, then it is clear that the Son of Man christology appeared relatively late in the exegetical tradition of the early church.

This conclusion is strengthened and further clarified by an aspect of my hypothesis regarding the origin of the Son of Man christology that is easily overlooked: this is my contention that the use of Psalm 8 to serve as a link between Ps 110:1 and Dan 7:3 could have occurred only among Greek-speaking, not Aramaic-speaking, Christians.[84] The basic argument here is that the requisite verbal parallels between Ps 110:1 and Ps 8:6 are to be found in the Greek, but not in the Hebrew, texts.[85] It should be noted, too, that other scholars have argued on quite different grounds for the Hellenistic origin of the Son of Man christology.[86] If this view is correct, then the Son of Man concept did not develop within the

---

83. Hahn, *Titles of Jesus in Christology*, esp. 129–35; cf. also, e.g., Fuller, *Foundations of New Testament Christology*, esp. 184–86.

84. Walker, "Origin of the Son of Man Concept," chap. 10 in this volume, pp. 190–91.

85. In the Hebrew, Ps 110:1 ends, *'ad-'āšît 'ōyĕbe(y)kā hădōm lĕragle(y)kā*, while Ps 8:6 (8:7) ends, *kōl šattâ taḥat-raglā(y)w*. Thus, the similarities are much less striking than in the Greek. Moreover, it should be noted that Ps 8:4 (8:5) uses *ben 'ādām* (Hebrew) for "son of man," while Dan 7:13 has the Aramaic *bar 'ĕnāš*; on this point, however, note the observation by Moloney ("Reinterpretation of Psalm VIII," 660–65) that the Aramaic targum on Ps 8:5 has *bar nāšā'* (in its present form, at least, this targum is late).

86. See, e.g., Teeple, "Origin of the Son of Man Christology," 238: "Since the Son of man logia originated in the church, there is no certainty that they ever existed in Aramaic. They may have originated in Greek. ... We conclude that the Son of man Christology did not begin with any sayings of Jesus nor even in the original Jerusalem church of Jesus' disciples. Instead, it began in Hellenistic Jewish-Christianity." Cf. also, p. 250 and cf., e.g., Boers, "Where Christology Is Real," 312: "The fact that the Son of man tradition appears to have been absent in the Hellenistic Christian atmosphere in which Paul was at home may be an indication that these traditions were not yet firmly established when Christianity started to move beyond the borders of Palestine. The Son of man sayings may thus not belong in the earliest phases of primitive Christianity." Casey (*Son of*

earliest Aramaic-speaking Palestinian church but rather among later Greek-speaking Christians, either Hellenistic-Jewish or non-Jewish.[87]

Proposition Six

Outside the canonical gospels, early Christian literature contains almost no traces of the Son of Man christology; therefore, it must be concluded that this christology never became widely established in the early church.

It has often been noted that, with only one exception, no New Testament writing other than the four gospels ever applies the term "Son of Man" to Jesus as a title.[88] The one exception is Acts 7:56,[89] with its unique reference to the Son of Man "standing" at the right hand of God.[90] Elsewhere, the phrase occurs in the anarthrous form (υἱὸς ἀνθρώπου rather than ὁ υἱὸς τοῦ ἀνθρώπου)[91]

Man, 234–35) concludes that the use of Dan 7:13 to form Son of Man sayings, while not original with Jesus himself, could have originated either in the Aramaic-speaking or in the Greek-speaking church (cf., e.g., pp. 168–71, 178, 183, 196–97).

87. Teeple ("Origin of the Son of Man Christology," esp. 247–50) argues for a Hellenistic-Jewish-Christian origin.

88. For the argument that, even in the canonical gospels, the term is not properly a title, see n. 26 above.

89. Even here, a few witnesses read "Son of God" rather than "Son of Man," and Kilpatrick argues that the former reading may well be original; see his "Acts vii.56," 209 and "Again Acts vii.56" According to Kilpatrick, the change to "Son of Man" in the textual tradition can be explained as an attempt both to avoid repeating the word "God" four times in two verses and to assimilate Acts 7:56 to Luke 22:60.

90. See, e.g., Owen, "Stephen's Vision in Acts 7.55–56"; Tödt, "Excursus II"; Barrett, "Stephen and the Son of Man."

91. In the gospels, except for John 5:27, and in Acts 7:56, the phrase is always arthrous (ὁ υἱὸς τοῦ ἀνθρώπου), and it has even been suggested that the ὅτι υἱὸς ἀνθρώπου ἐστίν of John 5:27 might be simply an idiomatic equivalent for ὅτι ἐστὶν ὁ υἱὸς τοῦ ἀνθρώπου; see Colwell, "Use of the Article in the Greek New Testament"; Harner, "Qualitative Anarthrous Predicate Nouns"; cf., however, Moule, *Origin of Christology,* 16–17 n. 15, where the idea is rejected. Moule argues that the arthrous form reflects some Aramaic expression that meant *"the* Son of Man" or even *"that* Son of Man" and was a direct reference to "the (well-known Danielic) Son of Man"; see his "Neglected Features in the Problem of 'the Son of Man'" and *Origin of Christology,* 10–22.

at Heb 2:6, which is a quotation of Ps 8:4, and at Rev 1:13; 14:14, which speak of "one like a son of man" (ὅμοιον υἱὸν ἀνθρώπου) and thus would appear to be direct references to Dan 7:13, with its ὡς υἱὸς ἀνθρώπου. It is not clear whether these passages reflect preliminary stages prior to the use of "Son of Man" as a christological title, independent appeals to the Old Testament in an attempt to portray the significance and role of Jesus, or possibly even later traces of an earlier titular use of the term. In any case, however, they do not use "Son of Man" as a title and thus cannot be regarded as evidence for a Son of Man christology in the earliest church. A number of scholars have suggested that Paul's designation of Jesus as ἄνθρωπος ("human being") and perhaps his concept of the "second Adam"[92] are related, either directly or indirectly, to the Son of Man christology,[93] but this view has been seriously questioned by, among others, Reginald H. Fuller, who concludes that the argument in its support "is much weaker than is generally supposed."[94] Barnabas Lindars has even argued that "what may be called a Son of Man christology is basic to the New Testament, being found in all the major theological strands."[95] In

---

92. See, e.g., Rom 5:12–21; 1 Cor 15:21–23, 45–50; cf. Phil 2:5–11.

93. See, e.g., Foakes Jackson and Lake, *Beginnings of Christianity*, 380: "All the essentials of the eschatological doctrine connoted by the apocalyptic Son of Man are found in Paul, but not the phrase itself. Is not this because he was too good a Grecian to translate *Bar-nasha* by so impossible a phrase as ὁ υἱὸς τοῦ ἀνθρώπου, and rendered it idiomatically by ὁ ἄνθρωπος?" Cf. also, e.g., Cullmann, *Christology of the New Testament*, esp. 141–52, 166–81.

94. Fuller, *Foundations of New Testament Christology*, 233–34; cf. e.g., Hahn, *Titles of Jesus in Christology*, 20; Boers, "Where Christology Is Real," 312: "The Son of Man tradition appears to have been absent in the Hellenistic Christian atmosphere in which Paul was at home." For the view that Paul's Adam typology is not a part of any Son of Man christology, see, e.g., Lindars, "Re-enter the Apocalyptic Son of Man," esp. 62 n. 2.

95. Lindars, "Re-enter the Apocalyptic Son of Man," 64; cf. 61–65; cf. also Smalley, "Johannine Son of Man Sayings," 300: "In this way we can see afresh that a Son of man christology belonged to the tradition (fostered by the Hellenists?) which was given expression and shape in the early kerygma, came into the substructure of the Gospels and Acts, and survived in the adaptations found in Rom. v and viii, Phil. ii, Col. i, 1

order to sustain his argument, however, Lindars is compelled to acknowledge that "this christology does not depend on the use of Son of Man as a title, so that the absence of it [i.e., the title] outside the gospels is no more significant than the absence of it from the major part of the relevant apocalyptic texts," and it becomes clear that what he regards as "basic to the New Testament" is really simply "the apocalyptic notion of the agent of divine intervention," which, only in the sayings tradition of the gospels, ever involves Son of Man terminology or imagery *per se*.[96]

Outside the New Testament, except in quotations from or allusions to the canonical gospels, the title "Son of Man" is found only once in its original eschatological sense. According to Hegesippus,[97] James the brother of Jesus, at the point of his own martyrdom, responded to a question regarding "the gate of Jesus" with the words: "Why do you ask me about the Son of Man (τοῦ υἱοῦ τοῦ ἀνθρώπου)? He, himself, is sitting at the right hand of the great power, and he will come on the clouds of heaven." Otherwise, the term is found in the esoteric Adam/Son of Man/ Prophet speculations of the Pseudo-Clementine literature and the literature of Christian Gnosticism, but in ways that are quite foreign to the New Testament usage, and in certain writings concerned with the debate over the human nature of Christ.[98] In the last instance, the title becomes simply "a designation for Jesus' humanity, contrasted with 'Son of God' as a designation for his divinity," and "any idea that it was originally a title of majesty is completely lost."[99]

Tim iii and so on." Similarly, Giles ("Son of Man in the Epistle to the Hebrews") argues that there was a widespread knowledge of the Son of Man tradition in the early church.

96. Lindars, "Re-enter the Apocalyptic Son of Man," 64, 61.

97. Eusebius, *Hist. eccl.* 2.23,13.

98. See, e.g., Colpe, "ὁ υἱὸς τοῦ ἀνθρώπου," 473–77.

99. Fuller, *Foundations of New Testament Christology*, 229. Note that *Barn.* 12:10 rejects "Son of Man" as a title for Jesus in favor of "Son of God." In the thought of Irenaeus, the Son of Man terminology figures prominently in the Adam/Christ typology, but, here too, the title designates the humanity of Christ in contrast to his deity.

Thus, the judgment holds that the Son of Man christology presented in the canonical gospels cannot be found with any certainty outside these gospels except at Acts 7:56 and in the Hegesippus report concerning James,[100] and, where the term continued to be used at all, it became either part of an elaborate metaphysical system of esoteric speculation or simply a cipher for the humanity of Jesus.[101] The almost inevitable implication is that the Son of Man christology reflected in the gospels' titular use of the term never became widely established in the early church.

Conclusion

Taken as a whole, the line of research that has been summarized appears to suggest rather clearly: (1) that the Son of Man title and concept originated within the limited circle of a particular christological exegetical tradition, (2) that they developed relatively late within this tradition, (3) that they never became widely known or accepted outside this limited circle, and (4) that their earliest form was eschatological in nature. My own suggestion, at this point, and it requires much further investigation, is that the Son of Man christology may have originated, flourished, and, for the most part, died within what can be called the "Q" community, i.e., the community from whose traditions the authors of both Matthew and Luke drew material for their respective gospels. This suggestion is supported, in my judgment, by some significant recent research regarding the Q community and its relationship to the Son of Man christology.[102] The suggestion also has some rather important implications regarding the Synoptic Problem[103] and the relationship between the Synoptic Gospels and the Fourth Gospel. These, however, cannot be explored in the present paper.

---

100. Note the similarity of these two passages: both are parts of martyrdom accounts, and both contain similar terminology and imagery.

101. For a brief summary of the argument that the absence of the Son of Man terminology and concept "is not as complete as is usually assumed," see, e.g., J. M. Robinson, *New Quest of the Historical Jesus*, 102–3 n. 2.

102. See, e.g., Schürmann, "Beobachtungen zum Menschensohn-Titel in der Redequelle."

103. See Walker, "Son of Man Question," chap. 12 in this volume.

Chapter 12

The Son of Man Question and the Synoptic Problem

Introduction

Recent discussion of the Synoptic Problem has made it increasingly clear that the problem has not been solved and that, indeed, there exists at the moment no scholarly consensus as to how it might be solved.[1] Reginald H. Fuller, among others, has called for what might be termed an "atomistic" approach, maintaining that advocates of a particular hypothesis must be prepared to "demonstrate its tenability pericope by pericope."[2] William R. Farmer, on the other hand, has rejected this "atomistic" or "pericope-by-pericope" approach on three grounds: (1) the time and energy required for its completion "would be virtually prohibitive"; (2) "it is at least equally possible" to demonstrate the tenability of rival

"The Son of Man Question and the Synoptic Problem." *NTS* 28 (1982) 374–88. Copyright © Cambridge University Press. Reprinted in slightly revised version as second part of "The Son of Man Question and the Synoptic Problem," in *New Synoptic Studies: The Cambridge Gospel Conference and Beyond* (ed. William R. Farmer. Macon, GA: Mercer University Press, 1983) 261–301. Reprinted with permission.

1. For the suggestion that the Synoptic Problem may finally be insoluble, see, e.g., Walker, "Unexamined Presupposition in Studies of the Synoptic Problem," chap. 6 in this volume, esp. 95–97 and the literature there cited.

2. Fuller, Sanders, and Longstaff, "Synoptic Problem," 67; cf. e.g., Fee, "Modern Text Criticism and the Synoptic Problem," 161, who expresses the same view (cf. also 167–69). For a "negative" application of this approach, see Talbert and McKnight, "Can the Griesbach Hypothesis Be Falsified?"; and Buchanan, "Has the Griesbach Hypothesis Been Falsified?"

solutions to the Synoptic Problem "pericope by pericope";[3] and (3) there are other relevant considerations "such as the argument from order, the weight of external evidence, or compositional and redactional factors," all of which "call for something more than a 'pericope by pericope' demonstration." Thus, for Farmer and others, the solution to the Synoptic Problem must be based primarily upon such "larger considerations," and the detailed analysis of individual pericopes can serve at best only to demonstrate and confirm the tenability of whatever solution has, on the basis of these "larger considerations," been found "most adequate to explain the data."[4] Farmer, in other words, calls for a more "holistic" approach to the Synoptic Problem.

I, myself, am inclined to agree with Farmer: If the Synoptic Problem is ever to be solved, it will not be done exclusively (or perhaps even primarily) upon the basis of an "atomistic" or "pericope-by-pericope" approach such as that advocated by Fuller.[5] Nevertheless, it is my judgment that such an approach should not be abandoned, because the cumulative weight of its results may eventually help in "tipping the scales" toward (or perhaps against) one or another of the proposed solutions. The purpose of this paper, however, is to propose a somewhat different type of "atomistic" approach from that advocated by Fuller and designated by the label, "pericope-by-pericope," and to illustrate this other type of "atomistic" approach by means of one among a number of possible examples.

-----

3. Cf. Fuller, Sanders, and Longstaff, "Synoptic Problem," 67: "We must even be prepared to find them [i.e., the direction indicators] working in opposite directions."

4. Farmer, "Basic Affirmation with Some Demurrals," 310; for the same view, see, e.g., Orchard, "J. A. T. Robinson and the Synoptic Problem." Farmer, himself, has tended to emphasize the "compositional and redactional factors"; see, e.g., his "Redaction Criticism and the Synoptic Problem." For a recent consideration of "the argument from order," see, e.g., Tyson, "Sequential Parallelism in the Synoptic Gospels." For a provocative treatment of "the weight of the external evidence," see G. A. Kennedy, "Classical and Christian Source Criticism," esp. 147–52.

5. It is instructive at this point to note that Fuller is much less confident than is Farmer regarding the possibility of finally solving the Synoptic Problem; see, e.g., Walker, "Introduction," 12.

The approach here proposed might be termed a "thematic" or "motif-by-motif" approach. It involves the attempt to determine which of the proposed solutions to the Synoptic Problem is most compatible (or perhaps least compatible) with what has been learned, quite independently of the Synoptic Problem, regarding the development of particular themes or motifs in early Christianity.[6] To be sure, the proposed treatment of any one theme or motif, or even of a number of them, cannot, in and of itself, be decisive in solving the Synoptic Problem; rather, as in the case of the "pericope-by-pericope" approach, the evidence gathered by means of this approach must be used in a cumulative fashion, and it may well be that, as in the case of the "pericope-by-pericope" approach, we must be prepared to find the evidence pointing in different directions, depending upon the particular theme or motif being investigated.[7] Nevertheless, the cumulative weight of this "thematic" or "motif-by-motif" approach, like that of the "pericope-by-pericope" approach, may eventually help in "tipping the scales" toward (or perhaps against) one or another of the proposed solutions to the Synoptic Problem.[8]

---

6. It is not necessarily true, of course, that literary development in the early church paralleled historical developments in every case (e.g., a relatively late document may well reflect a much earlier stage of historical development, or the same document may reflect more than one stage of historical development); nevertheless, it must surely be granted that, all other things being equal, a source theory that does parallel the most probable course of historical development would be more plausible than one that does not.

7. If such should, in fact, prove to be the case, the evidence would thereby be strengthened for a more complex relationship among the Synoptic Gospels than is generally assumed, and this more complex relationship would likely include some degree of "cross-fertilization" among the gospels; on this, see, e.g., Fuller, "Classics and the Gospels," 173–76.

8. In a conversation, M. Eugene Boring has suggested that, in proposing this new approach to the Synoptic Problem, I am actually proposing two different approaches, each of which may be helpful, but which might better be kept separate. One approach is to study a series of discrete sayings in the tradition, each containing a particular vocabulary; the other approach is to study a theme or motif in the tradition, not bound to a set of sayings containing a particular vocabulary. I find Boring's distinction helpful, but, at least for the moment, I prefer to treat the two as sub-categories under the general heading "thematic" or "motif-by-motif" approach.

Son of Man:
Some Recent Developments

Various themes or motifs immediately suggest themselves for possible consideration,[9] but the one chosen for treatment here is "Son of Man." The reasons for its selection include both the intrinsic importance and interest of the topic[10] and at least the possibility that the implications for Synoptic studies of certain highly significant developments in recent Son of Man research have been overlooked in contemporary New Testament scholarship. These developments, which, to be sure, come from only one "wing" of recent Son of Man research,[11] can be summarized in terms of six propositions, which, in this paper, cannot be explained or defended but only stated.[12] The six propositions are: (1) There was no Son of Man title or concept as such in first-century Judaism; therefore, the titular use of the term and the concept associated with it must have originated either with Jesus himself or within the early Christian community.[13] (2) No Son of Man title or concept as such can be detected in the authentic sayings of Jesus; therefore, the titular use of the term and the concept associated with it must have originated within the early Christian commu-

---

9. On November 18, 1978, during the annual meeting of the Society of Biblical Literature in New Orleans, Louisiana, the late Samuel Sandmel suggested that the subject of Christian attitudes toward Judaism and Jews might fruitfully be explored in this way.

10. The literature on the subject is massive. For two excellent recent bibliographies, see Casey, *Son of Man*, 241–59; and A. J. B. Higgins, *Son of Man in the Teaching of Jesus*, 159–68.

11. For example, the most recent book on the subject (Higgins, *Son of Man in the Teaching of Jesus*), does not accept any of these developments as valid. Nevertheless, there appears to be a growing consensus supporting at least some of the developments, and it is my own judgment that cogent arguments can be made for all of them.

12. For discussion and defense of the propositions, see Walker, "Son of Man: Some Recent Developments," chap. 11 in this volume.

13. See, e.g., Perrin, "Son of Man in Ancient Judaism and Primitive Christianity"; and Perrin, *Rediscovering the Teaching of Jesus*, 23–30; Vermes, "Appendix E"; and Vermes, *Jesus the Jew*, 160–91; Leivestad, "Exit the Apocalyptic Son of Man"; Casey, *Son of Man*, esp. 7–141.

nity.[14] (3) The origin of the Son of Man title and concept can be found within the early Christian community as the product of a *pesher*-type exegetical process similar to that which has been discovered among the sectaries of Qumran.[15] (4) Of the various types of Son of Man sayings preserved in the gospels, those that reflect the influence of Dan 7:13 and thus are eschatological in nature most nearly represent the earliest stage of the development of the Son of Man title and concept; all other types are secondary and derivative.[16] (5) Relatively speaking, the Son of Man christology originated and developed rather late within the exegetical tra-

---

14. See, e.g., Vielhauer, "Gottesreich und Menschensohn in der Verkündigung Jesu"; "Jesus und der Menschensohn"; and "Ein Weg der neutestamentlichen Theologie?" esp. 26–28. Cf. also, e.g., Käsemann, "Sentences of Holy Law in the New Testament," "Beginnings of Christian Theology," and "On the Subject of Primitive Christian Apocalyptic"; Conzelmann, "Present and Future in the Synoptic Tradition," and *Jesus: The Classic Article,* 43–46; Teeple, "Origin of the Son of Man Christology," 216–23. See also Perrin, "Mark XIV.62," " Son of Man in Ancient Judaism and Primitive Christianity," "Son of Man in the Synoptic Tradition," and *Rediscovering the Teaching of Jesus,* 164–99.

For a somewhat different line of approach, leading to similar conclusions, see, e.g., Vermes, *Jesus the Jew,* esp. 177–86; Casey, *Son of Man,* esp. 157–240.

15. See esp. the works by Perrin cited in n. 14 above; Walker, "Origin of the Son of Man Concept," chap. 10 in this volume; Perrin, "Postscript" to "Mark 14:62," 19, 21–22; and his "Son of Man," 835.

16. This proposition is based largely upon the view that the earliest use of "Son of Man" as a title and the earliest form of the concept associated with it originated as the product of a *pesher*-type combination of Ps 110:1 and Dan 7:13 (with Psalm 8 serving as the link between the two), as worked out in the literature cited in n. 15 above. There are other scholars, however, who do not share this view regarding the origin of the Son of Man christology, who, nevertheless, agree that the Son of Man title and concept, as such, were originally eschatological in nature; see, e.g., Tödt, *Son of Man in the Synoptic Tradition,* 224–31, who regards the eschatological Son of Man sayings as the oldest of the Son of Man materials but believes that some (which do not refer directly to Dan 7:13) are authentic sayings of Jesus; and Vermes and Casey (see their works cited in n. 14 above), who regard some of the earlier, non-eschatological, Son of Man sayings as authentic sayings of Jesus but argue that these, in their original form, did not involve the titular use of "Son of Man" or the concept associated with it.

dition of the early church, and it apparently originated among Greek-speaking, not Aramaic-speaking, Christians.[17] (6) Outside the canonical gospels, early Christian literature contains almost no traces of the Son of Man christology found in these gospels; therefore, it must be concluded that this christology never became widely established in the early church.[18]

For purposes of exploring the possible relationship between the Son of Man question and the Synoptic Problem, it must now simply be assumed that these six propositions are valid. The propositions, taken as a whole, suggest rather clearly: (1) that the Son of Man title and concept originated, developed, and flourished within the limited circle of a particular Christian exegetical tradition; (2) that they originated relatively late within this tradition; (3) that their earliest form was eschatological in nature; and (4) that they never became widely known or accepted in the early church as a whole. A probable corollary of this is (a) that, within the limited circle where the Son of Man christology originated, developed, and flourished, there would have been a tendency to create new Son of Man sayings and to add the title to already

---

17. This proposition is based upon three considerations: (1) The third proposition above implies at least two stages in the exegetical process that produced the Son of Man christology prior to the actual appearance of this christology. (2) Other research suggests that there were still more stages in the process; see, e.g., Boers, "Psalm 16"; "Where Christology Is Real," 310–12; Perrin, "Postscript," 19–21; Perrin, "Son of Man," 834–35; Walker, "Christian Origins and Resurrection Faith," chap. 17, pp. 340–43 in this volume; J. A. T. Robinson, "The Most Primitive Christology of All?"; Hahn, *Titles of Jesus in Christology*, 129–35; Fuller, *Foundations of New Testament Christology*, esp. 184–86. (3) There is evidence that the final stage of the process—the stage that actually produced the Son of Man christology on the basis of Dan 7:13—could have occurred only on the basis of the Greek, not the Hebrew (or Aramaic) text of the Jewish Scriptures; see Walker, "Origin of the Son of Man Concept," chap. 10, pp. 190–91 in this volume; cf. e.g., Teeple, "Origin of the Son of Man Christology," 238, 247–50.

18. For a survey of the data, see. E.g., Colpe, "ὁ υἱὸς τοῦ ἀνθρώπου," 461–64, 470–77. For the view that the Son of Man christology is absent from the letters of Paul, see, e.g., Fuller, *Foundations of New Testament Christology*, 233–34; cf. Hahn, *Titles of Jesus in Christology*, 20; Boers, "Where Christology Is Real," 312; Lindars, "Re-Enter the Apocalyptic Son of Man," esp. 62 n. 2.

existing sayings lacking it but (b) that, outside this circle, the tendency would have been to eliminate or change the Son of Man title where it was found.

The crucial question now is: Of the leading theories regarding Synoptic relationships, which is most compatible (or perhaps least compatible) with this picture of the origin and development of the Son of Man christology? It will not be possible, in this paper, to examine all of the possible Synoptic source theories; rather, I shall limit myself to the Two-Source Hypothesis and the Griesbach Hypothesis and then briefly suggest a third theory, which, in my judgment, would appear to be more nearly compatible with the evidence than either of these.

Son of Man and the Two-Source Hypothesis

The Two-Source Hypothesis offers the following picture of the development of Son of Man sayings: Mark, the earliest gospel, contains fourteen Son of Man sayings;[19] of the fourteen, only three are eschatological in nature,[20] while two speak of the present authority of the Son of Man,[21] and the remaining nine refer to his impending betrayal, rejection, suffering, death, and/or resurrection.[22] Matthew, for all practical purposes, takes over all fourteen of Mark's Son of Man sayings,[23] and Luke takes over most of them,[24]

---

19. Mark 2:10, 28; 8:31, 38; 9:9, 12, 31; 10:33, 45; 13:26; 14:21a, 21b, 41, 62.

20. Mark 8:38; 13:26; 14:62.

21. Mark 2:10, 28.

22. Mark 8:31; 9:9, 12, 31; 10:33, 45; 14:21a, 21b, 41.

23. Mark 2:10/Matt 9:6; Mark 2:28/Matt 12:8; Mark 8:38/Matt 16:27; Mark 9:9/Matt 17:9; Mark 9:12/Matt 17:12; Mark 9:31/Matt 17:22; Mark 10:33/Matt 20:18; Mark 10:45/Matt 20:28; Mark 13:26/Matt 24:30b; Mark 14:21a/Matt 26:24a; Mark 14:21b/Matt 26:24b; Mark 14:41/Matt 26:45; Mark 14:62/Matt 26:64. It is true that Mark 8:31 has "Son of Man," while the parallel, Matt 16:21, has the third-person personal pronoun, but Matthew does take over the Markan pericope (Mark 8:27–33/Matt 16:13–23), changing Mark's "Son of Man" to "him," probably because he has already, unlike Mark (and Luke), introduced the title "Son of Man" at the beginning of his pericope (Matt 16:13; cf. Mark 8:27/Luke 9:18) and simply does not wish to repeat the title in the same pericope.

24. Mark 2:10/Luke 5:24; Mark 2:28/Luke 6:5; Mark 8:31/Luke 9:22; Mark 8:38/Luke 9:26; Mark 9:31/Luke 9:44; Mark 10:33/Luke 18:31; Mark 13:26/Luke 21:27; Mark 14:21a/Luke 22:22a; Mark 14:62/Luke 22:69. In

omitting only five of the "suffering" sayings.[25] Q, the other source
used by both Matthew and Luke (which may or may not be earlier
in date than Mark),[26] contains at least eight and probably ten Son
of Man sayings;[27] of the ten, at least five and probably six are eschatological in nature,[28] while four speak of the present situation

---

one instance, Luke has simply avoided a redundant second reference to
Son of Man in the same verse (Luke 22:22b; cf. Mark 14:21b/Matt 26:24b),
and he has omitted one entire Markan pericope that contains two Son of
Man references (Mark 9:9–13/Matt 17:9–13). Where Mark's "Son of Man"
is missing from Luke, in every case except one (Mark 14:21b/Matt 26:24b/
Luke 22:22b; see above), either the entire Markan pericope is absent from
Luke (Mark 9:9–13/Matt 17:9–13; Mark 10:35–45/Matt 20:20–28/cf. Luke
22:24–27, which is a rather different version of the entire pericope) or
the section of the pericope containing the Son of Man reference is absent
from Luke (Mark 14:39–42/Matt 26:42–46).

25. Mark 9:9/Matt 17:9; Mark 9:12/Matt 17:12; Mark 10:45/Matt 20:28;
Mark 14:21b/Matt 26:24b; Mark 14:41/Matt 26:45.

26. See, e.g., Kümmel, *Introduction to the New Testament*, 70.

27. The eight are Matt 8:20/Luke 9:58; Matt 11:19/Luke 7:34; Matt 12:32/
Luke 12:10; Matt 12:40/Luke 11:30; Matt 24:27/Luke 17:24; Matt 24:37/
Luke 17:26; Matt 24:39/Luke 17:30; Matt 24:44/Luke 12:40 (some manu-
scripts also include Matt 18:11/Luke 19:10). In addition, there are two
Lukan Son of Man sayings (Luke 6:22; 12:8) where the Matthean parallels (Matt 5:11; 10:32) have the first-person personal pronoun; these passages almost certainly come from Q, and it would appear more likely that
Matthew has removed the title than that Luke has added it. Note also,
however, that Matt 10:32/Luke 12:8 has a partial parallel, including the
Son of Man reference, in Mark 8:38/Luke 9:25/cf. Matt 16:27 and thus may
reflect some degree of Markan influence.

28. The five are Matt 24:27/Luke 17:24; Matt 24:37/Luke 17:26; Matt
24:39/Luke 17:30; Matt 24:44/Luke 12:40; Luke 12:8/cf. Matt 10:32. In addition, while it is true that Matt 12:40 refers to the death and resurrection of the Son of Man, with little, if any, direct eschatological content,
its Lukan parallel (11:30) has no reference to death and resurrection and
probably should be regarded as eschatological in its thrust. Furthermore,
the pericope, Matt 12:38–42, begins with a request for a sign, refers to the
sign of Jonah as the only sign that will be given, suggests that Jonah's
three days and three nights in the whale was this sign, compares it to the
death and resurrection of the Son of Man, and then points to the eschatological judgment; in Matt 24:30a, "the sign of the Son of Man," which is
clearly an eschatological phenomenon, may refer to the same idea. Thus,
it would appear that Matthew has transformed an originally eschatological Son of Man saying into a reference to the death and resurrection of the
Son of Man.

or status of the Son of Man,[29] and no more than possibly one refers to his impending death and resurrection.[30] In addition to the Son of Man sayings from Mark and Q, Matthew has nine Son of Man sayings not found elsewhere; these presumably were taken from an unknown source or sources, were formulated by the Evangelist himself, and/or were taken from Q by the Evangelist but, for some reason, were omitted by Luke.[31] Of the nine, six are eschatological in nature,[32] while two speak of the present activity or situation of the Son of Man,[33] and the other, which may reflect Markan influence, refers to the impending death of the Son of Man.[34] In addition to the Son of Man sayings from Mark and from Q, Luke has six Son of Man sayings not found elsewhere; these presumably were taken from an unknown source or sources, were formulated by the Evangelist himself, and/or were taken from Q by the Evangelist but for some reason, were omitted by Matthew.[35] Of the six, three are eschatological in nature,[36] while two, which

---

29. Matt 8:20/Luke 9:58; Matt 11:19/Luke 7:34; Matt 12:32/Luke 12:10; Luke 6:22/cf. Matt 5:11.

30. Cf. n. 28 above on Matt 12:40/Luke 11:30.

31. Matt 10:23; 13:37, 41; 16:13, 28; 19:28; 24:30a; 25:31; 26:2.

32. Matt 10:23; 13:41; 16:28; 19:28; 24:30a; 25:31. Note that 16:28 and 24:30a both represent insertions of Son of Man references into otherwise Markan material (cf. Mark 9:1/Luke 9:27; Mark 13:26/Luke 21:27). Note, too, that 19:28 has a partial parallel, but without "Son of Man," in Luke 22:28–30; thus, it is possible that Matthew has introduced the title into or, more likely, that Luke has omitted it from Q material. The other three eschatological Son of Man references are in pericopes that are unique to Matthew.

33. Matt 13:37; 16:13. Note, however, that the former is followed almost immediately in the same pericope by an eschatological Son of Man reference (16:41); note, too, that the latter simply substitutes "Son of Man" for "me" in a Markan pericope (cf. Mark 8:27/Luke 9:18).

34. Matt 26:2; there is a partial parallel (with "Son of Man") in Mark 14:1/Luke 22:1 and close affinities in Mark 8:31/Matt 16:21/Luke 9:22; Mark 9:31/Matt 17:22/Luke 9:44; Mark 10:33/Matt 20:18/Luke 18:31; cf. also Luke 24:7.

35. Luke 17:22; 18:8; 19:10; 21:36; 22:48; 24:7.

36. Luke 17:22; 18:8; 21:36. Note that 17:22 connects material unique to Luke (17:7–21) with Q material (Matt 24:26–28/Luke 17:23–24), which also includes a Son of Man saying. The other two eschatological Son of Man references are in pericopes that are unique to Luke.

may reflect the influence of Mark, refer to the impending betrayal, death, and/or resurrection of the Son of Man,[37] and one speaks of the present situation of the Son of Man.[38]

In summary, the Two-Source Hypothesis suggests: (1) that Son of Man sayings were fairly widespread in the early church, being found in at least two strata of the Synoptic source material (Mark and Q) and perhaps as many as four or more (Mark, Q, Special Matthew, and Special Luke);[39] (2) that the Son of Man sayings in the earliest gospel (Mark) were primarily those speaking of the impending betrayal, rejection, suffering, death, and/or resurrection of the Son of Man,[40] while the Son of Man sayings in the other stratum or strata of source material (which may or may not be earlier in date than Mark)[41] were, to the contrary, primarily those of an eschatological nature; (3) that there was a tendency for the later gospels (Matthew and Luke) to add Son of Man materials to

---

37. Luke 22: 48; 24:7. The former has a distant parallel, without "Son of Man," in Matt 26:50 and thus may derive, at least in part, from Q. Probably more significant, however, is the fact that both Mark (14:41) and Matthew (26:45), but not Luke, have a similar reference to Son of Man earlier in the same pericope, suggesting that "Son of Man" in Luke 22:48 may well be a misplaced Markan reference. It is also true that Luke 22:48 is part of Luke's Passion Narrative, which many scholars believe to be based, at least in part, on a source other than the Markan Passion Narrative; see, e.g., Taylor, *Passion Narrative of St. Luke*. This suggests the possibility of yet another source containing Son of Man material. The second passage, Luke 24:7, has close parallels in Markan material (Mark 8:31/Luke 9:22/cf. Matt 16:21; Mark 9:31/Matt 17:22/Luke 9:44; Mark 10:33/Matt 20:18/Luke 18:31; cf. also Matt 26:2).

38. Luke 19:10. Note that, while the pericope, Luke 19:1–10, is unique to Luke, some manuscripts include a parallel to the Son of Man reference at Matt 18:11.

39. Special Matthew and Special Luke are probably not to be regarded as single sources; see, e.g., Kümmel, *Introduction to the New Testament*, 76. It is quite possible, of course, that all of the non-Markan Son of Man sayings come from Q but that some were omitted by either Matthew or Luke, in which case the Son of Man materials derive from only two sources, Mark and Q.

40. In Mark 64.3 percent (9) of the sayings are of this type, 21.4 percent (3) are eschatological, and 14.3 percent (2) refer to present authority, etc.

41. See, e.g., Kümmel, *Introduction to the New Testament*, 76.

their Markan source from one or more other sources; and (4) that the characteristic development from the earliest gospel (Mark) to the later gospels (Matthew and Luke) apparently represented a movement away from "suffering" Son of Man sayings and toward eschatological sayings.[42] Thus, the Two-Source Hypothesis would appear to conflict at crucial points with the six propositions regarding Son of Man formulated earlier in this paper, since these propositions suggest that the Son of Man christology originated, developed, and flourished only within the limited circle of a particular Christian exegetical tradition and thus was not at all widespread in the early church, that the eschatological Son of Man sayings represent the earliest stage in this christology, and that the tendency was increasingly to eliminate rather than to add Son of Man references to the tradition.

Son of Man and the Griesbach Hypothesis

In contrast to the Two-Source Hypothesis, the Griesbach Hypothesis offers the following picture of the development of the Son of Man sayings: Matthew, the earliest gospel, contains thirty Son of Man sayings;[43] of the thirty, thirteen are clearly eschatological in nature,[44] and it is possible that another was originally

---

42. It is possible, of course, that this apparent development is misleading and that Matthew and Luke were simply using another source or sources earlier in date than Mark, but the fact nevertheless remains that, according to the Two-Source Hypothesis, the later gospels (i.e., Matthew and Luke) reflect, in large measure, an eschatological Son of Man christology, while the earliest gospel (i.e., Mark) presents primarily a suffering Son of Man christology.

43. Matt 8:20; 9:6; 10:23; 11:19; 12:8, 32, 40; 13:37, 41; 16:13, 27, 28; 17:9, 12, 22; 19:28; 20:18, 28; 24:27, 30a, 30b, 37, 39, 44; 25:31; 26:2, 24a, 24b, 45, 64.

44. Matt 10:23; 13:41; 16:27, 28; 19:28; 24:27, 30a, 30b, 37, 39, 44; 25:31; 26:64; indeed, ten of the thirteen refer explicitly to the "coming" (ἔρχεσθαι or παρουσία) of the Son of Man (10:23; 16:27, 28; 24:27, 30b, 37, 39, 44; 25:31; 26:64), with two others speaking either of his kingdom (13:41) or of his sitting on a throne (19:28); both his "sitting" and his "coming" are present in 26:64.

so intended,[45] while ten (or possibly only nine) refer to the impending betrayal, rejection, suffering, death, and/or resurrection of the Son of Man,[46] and the remaining seven speak of the present situation, status, or authority of the Son of Man.[47] Luke takes over at least sixteen and possibly eighteen of Matthew's thirty Son of Man references,[48] including virtually all of his seven "present" Son of Man sayings,[49] seven of his thirteen eschatological Son of Man sayings,[50] and perhaps as many as six of his ten "suffering" Son of Man sayings.[51] Luke then adds the Son of Man title to three

---

45. On Matt 12:40, see n. 28 above.

46. The nine are Matt 17:9, 12, 22; 20:18, 28; 26:2, 24a, 24b, 45. On 12:40, see n. 28 above.

47. Matt 8:20; 9:6; 11:19; 12:8, 32; 13:37; 16:13.

48. The sixteen are Matt 8:20/Luke 9:58; Matt 9:6/Luke 5:24; Matt 11:19/Luke 7:34; Matt 12:8/Luke 6:5; Matt 12:32/Luke 12:10; Matt 12:40/Luke 11:30; Matt 16:27/Luke 9:26; Matt 17:22/Luke 9:44; Matt 20:18/Luke 18:31; Matt 24:27/Luke 17:24; Matt 24:30b/Luke 21:27; Matt 24:37/Luke 17:26; Matt 24:39/Luke 17:30; Matt 24:44/Luke 12:40; Matt 26:24a/Luke 22:22a; Matt 26:64/Luke 22:69. Two other Lukan Son of Man references are so reminiscent of Matthean Son of Man materials in other contexts as to suggest the possibility of dependence: Luke 19:10 (cf. Matt 20:28/Mark 10:45) and Luke 22:48 (cf. Matt 26:45/Mark 14:41 earlier in the same pericope). Note, too, that Luke takes over three Son of Man sayings from Matthew (or introduces very similar sayings) but drops the Son of Man title from the sayings (Matt 16:13/Luke 9:18; Matt 16:28/Luke 9:27; Matt 19:28/Luke 22:29–30).

49. Matt 8:20/Luke 9:58; Matt 9:6/Luke 5:24; Matt 11:19/Luke 7:34; Matt 12:8/Luke 6:5; Matt 12:32/Luke 12:10. It is true that Luke does not include the Son of Man references from Matt 13:37 and 16:13; the former, however, is part of a pericope (Matt 13:36–43) that, in its overall thrust, is eschatological rather than present and is omitted in its entirety by Luke, and, in the latter, Luke (like Mark) includes the saying but substitutes the first-person personal pronoun for "Son of Man" (Luke 9:18; cf. Mark 8:27); note, however, that both Luke (9:22) and Mark (8:31) have "Son of Man" a few verses later in the same passage, where Matthew (16:21) has the first-person personal pronoun.

50. Matt 16:27/Luke 9:26; Matt 24:27/Luke 17:24; Matt 24:30b/Luke 21:27; Matt 24:37/Luke 17:26; Matt 24:39/Luke 17:30; Matt 24:44/Luke 12:40; Matt 26:64/Luke 22:69. On Matt 12:30/Luke 11:30, see n. 29 above. Note that, in two additional instances, Luke has the saying (or a similar saying) but without the title (Matt 16:28/Luke 9:27; Matt 19:28/Luke 22:29–30).

51. Matt 17:22/Luke 9:44; Matt 20:18/Luke 18:31; Matt 26:24a/Luke 22:22a; in addition, Luke 19:10 may well reflect Matt 20:28, Luke 22:22b

sayings where Matthew has used the first-person personal pronoun (one of them apparently a "present" saying, one a "suffering" saying, and one an eschatological saying),[52] introduces three new Son of Man sayings, all of them eschatological in nature,[53] and transforms one of Matthew's "suffering" Son of Man sayings into an eschatological saying.[54] In short, Luke retains almost all of Matthew's "present" Son of Man sayings and more than one-half of his "suffering" and eschatological Son of Man sayings; in addition, he introduces three new Son of Man sayings, all of them eschatological in nature, adds the Son of Man title to three of the Matthean sayings lacking it (in only one instance does he retain a Matthean Son of Man saying but eliminate the title),[55] and changes one "suffering" Son of Man saying into an eschatological saying. Mark takes over at least eight and possibly ten of the at least sixteen and possibly eighteen Son of Man references common to Matthew and Luke;[56] only three of these are eschatological in nature,[57] while two refer to the present authority of the Son of

---

simply has the third-person personal pronoun in place of the redundant "Son of Man" of Matt 26:24b, and Luke 22:48 apparently is based upon Matt 26:45. On Matt 12:40/Luke 11:30 ("suffering" in Matthew but eschatological in Luke), see n. 29 above.

52. Luke 6:22/Matt 5:11; Luke 9:22 (cf. Mark 8:31)/Matt 16:21; Luke 12:8/Matt 10:32.

53. Luke 17:22; 18:8; 21:36. Three additional Son of Man sayings are not included as new Lukan material because they are so reminiscent of similar Matthean material in other contexts as to suggest dependence; the three are Luke 19:10 (cf. Matt 20:28/Mark 10:45); Luke 22:48 (cf. Matt 26:45/Mark 14:41 earlier in the same pericope); and Luke 24:7 (cf. such passages as Matt 16:21/Mark 8:31/Luke 9:22; Matt 17:22–23/Mark 9:31/Luke 9:44b; Matt 20:18–19/Mark 10:33–34/Luke 18:31–33).

54. Matt 12:40/Luke 11:30; see n. 28 above.

55. Luke 9:18; cf. Matt 16:13.

56. Matt 9:6/Luke 5:24/Mark 2:10; Matt 12:8/Luke 6:5/Mark 2:28; Matt 16:27/Luke 9:26/Mark 8:38; Matt 17:22/Luke 9:44/Mark 9:31; Matt 20:18/Luke 18:31/Mark 10:33; Matt 24:30b/Luke 21:27/Mark 13:26; Matt 26:24a/Luke 22:22a/Mark 14:21a; Matt 26:64/Luke 22:69/Mark 14:62. Note also the possibility that Luke 19:10 is based upon Matt 20:28 (cf. Mark 10:45) and Luke 22:48 upon Matt 26:45 (cf. Mark 14:41); see nn. 49 and 53 above.

57. Matt 16:27/Luke 9:26/Mark 8:38; Matt 24:30b/Luke 21:27/Mark 13:26; Matt 26:64/Luke 22:69/Mark 14:62.

Man,[58] and at least three and possibly five refer to the impending betrayal, rejection, suffering, death, and/or resurrection of the Son of Man.[59] In addition, Mark also includes five (or possibly as few as three) of the fourteen (or possibly as few as twelve) Son of Man references found in Matthew but not in Luke,[60] all five of them speaking of the impending betrayal, rejection, suffering, death, and/or resurrection of the Son of Man, and one Son of Man reference that Luke has substituted for the first-person personal pronoun in Matthew,[61] this reference also speaking of the impending suffering, death, and resurrection of the Son of Man. In short, Mark never includes a Son of Man saying unless he finds it already present in one or, in most cases, both of his sources, and he includes eschatological Son of Man sayings or "present" Son of Man sayings only when these sayings occur in both of his sources (and not always then), but he occasionally includes a "suffering" Son of Man sayings that is found in only one of his sources. Altogether, nine of Mark's fourteen Son of Man sayings refer to the impending betrayal, rejection, suffering, death, and/or resurrection of the Son of Man, while only two speak of his present authority and only three are eschatological in nature. It may also be relevant to note at this point that, with only one exception,[62] wherever Matthew and Luke have a Son of Man saying in the same relative sequence with other Son of Man sayings, Mark includes it, but he never includes such a saying when they have it in a different sequence.[63]

---

58. Matt 9:6/Luke 5:24/Mark 2:10; Matt 12:8/Luke 6:5/Mark 2:28.

59. Matt 17:22/Luke 9:44/Mark 9:31; Matt 20:18/Luke 18:31/Mark 10:33; Matt 26:24a/Luke 22:22a/Mark 14:21a. On Matt 20:28/Luke 19:10/Mark 10:45; Matt 26:45/Luke 22:48/Mark 14:41, see nn. 48 and 53 above.

60. The three are Matt 17:9/Mark 9:9; Matt 17:12/Mark 9:12; Matt 26:24b/Mark 14:21b. On Matt 20:28/Luke 19:10/Mark 10:45; Matt 26:45/Luke 22:48/Mark 14:41, see nn. 48 and 53 above.

61. Luke 9:22/Mark 8:31; cf. Matt 16:21.

62. Matt 24:27, 37, 44; Luke 17:24, 26, 30 (three Son of Man references in the same immediate context).

63. Matt 8:20/Luke 9:58; Matt 11:19/Luke 7:34; Matt 12:32/Luke 12:10; Matt 12:40/Luke 11:30; Matt 24:44/Luke 12:40.

In summary, the Griesbach Hypothesis suggests: (1) that Son of Man sayings were fairly widespread in the early church, being found in two strata of the Synoptic source material (Matthew and, at least to some extent, Special Luke);[64] (2) that approximately one-half of the Son of Man sayings in the earliest gospel (Matthew) were eschatological in nature, with the others being divided fairly evenly between "suffering" and "present" Son of Man sayings, while the Son of Man sayings in the other stratum of source material (Special Luke, which may or may not be earlier in date than Matthew)[65] were, to the contrary, primarily those of an eschatological nature; and (3) that the characteristic development from the earliest gospel (Matthew) through the second (Luke) to the third (Mark) was a movement generally away from eschatological Son of Man sayings and toward "suffering" sayings (this general development is not consistent, however, because the second gospel, Luke, introduces new eschatological sayings not found in the first gospel, Matthew).[66] Thus, the Griesbach Hypothesis would appear to be more nearly compatible with the six propositions regarding Son of Man formulated earlier in this paper than is the Two-Source Hypothesis, particularly in its implication that the general development was away from eschatological Son of Man sayings and toward "suffering" Son of Man sayings and in its view that the gospel emphasizing this latter type (Mark) was written at a date later than were the gospels emphasizing the other types

---

64. Even if Luke has simply created his Son of Man *Sondergut*, perhaps on the basis of the Matthean Son of Man materials, this suggests a tendency on the part of a later writer to introduce new Son of Man sayings, which would appear to be contrary to the more likely tendency implied by the six propositions formulated earlier in this paper regarding Son of Man, namely, the tendency to eliminate or change the Son of Man title where it was found in the source material.

65. See, e.g., Kümmel, *Introduction to the New Testament*, 76; cf. also, however, n. 64 above.

66. It is possible, of course, that Luke was simply using another source or sources earlier in date than Matthew, but the fact nevertheless remains that, according to the Griesbach Hypothesis, the second gospel to be written (i.e., Luke) introduces eschatological Son of Man sayings not present in the first (i.e., Matthew).

(Matthew and Luke). Nevertheless, there remains the problem that, according to the Griesbach Hypothesis, Son of Man sayings are found in both strata of the Synoptic source material, whereas the six propositions suggest that the Son of Man Christology originated, developed, and flourished only within the limited circle of a particular Christian exegetical tradition and thus might be expected to be reflected in only one stratum of source material.

Son of Man and
a Third Alternative

Because neither the Two-Source Hypothesis nor the Griesbach Hypothesis is completely compatible with the six propositions regarding Son of Man formulated earlier in this paper, I now wish to propose a third hypothesis, which, in my judgment, is more nearly compatible with the propositions. According to this third hypothesis, Matthew and Luke both used a common source, which, for lack of a better title, will hereafter be referred to as "Q." Whether this Q was written or oral, whether Matthew and Luke made independent use of it or one of the two also knew and used the other, and whether Matthew and/or Luke also used other sources, perhaps even one or more other sources common to both, are not important for our purposes. Mark was written later than both Matthew and Luke, and the author used Matthew and Luke as his principal, probably sole, sources. Thus, my third hypothesis shares with the Two-Source Hypothesis its postulation of a Q source behind Matthew and Luke, and it shares with the Griesbach Hypothesis its postulation of Matthew and Luke as sources for Mark.

According to this hypothesis, all of the Son of Man sayings common to Matthew and Luke come from Q. There are sixteen of these sayings.[67] In addition, Matthew has seven Son of Man

---

67. Matt 8:20/Luke 9:58; Matt 9:6/Luke 5:24; Matt 11:19/Luke 7:34; Matt 12:8/Luke 6:5; Matt 12:32/Luke 12:10; Matt 12:40/Luke 11:30; Matt 16:27/Luke 9:26; Matt 17:22/Luke 9:44; Matt 20:18/Luke 18:31; Matt 24:27/Luke 17:24; Matt 24:30b/Luke 21:27; Matt 24:37/Luke 17:26; Matt 24:39/Luke 17:30; Matt 24:44/Luke 12:40; Matt 26:24a/Luke 22:22a; Matt 26:64/Luke 22:69.

sayings not found in Luke that apparently come from Q,[68] and Luke has seven Son of Man sayings not found in Matthew that apparently come from Q.[69] Thus, altogether, there are some twenty-seven Son of Man sayings in Matthew and/or Luke that either clearly or apparently come from Q.[70] Of these twenty-seven, eleven are clearly eschatological in nature and a twelfth is probably so,[71] eight refer to the present situation, status, or authority of the Son of Man,[72] and seven speak of the impending betrayal, rejection, suffering, death, and/or resurrection of the Son of Man.[73]

---

68. Matt 16:13; 26:24b have Lukan parallels with the personal pronoun rather than the title (Luke 9:18; 22:22b); Matt 16:28; 19:28; 20:28; 26:2 have Lukan parallels without the specific Son of Man reference (Luke 9:27; 22:29–30; 22:27 but cf. also 19:10; 22:1); and Matt 26:45 has what appears to be a parallel (although in a different context) at Luke 22:48.

69. Luke 6:22; 9:22; 12:8 have Matthean parallels with the personal pronoun rather than the title (Matt 5:11; 16:21; 10:32); Luke 17:22 is in the midst of Q material; Luke 19:10 is reminiscent of Matt 20:28; and Luke 22:48; 24:7 have what appear to be parallels (although in different contexts) at Matt 26:45 and Matt 17:22; 20:18.

70. The twenty-seven (allowing for some overlap among sayings in nn. 67, 68, and 69 above) are: Luke 6:22/cf. Matt 5:11; Matt 8:20/Luke 9:58; Matt 9:6/Luke 5:24; Luke 12:8/cf. Matt 10:32; Matt 11:19/Luke 7:34; Matt 12:8/Luke 6:5; Matt 12:32/Luke 12:10; Matt 12:40/Luke 11:30; Matt 16:13; cf. Luke 9:18; Luke 9:22/cf. Matt 16:21; Matt 16:27/Luke 9:26; Matt 16:28/ cf. Luke 9:27; Matt 17:22/Luke 9:44 and cf. Luke 24:7; Matt 19:28/cf. Luke 22:29–30; Matt 20:18/Luke 18:31 and cf. Luke 24:7; Matt 20:28/Luke 19:10 and cf. Luke 22:27; Luke 17:22; Matt 24:27/Luke 17:24; Matt 24:30b/Luke 21:27; Matt 24:37/Luke 17:26; Matt 24:39/Luke 17:30; Matt 24:44/Luke 12:40; Matt 26:2/cf. Luke 22:1; Matt 26:24a/Luke 22:22a; Matt 26:24b/cf. Luke 22:22b; Matt 26:45/Luke 22:48; Matt 26:64/Luke 22:69.

71. The eleven are Luke 12:8/cf. Matt 10:32; Matt 16:27/Luke 9:26; Matt 16:28/cf. Luke 9:27; Matt 19:28/cf. Luke 22:29–30; Luke 17:22; Matt 24:27/ Luke 17:24; Matt 24:30b/Luke 21:27; Matt 24:37/Luke 17:26; Matt 24:39/ Luke 17:30; Matt 24:44/Luke 12:40; Matt 26:64/Luke 22:69. Initially, Matt 12:40 apparently refers to the impending death and resurrection of the Son of Man, but the parallel, Luke 11:30, has no such reference, and the overall thrust of the pericope, both in Matthew and in Luke, is clearly eschatological; see n. 28 above.

72. Luke 6:22/cf. Matt 5:11; Matt 8:20/Luke 9:58; Matt 9:6/Luke 5:24; Matt 11:19/Luke 7:34; Matt 12:8/Luke 6:5; Matt 12:32/Luke 12:10; Matt 16:13/cf. Luke 9:18; Matt 20:28/Luke 19:10 and cf. Luke 22:27.

73. Luke 9:22/cf. Matt 16:21; Matt 17:22/Luke 9:44 and cf. Luke 24:7; Matt 20:18/Luke 18:31 and cf. Luke 24:7; Matt 26:2/cf. Luke 22:1; Matt 26:24a/Luke 22:22a; Matt 26:24b/cf. Luke 22:22b; Matt 26:45/Luke 22:48.

In addition to the Son of Man sayings that are clearly or apparently from Q, Matthew contains only seven other Son of Man sayings (actually representing only five different pericopes),[74] and Luke contains only two;[75] of the seven Matthean sayings, five are eschatological in nature,[76] with the other two (both in the same pericope) speaking of the suffering and resurrection of the Son of Man,[77] and both of the Lukan sayings are eschatological. It is possible, of course, that these nine Son of Man sayings in Matthew and Luke come from a source or sources other than Q or that they were formulated by the Evangelists themselves, but a strong case can be made that they, like the others, come from Q and, for some reason, have simply been omitted by one or the other of the Evangelists, who clearly did not include all of their available source material in their respective gospels. If this is true, then all of the thirty-six[78] Son of Man sayings in Matthew and/or Luke (and thus also all of those in Mark, since Mark has none that is not also present in either Matthew or Luke or, in most cases, both) come from a single source, Q. Of these thirty-six sayings, nineteen are eschatological,[79] while only nine refer to the impending betrayal, rejection, suffering, death, and/or resurrection of the Son of Man,[80] and only eight speak of his present situation, status, or authority.[81] This, of course, is quite compatible with the view that the Son of Man christology originated, developed, and flourished within the limited circle of a particular Christian exegetical tradition (perhaps the Q community?) and that the eschatological Son of Man sayings represent the earliest stage in this christology. According to this hypothesis, Mark, using Matthew and Luke as

---

74. Matt 10:23; 13:37, 41; 17:9, 12; 24:30a; 25:31.
75. Luke 18:8; 21:36.
76. Matt 10:23; 13:37, 41; 24:30a; 25:31.
77. Matt 17:9, 12.
78. I.e., the sixteen from n. 67 plus the seven from n. 68, plus the four from n. 69 that do not appear to have parallels in Matthew, plus the seven from n. 74, plus the two from n. 75.
79. See nn. 71, 75, and 76 above.
80. See nn. 73 and 77 above.
81. See n. 72 above.

his sources, takes over eight of the nine "suffering" Son of Man sayings[82] but only two of the eight "present" sayings[83] and only three of the nineteen eschatological sayings.[84] In the case of the "present" and eschatological sayings, Mark never includes them unless *both* Matthew and Luke have them and, even then, very sparingly; in the case of the "suffering" sayings, however, with only one exception,[85] Mark includes them whenever *either* of his sources has them. Mark *never* introduces a Son of Man saying unless he finds it in at least one (in most cases, both) of his sources. In my judgment, this suggests rather clearly that, by the time Mark wrote, the creation of Son of Man sayings had ceased and that the characteristic movement had been away from eschatological Son of Man sayings in the direction of "suffering" Son of Man sayings. This, too, of course, is completely compatible with the picture suggested by the six propositions regarding Son of Man formulated earlier in this paper.

In conclusion, then, I suggest that the Synoptic source hypothesis most nearly compatible with the six propositions regarding Son of Man is the following: Matthew and Luke both used a common source, which I have chosen to call "Q," and Mark used both Matthew and Luke as sources.

As noted earlier, however, the treatment of this one theme or motif, in and of itself, is by no means decisive in solving the Synoptic Problem; rather, the approach here proposed must be applied independently to a number of other themes or motifs in the hope that the cumulative weight of its results will eventually help in "tipping the scales" toward (or perhaps against) one or another of the possible solutions. Furthermore, it is likely that many

---

82. Luke 9:22/cf. Matt 16:21/Mark 8:31; Matt 17:9/Mark 9:9; Matt 17:12/Mark 9:12; Matt 17:22/Luke 9:44 (cf. Luke 24:7)/Mark 9:31; Matt 20:18/Luke 18:31 (cf. Luke 24:7)/Mark 10:33; Matt 26:24a/Luke 22:22a/Mark 14:21a; Matt 24:24b/Luke 22:22b/Mark 14:21b; Matt 26:45/Luke 22:48/Mark 14:41.

83. Matt 9:6/Luke 5:24/Mark 2:10; Matt 12:8/Luke 6:5/Mark 2:28.

84. Matt 16:27/Luke 9:26/Mark 8:38; Matt 24:30b/Luke 21:27/Mark 13:26; Matt 26:64/Luke 22:69/Mark 14:62.

85. Matt 26:2 (cf. Luke 22:1 and Mark 14:1).

of the data included in this study will need further refinement and that more attention will need to be paid to such features as sequence, inclusion or omission of entire pericopes, and the like. Nevertheless, it is my hope that this study will mark the beginning of a new and fruitful approach to the Synoptic Problem.

Chapter 13

John 1:43–51 and "The Son of Man" in the Fourth Gospel

Contemporary New Testament scholarship is in general agreement that the christology of the Fourth Gospel is essentially incarnational in nature—that is, that "the Gospel in its final form intends to present Jesus as the incarnation of God's Word or Son."[1] Because the title "Son of Man"[2] appears thirteen times in the Fourth Gospel,[3] one would assume, on *a priori* grounds, that it plays a significant role in this gospel's christological thought.

"John 1:43–51 and 'The Son of Man' in the Fourth Gospel." *JSNT* 56 (1994) 31–42. Copyright © 1994 Sage Publications. Reprinted with Permission.

1. Hare, *Son of Man Tradition*, 79. Hare recognizes the complexity of the Fourth Gospel's literary history and the resulting possibility that various strata contain differing and even conflicting christologies. Nevertheless, he proposes to "concentrate upon the Gospel as we now have it," that is, in its final redaction. I intend to do the same.

2. Following the conventional usage, I am translating ὁ υἱὸς τοῦ ἀνθρώπου as "the Son of Man." The more accurate and exact translation, however, would be "the Son of the Human."

3. John 1:51; 3:13, 14; 5:27; 6:27, 53, 62; 8:28; 9:35; 12:23, 34 (*bis*); 13:31. By way of comparison, it should be noted that "Son of God" appears only nine times: John 1:49; 3:18; 5:25; 10:36; 11:4, 27; 17:1; 19:7; 20:31 (most manuscripts also include 1:18, where, however, the best witnesses read μονογενὴς Θεός; 1:34, where the preferable reading may be ὁ ἐκλεκτὸς τοῦ Θεοῦ; and 6:69, where the preferable reading is ὁ ἅγιος τοῦ Θεοῦ; see, e.g., Brown, *Gospel according to John (i–xii)*, 17, 57, 198). There are at least sixteen other instances, however, where the context suggests that "Son" is simply an abbreviated version of the fuller title "Son of God": John 3:16, 17, 35, 36 (*bis*); 5:19 (*bis*), 20, 21, 22, 23 (*bis*), 26; 6:40; 14:13; 17:1; it is not clear whether 8:35, 46 refers directly to Jesus.

There is no scholarly consensus, however, regarding the precise relation between "Son of Man" and John's incarnational portrayal of Jesus.[4] Indeed, some have argued that "Son of Man" in the Fourth Gospel is simply a literary variation for "Son of God" and that this gospel has no distinctive "Son of Man" christology.[5]

I am not persuaded, however, that "Son of Man" is simply a literary variation for "Son of God" in the Fourth Gospel.[6] In the first place, I find few if any direct clues suggesting such an identification of the two.[7] In the second place, there are intimations in the Fourth Gospel that the identity of the "Son of Man" is problematic in a way that is not true of the "Son of God." For example, in John 9:35 Jesus asks the recently healed blind man, "Do you believe in the Son of Man?"[8] The man answers (v. 36), "And who is he, sir, that I may believe in him?" Similarly, in 12:34 the crowd asks, "How can you say that the Son of Man must be lifted up? Who is this Son of Man?" The fact that no such questions are raised regarding the "Son of God" would appear to suggest that "Son of

---

4. See, e.g., Hare, *Son of Man Tradition*, 79: "The consensus breaks down, however, as soon as a question is raised concerning the relationship between 'the Son of man' and John's incarnational Christology"; cf. pp. 80–82.

5. Freed, "Son of Man in the Fourth Gospel"; cf., e.g., Barrett, *Gospel according to St John*, 2nd ed., 73: "So much is in fact predicated of Jesus as the Son of man that it is doubtful whether the title as such has any distinctive significance." For a recent argument that "Son of Man" in the Fourth Gospel actually *means* "Son of God," see Burkett, *Son of Man in the Gospel of John*.

6. Cf., e.g., Painter, "Enigmatic Johannine Son of Man," 1870: "Thus there is no Son of Man christology though the Son of Man motifs are a constituent part of John's christology. But contrary to E. D. Freed, Son of Man is not simply a stylistic variant on Son and Son of God."

7. E.g., there is nothing like the apparent equation of "Christ" and "Son of God" in 11:27 and 20:31, or of "Son of God" and "King of Israel" in 1:49. Without some such clues, it could hardly be assumed that readers of the Fourth Gospel (either then or now) would recognize "Son of God" and "Son of Man" as virtual synonyms.

8. Some of the manuscripts read "Son of God," but "Son of Man" is much better attested and, in addition, has the advantage of being the *lectio difficilior*.

Man" is not simply a literary variation for "Son of God."[9] In the third place, and most importantly, I intend to argue in this paper that "Son of Man" does, in fact, play a highly significant role in the incarnational christology of the Fourth Gospel—a role different from but complementary to that played by "Son of God."[10]

If "Son of Man" does play an important role in the Fourth Gospel's christology, it would not be unreasonable to expect the author[11] to provide some clue regarding the nature of this role. Moreover, a natural place to look for such a clue might well be the pericope in which the title first appears: John 1:43–51.[12] Thus, I turn now to a consideration of this pericope. I should note at the outset, however, that this pericope contains *not only* the first "Son of Man" reference in the Fourth Gospel but *also* the first explicit identification of Jesus as "Son of God"; in addition, the pericope refers to Jesus, for the first time in the Fourth Gospel, as "Son of Joseph." I find it difficult to believe that such a juxtaposition— the *first* occurrence of each title, in the *same* pericope, in the *first* chapter of the Fourth Gospel—could be merely coincidental. It would appear to reflect a deliberate literary/rhetorical/theological decision on the part of the author. Thus, I propose to structure my consideration of John 1:43–51 in terms of the three titles: "Son of God," "Son of Joseph," and "Son of Man."

---

9. It should also be noted that a simply equation of "Son of God" and "Son of Man" appears problematic if for no other reason than the fact that such an equation might imply too close an identification of "God" and "Man" in the two titles.

10. Cf., e.g., Painter ("Enigmatic Johannine Son of Man," 1869–70), who suggests that the "Son of Man" sayings in the Fourth Gospel "provide a corrective to inadequate christological views," that they serve "as a corrective to inadequate perceptions of Jesus and confessions of faith in him."

11. For reasons already noted (see n. 1), I am using the term "author" as a virtual synonym for "final redactor."

12. See, e.g., Painter, "Enigmatic Johannine Son of Man," 1872: "Given that the Son of Man is introduced for the first time at the end of chapter one we might expect 1, 51 to provide a key to the evangelist's use of this term."

"Son of God" in John 1:43–51

As already noted, John 1:43-51 contains the first explicit identification of Jesus as "Son of God" in the Fourth Gospel (v. 49).[13] This is
in Nathanael's confession: "Rabbi, you are the Son of God, you are
King of Israel." "Son of God" is an important—perhaps the most
important—christological title in the Fourth Gospel.[14] Indeed,
although "Son of God" and "King of Israel" appear here to be
virtual synonyms,[15] it is clear that, in the Fourth Gospel, "King
of Israel" (that is, "Christ"/"Messiah" is to be understood in light
of "Son of God," not *vice versa*, and that the latter represents a
quite "high" christology. Whatever "Messiah" or "Son of God"
may have meant in first-century Judaism or in pre-Johannine
Christianity, both are to be understood in the Fourth Gospel in
more-than-human terms—as designating the pre-existent heavenly figure who came from God and returns to God, the incarnation of the divine Logos.[16] Thus, Nathanael's confession of Jesus

13. Most manuscripts have ὁ μονογενὴς υἱός at John 1:18, but the
preferable reading is μονογενὴς Θεός; and some have ὁ υἱὸς τοῦ Θεοῦ
at 1:34, but the preferable reading may be ὁ ἐκλεκτὸς τοῦ Θεοῦ; see n. 3.

14. Indeed, the stated purpose of the Fourth Gospel is that its readers
"may believe that Jesus is the Christ, the Son of God, and, believing, may
have life in his name" (John 20:31); cf., e.g., Barrett, *Gospel according to St
John*, 2nd ed., 575: "Both the purpose of the gospel and the author's theology are summed up in this verse." Thus, it is appropriate that Robert
Kysar (*John, the Maverick Gospel*) entitles his chapter on Johannine christology "The Father's Son—Johannine Christology."

15. Cf. also John 11:27 and 20:31, where "Son of God" and "Christ"
(i.e., "Messiah") appear as virtual synonyms.

16. Cf., e.g., Brown, *Gospel according to John (xiii–xxi)*, 1060: "certainly
the evangelist has not been satisfied with presenting Jesus as the Messiah
in any minimalist sense. ... Throughout the Gospel John demands not
only belief that Jesus is the Messiah predicted by the prophets (that is,
as the prophets were understood in NT times), but also belief that Jesus
came forth from the Father as His special representative in the world (xi
42, xvi 27, 40, xvii 8), that Jesus and the Father share a special presence to
one another (xiv 11), and that Jesus bears the divine name 'I AM' (viii 24,
xiii 19). Having had Thomas confess Jesus as Lord and God by way of a
climactic Christian response to the presence of the risen Jesus through the
Spirit, the evangelist can scarcely have stated in xx 31 that he wrote his
Gospel to bring about faith in Jesus simply as the Messiah."

as "Son of God" and "King of Israel" in 1:49 appears to express in succinct form the very heart of Johannine christology. Indeed, one might well have expected that this confession would serve as the rhetorical climax of John 1:43–51. Such, however, appears not to be the case. The identification of Jesus as "Son of God" is of critical importance for a proper understanding of the pericope: it is intended, in my judgment, to emphasize the *heavenly* origin and *divine* nature of Jesus. This identification is followed, however, by a "Son of Man" saying (v. 51), and it would be difficult to argue that the latter is intended as in any way anti-climactic.

"Son of Joseph" in John 1:43–51

Prior to the appearance of either "Son of God" or "Son of Man" in John 1:43–51, Jesus is identified as "Son of Joseph" (v. 45). It is commonly assumed that "Son of Joseph," like the immediately following "from Nazareth," is essentially simply part of Jesus' *name* (that is, "Jesus of Nazareth, Son of Joseph")—perhaps as a "way of distinguishing this particular Jesus from others of the same name (at Nazareth?)."[17] According to this view, "Son of Joseph" is *not* a title and is therefore in no way parallel with "Son of God" and "Son of Man," which clearly *are* titles. I submit, however, that such an understanding of "Son of Joseph" in John 1:45 is almost certainly inadequate.

In the first place, it is unclear why "son of Joseph" would be needed to distinguish "this particular Jesus from others of the same name," given the fact that no other "Jesus" is mentioned in the narrative.[18] This suggests that the phrase has some other

---

17. Brown, *Gospel according to John (xiii–xxi)*, 82.

18. The same is true, of course, of "the son of John" in John 1:42, but there the principal point of emphasis has to do with Simon's name (or, rather, his change of names); such is not the case with "son of Joseph" in 1:45. Furthermore, "son of John" (*bar-Jonah*) was apparently rather firmly fixed in the tradition as a part of Simon's name (cf. Matt 16:17, etc.), but there is no evidence that this was true of "son of Joseph" in connection with Jesus. The phrase appears elsewhere in the New Testament only at Luke 4:22 (cf. 2:33, where Joseph is referred to as "his [i.e., Jesus'] father," and 3:23, where, in Luke's genealogy, Jesus is identified as "son, as was being supposed, of Joseph"); John 1:45; 6:42. Thus, the apparent parallel

function. Perhaps more importantly, it is far from clear that "from Nazareth" functions in 1:45 simply as a part of Jesus' name. To be sure, Jesus is three times referred to as "Jesus the Nazarene" later in the Fourth Gospel,[19] and "the Nazarene" may well be intended there as part of his name. The wording in 1:45, however, is not "Jesus the Nazarene" but rather "Jesus the one from Nazareth." Jesus is not simply identified by name; rather, something specific is said about his *place of origin*: he is "from Nazareth." Furthermore, it is clear from what follows that this is regarded as problematic. In the next verse, Nathanael asks, "Can anything good be from Nazareth?" More pointedly, later in the Fourth Gospel people ask, "Is the Christ to come from Galilee? Has not the scripture said that the Christ is descended from David, and comes from Bethlehem, the village where David was?"[20] Then, a few verses later, the Pharisees challenge Nicodemus: "Search and you will see that no prophet is to rise from Galilee."[21] In other words, Jesus cannot be the Messiah because he comes from Nazareth in Galilee, not from Bethlehem in Judea. The objection regarding Jesus' place of origin appears at a more profound level, however, when people in Jerusalem, considering the possibility of Jesus' messiahship, observe, "Yet we know where this man comes from; and when the Christ appears, no one will know where he comes from."[22] At either level, the point is that Jesus cannot be the Messiah because

---

between "the son of John" in 1:42 and "son of Joseph" in 1:45 may be *only* apparent. To be sure, if the pericope in question were to be regarded as based upon (someone's) actual historical memory, it might be argued that the words are included simply because they were *said*. In my judgment, however, the general problem of the historicity of the Fourth Gospel makes this highly unlikely.

19. John 18:5, 7; 19:19. Many translations read, incorrectly, "Jesus of Nazareth."

20. John 7:41b–42.

21. John 7:52b. The cumulative force of the three objections appears to be essentially the following: "Nothing good can come from Nazareth—certainly not a prophet, and absolutely not the Messiah!" (It may be, however, that "prophet" [i.e., "*the* Prophet"] and "Messiah" are intended as virtual synonyms.)

22. John 7:25–27.

he comes from Nazareth in Galilee. Thus, for the author of the Fourth Gospel, "from Nazareth" is more than simply a part of Jesus' *name*; it says something significant (and problematic) about his *origin* and thus about his real identity: he is "the one from Nazareth," and this is regarded as troublesome.

If, then, "from Nazareth" is intended in 1:45 as more than simply a part of Jesus' name, the same may well be true of "Son of Joseph." In this regard, it is instructive to note the only other reference in the Fourth Gospel to Jesus as "Son of Joseph": John 6:42. In response to Jesus' claim that he is "the bread that came down from heaven"[23] "and gives life to the world,"[24] the Jews ask, "Is not this Jesus, the Son of Joseph, whose father and mother we know? How can he now say, 'I have come down from heaven'"? It appears, therefore, that "Son of Joseph" is intended, at least at 6:42, to say something significant (and problematic) about Jesus' *origin* and thus about his *identity*: he is the son of a human father. If such is the case at 6:42, it may well also be the case at 1:45, particularly in light of the fact that "from Nazareth" apparently has a similar import at 1:45.

In short, I suggest that "Son of Joseph" — like "from Nazareth" — functions at 1:45 as much more than simply a part of Jesus' *name*: it is intended to say something important about his *origin* and thus about his *identity* and, in this sense, is at least similar to a *title*.[25] If this suggestion is correct, then "Son of Joseph" would, from a functional standpoint, appear to be more-or-less parallel with "Son of God" and "Son of Man" in John 1:43–51.

A further consideration — and this, in my judgment, is highly significant — is that the identification of Jesus as "Son of Joseph" in John 1:45 appears at a point in the narrative where one might

---

23. John 6:41.

24. John 6:33.

25. It may well be that a sharp distinction between *name* and *title* represents a modern imposition upon an ancient text; see, e.g., Huffmon, "Names, Religious Significance of," 619: "The giving of personal names in ancient Israel was not merely for the purpose of providing a distinctive label for an individual but was also commonly an occasion for expressing religious convictions associated with the birth of a child or its future."

more naturally have expected "Son of God" or some other "messianic" title.[26] Already in the Fourth Gospel Jesus has been identified as "Christ" or "Messiah,"[27] "Lamb of God who takes away the sin of the world,"[28] and "Chosen One of God";[29] in addition, his identity as the incarnation of the pre-existent heavenly Logos/ Light has been made clear.[30] Even here, in 1:45, Philip's statement to Nathanael *begins* with what appears to be a "messianic" identification of Jesus: "We have found him about whom Moses in the law, and also the prophets, wrote." Moreover, the expected "messianic" identification of Jesus does, in fact, occur only a few verses later in the pericope (v. 49) with Nathanael's confession: "Rabbi, you are the Son of God, you are King of Israel." Thus, the identification of Jesus as "Son of Joseph" in v. 45 represents a somewhat surprising and even jarring interruption in an otherwise rather straightforward confession of Jesus as "Son of God" and "King of Israel." Indeed, unless one knew otherwise, it might almost be assumed that "Son of Joseph" was itself a "messianic" title (like "Son of David").[31] I suggest, therefore, that the appearance of "Son of Joseph" at 1:45 (a point where one would expect "Son of God" or some equivalent title) represents a deliberate literary/ rhetorical/theological device on the part of the author—indeed, that it is intended to make an important christological point—not, however, the final or most important point in the pericope. Just as "Son of God" in v. 49 is intended to emphasize the *heavenly* origin and *divine* nature of Jesus, so, I suggest, "Son of Joseph" in v. 45 is intended to emphasize the *earthly* origin and *human* nature of Jesus.

---

26. Note 1:44, where Andrew says to Simon, "We have found the Messiah, which is translated 'Christ.'" Indeed, there are some indications—both structurally and verbally—that John 1:43–51 may have been constructed with 1:35–42 as a model.

27. John 1:17, 41.

28. John 1:29, 36.

29. John 1:34; as already noted (see n. 3), most manuscripts read ὁ υἱὸς τοῦ Θεοῦ, but ὁ ἐκλεκτὸς τοῦ Θεοῦ may be the preferable reading.

30. John 1:1–18.

31. For an argument that "Son of Joseph" was, in fact, a "messianic" title in the first century, see Knohl, "Messiah Son of Joseph."

"Son of Man" in John 1:43–51

As already noted, John 1:43–51 contains not only the first explicit reference in the Fourth Gospel to Jesus as "Son of God" and the first reference to him as "Son of Joseph" but also the first "Son of Man" saying (v. 51). Although the title is not explicitly applied here to Jesus, the identification is clear elsewhere in the Fourth Gospel. Particular emphasis is placed on the "Son of Man" reference by the fact that it alone of the appellations comes from the lips of Jesus himself. It is significant, however, that the "Son of Man" saying comes at the very end of the pericope, and its relation to the remainder of the pericope is far from clear. Indeed, there are a number of indications that v. 51 has not "always been associated with the context in which it is now found"[32] — that it represents, in fact, a traditional "Son of Man" saying and has been somewhat artificially added to the narrative at this point. These indications include the following: (1) the transition between v. 50 and v. 51 ("and he said") is rough, and there is no indication of the subject of the verb; (2) the verb λέγει (v. 51) is in the present tense, while the verbs in v. 50 are aorist; (3) the verb ὄψεσθε (v. 51) is plural, while ὄψῃ (v. 50) is singular; (4) v. 51 is not needed to complete the pericope; "Greater things than these you will see" (v. 50) provides a most appropriate ending to the pericope and transition from ch. 1 into what many have called "The Book of Signs," which begins with the miracle at Cana (2:1–11); (5) there is nothing in the Fourth Gospel to indicate that the promise of v. 51 is ever fulfilled — certainly not in any literal sense; (6) on the one hand, similarities between v. 51 and Matt 26:64[33] suggest a connection with references to Jesus' post-crucifixion exaltation; and (7) on the other hand, similarities between v. 51 and the Synoptic baptism narratives suggest a possible connection with Jesus' baptism.[34]

---

32. Brown, *Gospel according to John (i–xii)*, 88, cf. 88–89.

33. Cf. Matt 16:27–28; Acts 7:56.

34. Note, however, the parallel structure of the entire pericope with Peter's "messianic" confession followed by a "Son of Man" saying (Mark 8:27–31; Luke 9:18–22).

Without the "Son of Man" saying, John 1:43–51 would appear to reach its rhetorical climax with the confession that Jesus is "Son of God" and "King of Israel." Why, then, would the author add the "Son of Man" saying? Perhaps for the same reason that a "Son of Man" reference immediately follows the Synoptic accounts of Peter's confession of Jesus as the Messiah.[35] There, however, the reference to "the Son of Man" appears much less artificial and contrived than in John 1:51. Thus, I suggest that the author of the Fourth Gospel has added v. 51 with its "Son of Man" reference precisely for the purpose of making an important literary/rhetorical/theological and, indeed, christological point, and that this point is somehow to be found in the careful juxtaposition in John 1:43–51 of the three titles "Son of God," "Son of Joseph," and "Son of Man."

Conclusion

As already indicated, it is my judgment that this careful juxtaposition of the three titles—"Son of God," "Son of Joseph," and "Son of Man"—early in the narrative (the first occurrence of each title), in the same pericope, can hardly be merely coincidental. The author almost certainly has some important literary/rhetorical/theological—and, I believe, christological—purpose in mind.

In this light, the pericope can be summarized as follows: John 1:43–51 begins, following Jesus' initial call of Philip (v. 43), with what one would expect to be a rather straightforward confession of Jesus as the Messiah and, indeed, as the divine "Son of God" (vv. 44–45a). This confession is interrupted, however, by the unexpected and somewhat surprising characterization of Jesus as the human "Son of Joseph," the one from Nazareth (v. 45b). This poses a serious christological problem, only hinted at in the actual wording of Nathanael's objection (v. 46a) but made clear elsewhere in the Fourth Gospel. The problem is how the *earthly* and *human* "Son of Joseph" can possibly be the *heavenly* and *divine* "Son of God." Philip is unable to answer the objection; he

---

35. Mark 8:31; Luke 9:22; cf. Matt 16:21.

can only say to Nathanael, "Come and see" (v. 46b). The problem is then addressed in a preliminary way by the indication that the human Jesus possesses greater-than-human power: he could see Nathanael under the fig tree before Philip called him (vv. 47–48). This enables Nathanael to complete the confession earlier initiated by Philip by declaring that Jesus is "Son of God" and "King of Israel" (v. 49). Jesus suggests, however, that Nathanael's new faith is somehow still inadequate: "Do you believe because I said to you that I saw you under the fig tree? You will see greater things than these" (v. 50). Thus, at the end of v. 50, there remains a clear christological tension. The confession of Jesus as the *divine* "Son of God" has been completed, but the objection that he is the *human* "Son of Joseph" has not adequately been answered. The pericope then ends with the emphatic introduction (for the first time) of the title "Son of Man" (v. 51). Surely, this "Son of Man" saying represents the rhetorical climax of the pericope!

What, then, is the point of the "Son of Man" saying? My suggestion is that it is intended to resolve, in almost Hegelian fashion, the apparent contradiction between the christological confession of faith that Jesus is the *divine* "Son of God" (*thesis*) and the irrefutable historical fact that Jesus is the *human* "Son of Joseph" (*antithesis*). The *synthesis* is the identification of Jesus as "Son of Man."

Whatever else may be said regarding the history of the term "Son of Man" prior to the composition of the Fourth Gospel, three things are clear: (1) in ordinary Hebrew and Aramaic usage, the term meant simply a "human being";[36] (2) with reference to Dan 7:13–14, however, the term had come to designate a more-than-human heavenly, eschatological, and at least quasi-messianic figure—probably not in pre-Christian Judaism or even within Jesus' lifetime, but certainly in at least some streams of pre-Johannine Christianity; and (3) the term had already, prior to the composition of the Fourth Gospel, been applied to Jesus—probably not

---

36. The reference could be either to *any* human being or to some *particular* person. It is also possible that "son of man" could be used as a circumlocution for the first-person singular pronoun, though this is a matter of debate among scholars.

by Jesus himself but certainly within the pre-Johannine church. Thus, the author of the Fourth Gospel had, ready at hand, a title that could signify either an earthly or a heavenly figure and that had already been applied to Jesus. The title "Son of Man," therefore, could be used to bridge the gap between the divine ("Son of God") and the human ("Son of Joseph"). This, indeed, is precisely the point of the Fourth Gospel's first "Son of Man" reference in John 1:51: "Truly, truly, I say to you, you will see the heaven opened and the angels of God ascending and descending upon the Son of Man."[37] It is precisely as "Son of Man" — a figure both *earthly* and *heavenly*, both *human* and *divine* — that Jesus is the "ladder" between the heavenly and the earthly. He is *both* "Son of God" *and* "Son of Joseph" *because* he is "Son of Man."[38]

Having once established that Jesus can be *both* "Son of God" *and* "Son of Joseph" precisely *because* he is "Son of Man," the author can then virtually drop the title "Son of Joseph" from further

---

37. The relation of this verse to Gen 28:12 ("Jacob's ladder") has occasionally been questioned (see, e.g., Hare, *Son of Man Tradition*, 82–85; cf., e.g., Brown, *Gospel according to John (i–xii)*, 89–91), but I am unpersuaded by the objections. Indeed, in company with most scholars, I see the verse as a "midrashic" treatment of Gen 28:12. Particularly striking, in my judgment, is the parallel between καὶ οἱ ἄγγελοι τοῦ Θεοῦ ἀνέβαινον καὶ κατέβαινον ἐπ᾽ αὐτῆς (Gen 28:12 LXX) and καὶ τοὺς ἀγγέλους τοῦ Θεοῦ ἀναβαίνοντας καὶ καταβαίνοντας ἐπὶ τὸν υἱὸν τοῦ ἀνθρώπου (John 1:51).

38. Such, indeed, may well be the meaning of the Johannine characterization of Jesus as "μονογενής Son of God" — a characterization that occurs in the New Testament *only* in the Johannine literature and primarily in the Fourth Gospel (John 1:14 [contrary to most translations, the Greek of 1:14 does not include υἱός with μονογενής]; 3:16, 18; 1 John 4:9; as already noted [n. 3], most manuscripts read ὁ μονογενὴς υἱός rather than μονογενὴς Θεός at 1:18, but the latter is the preferable reading). It is now generally agreed that μονογενής should be translated as "only" rather than "only-begotten"; see, e.g., Moody, "God's Only Son." My own judgment, however, is that μονογενής, as applied to Jesus, should be translated as "only one of his kind" or "unique"; see, e.g., Brown, *Gospel according to John (i–xii)*, 13: "μονογενής describes a quality of Jesus, his uniqueness." Jesus' uniqueness consists in the fact that he is *both* the *human* Son of Joseph *and* the *divine* Son of God. Whether the Gospel and the three Johannine epistles have the same author is a matter of dispute; see, e.g., Brown, *Epistles of John*, 14–35.

consideration[39] and employ "Son of Man" in later contexts—almost interchangeably with "Son of God"—without the necessity of re-establishing its point of reference. Thus, after speaking of "the angels of God ascending and descending upon the Son of Man,"[40] the Fourth Gospel can indicate that the "Son of Man" himself both "descended from heaven" and "will ascend into heaven,"[41] that he is to be "lifted up" (a double entendre referring to both crucifixion and resurrection/ascension)[42] and "glorified,"[43] that he will give his flesh and blood as food and drink[44] "that endures for eternal life,"[45] and that he is the appropriate object of faith.[46] Perhaps most interesting for the present discussion is the fact that he is identified as the life-giving "Son of God" to whom "the Father" as given "authority to execute judgment, *because he is a Son of Man* (that is, because he is of both *human* and *divine* origin)."[47] Thus, all of the "Son of Man" references in the Fourth Gospel appear to have in mind the paradox of Jesus' divine and human origin: it is precisely the *human* Son who is also the *divine* Son.

Clearly, such an understanding of "Son of Man" makes sense within the context of the Fourth Gospel's incarnational christology and indeed, contrary to what others have argued, suggests a specific and important role for the title "Son of Man" within the christology of the Fourth Gospel.

---

39. It does surface again, of course, in John 6:41–59, where the problem is essentially the same as that suggested in 1:43–51: How can the *earthly* and *human* Son of Joseph possibly be the *heavenly* and *divine* Son of God? Note, also, that here too the resolution of the problem involves use of the title "Son of Man" (v. 53).

40. John 1:51.

41. John 3:13; cf. 6:62.

42. John 3:13; 8:28; 12:34.

43. John 12:23; 13:31.

44. John 6:53.

45. John 6:27.

46. John 3:15; 9:35.

47. John 5:27. Neither "son" (υἱός) nor "man" (ἀνθρώπου) has the article; thus, the most obvious translation would be "a son of a man," or, more correctly, "a son of a human" (i.e., "a human being"). It is not certain, however, that the anarthrous nature of the title here has any real significance; see, e.g., Brown, *Gospel according to John (i–xii)*, 215, 220–21.

PART FOUR

Special Topics
in the Gospels

Chapter 14

Κύριος and Ἐπιστάτης as Translations of *Rabbi/Rabbouni*

In the Gospels of Matthew, Mark, and John (but not in Luke), Jesus is occasionally addressed as *rabbi* or *rabbouni* (Aramaic for "my great one," "my lord," or "my master").[1] More frequently, in all of the canonical gospels, he is addressed as διδάσκαλος (Greek for "teacher").[2] Most scholars assume—correctly in my judgment—that διδάσκαλος is here to be regarded as the Greek equivalent

"Κύριος and Ἐπιστάτης as Translations of *Rabbi/Rabbouni*." *JHC* 4, 1 (Spring 1997) 56–77. Copyright © 1997 Institute for Higher Critical Studies. Reprinted (in slightly revised version) with permission.

1. *Rabbi*: Matt 26:25, 49; Mark 9:5; 11:21; 14:45; John 1:38, 49; 3:2; 4:31; 6:25; 9:2; 11:8. *Rabbouni*: Mark 10:51; John 20:16. *Rabbouni* is a variant form of *rabbi*. The correct transliterations from the New Testament Greek would be *hrabbi* (ῥαββί) and *hrabbouni* (ῥαββουνί); in deference to common usage, however, I shall employ *rabbi* and *rabbouni*. Other than Jesus, only John the Baptist is addressed in the New Testament as *rabbi* (John 3:26), and no one other than Jesus is addressed as *rabbouni*. In Matt 23:7–8 (the only other occurrence of *rabbi* in the New Testament), Jesus tells his disciples that they, unlike the scribes and Pharisees, are not to be called *rabbi*.

2. Matt 8:19; 9:11; 12:38; 17:24; 19:16; 22:16, 24, 36; 26:18 (also Matt 10:24–25 but not directly as a title of address for Jesus); Mark 4:38; 5:35; 9:17, 38; 10:17, 20, 35; 12:14, 19, 32; 13:1; 14:14; Luke 7:40; 8:49; 9:38; 10:25; 11:45; 12:13; 18:18; 19:39; 20:21, 28, 39; 21:7; 22:11 (also Luke 6:40 but not directly as a title of address for Jesus); John 1:38; 3:2; 11:28; 13:13–14; 20:16. Except at John 11:28; 13:13–14, διδάσκαλος serves in the Fourth Gospel simply as a translation or synonym for *rabbi* or *rabbouni*; at 11:28, it may be essentially a synonym for or variant of κύριος (cf. 11:21, 27, 32, 34, 39).

of the Aramaic *rabbi/rabbouni*.³ Thus, it would appear that *rabbi/ rabbouni* as a title of address for Jesus was somewhat more wide- spread in the early tradition than the occasional appearance in the gospels of the Aramaic forms might initially suggest. In short, it is likely that a characteristic address for Jesus in the early tradi- tion was *rabbi/rabbouni* and that, as the tradition was transmitted in Greek, this title was sometimes simply transliterated but more often was translated as διδάσκαλος.

In all of the canonical gospels except Mark, however, Jesus is also rather frequently addressed as κύριος (Greek for "lord" or "master");⁴ in addition, he is addressed six times in Luke as

---

3. E.g., Lohse, "ῥαββί, ῥαββουνί," 964. The Fourth Gospel explicitly states that διδάσκαλος is the translation of *rabbi* and *rabbouni* (John 1:38, the first occurrence of *rabbi* in the Fourth Gospel, and John 20:16, the only occurrence of *rabbouni* in the Fourth Gospel). The same is perhaps im- plied at John 3:2, where *rabbi* and διδάσκαλος are juxtaposed as apparent synonyms; cf. also Matt 23:8, where *rabbi* and διδάσκαλος may be in- tended as synonyms. Despite its originally broader meaning, *rabbi* came to be applied (probably not, however, in the lifetime of Jesus) almost ex- clusively to teachers of Torah. Solomon Zeitlin ("A Reply," 348) main- tains that "[διδάσκαλος] was used by the Jews during the Hellenistic and Roman periods for the Hebrew *morêh* teacher"; Raymond E. Brown (*Gospel according to John (i–xii)*, 74), however, suggests that διδάσκαλος may also have served in the pre–70 CE period as a translation of *rabbi*.

4. Matt 7:21, 22; 8:2, 6, 8, 21, 25; 9:28; 12:8 (perhaps not a title of ad- dress); 14:28, 30; 15:22, 25, 27; 16:22; 17:4, 15; 18:21; 20:31, 33; 21:3 (perhaps not a title of address); 22:43, 44, 45; 24:42 (perhaps not a title of address); 25:37, 44; 26:22; Luke 1:43; 2:11; 5:8, 12; 6:5 (perhaps not a title of address), 46; 7:6, 13, 19; 9:54, 59, 61; 10:1, 17, 39, 40, 41; 11:1, 39; 12:41, 42; 13:15, 23; 17:5, 6, 37; 18:6, 41; 19:8 (*bis*), 31 (perhaps not a title of address), 34 (perhaps not a title of address); 20:42, 44; 22:33, 38, 49, 61 (*bis*); 24:34; John 4:11, 15, 19, 49; 5:7; 6:23, 34, 68; 9:36, 38; 11:2, 3, 12, 21, 27, 32, 34, 39; 12:21; 13:6, 9, 13, 14, 25, 36, 37; 14:5, 8, 22; 20:2, 13, 15, 18, 20, 25, 28; 21:7 (*bis*), 12, 15, 16, 17, 20, 21. In Luke and to a lesser degree John (unlike Matthew and Mark), a number of the occurrences of κύριος represent the author's designation of Jesus absolutely as ὁ κύριος, not an address by a character in the narrative (Luke 7:13, 19; 10:1, 39, 41; 11:39; 12:42; 13:15; 17:5, 6; 18:6; 19:8; 22:61 (*bis*); John 6:23; 11:2; 20:20; 21:7, 12).

In Mark, the only certain reference to Jesus as κύριος is at 7:28; other apparent references are at 2:28; 12:36–37; and perhaps 11:3. Textual vari- ants provide other possible references at Mark 1:40; 9:24; 10:51.

ἐπιστάτης (Greek for "master").[5] It has occasionally been proposed that ἐπιστάτης in Luke might reflect an earlier *rabbi/
rabbouni* in the tradition.[6] Only rarely, however, has it been suggested—and, at least to my knowledge, never argued in detail—
that κύριος might also reflect an earlier *rabbi/rabbouni*—in other
words, that *rabbi/rabbouni* might also have been translated into
Greek as κύριος.[7] Rather, it is generally assumed that κύριος
(and probably ἐπιστάτης as well) reflect an earlier use of some
Aramaic term such as *mar* ("lord," "master") or *marî* ("my lord,"
"my master").[8]

---

5. Luke 5:5; 8:24 (*bis*), 45; 9:33, 49; 17:13.

6. Observing that ἐπιστάτης corresponds once to the Markan *rabbi*
(Luke 9:33/Mark 9:5) and twice to the Markan διδάσκαλος (Luke 8:24/
Mark 4:38; Luke 9:49/Mark 9:38) and that "apparently it covers much of
the same semantic field as *rab*," Hayim Lapin ("Rabbi," 601–2) concludes:
"It is possible that the Lukan ἐπιστάτης reflects (as it clearly seems to
in Luke 9:33) sources which used the Heb/Aram *rabbi*." Albrecht Oepke
("ἐπιστάτης," 622–23) appears to be certain of this translation. For each
occurrence of ἐπιστάτης, an original *rabbi/rabbouni* would make perfectly
good sense.

7. E.g., Hahn, *Titles of Jesus in Christology*, 78–79: "In view of the re-
placement of ῥαββουνί in Mk. 10:51 by κύριε in Lk. 18:41, we might
wonder whether κύριε might also be traced back to an original *rabbi* especially as διδάσκαλε was only an inadequate translation of *rabbi*. Yet
διδάσκαλε as a rendering of *rabbi* came to prevail and another equivalent
of κύριε must be assumed. Behind the use of 'Lord' as a form of address
there stands the Aramaic *marah* whose later form *mar* was a word, which
like *rab* was not used absolutely without a dependent substantive or suf-
fix."

8. Indeed, Hahn (*Titles of Jesus in Christology*, 79; cf. the entire discussion, 73–89) concludes: "we must suppose that [the historical] Jesus was
addressed not only as *rabbi* but also as *marî*." If this was indeed the case,
the two titles were likely regarded as virtual synonyms. Cf., however,
Oepke, "ἐπιστάτης," 623: "In some cases (Mk. 11:3 and par.; Lk. 5:8; Mt.
7:21 and par.?), *mar* or *marî*, *marana* may be the original of κύριος, but this
can hardly be true of ἐπιστάτης. Nor is *moreh* a likely original." Joseph
A. Fitzmyer has noted that the Greek κύριος (as a loan-word) was apparently already being applied to God by first-century Aramaic-speaking
Palestinian Jews; see his "Semitic Background of the New Testament
Κύριος-Title"; "New Testament Κύριος and *Maranatha*," 220–23; and
"κύριος, κυριακός," 330; cf. Vermes, *Jesus the Jew*, 113.

It is not my purpose in this paper to raise the question of how
the historical Jesus was addressed by his contemporaries during
his lifetime.[9] Neither do I propose to deal with the Aramaic *mar* as
it is applied to the risen Christ in 1 Cor 16:22 and Did 10:6 (cf. Rev
22:20).[10] Rather, it is my intention to argue that both ἐπιστάτης
and κύριος as titles of address for Jesus in the gospels are to be
seen as reflecting the use in the pre-gospel tradition of *rabbi/rab-
bouni*—in other words, that *rabbi/rabbouni* was translated into
Greek not only as διδάσκαλος but also as κύριος and ἐπιστάτης.
In my judgment, there are eight lines of evidence that, when
viewed cumulatively, support this argument.

I

If our only source were the Gospel of Mark, which is still regarded
by most scholars as the earliest of the gospels,[11] we would almost

---

9. Hahn (*Titles of Jesus in Christology*, 79), apparently in agreement
with most scholars, asserts: "It is certain that in His own lifetime Jesus
was addressed as '*Rabbi*.'" Arguments for this conclusion include: (1) the
title is Aramaic and not Greek (at least for the most part, the movement in
the transmission of early Christian traditions appears to have been from
Aramaic to Greek, not *vice versa*); (2) its application to Jesus is attested in
both the Synoptic and the Johannine traditions; (3) it is difficult to account
for the title's introduction into the tradition after the lifetime of Jesus; (4)
the title is not applied to Jesus outside the Synoptic and Johannine traditions (i.e., for the most part, it appears to have dropped from use relatively early); and (5) even where it occurs in the gospels, the title appears
to play no significant christological role. As to whether "*rabbi*" as a form
of address in the gospels is anachronistic, see, e.g., Shanks, "Is the Title
'*Rabbi*' Anachronistic?"; Zeitlin, "A Reply"; Shanks, "Origins of the Title
'*Rabbi*'"; Zeitlin, "The Title *Rabbi* in the Gospels Is Anachronistic." Brown
(*Gospel according to John [i–xii]*, 74), however, cautiously concludes that
the New Testament usage of *rabbi* may not be anachronistic.

10. The appearance of *maranatha* ("Our lord, come!") in 1 Cor 16:22 and
Did 10:6 would appear to suggest that Jesus was sometimes addressed
in the tradition as *mar*; see, e.g., Fitzmyer, "New Testament *Kyrios* and
Maranatha," 223–29. It should be noted, however, that there is no direct
evidence of *mar* in the traditions that underlie the gospels and, indeed,
that 1 Corinthians and the Didache apply the title to the risen Christ, not
the pre-Easter Jesus.

11. This, of course, has been vigorously challenged particularly by the
proponents of the Griesbach (or Two-Gospel) Hypothesis, which holds

certainly assume that Jesus was characteristically addressed as *rabbi/rabbouni* and that he was rarely if ever addressed by any other title.

In Mark, Jesus is addressed as *rabbi* or *rabbouni* four times (*rabbi*: Mark 9:5; 10:51; 11:21; 14:45) and as διδάσκαλος (almost certainly to be regarded as the Greek translation of *rabbi*) twelve times (Mark 4:38; 5:35; 9:17, 38; 10:17, 20, 35; 12:14, 19, 32; 13:1; 14:14). The address ἐπιστάτης does not appear in Mark, and only once is it certain that κύριος is a title of address for Jesus.[12] This is at Mark 7:28, where he is so addressed by a woman specifically identified as "a Greek, a Syrophoenician by birth" (v. 26).[13] For a non-Jew to address Jesus as *rabbi/rabbouni* would, no doubt, have been regarded as inappropriate, both in the earlier tradition and by the author of Mark, and, in the context, even διδάσκαλος might appear somewhat surprising. Thus, in my judgment, the use of κύριος in this pericope by no means points to some Aramaic title of address other than *rabbi/rabbouni* (e.g., *mar* or *marî*) in the earlier tradition.

Elsewhere in Mark, apparent references to Jesus as κύριος appear only at Mark 2:28 ("the Son of Man is lord [κύριος] of the

---

that Matthew was the earliest of the Synoptic Gospels, that it served as a primary source for Luke, and that Mark represents a conflated abbreviation of Matthew and Luke. As I began the research for this paper, I presupposed no particular solution to the Synoptic Problem. As the research proceeded, however, and for reasons that will become obvious, I became increasingly convinced that the data relating to the topic of the paper could best be accounted for by assuming either some form of Markan priority or some type of "ur-gospel" hypothesis.

12. Textual variants provide other possible references at Mark 1:40 (both of the parallels, Matt 8:2 and Luke 5:12, have κύριος); Mark 9:22 (no parallel in Matthew or Luke); Mark 10:51 (the best reading in Mark is *rabbi*, but both of the parallels, Matt 20:33 and Luke 18:41, have κύριος; in each case, however, the textual evidence for κύριος is tenuous). Cf., however, Vermes, *Jesus the Jew*, 122–28, who argues that "if all the Marcan witnesses [i.e., textual variants] are allowed to testify, the old axiom [that 'lord' appears only in the mouth of Gentiles in the earliest gospel tradition] will have to be discarded."

13. Parallel in Matt 15:27 (including κύριος both here and earlier in vv. 22, 25), but the entire pericope is missing from Luke.

Sabbath"; parallels at Matt 12:8 and Luke 6:5); Mark 11:3 ("the
lord [κύριος] has need of [the colt]"; parallels in Matt 21:3 and
Luke 19:31; cf. also Luke 19:34), and Mark 12:36–37, a quotation
from the LXX of Ps 110:1 ("The Lord said to my lord [κύριος] …")
and a comment regarding the quotation ("David himself calls him
lord [κύριος]").[14] In none of these references, however, is κύριος
directly applied to Jesus as a title of address; indeed, in each case,
κύριος appears on the lips of Jesus himself. Moreover, although
it is clear that the author of Mark regards κύριος as referring to
Jesus, this may well not have been the case in the earlier tradition.[15]

In short, the evidence in the Gospel of Mark suggests (1) that
Jesus was characteristically addressed in the early tradition as
rabbi/rabbouni and not by any other Aramaic title and (2) that *rabbi*
was sometimes simply transliterated into Greek but more often
was translated as διδάσκαλος.

II

In at least two respects, the Markan portrayal of Jesus as *rabbi/
rabbouni* appears to find confirmation in the Gospels of Matthew
and John.

It is obviously significant that Jesus is addressed as *rabbi/rab-
bouni* not only in the Gospels of Mark and Matthew but also in
John (i.e., in both the Synoptic and the Johannine traditions). This
suggests, in my judgment, that the title was rather deeply imbedded in a relatively early stratum of the Jesus tradition.

---

14. The fact that the quotation is from the LXX may suggest that the
entire pericope originated in the Greek-speaking, not the Aramaic-
speaking, church.

15. In Mark 2:28, "the son of man" may, in the earlier tradition, have
been nothing more than a circumlocution for "a human being." In Mark
11:3, "the lord" may refer either to Jesus or to the owner of the animal;
even if it refers to Jesus, however, it may refer to him simply as the (alleged) owner of the animal. In Mark 12:36–37, the reference, at least
overtly, is simply to "the Christ," who is here not specifically identified
with Jesus.

Somewhat less obvious, but perhaps of equal importance, however, is the fact that Mark, Matthew, and John disagree regarding who it is that addresses Jesus as *rabbi/rabbouni*. In Mark 9:5 and 11:21, Jesus is so addressed by Peter (one of the disciples); in Mark 10:51 by Bartimaeus (a potential disciple); and in Mark 14:45 by Judas Iscariot (the disciple who betrayed Jesus). Thus, the use of the title in Mark appears to suggest no particular christological agenda; it simply represents, in quite neutral fashion, the typical form of address applied to Jesus by other characters in the narrative. In the Fourth Gospel, only the positive side of the Markan picture is picked up, and this side is extended: With but one exception, Jesus is addressed as *rabbi/rabbouni* only by his followers or potential followers (*rabbi*: John 1:38, 49; 3:2; 4:31; 9:2; 11:8; *rabbouni*: John 20:16).[16] In Matthew, however, it is only the negative side of the Markan picture that appears: Jesus is addressed as *rabbi* only by Judas Iscariot (Matt 26:25, 49), and it is clear that the title has a pejorative connotation for Matthew.[17] In other words, both Matthew and John have schematized the *rabbi/rabbouni* tradition reflected in Mark, but in opposite directions: John reflects the positive side, and Matthew the negative. This bifurcation, in my judgment, is most naturally explained by assuming that the earlier tradition included both sides. In short, the pointed difference between Matthew and John at this point provides apparent support for the fuller Markan picture, in which Jesus is addressed as *rabbi/rabbouni* by friend and foe alike.

Thus, the Markan portrayal of Jesus as *rabbi/rabbouni* finds support in Matthew and John. This suggests that *rabbi/rabbouni*

---

16. The one exception is John 6:25, where it is "the crowd" who address him as *rabbi*. Even "the crowd," however, has gone to Capernaum looking for Jesus and thus, at this point in the narrative, can hardly be regarded as hostile to him. The term thus appears to have a quite positive connotation in John. Note also John 20:16, where Mary initially addresses Jesus as κύριος (perhaps meaning only "sir") and then, after she recognizes him, as *rabbouni*, which perhaps implies that *rabbouni* is an even "higher" title than κύριος.

17. In Matt 23:7–8, Jesus tells his disciples that they, unlike the scribes and Pharisees, are not to be called *rabbi*.

was a characteristic title (probably *the* characteristic title) of address for Jesus in the early tradition and that, in this tradition, Jesus was so addressed by all sorts of people.

III

Although, with only one exception (Matt 26:26; see below), Jesus is never directly addressed as *rabbi/rabbouni* in the so-called "Q," "M," and "L" materials, there is little if anything in these materials that would serve to contradict the Markan portrayal of Jesus as *rabbi/rabbouni*.[18]

Neither *rabbi* nor *rabbouni* appears in the "Q" materials in Matthew and Luke, and διδάσκαλος certainly appears only once (Matt 10:24–25/Luke 6:40), where it is not explicitly or directly a title of address for Jesus and, taken out of context, need not necessarily even refer to Jesus.[19] Κύριος, however, appears a number of times as a title of address for Jesus.

With regard to κύριος, it is instructive to note how Matthew and Luke deal with their Markan source.[20] The clear tendency of

------

18. As noted above (n. 11), I initially intended to presuppose no particular solution to the Synoptic Problem in this paper. Once I became convinced, however, that the best sense could be made of the *rabbi/rabbouni* data by assuming either some sort of Markan priority of some type of "ur-gospel" hypothesis, it then became necessary to make some decision regarding the non-Markan materials in Matthew and Luke. In what follows, therefore, I am assuming that Matthew and Luke used some common non-Markan source material ("Q") and that each also used some additional non-Markan source material and/or created some material *de novo* ("M" and "L"). The following questions remain open, however, so far as this paper is concerned: (a) whether some or possibly even all of the so-called "Q," "M," and "L" material might have come from an "ur-gospel" also used by Mark, (b) whether some or possibly even all of the so-called "M" and "L" material might also have come from "Q," (c) whether "Q" refers to one or more written sources and/or a body of oral tradition, and (d) whether "Q" itself might in some way have been related to or a part of source material used by Mark.

19. The address διδάσκαλος appears also at Matt 8:19 but not in the parallel, Luke 9:57.

20. By "Markan source," I mean either the Gospel of Mark itself (whether in essentially its canonical form or in some earlier form is a question to be considered later in this paper) or some earlier source material ("ur-gospel") used by Mark.

both Matthew and Luke is (1) to reproduce κύριος whenever it appears in Mark[21] and (2) sometimes to add κύριος where it does not appear in Mark.[22] If Matthew and Luke deal similarly with κύριος in the "Q" material, the following conclusions would appear warranted: (1) where κύριος appears in neither the Matthean nor the Lukan version of the "Q" material, it almost certainly did not appear in "Q"; and (2) where κύριος appears only in the Matthean or only in the Lukan version of the "Q" material, it probably did not appear in "Q."[23] To state the matter positively: Because of Matthew's and Luke's apparent propensity for using κύριος as a title of address for Jesus whenever it is found in their sources, it is likely that κύριος appeared in "Q" only at those points where both Matthew and Luke include it.[24] This occurs in only three pericopes (Matt 7:21–22/Luke 6:46; Matt 8:8/Luke 7:6; Matt 8:21/Luke 9:59). In each of these pericopes, however, it is simply impossible to know what Aramaic term, if any, might lie behind κύριος, either in the tradition behind "Q" or possibly even

---

21. Matthew reproduces all four of the (apparent) Markan references to Jesus as κύριος (Matt 15:27/Mark 7:28; Matt 12:8/Mark 2:28; Matt 21:3/ Mark 11:3; Matt 22:44–45/Mark 12:36–37). Luke reproduces three of the four (Luke 6:5/Mark 2:28; Luke 19:31/Mark 11:3; Luke 20:42–44/Mark 12:36–37) but omits the entire pericope containing the fourth (Mark 7:24–30)—possibly because of its apparently anti-Gentile bias (note, however, that this pericope is a part of the so-called "Great Omission" in Luke [Mark 6:45–8:26]).

22. Six times in Matthew: Matt 8:21 (cf. Mark 1:40); twice in the pericope Matt 15:21–28 (cf. Mark 7:24–30), at vv. 22 and 25 (Mark has it at v. 28, followed by Matthew at v. 27); Matt 16:22 (cf. Mark 8:32); Matt 20:3 (cf. Mark 10:48); Matt 22:43 (cf. Mark 12:36; Mark has it at vv. 36 and 37, followed by Matthew at vv. 44 and 45). Note also Matt 24:42 (cf. Mark 13:35), where Matthew may have changed κύριος as an apparent reference to someone other than Jesus to κύριος as a direct reference to Jesus. Four times in Luke: Luke 5:12 (cf. Mark 1:40); Luke 19:34 (cf. Mark 11:6); Luke 22:61 (cf. Mark 14:72).

23. Unless, of course, Matthew or Luke had some compelling reason for omitting it, as is perhaps the case with Luke's omission of the entire pericope Mark 7:24–30 because of its apparently anti-Gentile bias.

24. Even this must remain somewhat suspect, however, because both Matt 8:2 and Luke 5:12 have a leper address Jesus as κύριος but the parallel, Mark 1:40, does not (i.e., both Matthew and Luke have added κύριος to their Markan source).

in "Q" itself. The term might be *mar/marî*, but it equally well might be *rabbi/rabbouni*.[25] In short, the three "Q" passages in which both Matthew and Luke have Jesus addressed as κύριος do not, in my judgment, provide any real evidence that Jesus was addressed by

---

25. In Matt 7:21–22/Luke 6:46; Luke 13:25, the one being addressed is the one who tells (teaches?) people how they should live; at the time when Matthew and Luke were written, *rabbi* or *rabbouni* would be appropriate here. In Matt 8:8/Luke 7:6, where Jesus is addressed as κύριος by the Roman centurion, it may have been regarded as inappropriate for Jesus to be addressed as *rabbi* or *rabbouni* by a non-Jew (see above on Mark 7:28), and, indeed, if the pericope has any basis in historical fact, the Greek κύριος may well have been the actual term of address used. In short, there may be no Aramaic term at all behind the κύριος of this passage. In Matt 8:21/Luke 9:59 ("Lord, let me first go and bury my father"), it should be noted that at the beginning of the pericope (and in a somewhat parallel statement), Matthew has Jesus addressed as διδάσκαλος, presumably the equivalent of *rabbi* or *rabbouni* (v. 19). Thus, it is possible that "Q" read διδάσκαλος throughout the pericope and that Matthew and Luke have variously either simply reproduced the διδάσκαλος (Matt 8:19), eliminated the διδάσκαλος altogether (Luke 9:57), changed the διδάσκαλος to κύριος (Matt 8:21 and Luke 9:59), and added yet another κύριος to the pericope (Luke 9:61). It is also possible, however, that "Q" read *rabbi* or *rabbouni* throughout the pericope and that Matthew and Luke have variously translated the *rabbi* or *rabbouni* as διδάσκαλος (Matt 8:19), eliminated the *rabbi* or *rabbouni* altogether (Luke 9:57), translated the *rabbi* or *rabbouni* as κύριος (Matt 8:21 and Luke 9:59), and added yet another κύριος to the pericope (Luke 9:61).

At this point, a closer examination of the entire pericope (Matt 8:18–22/Luke 9:57–62) may be helpful. In its Lukan version, three people address Jesus; the second and third call him κύριος, but, in the better manuscripts, the first uses no title of address at all. In the Matthean version, only two people address Jesus (Luke's third person is missing); the second (the same as Luke's second) calls him κύριος, but the first (the same as Luke's first) calls him διδάσκαλος. Thus, for the first person, Matthew has διδάσκαλος but Luke apparently has no title of address. There is some manuscript evidence, however, for the first person in Luke addressing Jesus as κύριος. If this reading is original, then Matthew reads διδάσκαλος and Luke reads κύριος at the same point in the narrative. This might well reflect a situation in which the original was *rabbi* or *rabbouni* and the *rabbi* or *rabbouni* was variously translated as διδάσκαλος (Matthew) and κύριος (Luke). The terms διδάσκαλος and κύριος are, of course, by no means synonymous, but either of them could (and apparently did) serve as a translation of *rabbi* or *rabbouni*. In short, it is at least possible that *rabbi* or *rabbouni* underlies the κύριος of Matt 8:21/Luke 9:59.

some Aramaic term other than rabbi/*rabbouni* in the "Q" source.

In the "M" material, Jesus is addressed as *rabbi* only once, at Matt 26:25 (*rabbouni* does not appear in the "M" material). My own judgment is that this verse, which appears neither in Mark nor in Luke, is almost certainly a Matthean creation and is intended to reinforce the Matthean idea that only Judas Iscariot addresses Jesus as *rabbi*. Only twice in the "M" material is Jesus addressed as διδάσκαλος (Matt 12:38, which is a Matthean addition to "Q" material, and 17:24). In three pericopes, he is addressed as κύριος. The first is Matt 9:27–31 (κύριος in v. 28). This pericope, however, may well be a doublet of Matt 20:29–34/ Mark 10:46–52/Luke 18:35–43, in which case κύριος apparently represents simply Matthew's translation of the Markan *rabbouni*. The second pericope is Matt 14:28–31 (κύριος in vv. 28 and 30), which is a Matthean addition to a Markan pericope (Mark 6:45-52/ Matt 14:22–33/Luke 6:16–21). The third pericope is Matt 25:31–46 (κύριος in vv. 37 and 44), which has no parallel of any sort in either Mark or Luke. In the latter two pericopes, there is no way to tell what Aramaic term, if any, lies behind Matthew's κύριος. It could have been *mar/marî*, but it equally well could have been *rabbi/rabbouni*; or finally, of course, κύριος could reflect only the redactional hand of the author.

Neither *rabbi* nor *rabbouni* appears in the "L" material, but Jesus is addressed as διδάσκαλος six times (Luke 7:40; 11:45; 12:13; 19:39; 20:39; 21:7 [a Lukan addition to Markan material]). Κύριος is much more frequent in "L" than in "M" or "Q," and Jesus is addressed six times as ἐπιστάτης (Luke 5:5; 8:24 [*bis*], 45; 9:33, 49; 17:13). In a number of cases, however, κύριος is simply the author's designation of Jesus absolutely as ὁ κύριος, not a direct title of address used by a character in the narrative (Luke 7:13; 10:1, 39, 41; 11:39; 12:42; 13:15; 17:5, 6; 18:6; 19:8; 22:61 [*bis*]; 24:34). In two other cases, Jesus is addressed as κύριος in Lukan additions to Markan or "Q" materials (Luke 9:6, after Matt 8:22 = "Q," and Luke 19:34, after Mark 11:6 = Mark), and these additions likely reflect no source other than the redactional hand of the author of Luke. Finally, in two cases, it is the as-yet-unborn or newly-born Jesus who is referred to as ὁ κύριός μου (Luke 1:43) or as κύριος

(Luke 2:11). There remain twelve passages in the "L" material in which the adult Jesus is addressed as κύριος (Luke 5:8; 9:54; 10:17, 40; 11:1; 12:41; 13:23; 17:37; 19:8; 22:33, 38, 49) and the six passages in which he is addressed as ἐπιστάτης. As in the case of the "M" material, however, there is no way to know what Aramaic term, if any, lies behind Luke's use of either κύριος or ἐπιστάτης at these points. In at least two of the passages, however, *rabbi/rabbouni* would appear more likely than *mar/marî*; these are Luke 11:1, where the disciples address Jesus as κύριος and say, "Teach us to pray, as John taught his disciples,"[26] and at Luke 12:41, where Peter, addressing Jesus as κύριος, asks him, "Are you telling this parable for us or for everyone?" In these passages, it is clear that Jesus is viewed as teacher/teller of parables (i.e, *rabbi/rabbouni*). Moreover Simon Peter's designation of Jesus as κύριος at Luke 5:8 is preceded in the same periscope (v. 5) by his designation of Jesus as ἐπιστάτης. The appearance of these essentially synonymous terms in the same pericope might well indicate a common Aramaic term in the tradition (translated into two different Greek terms perhaps for the same of literary variety), and *rabbi/rabbouni* would appear to be a more likely candidate than *mar/marî*,

A major problem with both the "M" and the "L" material, of course, is the impossibility of knowing at any given point whether a source is being used or the author is simply creating the material (or at least the title of address) *de novo*. In any case, however, there is little if any evidence that κύριος or ἐπιστάτης in the "M" and "L" material reflect some earlier Aramaic term other than *rabbi/ rabbouni*.

IV

Both κύριος and ἐπιστάτης clearly would have been regarded as appropriate Greek translations of *rabbi/rabbouni*—indeed, in the earlier period of Christian tradition, better translations than διδάσκαλος.

---

26. Note δίδαξον and ἐδίδαξεν, cognates of διδάσκαλος.

The root meaning of *rab* is "great one" (*rabbi* and *rabbouni* mean "my great one"), and the title is applied to "someone who occupies a high and respected position."[27] Inscriptional and other evidence suggests that, at the time of Jesus, the term was "an honorific roughly equivalent to 'sir,' with no explicit connection to either teaching or adjudication" and thus was "much like the colloquial use" of the Greek κύριος[28] (and ἐπιστάτης). Apparently, it was only later that its use was restricted primarily to recognized experts on the Law.[29] Thus, particularly in the pre-70 CE period, κύριος and ἐπιστάτης would appear to have been more appropriate then διδάσκαλος as translations of *rabbi/rabbouni*. Indeed, Ferdinand Hahn notes that "in the synoptic tradition there is a surprising parallelism" between διδάσκαλος (which he assumes to be a translation of *rabbi/rabbouni*) and κύριος.[30] Hahn fails, however, to draw what would appear to be a logical inference from this observation, namely, that *both* κύριος *and* διδάσκαλος are Greek translations of *rabbi/rabbouni*.

V

The manuscript tradition of the gospels indicates confusion at certain points as to whether Jesus is addressed as διδάσκαλος, ἐπιστάτης, or κύριος, and this may suggest that the terms were regarded as, if not synonymous, at least interchangeable titles of address (perhaps as alternative translations of *rabbi/rabbouni*):

(1) At Luke 5:5, a few "Western" texts[31] have Simon address Jesus as διδάσκαλος rather than ἐπιστάτης. Because there is no parallel in Matthew or Mark, this cannot be regarded as an instance of direct textual assimilation. Although an original

---

27. Lohse, "ῥαββί, ῥαββουνί," 961.

28. Lapin, "Rabbi," 601; cf. Cohen, "Epigraphical Rabbis." Note the roughly equivalent use of the Spanish *señor*.

29. See, e.g., Hahn, *Titles of Jesus in Christology*, 74; cf. also Vermes, *Jesus the Jew*, 115.

30. Hahn, *Titles of Jesus in Christology*, 73–74.

31. Including D (fifth/sixth century).

ἐπιστάτης might have been changed to διδάσκαλος simply because the latter is the more common title of address for Jesus, the
appearance of ἐπιστάτης in some manuscripts and διδάσκαλος
in others suggests that the two terms were regarded as either synonymous or interchangeable. In either case, the Aramaic *rabbi/rab-
bouni* would be the most likely candidate for translation as either
ἐπιστάτης or διδάσκαλος and might suggest the presence of an
original *rabbi/rabbouni* in the "L" material.

(2) At Luke 8:24, a few "Western" texts[32] have the disciples
address Jesus as κύριος rather than ἐπιστάτης. This, of course,
may be an assimilation to Matthew's κύριος in the parallel passage (Matt 8:25). Because the parallel passage in Mark (4:38) has
διδάσκαλος, however, κύριος may represent an independent rendition either of the Markan διδάσκαλος or possible of *rabbi/rab-
bouni* in the original source material.[33]

(3) At Luke 9:33, a few manuscripts (one of them 𝔓[45], dated in
the third century) have Peter address Jesus as διδάσκαλος rather
than ἐπιστάτης. Because the parallels have κύριος (Matt 17:4) and
rabbi (Mark 9:5), this cannot be regarded as an instance of textual
assimilation. Thus, it may be that διδάσκαλος here represents an
independent (perhaps earlier) rendition of the Markan *rabbi*. If, as
most scholars still maintain,[34] Mark is the earliest of the gospels,
it is significant that the earliest gospel has *rabbi* while the later
gospels have either κύριος (Matthew), ἐπιστάτης (the best manuscripts of Luke), or διδάσκαλος (a few manuscripts of Luke). This
suggests that *rabbi* could be translated by any one of the three
Greek terms.

(4) At Luke 9:49, a few manuscripts (again, one of them being 𝔓[45]) have John address Jesus as διδάσκαλος rather than
ἐπιστάτης. This, of course, may be an assimilation to the Markan
διδάσκαλος (Mark 9:38; no parallel in Matthew). Again, it is pos-

---

32. Including D.

33. On the possibility that this "original source material" might have
been either an earlier version of Mark or some type of "ur-gospel," see
below.

34. See n. 11.

sible that διδάσκαλος was the original reading in Luke and that it reflects an earlier *rabbi/rabbouni*. In any case, it appears that διδάσκαλος and ἐπιστάτης were regarded as either synonymous or interchangeable, and the Aramaic *rabbi/rabbouni* would be the most likely candidate for translation by either of the two Greek terms.

VI

At least four pericopes in the "established" text of the gospels appear to reflect, if not a synonymous, at least an interchangeable use of *rabbi/rabbouni*, διδάσκαλος, and/or κύριος as titles of address for Jesus:

(1) It is possible that *rabbi* and κύριος in Matt 26:20–25 reflect an interchangeable usage of the two terms (as already indicated, they have essentially the same meaning). Following Jesus' announcement that one of the twelve disciples will betray him (v. 21 = Mark 14:18/Luke 22:21), first the disciples ask, "Is it I, κύριος?" (v. 22),[35] and then Judas asks, "Is it I, *rabbi*?" (v. 25).[36] Although the author may have intended a distinction between κύριος on the lips of the other disciples and *rabbi* on the lips of Judas,[37] the distinction is a subtle one and in fact would appear to "work" as a piece of literary irony only if the titles have essentially the same meaning. Thus, it may well be the case that κύριος and *rabbi* would, in other contexts, be regarded as synonymous or at least interchangeable titles of address. If so, then it would not be surprising to find *rabbi/rabbouni* translated into Greek elsewhere as κύριος.

(2) Similarly, it is possible that διδάσκαλος (likely regarded as the equivalent of *rabbi/rabbouni*) and κύριος in Matt 8:19–22 (= Luke 9:57–62) reflect an interchangeable usage of the two terms. Here, a scribe addresses Jesus as διδάσκαλος (v. 19; no title in

---

35. There is no use of the title in Mark 14:19 or Luke 22:23.

36. No parallel in Mark or Luke.

37. Neither the Markan nor the Lukan parallel has any title of address. As already noted, Matthew appears to have an aversion to *rabbi* and *rabbouni* as titles of address for Jesus. For him, the most appropriate term of address appears to be κύριος.

Luke 9:57), and "another of the disciples" addresses him as κύριος
(v. 21 = Luke 9:59). Again, it may be that the author intended a distinction between διδάσκαλος on the lips of the scribe and κύριος
on the lips of the disciple,[38] but, if so, the distinction is again a
subtle one, and it is at least possible that διδάσκαλος and κύριος
are here used interchangeably (i.e., both as the equivalent of *rabbi/
rabbouni*).

(3) Again, it may be that διδάσκαλος (likely a translation
of *rabbi/rabbouni*) and κύριος are used interchangeably in John
13:13–14 ("You call me ὁ διδάσκαλος and ὁ κύριος").[39]

(4) In John 11:17–44 (the account of the raising of Lazarus),
Jesus is five times addressed as κύριος (by Martha in vv. 21, 27,
and 39; by Mary in v. 32; and, presumably, by "the Jews" in v. 34)
and once referred to as ὁ διδάσκαλος (by Martha, speaking to
Mary in v. 28). There is no apparent reason for the change, and it
may be that κύριος and διδάσκαλος are here regarded as essentially interchangeable titles of address.

VII

There appear to be at least five and probably as many as eight
instances in the gospels in which an original *rabbi/rabbouni* was in
fact translated into Greek as κύριος and/or ἐπιστάτης. These fall
into three groups:

(1) Most striking are two passages in which Jesus is addressed
as *rabbi* in Mark but as either κύριος or ἐπιστάτης in the Matthean
and Lukan parallels. In the accounts of the Transfiguration, Mark
9:5 has Peter address Jesus as *rabbi* while Matt 17:4 has κύριος and

---

38. Note, however, that it is "another of the disciples" who addresses
Jesus as κύριος; this would appear to suggest that the "scribe" who addresses him as διδάσκαλος is also one of "the disciples." If so, there
would be no apparent reason for a distinction between διδάσκαλος and
κύριος.

39. But see, e.g., Brown, *Gospel according to John (xiii–xi)*, 553: "Both
titles (*rab, mar*) were given to *rabbis* by their disciples. ... The order in
which the two titles are mentioned may reflect the development of the
disciples' understanding, for 'Teacher' is more common in the earlier
chapters of the Gospel and 'Lord' in the later chapters."

Luke 9:33 has ἐπιστάτης.[40] Similarly, in the accounts of the healing of the blind Bartimaeus (Mark) or the unnamed blind man (Luke) or men (Matthew), Mark 10:51 has Bartimaeus address Jesus as *rabbi* while both Matt 20:33 and Luke 18:41 have κύριος. In both cases, it appears more likely, on *a priori* grounds, that an original Aramaic *rabbi* would have been variously rendered into Greek as κύριος and ἐπιστάτης than *vice versa*. Thus, at least for the title of address in these two pericopes, I assume that Mark preserves the earliest version and that Matthew and Luke have, respectively, translated the Markan *rabbi* as κύριος and ἐπιστάτης.

At this point, it might be argued, however, that Matthew and Luke were not translating the Markan *rabbi* but rather were replacing the Aramaic term with Greek titles more compatible with their own christological or other agendas.[41] Indeed, as already noted, Luke never has Jesus addressed as *rabbi/rabbouni*, and Matthew has him so addressed only by Judas Iscariot. Moreover, κύριος would appear to fit better with Matthew's and Luke's christological interests than would *rabbi/rabbouni*.[42] It is less apparent, however, that ἐπιστάτης reflects any particular christological or other agenda on the part of Luke. In addition, it is significant that Luke 9:33 changes the Markan *rabbi* to ἐπιστάτης while Luke 18:41 changes it to κύριος. This suggests that the author of Luke regards both ἐπιστάτης and κύριος as appropriate translations of *rabbi*. Thus, it is my judgment that Matthew and Luke were, in fact, *translating* the Markan *rabbi* as, respectively, κύριος and ἐπιστάτης, not *substituting* these titles for *rabbi*.

In addition, if, for christological or other reasons, Matthew and Luke were substituting some other title of address for the Markan *rabbi* rather than simply translating it, it might be reasonable to expect that they would regularly make the same or a

---

40. A few manuscripts, including 𝔓[45] (third century), have διδάσκαλος at Luke 9:33 (see above).

41. This was suggested by Francis Watson in a letter to me dated March 7, 1996.

42. The Tetragrammaton *YHWH* is, of course, regularly translated in the LXX as κύριος.

similar substitution when διδάσκαλος appears in Mark. After all, διδάσκαλος would appear to be, if anything, even less useful for christological purposes than *rabbi/rabbouni!*[43] This, however is not generally the case. For the most part, neither Matthew nor Luke replaces the Markan διδάσκαλος with another title of address for Jesus. In four cases, both Matthew and Luke repeat Mark's διδάσκαλος,[44] and in two other instances Luke alone does so.[45] In four cases, both Matthew and Luke simply omit the Markan διδάσκαλος,[46] and Matthew alone does so once.[47] This, however is probably not significant because, except in one case, either the entire sentence or the entire pericope is omitted, not just the title of address, and in this one case both Matthew and Luke have used the title διδάσκαλος just a few verses earlier in the same pericope.[48] In only three pericopes do Matthew (once) or Luke (once) or both (once) change the Markan διδάσκαλος to some other title of address,[49] and I shall suggest below than even here they are not substituting but rather translating from an earlier source (either an earlier version of Mark or some type of ur-gospel) that read *rabbi/rabbouni* rather than διδάσκαλος. Moreover, both Matthew

---

43. As already noted, the root meaning of *rabbi/rabbouni* is essentially the same as that of both ἐπιστάτης and κύριος but not of διδάσκαλος.

44. Mark 10:17/Matt 19:16/Luke 18:18; Mark 12:14/Matt 22:16/Luke 20:21; Mark 12:19/Matt 22:24/Luke 20:28; Mark 14:14/Matt 26:18/Luke 22:11.

45. Mark 5:35/Luke 8:49/verse missing in Matthew; Mark 9:17/Luke 9:38/Matt 17:15 has κύριος.

46. Mark 10:20/Matt 19:20/Luke 18:21 (note, however, that διδάσκαλος is present in both Matthew and Luke just a few verses earlier [in the same pericope]); Mark 10:35/entire sentence missing in Matthew/entire pericope missing in Luke; Mark 12:32/entire pericope missing in both Matthew and Luke; Mark 13:1/entire sentence missing in both Matthew and Luke.

47. Mark 5:35/Luke 8:49/entire verse missing in Matthew.

48. Mark 10:20/Matt 19:20/Luke 18:21; cf. Mark 10:17/Matt 19:16/Luke 18:18.

49. Mark 4:38 (διδάσκαλος)/Matt 8:25 (κύριος)/Luke 8:24 (ἐπιστάτης); Mark 9:17 (διδάσκαλος)/Matt 17:15 (κύριος)/Luke 9:38 (διδάσκαλος); Mark 9:38 (διδάσκαλος)/Luke 9:49 (ἐπιστάτης)/entire pericope missing in Matthew.

and Luke have Jesus addressed as διδάσκαλος in non-Markan materials,[50] and, indeed, both Matthew (twice) and Luke (once) even add διδάσκαλος to Markan material.[51] Thus, in my judgment, there is little if any evidence that either Matthew or Luke has any inclination to change the Markan διδάσκαλος to some other title of address. It may well be the case, therefore, that they would also be less inclined to substitute some other title of address for the Markan *rabbi* than simply to translate it into its Greek equivalent (i.e., either κύριος or ἐπιστάτης).

In short, it is my judgment that the Aramaic *rabbi* at Mark 9:5 and 10:51 has been translated into Greek as κύριος at Matt 17:4, as ἐπιστάτης at Luke 9:33, and as κύριος in both Matt 20:33 and Luke 18:41.

(2) In a second group of passages, it appears that κύριος was regarded, at least by some later copyists, as an appropriate translation of *rabbi/rabbouni*:

At John 20:15, Mary Magdalene, not recognizing the risen Jesus, addresses him as κύριε;[52] then, having recognized him (v. 16), she addresses him as *rabbouni*. There are three points of interest here: (1) the possible intimation that *rabbouni* is somehow a more "exalted" title than κύριος;[53] (2) the statement that *rabbouni* is to be translated into Greek as διδάσκαλος; but (3) the reading in some "Western" texts (including D, dated in the fifth or sixth century) of κύριε διδάσκαλε as the translation of *rabbouni*.[54] As

---

50. Matt 8:19; 12:38; 17:24; Luke 7:40; 11:45; 12:13; 19:39; 20:39.

51. Matt 9:11; 22:36; Luke 21:7.

52. Here, most English translations read "sir."

53. Contrary to what one might expect. If κύριος is regarded as a translation of *mar*, this would appear to contradict Vermes' suggestion (*Jesus the Jew*, 118–21) that *mar* is a title superior to *rabbi*. To be sure, Vermes specifies (p. 118) that he has in mind situations in which "'*rabbi*' and '*mar*' appear together but refer to different persons" (p. 118), but, by extension, the same might apply in cases where the two terms apply to the same person.

54. See, e.g., Brown, *Gospel according to John (xiii–xxi)*, 992: "Perhaps precisely because of the simplicity of the address, some Western witnesses add 'Lord' or substitute it for 'Teacher'. In fact, however, 'lord, master' is a more literal rendering of *rabbi* than 'teacher.'"

regards the third point, κύριε may well originally have been a marginal gloss, intended to clarify or even correct the text's translation of *rabbouni* as διδάσκαλε, that was later copied into the text. In any case, however, it appears clear that someone here regarded κύριος as an appropriate translation of *rabbouni*.

At Mark 10:51, some "Western" texts have the blind Bartimaeus address Jesus as "κύριε *rabbi*."[55] It is possible that κύριε *rabbi* is simply a conflation of the Markan *rabbouni* and the Matthean/Lukan κύριε. Given the fact that this reading appears in the same manuscripts that translate *rabbouni* as κύριε διδάσκαλε at John 20:16, however, I regard it as more likely that κύριε here too was originally a gloss, intended to explain the meaning of *rabbouni*. If so, here again someone apparently regarded κύριος as an appropriate translation of *rabbi*.

Similarly, an apocryphal gospel fragment has Nathanael address Jesus as "*rabbi* κύριε" (cf. John 1:49).[56] Here too, it is at least possible that κύριε was originally a gloss, intended to explain the meaning of *rabbi*, that was later copied into the text.

(3) In a third group of passages, also three in number, Jesus is addressed as διδάσκαλος in Mark but as either κύριος or ἐπιστάτης in the Matthean and Lukan parallels. In the accounts of the stilling of the storm, Mark 4:38 has the disciples address Jesus as διδάσκαλος while Matt 8:25 has κύριος and Luke 8:24 has ἐπιστάτης.[57] Similarly, in the accounts of the healing of the epileptic boy, both Mark 9:17 and Luke 9:38 have the boy's father address Jesus as διδάσκαλος while Matt 17:15 has κύριος. Finally, in the accounts of the strange exorcist, Mark 9:38 has John address

---

55. Indeed, the same manuscripts that have κύριε διδάσκαλε at John 20:16 (see above). Note that most manuscripts of Mark have *rabbouni* while both Matthew and Luke have κύριος.

56. Berlin Papyrus 11710, cited by Lohse, "ῥαββί, ῥαββουνί," 964 n. 35; cf. Hans Lietzmann ("Notizen"). The reading is actually *hrambiou*, explained as a vocative form of *hrambis*, which is a variant of *rabbi* (*hrabbi*).

57. Note, however, that some manuscripts, including D (fifth/sixth century) read κύριος rather than ἐπιστάτης in Luke.

Jesus as διδάσκαλος while Luke 9:49 has ἐπιστάτης (the entire pericope is absent from Matthew).[58]

To be sure, *rabbi/rabbouni* appears in none of the parallels in this third group of passages. Two points, however, call for attention: In the first place, because ἐπιστάτης and especially κύριος would appear to represent a "higher" christology than διδάσκαλος, it appears inherently more likely that, in the developing tradition of the church, διδάσκαλος would have been changed to κύριος or ἐπιστάτης than that the reverse would have occurred. Thus, it would appear that Matthew's and Luke's κύριος and ἐπιστάτης do not represent the earliest version of the tradition in these passages.

In the second place, however, it is at least possible that Mark's διδάσκαλος also represents a secondary version of the tradition in these passages and that the original—either an earlier version of Mark or some type of ur-gospel—actually read *rabbi* or *rabbouni* rather than διδάσκαλος.[59] This possibility, which I regard as indeed a probability, is based upon the following considerations: (1)

---

58. The entire pericope is absent in Matthew. Note that a few manuscripts, including 𝔓⁴⁵ (third century), read διδάσκαλος at Luke 9:49.

59. If some earlier version of Mark (or a source used by Mark) read *rabbi* or *rabbouni* rather than διδάσκαλος not only in these passages but at other points as well, an otherwise puzzling feature of the Gospel of Mark might thereby by explained: although Mark refers rather frequently to Jesus as διδάσκαλος ("teacher"), he includes relatively little of Jesus' actual διδαχή or διδασκαλία ("teaching"). Perhaps, however, the original text of Mark (or a source used by Mark) read *rabbi* or *rabbouni* and *rabbi/ rabbouni* had not yet taken on the restricted meaning "teacher." As to why *rabbi* and/or *rabbouni* might, in a later version of Mark, have been changed to διδάσκαλος (not κύριος or ἐπιστάτης), one can only speculate. It may be, however, that the change occurred at a time when *rabbi/rabbouni* had already taken on the restricted meaning "teacher" and διδάσκαλος would therefore have been the most appropriate Greek equivalent. This might also explain why, in the Fourth Gospel, διδάσκαλος is explicitly designated as the translation of *rabbi/rabbouni*. Another possibility, of course, is that the Aramaic term increasingly applied to Jewish teachers would simply have been seen by Christians as inappropriate when applied to Jesus.

As already noted, both Matthew and Luke use διδάσκαλος as a title of address for Jesus fairly frequently; thus, it would appear that neither has any particular aversion to the term as applied to Jesus or any compelling reason for changing an original διδάσκαλος to κύριος or ἐπιστάτης.[60] (2) Both Matthew and Luke, however, do have an apparent aversion to the title *rabbi/rabbouni*.[61] Luke never uses it, and it occurs in Matthew only in a pejorative sense (Matt 23:7–8),[62] or in a possibly ironic sense on the lips of Judas Iscariot (Matt 26:25, 49).[63] Thus, both Matthew and Luke would appear to have good reason for changing an original *rabbi/rabbouni* to some other title of address. Thus, on the face of it, I regard it as more likely that κύριος at Matt 8:25 and ἐπιστάτης at Luke 8:24 represent independent translations of an original *rabbi/rabbouni* than that they are substitutions for an original διδάσκαλος (as in Mark 4:38). If this is the case, then κύριος at Matt 17:15 and ἐπιστάτης at Luke 9:49 should also be regarded as translations of an original *rabbi/rabbouni*, not substitutes for an original διδάσκαλος (as in Mark 9:17/Luke 9:38 and Mark 9:38). In short, it is my judgment

60. Günther Bornkamm ("End-Expectation and Church in Matthew," 41) has suggested that in Matthew only "outsiders" call Jesus διδάσκαλος (his disciples call him κύριος). Thus, in his view, Matthew does not regard διδάσκαλος as an adequate title of address for Jesus. Cf., however, Kingsbury, *Matthew: Structure, Christology, Kingdom*, 103–13, for a somewhat different interpretation of the matter and, for a refutation of Bornkamm's view, see Gundry, "On True and False Disciples in Matthew 8.18–22," 439–40.

61. On the one hand, this may reflect the post-70 CE situation with its growing tension between Judaism and Christianity and the increasing use of *rabbi* as a technical term for Jewish teachers. On the other hand, it is possible that Mark and John might reflect the later situation when *rabbi* was applied more specifically to Jewish teachers.

62. Here, it is perhaps implied that διδάσκαλος is a more appropriate title for Jesus than *rabbi*. The term καθηγητής (Matt 23:10) literally means "leader" or "guide" but "is used frequently in Hellenistic literature of the authority of teachers and of those whose actions are given as models" (Anonymous, "καθηγητής, οῦ, ὁ," 222); thus, it is a virtual synonym of *rabbi* and διδάσκαλος in vv. 7–8.

63. Here, there may be a deliberate distinction between *rabbi* on the lips of Judas Iscariot (the betrayer) and κύριος on the lips of the (other) disciples (v. 22).

that the three passages in this third group also reflect instances in which an original *rabbi/rabbouni* has been translated into Greek as either κύριος or ἐπιστάτης.

To be sure, the notion that Matthew and Luke used a version or versions of Mark earlier than canonical Mark or that all three of the Synoptic Gospels used a common source or ur-gospel is not widely accepted today. There is considerable evidence, however, that two or more versions of Mark existed at least by the second century, and, in my judgment, Helmut Koester has made a strong case for the view that Matthew and Luke used different versions of Mark that were earlier than canonical Mark.[64] If Koester is correct,[65] as I believe may well be the case,[66] then I regard it as highly likely, for the reasons noted above, that the reading of the source(s) behind Mark 4:38; 9:17; and 9:38 was *rabbi/rabbouni*, not

---

64. Koester, *Introduction to the New Testament*, 168–69: "I have no doubt ... that the two-source hypothesis is essentially correct. Both Matthew and Luke have used Mark. But which 'Mark'? ... 'Ur-Markus' hypotheses are not popular. But is it possible to assume that the Markan text which is transmitted in most of our New Testament manuscripts, i.e., 'canonical Mark,' was the text used by Matthew and Luke? ... The well-known common omissions of Matthew and Luke (e.g., Mk. 4:26–29; 8:22–26), but also such details as 'Is not this the carpenter, the son of Mary?' in Mk. 6:3 as compared to Mt.'s and Luke's 'Is not this the son of the carpenter (Joseph)?'; are significant indicators of the problem. Furthermore, does Luke's omission of Mk. 6:45–7:26 indicate that his 'Mark' was different from, and more original than Matthew's? This would lead us to assume that there were at least two different copies of Mark in existence in the first century A.D. But also 'canonical Mark' may be based on an older copy which existed in the first century, and Matthew and Luke could be considered as Markan 'revisions,' albeit rather substantial revisions of Mark." Cf. also Koester, "Response," 29. For a fuller exposition, see his "History and Development of Mark's Gospel" and *Ancient Christian Gospels*, 273–303.

65. For a penetrating critique of an early presentation of Koester's position, see Peabody, "Late Secondary Redaction of Mark's Gospel."

66. It appears to me that Koester's position is not very different from an "ur-gospel" hypothesis. Both assume that canonical Mark, canonical Matthew, and canonical Luke used (some of) the same source material, and both generally assume that canonical Mark reflects this common source material, at least at many points, more faithfully than do Matthew and Luke.

διδάσκαλος and that Matthew and Luke, in their parallel passages, have translated *rabbi/rabbouni* as κύριος or ἐπιστάτης.

In summary, there appear to be at least five and probably as many as eight instances in the gospels in which an original *rabbi/rabbouni* was in fact translated into Greek as κύριος or ἐπιστάτης.

VIII

In every case where a specific Aramaic term has, with any significant degree of probability, been identified behind Matthew's or Luke's κύριος or ἐπιστάτης, this term has been *rabbi/rabbouni*. In the absence of evidence to the contrary, this suggests that the only Aramaic title of address for Jesus reflected by Matthew's and Luke's κύριος and ἐπιστάτης was likely to have been *rabbi/rabbouni*.

As indicated in the preceding section, there appear to be at least five and probably as many as eight instances in the gospels in which *rabbi/rabbouni* was in fact translated into Greek as κύριος and/or ἐπιστάτης. Moreover, there are no examples in the gospels in which κύριος or ἐπιστάτης necessarily—or, in my judgment, even likely—reflect any Aramaic term other than *rabbi/rabbouni* in the earlier tradition. Thus, in light of the supporting evidence and in the absence of any evidence to the contrary, I conclude that each instance of κύριος or ἐπιστάτης in Matthew and Luke probably reflects either an earlier *rabbi/rabbouni* in the tradition or a redactional addition by the particular evangelist.

Conclusion and Implications

In summary: (1) if our only source were the Gospel of Mark (still regarded by most scholars as the earliest of the gospels), we would almost certainly assume that Jesus was characteristically addressed as *rabbi/rabbouni* and that he was rarely if ever addressed by any other title; (2) in at least two respects, the Markan portrayal of Jesus as *rabbi/rabbouni* appears to find confirmation in the Gospels of Matthew and John; (3) although, with only one exception, Jesus is never directly addressed in the so-called "Q," "M," and "L" materials as *rabbi/rabbouni*, there is little if anything in these materials that would serve to contradict the Markan portrayal of Jesus as *rabbi/rabbouni*; (4) both κύριος and ἐπιστάτης

clearly would have been regarded as appropriate Greek translations of *rabbi/rabbouni*—indeed, in the earlier period of Christian
tradition, better translations than διδάσκαλος; (5) the manuscript
tradition of the gospels indicates confusion at certain points as
to whether Jesus was addressed as διδάσκαλος, ἐπιστάτης, or
κύριος, and this may suggest that the terms were regarded as,
if not synonyms, at least interchangeable titles of address (perhaps as alternative translations of *rabbi/rabbouni*); (6) at least four
pericopes in the "established" text of the gospels appear to reflect, if not synonymous, at least interchangeable use of *rabbi/rab-
bouni*, διδάσκαλος, and/or κύριος as titles of address for Jesus;
(7) there appear to be at least five and probably as many as eight
instances in the gospels in which *rabbi/rabbouni* was in fact translated into Greek as κύριος and/or ἐπιστάτης; and (8) in every case
where a specific Aramaic term has, with any significant degree
of probability, been identified behind Matthew's or Luke's κύριος
or ἐπιστάτης, this term has been *rabbi/rabbouni*; in the absence of
evidence to the contrary, this suggests that the only Aramaic title
of address for Jesus reflected by Matthew's and Luke's κύριος and
ἐπιστάτης was likely to have been *rabbi/rabbouni*.

Given this array of evidence, the following reconstruction of
the gospel tradition appears likely: The most characteristic title
by which Jesus was addressed in the tradition of the Aramaic-
speaking church was *rabbi/rabbouni*. In the Greek-speaking church,
rabbi/rabbouni was sometimes simply transliterated into Greek
and retained as a title of address for Jesus, but increasingly it was
translated into Greek. Initially, it probably was translated into the
Greek terms most nearly synonymous with the root meaning of
rabbi/rabbouni: either κύριος or ἐπιστάτης. At this point, the meaning of κύριος (and ἐπιστάτης) would have been no different from
that of *rabbi/rabbouni*; that is, the Greek terms would have carried
no christological implications, just as *rabbi/rabbouni* carried none[67]

---

67. It is barely possible that the author of the Fourth Gospel has some
christological implications in mind when he has Mary Magdalene address the resurrected Jesus as *rabbouni* after she has recognized who he is
(John 20:16).

(clearly, however, κύριος would have lent itself to later christological development in a way that *rabbi/rabbouni* would not).[68] The
translation of *rabbi/rabbouni* as διδάσκαλος would then appear to
reflect a later situation in which the Aramaic *rabbi/rabbouni* came
to be applied primarily to Jewish religious leaders (i.e., experts
regarding Torah).

In short, it is likely that references in the gospels to Jesus as
κύριος and ἐπιστάτης reflect either an earlier Aramaic *rabbi/
rabbouni* in the tradition or simply the redactional additions of
Matthew and Luke. In the former case, the titles probably carry
no particular christological significance; in the latter, they may
or may not carry such significance, and each instance must be
judged on its own merits. In any case, it would appear that the
origin of κύριος and ἐπιστάτης as titles of address for Jesus in the
gospels is to found in his earlier designation as *rabbi/rabbouni* and
not in the application to him of some other Aramaic term such as
mar or *marî*.

As to why *rabbi/rabbouni* almost disappeared from the tradition, one can only speculate. One factor almost certainly was
simply the impulse (in the Greek-speaking church) to translate
Aramaic terms into their Greek equivalents (as, for example,
the move from "Messiah" to "Christ"). In the earlier period, this
would have produced ἐπιστάτης and particularly κύριος, which
correspond to the root meaning of *rabbi/rabbouni*; at a later period,
it would have produced διδάσκαλος, which reflects the more restricted meaning of *rabbi/rabbouni*. In addition, as the gap wid-
ened between developing Christianity and continuing Judaism,
the designation of Jesus by an Aramaic title increasingly reserved
for Jewish religious leaders would have been regarded as inap-

---

68. Κύριος was applied to various of the Hellenistic deities and to the
Roman Emperor. According to Joseph A. Fitzmyer ("Semitic Background
of the New Testament Κύριος-Title," 115–26), it was beginning to be applied to God in pre-Christian Palestinian Judaism. Contrary to common
assumptions, however, (ὁ) κύριος first appears in the LXX as a translation of the Tetragrammaton *YHWH* only in the fourth- and fifth-century
Christian copies.

propriate and even offensive to some Christians. Finally, it is clear that *rabbi/rabbouni* did not lend itself to christological development in the way that κύριος did. Because this last point would appear to be equally applicable to διδάσκαλος, however, it is my judgment that the first and second considerations were probably more important.

Chapter 15

Jesus and the
Tax Collectors

S. G. F. Brandon, among others, has maintained that, whatever else he may have been, Jesus was a social-political revolutionary who was generally sympathetic with and, to some extent, associated with the first century Palestinian liberation movement popularly known as the "Zealots"[1] and that, for this reason, he was executed by the Roman authorities as an insurrectionist.[2] One of Brandon's arguments for associating Jesus with the Zealots is the apparent fact that at least one member of Jesus' closest circle of followers, Simon the Zealot,[3] belonged to the revolutionary movement. This,

---

"Jesus and the Tax Collectors." *JBL* 97,2 (June 1978). Copyright © 1978 Society of Biblical Literature. Reprinted with permission.

1. Debate continues regarding the origin and history of the Zealot movement and the relationship between Zealots and "Sicarii." Morton Smith ("Zealots and Sicarii,") and Günther Baumbach ("Zeloten und Sikarier"), among others, argue that the Zealot group did not come into existence until 67–68 CE and should be distinguished from the Sicarii, who first followed Judas the Galilean in 6 CE. Martin Hengel (*Die Zeloten*), on the other hand, traces the origin of the Zealot movement directly to Judas the Galilean in 6 CE (cf. also his *Was Jesus A Revolutionist?* 10–14, esp. 11 n. 39). S. G. F. Brandon (*Jesus and the Zealots*), among others, agrees with Hengel on this point. In this paper, the term "Zealot" will be used indiscriminately to designate "all the resistance fighters without wishing to deny the differences which may have existed between them" (Cullmann, *Jesus and the Revolutionaries*, 4).

2. Most important among his writings on the subject is *Jesus and the Zealots: A Study of the Political Factors in Primitive Christianity*.

3. Luke 6:15 identifies Simon as "the one called Zealot" (*ton kaloumenon zēlōtēn*), and Acts 1:13 refers to him as "the Zealot" (*ho zēlōtēn*). Matt 10:4/ Mark 3:19, however, identify him as *ho kananaios* (usually translated as "the Cananaean"), but Brandon (*Jesus and the Zealots*, 42–44, 244) and

according to Brandon, shows that Jesus' own convictions and intentions were not incompatible with those of the Zealots.

In response to Brandon's argument, some scholars simply deny that the term *zēlōtēs* (or *kananaios*) as applied to Simon carries any political overtones,[4] and others suggest that, while Simon may have been a political revolutionary *before* becoming a follower of Jesus, his association with Jesus would necessarily have ruled out the possibility of any *continuing* Zealot activities or sentiments.[5] The most characteristic means, however, of attempting to refute Brandon's use of Simon as an indication of Jesus' Zealot affinities is to point out that, according to the gospels, Jesus also extended fellowship and even discipleship to tax collectors,[6] a class of people whom no Zealot or Zealot sympathizer would ever have accepted.[7] As Oscar Cullmann observes, "Greater enemies

most other scholars regard this as simply the Greek transliteration of the Aramaic word *qane'ānā'*, which means "zealot." Oscar Cullman (*State in the New Testament*, 18), who heatedly disputes Brandon's basic thesis regarding Jesus, agrees on this point regarding Simon and suggests (18–20) the possibility that still others of the Twelve, including Judas Iscariot, Simon Peter, and James and John the sons of Zebedee, were Zealots or former Zealots (cf. Brandon, *Jesus and the Zealots*, 203–5).

4. E.g., Edwards, *Jesus and the Politics of Violence*, 57; and Richardson, *Political Christ*, 41–44.

5. Cullmann (*Jesus and the Revolutionaries*, 44) says that "among the Twelve was one or more *former* Zealots" (emphasis added), and Hengel (*Was Jesus a Revolutionist?* 10 n. 34), among others, implies the same suggestion. For Brandon's opposing argument, see *Jesus and the Zealots*, 201 esp. n. 4, and for a response to Brandon, see Edwards, *Jesus and the Politics of Violence*, 55–56.

6. The Greek word *telōnēs* (plural *telōnai*) is usually translated as "tax collector," but a distinction should be made between "tax collector" and "toll collector." The former collected "the directed taxes, the poll or head tax and the land tax for the current rulers," while the latter collected "the myriad of minor taxes, sales taxes, customs taxes, taxes on transport" (Donahue, "Tax Collectors and Sinners," 42). It is generally to this latter group that the term *telōnēs* was applied in first-century Palestine, but, for the sake of simplicity, this paper will follow the usual custom and translate *telōnēs* as "tax collector."

7. E.g., Hengel, review of *Jesus and the Zealots*, 236; Edwards, *Jesus and the Politics of Violence*, 58; Cullmann, *Jesus and the Revolutionaries*, 10, 44; cf. Klassen, "Jesus and the Zealot Option," 16–17.

than Zealots and tax-collectors cannot be imagined,"[8] because tax collectors worked for the hated Roman authorities, while Zealots were dedicated to the overthrow of the Romans. It would seem that if Jesus did, in fact, include both a Zealot and a tax collector among the circle of his disciples, either one or the other or perhaps both must have renounced their previous commitments upon joining his band.

Brandon himself gives little attention to this problem, but he does suggest that the individual tax collectors who followed Jesus, such as Zacchaeus[9] and Levi or Matthew,[10] as well as the unnamed tax collectors with whom he associated,[11] sensed an "incompatibility" between their profession and Jesus' call and thus needed a "conversion" that involved "repentance," while a Zealot, such as Simon, felt no such need.[12] The late Bishop James A. Pike even

---

There has been some debate in recent years regarding the specific reasons for the juxtaposition of *telōnai* with "sinners" (*hamartōloi*), "Gentiles" (*ethnikoi*), and "prostitutes" (*pornai*) in the Synoptic Gospels and for the generally negative view taken of them, not only in the gospels but also in Jewish literature. Norman Perrin (*Rediscovering the Teaching of Jesus,* 92–102), for example, sees the *telōnai* as Jews who have betrayed their heritage by living like Gentiles; cf. also Farmer, "Who are the 'Tax Collectors and Sinners'?" Joachim Jeremias (*Jerusalem in the Time of Jesus,* 303–12; "Zöllner und Sünder"), on the other hand, regards them as persons following an occupation that led to dishonesty. Donahue ("Tax Collectors and Sinners," 59–61) concludes that, during the historical ministry of Jesus in Galilee, his association with the *telōnai* would have been seen primarily as association with persons scorned because of their real or suspected dishonesty, but that there were periods in the formation of the gospel tradition when fellowship with *telōnai* would have been construed as fellowship with those in the service of the Roman oppressors.

8. Cullmann, *State in the New Testament,* 22.

9. Luke 19:1–10.

10. Matt 9:9/Mark 2:14/Luke 5:27–28; cf. Matt 10:3.

11. Matt 9:10–13/Mark 2:15–17/Luke 5:29–32; Matt 11:19/Luke 7:34; Luke 15:1–2.

12. Brandon, *Jesus and the Zealots,* 201 and esp. n. 4; for a response, see Edwards, *Jesus and the Politics of Violence,* 55–56. Otto Michel ("τελώνης," 105) states "that quite obviously neither John nor Jesus demanded in principle that toll-collectors should give up their profession."

suggested that Matthew/Levi might have been a secret member of the "underground" revolutionary (i.e., Zealot) movement, with which he also associated Jesus,[13] and that Jesus' association with such people as the tax collector Zacchaeus might have been motivated in part by his need to obtain monetary contributions for the support of his movement.[14] Pike's suggestions are little more than speculation, however, and Brandon cites no real evidence to support his view that the tax collectors underwent "conversion" upon becoming disciples while the Zealots did not. Thus, in order to resolve the conflicting claims that Jesus had one or more disciples who were Zealots and that he associated with tax collectors, as well as for its intrinsic importance, it is necessary to explore the crucial question: What was the relationship between Jesus and tax collectors?

On the face of it, there appears to be solid evidence in the gospels that Jesus not only associated and even ate with tax collectors, thus drawing upon himself the wrath of the Pharisees (and surely also of the Zealots!), but that he even chose a tax collector as a member of his inner circle of the Twelve.[15] A careful examination of the relevant materials in the gospels, however, suggests that the evidence is by no means as solid or unambiguous as has generally been assumed. The following points emerge from such an examination.

---

13. Pike and Kennedy, *The Wilderness Revolt*, 126.

14. Pike and Kennedy, *The Wilderness Revolt*, 153. Note that Zacchaeus was "rich."

15. The relevant passages are Matt 9:9–13/Mark 2:13–17/Luke 5:27–32; Matt 5:46–47 (cf. Luke 6:32–34); Matt 11:18–19a/Luke 7:33–34; Matt 10:3 (cf. Mark 3:18/Luke 6:15/Acts 1:13b); Matt18:15–17 (cf. Luke 17:3–4); Matt 21:31b–32/Luke 7:29–30; Luke 3:12–14; Luke 15:1–2; Luke 18:9–14; Luke 19:1–10. For the historicity and centrality of this feature of Jesus' ministry, see, e.g., Bornkamm, *Jesus of Nazareth*, esp. 78–81; Farmer, "Historical Essay on the Humanity of Jesus Christ," esp. 110–26; Perrin, *Rediscovering the Teaching of Jesus*, 102–8; Jeremias, *The Parables of Jesus*, 124–46. On the general attitude toward tax collectors in the ancient world, as well as the specifically Jewish attitude, see, e.g., Michel, "τελώνης," 99–103.

I

The first point to be noted is that traditions regarding Jesus' association with tax collectors are found only in the Synoptic Gospels. Such traditions are absent from the Fourth Gospel and, for that matter, from all of the other New Testament writings. In the Fourth Gospel, there is no mention at all of tax collectors, and the criticisms that are raised against Jesus have very little to do with his associations,[16] focusing rather on such matters as his claim to divine sonship,[17] his place of origin,[18] his practice of healing on the Sabbath,[19] and the charge that he was a Samaritan and/or was demon-possessed.[20] The historical value of the Fourth Gospel is, if course, a matter of considerable scholarly debate,[21] and arguments from silence carry relatively little weight, but it is of interest and perhaps significant that there is at least one line of tradition that preserves no reference to Jesus associating with tax collectors.

II

The second point to be noted is that the Synoptic Gospels preserve traditions suggesting that Jesus held a highly negative view

---

16. Note, however, Judas' criticism of Jesus for allowing Mary to anoint his feet with expensive ointment (John 12:2–8; cf. Matt 26:6–13/Mark 14:3–9/Luke 7:37–50; in Luke's version, it is stated and emphasized that the woman is a "sinner"). Cf. also the wedding in Cana (John 2:1–11) and Jesus' association with the (immoral) Samaritan woman (John 4:7–42), which may hint at the kinds of associations that, in the Synoptic Gospels, make Jesus the object of Pharisaic criticism. The story of the woman taken in adultery (John 7:53–8:11) might also be relevant here; although the manuscript evidence weighs heavily against its inclusion, it does preserve a tradition of Jesus dealing sympathetically with a woman who was a "sinner."

17. John 5:18; 10:33, 36; 19:7; cf. 6:41, 42.

18. John 1:46; 7:26, 41, 42, 52.

19. John 5:9, 16, 17; 7:23; 9:14–16.

20. John 7:20; 8:48, 52; 10:20. The charge that he was a Samaritan might also be related to the view that he associated with "outcasts"; note also the charge that he himself was a "sinner" (John 9:17, 24).

21. See, e.g., Dodd, *Historical Tradition in the Fourth Gospel*.

regarding tax collectors. Such traditions appear particularly, but not exclusively, in Matthew. Matt 5:46–47, for example, has Jesus juxtaposing tax collectors with Gentiles in a manner that is most unflattering to both:

> For if you love those who love you, what reward have you? Do not even the tax collectors do the same? And if you salute only your brothers, what more are you doing than others? Do not even the Gentiles do the same?

Such an association of tax collectors and Gentiles would apparently have been widely accepted in first-century Palestinian Judaism,[22] but it does, for most modern readers, sound strange on the lips of Jesus. A comparison of Matt 5:46–47 with the parallel in Luke 6:32–34 is instructive: Luke has "sinners" where Matthew has "tax collectors" and "Gentiles." The problem of the chronological and literary relationship between Matthew and Luke cannot be treated here, but, on the face of it, it appears more likely that the later tradition would have substituted "sinners" for "tax collectors" and "Gentiles" than *vice versa*.[23] Even if the opposite is assumed, however, or if the two versions are assumed to have derived from separate sayings of Jesus, or even if the authenticity of both is denied, the highly derogatory nature of the reference to "tax collectors" and "Gentiles" is clear: Someone thought, correctly or incorrectly, that such a reference on the lips of Jesus was not inappropriate.[24]

---

22. See, e.g., Michel, "τελώνης," 101–3; Jeremias, *Jerusalem in the Time of Jesus*, 310–22; Perrin, *Rediscovering the Teaching of Jesus*, 93–94.

23. For further arguments regarding the priority of the Matthean version, see, e.g., Michel, "τελώνης," 103 and esp. n. 146; Black, *Aramaic Approach*, 179–81.

24. William R. Farmer (letter to me dated April 28, 1976) maintains that the references to tax collectors and Gentiles in this logion would not have been inconsistent with accounts of Jesus eating and otherwise associating with tax collectors: "Consider this: A pastor in Norway during the occupation by the Nazis addresses his flock: 'If you love those who love you what reward have you? Do not even Quisling and his associates do the same? And if you salute only those of your ethnic group, what are you

Similarly, Matt 18:15–17 has Jesus associating tax collectors with Gentiles in a most unflattering manner:

> If your brother sins against you, go and tell him his fault, between you and him alone. If he listens to you, you have gained your brother. But if he does not listen, take one or two others along with you, that every word may be confirmed by the evidence of two or three witnesses. If he refuses to listen to them, tell it to the church; and if he refuses to listen even to the church, let him be to you as a Gentile and a tax collector.

Luke 17:3 is parallel to the first part of this passage, but Luke has no parallel to the latter part with its reference to "a Gentile and a tax collector." This fact, together with Matthew's use of the word "church" (*ekklēsia*) and the implication of an organized institution, has led many modern scholars to deny that the latter part of the passage preserves an authentic saying of Jesus.[25] It appears clear, however, that Matthew's material does come from a Palestinian, not a Hellenistic, milieu,[26] and the possibility can by no means be ruled out that the passage contains traces of an authentic saying or at least an authentic motif in the teaching of Jesus. In any case, here, as in Matt 5:46–47, someone thought, correctly or incorrectly, that such a reference to "a Gentile and a tax collector" on the lips of Jesus was not inappropriate.[27]

---

doing more than others, do not even the Nazis do this much? You must love your enemies.' It would have been scandalous for such a pastor to have been seen eating with collaborators—but it would not have been inconsistent with the teaching in this logion. This is prophetic irony and is characteristic of Jesus."

25. E.g., Bultmann, *History of the Synoptic Tradition*, rev. ed., 146, 409. For an opposing view, see, e.g., Kistemaker, *Gospels in Current Study*, 83.

26. Bultmann (*History of the Synoptic Tradition*, rev. ed., 141) agrees; see also, e.g., Michel, "τελώνης," 103–4 esp. n. 147.

27. Bultmann (*History of the Synoptic Tradition*, rev. ed., 141) believes that the Lukan parallel to the first verse of the passage was based on an "older version" than the Matthean passage, but he "can offer no conjecture as to the origin of the older version"; he suggests no similar view regarding the latter part of the Matthean passage, however.

It is true, of course, that both of the unflattering references
to tax collectors just cited are found only in Matthew, with the
Lukan parallels not containing such references and Mark having
no parallels. Thus, it is possible that the references express only
the particular views of Matthew[28] or of his source(s) or perhaps of
the Palestinian church. There are other passages in the Synoptic
Gospels, however, that have generally been interpreted as associating Jesus more positively with tax collectors but that, upon
closer examination, are at least ambiguous and more likely even
derogatory. One such passage is Matt 11:18–19a, with its virtually
identical parallel in Luke 7:33–34. Here, Jesus complains of his critics: "For John came neither eating nor drinking, and they say, 'He
has a demon'; the Son of Man came eating and drinking, and they
say, 'Behold, a glutton and a drunkard, a friend of tax collectors
and sinners!'" The association of tax collectors with "sinners," the
primary parallelism between "a glutton and a drunkard"[29] and
"a friend of tax collectors and sinners," and the secondary parallelism between the entire epithet and the charge that John had a
"demon" all indicate the extremely serious and derogatory nature
of the charge against Jesus. Furthermore, it must be clear that the
charge of demon possession against John is regarded by the tradition as untrue, and this may well imply that the parallel charge
of being "a glutton and a drunkard, a friend of tax collectors and
sinners" against Jesus was originally regarded by the tradition as
equally untrue.[30] In any case, the passage, in and of itself, cannot

---

28. The names "Matthew," "Mark," and "Luke" will henceforth be
used to designate the authors of the Synoptic Gospels, without in any
way, however, implying an acceptance of the traditional views regarding
authorship.

29. Farmer ("Who are the 'Tax Collectors and Sinners'?" 4) insists that
anthrōpos phagos kai oinopotēs should be translated not "a glutton and a
drunkard" as in the RSV but simply "a man who eats, and drinks wine,"
namely with tax collectors and sinners. Cf. also Perrin, *Rediscovering the
Teaching of Jesus*, 105–6. In reply, it can only be pointed out that the terms
normally mean "glutton and drunkard" (see, e.g., BAG 564, 859).

30. See below on this point. Bultmann (*History of the Synoptic Tradition*,
rev. ed., 172, 165, cf. 155–56) insists that the passage is "a community
product." Perrin (*Rediscovering the Teaching of Jesus*, 120–21), on the other
hand, argues strongly for its authenticity.

be regarded as necessarily suggesting that Jesus associated with tax collectors. Indeed, just as Matt 5:46–47 and 18:15–17 place on the lips of Jesus a highly unflattering association of tax collectors with Gentiles, this passage similarly places on his lips an association of tax collectors with sinners.

A second passage that is often interpreted as attributing to Jesus a sympathetic attitude toward tax collectors is Matt 21:31b–32, which reads:

> Jesus said to them, "Truly I say to you, the tax collectors and the harlots go into the kingdom of God before you. For John came to you in the way of righteousness, and you did not believe him, but the tax collectors and the harlots believed him; and even when you saw it, you did not afterward repent and believe him."

Here, tax collectors are associated with "harlots" in much the same way as Matt 5:46–47 and 18:15–17 associate them with Gentiles and Matt 11:18–19a/Luke 7:33–34 associate them with "sinners."[31] Although this passage does speak of tax collectors believing John and thus entering the kingdom of God,[32] the implication appears clear that this is regarded by all parties concerned as a highly unusual and surprising development. The saying, taken on its own terms, is by no means a commendation of tax collectors and harlots; rather, it is a ringing condemnation of the Jewish religious leaders, who are regarded as *even worse* than the tax collectors

---

31. Note that the rather indirect Lukan parallel (7:29) associates tax collectors not with harlots but with "all the people." A similar tendency is seen in Luke 5:29, which reads "tax collectors and others" where Matt 9:10/Mark 2:15 have "tax collectors and sinners."

32. The fact that Matthew here uses "kingdom of God" rather than his more usual term, "kingdom of heaven," may indicate that this saying came to him rather firmly fixed in the tradition. The saying does not occur, however, in the other gospels. Jeremias (*Parables of Jesus*, 80–81) argues cogently that v. 32 was originally a separate saying that has become attached to v. 31b (probably in the pre-Matthean tradition) through verbal association ("the tax collectors and the harlots"). He regards v. 31b as the original conclusion of the preceding parable regarding the two sons (Matt 21:28–31a). See also Perrin, *Rediscovering the Teaching of Jesus*, 119, cf. 75, where he maintains the authenticity of v. 32.

and harlots. The first part of the saying might accurately be paraphrased: "Why, I tell you, *even* the tax collectors and the harlots go
into the kingdom of God before you!"[33]

At this point in the discussion, specific attention must be called
to the general tendency of the Synoptic tradition, not only in the
passages already noted but elsewhere as well, to associate tax collectors in an unflattering manner with "Gentiles,"[34] "sinners,"[35]
and "harlots."[36] Joachim Jeremias asserts that "the deep contempt
expressed in such designations shows that these phrases were
coined by Jesus' opponents."[37] This can only be assumed, however, if the prior assumption is made that Jesus in no way shared
the popular view regarding tax collectors, and, as yet, no compelling evidence for this prior assumption has appeared. Thus, the
question at least remains open.

It should also be noted that tax collectors are contrasted with
"the righteous" and are regarded, as least in Luke, as need-
ing "repentance." Jesus is represented as comparing himself to
a "physician," the tax collectors and sinners to "those who are
sick," and perhaps, by implication, the scribes and/or Pharisees to
"those who are well"; he also refers to the tax collectors as "sinners" and perhaps, again by implication, to the Pharisees as "the
righteous."[38] It is, of course, possible that a form of sarcasm is intended and that the real meaning is something such as "so-called
sinners" and "self-styled" or "so-called righteous," but there is
nothing in the text of this particular passage that either necessi-
tates or implies such an interpretation. The words, if taken simply
at face value, assume the popular distinction between "sinners"
and "righteous" and assign the tax collectors to the former
group.[39] Similarly, the emphasis, either explicit or implicit, upon

---

33. The presence of *amen* ("truly") appears to indicate not merely a
casual comment but rather a solemn pronouncement.

34. Matt 5:46–47; 18:15–17.

35. Matt 11:18–19a/Luke 7:33–34; Matt 9:10–13/Mark 2:14–17/Luke
5:29–32; Luke 15:1–2; 18:9–14; 19:1–10.

36. Matt 21:31b–32.

37. Jeremias, *New Testament Theology*, 109. See, e.g., Matt 11:18–19a/
Luke 7:33–34.

38. Matt 9:12–13/Mark 2:17/Luke 5:31–32.

39. Note a similar distinction, e.g., Luke 15:7.

"repentance" as associated with tax collectors, even though it is largely confined to Luke, is significant.[40]

Finally, it must be pointed out that a careful examination even of the Lukan materials, which have most often been interpreted as revealing a more sympathetic attitude toward tax collectors,[41] shows at least traces of essentially the same negative evaluation of tax collectors as has been found in the other materials already discussed. To be sure, there are certain features in Luke that might suggest a more positive attitude toward tax collectors than is found, for example, in Matthew.[42] Nevertheless, an

---

40. Luke 15:1–2 (note the immediately following parable of the lost sheep, lost coin, and prodigal son, with the words of "application" in vv. 7, 10); 18:9–14; 19:1–10.

41. Luke's interest in and concern for the poor, women, Samaritans, Gentiles, sinners and other "outcasts" (such as tax collectors) have often been noted; see, e.g., Taylor, "Luke, Gospel of," 183.

42. In three of the four Matthean passages expressing or implying a negative attitude toward tax collectors, Luke either has no parallel to the reference to tax collectors (Matt 18:15–17/Luke 17:3) or his version reads so as to imply no such negative attitude toward tax collectors (Matt 5:46–47/Luke 6:32–34; Matt 21:31b–32/Luke 7:29–30). Similarly, in the only passage regarding tax collectors found in all three of the Synoptic Gospels (Matt 9:9–13/Mark 2:13–17/Luke 5:27–32), Luke is the only one of the three to explicitly identify the man called by Jesus as "a tax collector," and, at one point in the story (v. 29), Luke has "tax collectors and others," where both Matthew and Mark have "tax collectors and sinners" (Luke does at times refer to "tax collectors and sinners" [5:30; 7:33–34; 15:1–2; cf. 18:9–14; 19:10], but this association occurs initially on the lips of Jesus' critics [5:30; 7:33–34; 15:2; cf. 19:7] and probably came to Luke already a firm part of the tradition). Finally, it should be noted that in Luke 3:12–14 John the Baptist apparently accepts and baptizes tax collectors (cf. Matt 21:31b–32; Luke 7:29–30), without stating or implying that they should renounce their occupation. The authenticity of this last passage, however, is hotly debated, with Bultmann (*History of the Synoptic Tradition*, rev. ed., 145, 147), among others, tending to regard it as a "Christian construction"; Jeremias (*New Testament Theology*, 48 and esp. n. 4), however, regards the tradition as authentic and refers to Sahlin, "Die Früchte der Umkehr," for a discussion of the matter. (The late Bishop James A. Pike [Pike and Kennedy, *The Wilderness Revolt*, 81–83] cited, with cautious approval, the earlier view of Robert Eisler that the "conversion" of the tax collectors meant that the revenues, which they would continue to collect, would now be delivered not to the Roman authorities as before, but rather to the "liberation movement.")

examination of a number of passages, some of them found *only* in Luke, greatly weakens the force of any such suggestions. In the parable of the Pharisee and the tax collector,[43] for example, Jesus contrasts favorably a tax collector who repents with a Pharisee who does not.[44] It should be noted, however, that the tax collector is placed in the same category with "extortioners," "unjust," and "adulterers" and that he accepts and emphasizes this categorization by referring to himself as "the sinner" and praying for mercy. The parable, then, is not a commendation of the tax collector, except insofar as he recognizes his sinful state, but rather a ringing condemnation of the Pharisee and a call for repentance. In this respect, it is quite similar to Matt 21:31b, which has earlier been paraphrased as: "Why, I tell you, *even* the tax collectors and the harlots go into the kingdom of God before you!" Indeed, it is even possible that the parable of the Pharisee and the tax collector was created within the early church on the basis of the saying in Matt 21:31b. Similarly, in the story of Zacchaeus,[45] Jesus eats in the home of a tax collector, who repents and receives "salvation." I shall suggest later that this story may well be simply a variant version of the call of Levi/Matthew.[46] Let it suffice here to note that Zacchaeus is referred to as "a sinner," that Jesus does not challenge this judgment but rather confirms it by speaking of him as one of "the lost," and that Zacchaeus does, in fact, "repent" (whether this "repentance" includes a renunciation of his occupation is not clear). The parable of the Pharisee and the tax collector and the story of Zacchaeus cannot, therefore, be used to show that Jesus was sympathetic to or associated with tax collectors without explicit "repentance" on their part. Furthermore, it should be noted that Luke prefaces the parables of the lost sheep, the lost

43. Luke 18:9–14.

44. Both Jeremias (*Parables of Jesus,* 139–44) and Perrin (*Rediscovering the Teaching of Jesus,* 122) have argued strongly for the essential authenticity of the parable as a saying of Jesus, acknowledging, however, that "the generalizing conclusion" in v. 14b is an independent saying that was not originally a part of the parable (cf. Luke 14:11; Matt 23:12; 18:4 for other occurrences of essentially the same saying).

45. Luke 19:1–10.

46. Matt 9:9–13/Mark 2:13–17/Luke 5:27–32.

coin, and the prodigal son with the report that the Pharisees were criticizing Jesus for associating with tax collectors and sinners[47] and that two of the parables are followed immediately by specific words of "application" that speak of sinners who repent.[48] Clearly, Luke intends these parables to explain and justify Jesus' association with tax collectors and sinners, but these tax collectors and sinners are obviously regarded as standing in need of repentance. Thus, it is not at all clear that the traditions included in Luke are significantly more sympathetic toward tax collectors than are those found in Matthew; the only real difference is that Luke does not have the *explicitly* derogatory references, and this fact probably reflects more the situation and views of a redactor than the situation and views of the historical Jesus.[49]

III

The third point to be noted is that the references to intimate contacts between Jesus and tax collectors appear, for the most part, in the form of accusation on the lips of others, and it is not at all clear that these accusations are based upon fact. Reference has already been made to the saying attributed to Jesus in Matt 11:18–19a, with its virtually identical parallel in Luke 7:33–34: "For John came neither eating nor drinking, and they say, 'He has a demon'; the Son of Man came eating and drinking, and they say, 'Behold, a glutton and a drunkard, a friend of tax collectors and sinners!'" The essentially negative view of tax collectors reflected in this passage has already been discussed. Norman Perrin, among others, has argued that the charge against Jesus must have been based upon fact and that "it refers to the practice of Jesus in holding table-fellowship with 'tax collectors and other Jews who had made themselves as Gentiles.'"[50] I have already suggested, however, that the implication in this passage is that the charge against Jesus

---

47. Luke 15:1–2.

48. Luke 15:7, 10.

49. Michel ("τελώνης," 104) agrees that "Lk's approach is not in the last analysis much different [from Matthew's]."

50. Perrin, *Rediscovering the Teaching of Jesus*, 106; cf. the entire discussion, 105–6.

is *not* true. Surely, it is not necessary to assume that every charge made against Jesus was true! Most scholars assume, for example, that the charge of sedition was untrue, and it is not widely held that Jesus cast out demons by the power of Satan. In this particular case, the parallelism in the passage may well suggest that the charge is regarded as false. It is clear that the charge against John is regarded by the tradition as untrue, and this suggests that the parallel charge against Jesus was originally regarded by the tradition as equally untrue. At a later stage of transmission, the church may have come to believe that the charge had been based upon actual fact; indeed, the charge itself might reflect a charge that was later brought against the church rather than a charge against the historical Jesus.[51]

Such an interpretation, of course, leaves unanswered the question of the basis of the charge, but several possibilities suggest themselves. *First*, the passage itself calls attention to the contrast between John and Jesus, and the charge may be based on nothing more than the fact that Jesus was not an ascetic, as John apparently was. *Second*, there may have been something about Jesus' eating and drinking habits—e.g., the fact that he apparently was not overly punctilious regarding the prescribed fasts, ritual purifications, and the like[52]—that provoked the charge. *Third*, the phrase, "a friend of tax collectors and sinners," may have been used in somewhat the same way as "nigger-lover" has been used, particularly in the southern part of the United States (anyone who lived in certain sections of the South during the 1950s and early 1960s, for example, knows that it did not require extensive or intimate contact with black people, and certainly not eating with them, to gain the epithet for oneself). *Fourth*, it may be that some "tax collectors and sinners" actually were attracted by Jesus' message and that they did at times come to hear him, but this does not necessarily imply that he ate with

---

51. This might reflect the situation of the Palestinian church during the chaotic period immediately preceding the Jewish War, particularly if the church, as is often held, refused to participate in the uprising of the Jews.

52. See, e.g., Matt 15:1–20/Mark 7:1–23; cf. Luke 11:37–40.

them or in any other way associated intimately with them. Luke 15:1–2, with its interesting *non sequitur*, is instructive here: "Now the tax collectors and sinners were all *drawing near to hear him*. And the Pharisees and the scribes murmured, saying, 'This man *receives sinners and eats with them*.'" The report is simply that "the tax collectors and sinners were all *drawing near to hear him*," but the charge is that "this man *receives sinners and eats with them*." It is not at all uncommon for charges against individuals to be exaggerated, and this may well have happened in the case of Jesus and tax collectors: It may have been true that "tax collectors and sinners" came to hear him and that he did not turn them away (thus, in a sense, "receiving" them) but still untrue that he ate with them. As a basis for provoking public sentiment against him, however, the latter charge (whether true or false) would have carried great power. *Fifth*, it is possible that Jesus did refer to tax collectors in his preaching, not in any positive manner but simply to emphasize the extreme obstinacy of his critics, who refused to accept his message of the coming kingdom.[53] *Sixth*, it should be noted that Matt 11:18–19a/Luke 7:33–34 does not even charge that Jesus *ate* with tax collectors and sinners but only that he was their "friend"; the *eating* charge may be a later development[54] and may have been based upon a combination of the former charge and complaints about his general eating habits. In short, if it were not for the presence in the gospels of two reports that Jesus actually did eat with tax collectors[55] and the reference to the presence of a tax collector among the Twelve,[56] I strongly suspect that the charges against Jesus of associating with tax collectors would quite generally be dismissed as untrue, or at least as exaggerations.

---

53. Matt 21:31b ("Truly, I say to you, [even] the tax collectors and the harlots go into the kingdom of God before you") and 5:46–47 ("Do not even the tax collectors [and Gentiles] do the same?") appear to suggest this, as well as perhaps the parable of the Pharisee and the tax collector (Luke 18:9–14).

54. Cf. again Luke 15:1–2.

55. Matt 9:9–13/Mark 2:13–17/Luke 5:27–32; Luke 19:1–10.

56. Matt 10:3; cf. Mark 3:18; Luke 6:15; Acts 1:13b.

IV

The fourth point to be noted is that only two passages in the gospels actually report that Jesus *did*, in fact, hold table fellowship with tax collectors (elsewhere, this is only *charged* by his critics), and both of these passages can quite plausibly be regarded as artificial constructions by either the gospel writers or their sources. The first of these passages is Matt 9:9–13/Mark 2:13–17/ Luke 5:27–32, which is the only reference to tax collectors found in all three of the Synoptic Gospels (it is also the only reference to tax collectors in Mark). The passage reports the call of Levi (or Matthew), who was "sitting at the tax office," together with an occasion when Jesus was criticized by Jewish religious leaders for "eating with tax collectors and sinners" and replied by making his famous distinction between "those who are well" (the "righteous") and "those who are sick" (the "sinners"). Because only Luke connects the call story and the meal story in anything other than a quite abrupt and awkward manner, it is widely held that the call story and the meal story were originally separate traditions.[57] The present discussion, therefore, will deal only with the latter tradition concerning Jesus eating with tax collectors and sinners, with the call story being reserved for later treatment.

The passage, as it now stands, displays a somewhat ambivalent attitude toward tax collectors, and it is this attitude that has been almost universally accepted as reflecting the views of Jesus himself. On the negative side, tax collectors are associated with "sinners" (as opposed to the "righteous"), described as "those who are sick" and who thus "need a physician" (as opposed to "those who are well" and who thus do not need a "physician"), and, at least in Luke's version, are regarded as in need of "repentance." This is all what would be expected in the light of the other materials that have been examined. On the positive side, however, we find, for the first time in our study, that Jesus does, in fact, eat with them and that he verbally defends his action before his critics.

---

57. See, e.g., Anderson, *Gospel of Mark*, 102–3.

It is my judgment, however, although I obviously cannot conclusively demonstrate it, that this passage is an artificial construction,[58] based upon a saying that the tradition attributes to Jesus ("Those who are well have no need of a physician, but those who are sick do"),[59] combined with the charge, already observed elsewhere, of Jesus' critics ("He is eating with tax collectors and sinners").[60] The charge has already been discussed, and it has been suggested that it may very well have been a false charge. Regarding the artificial construction of the passage, Bultmann summarizes the evidence as it relates to Mark's version, which he regards as the earliest:

> The point of the story, expressed in Jesus' words in v. 17, has no very close connection with the situation described. *The saying was thus originally unattached, and v. 15 is simply a story designed for it.* The situation comes about through the quite impossible appearance of the γραμματεῖς τῶν Φαρισαίων[61] and the fact that the disciples are questioned and Jesus answers.[62] The meal seemed to be a suitable occasion, since

58. Bultmann (*History of the Synoptic Tradition*, rev. ed., 47) asserts that "the artificiality of the composition is clear as day."

59. The authenticity of the saying itself is debated; see, e.g., Bultmann, *History of the Synoptic Tradition*, rev. ed., 104–5. It is possible that the saying may also have included the words, "I came not to call the righteous, but sinners." Bultmann (155–56, cf. 412), however, argues that all sayings that speak of Jesus having "come" are likely church products because such terminology indicates a view of "the historical appearance of Jesus as a whole" in the past, and he regards these words as "a secondary explanation of the saying about the physician" (92), which, however, probably originated in the Palestinian rather than the Hellenistic church (163). On this, cf. also Anderson, *Gospel of Mark*, 105.

60. Luke 15:2; cf. 19:7.

61. See Bultmann, *History of the Synoptic Tradition*, rev. ed., 18 n. 3: "The situation is quite impossible. Whence and why do the Pharisees come? Do they arrive during the meal, or when it is over? It is unthinkable that they should be part of the company sitting at meat! Moreover the article in οἱ γραμματεῖς shows that they are the enemies of Jesus who were well known to the hearers of the story." See further, p. 66.

62. Bultmann, (*History of the Synoptic Tradition*, rev. ed., 49) suggests that the fact of the question about Jesus' conduct being put to the disciples rather than directly to Jesus indicates the secondary nature of the

Jesus' use of καλεῖν would be understood as reflecting its use in an invitation to table fellowship, and since table fellowship in general is used symbolically for fellowship as such. A primitive sensitiveness would not feel that it was the wrong place for the saying in v. 17. It is instructive for the history of the tradition to note that copyists like Matthew and Luke take pains to make the incomprehensible situation of vv. 15f. somewhat more understandable; and equally that Matthew at this point uses the quotation from scripture that he also inserts into Mark's text at 12.7.[63] (*Emphasis added*)

If this suggestion is accepted, then the narrative portion of the passage, which reports that Jesus actually ate with tax collectors and sinners, is a creation of the early church,[64] and we are left simply with the charge against Jesus that he ate with tax collectors and sinners and the saying of Jesus, which originally circulated independently and may or may not have had anything to do with the charge (which, itself, may well have been untrue).

The second passage actually reporting that Jesus ate with tax collectors, the story of Zacchaeus (Luke 19:1–10), has also been examined carefully by Bultmann, who concludes that it is "not an unitary composition":

Vv. 9f. follows on v. 7. This means that either vv. 7, 9f. must be regarded as secondary, or—much more probably—v. 8.

---

tradition, for here "the Church is the means by which man's relation to Jesus is mediated to those outside." It may be, too, that the real criticism was intended against the conduct of the church in its dealings with "sinners" rather than against the historical Jesus, which, again, would be an indication of the secondary nature of the tradition.

63. Bultmann, *History of the Synoptic Tradition*, rev. ed., 18, cf., e.g., 47, 48, 61, 331. It is clear that Bultmann regards the Markan version as the source for the Matthean and Lukan versions, but this assumption is not essential to his basic argument here. See Bultmann, 384, 395, for views of other scholars regarding the unity of the passage.

64. Bultmann (*History of the Synoptic Tradition*, rev. ed., 39–69) discusses "The Form and History of Apophthegms," showing how, in his view, narrative settings often were created by the church for sayings attributed to Jesus.

In v. 9 πρὸς αὐτόν cannot mean 'with reference to him' but only 'to him'; if this is to be eliminated according to some MSS then the difficulty arises that Jesus suddenly begins to talk about Zacchaeus in the third person to those who are present, and this is much more possible if, with some texts, we read πρὸς αὐτούς. Further, Jesus does not establish his relationship to Zacchaeus by appealing to his morality, as v. 8 seems to suppose, but on the simple fact that Zacchaeus is as much a Jew as the rest. The detailed introduction is far better matched with v. 9 as its point than with v. 8. And so we may hold Luke himself responsible for this latter verse; and its moral suits him. Likewise we can ascribe the addition of v. 10 to him, a verse which is appended in different texts to 9.56 and Matt. 18.11 as well. *What is left is a scene that is unitary in conception, though manifestly imaginary, an extended version of Mk. 2.14 which, combined with vv. 15–17 gave rise to this story.* That Zacchaeus did not, like Levi, 'follow' Jesus is hardly due to his being converted with his family, as Wellhausen mistakenly supposed from τῷ οἴκῳ τούτῳ in v. 9, but rather to the fact that the story had its origin much later, when 'following' could less easily be symbolized by the physical act.[65] (*Emphasis added*)

If, then, this story is an extended version of Matt 9:9–13/Mark 2:13–17/Luke 5:27–32, as Bultmann suggests,[66] it obviously provides no independent testimony regarding Jesus' possible association with tax collectors. Certain problems remain, however,

---

65. Bultmann, *History of the Synoptic Tradition*, rev. ed., 33–34, but cf. 388, where he mentions other scholars who regard the story as based upon actual facts.

66. Bultmann (*History of the Synoptic Tradition*, rev. ed., 62) calls attention to "variation in motif" as one evidence of "the generating power" of the apophthegms and cites Mark 2:15–17 and Luke 19:1–10 as examples of "the theme of a visit to a tax-gatherer." He also (pp. 56–57) lists this passage as an example of an "ideal" apophthegm (i.e., one that embodies "a truth in some metaphorical sort of situation which, by reason of its wider reference, gives the apothegms their symbolic character").

relating primarily to the source of the place name, Jericho, and the personal name, Zacchaeus. The place name may have been added to the tradition quite arbitrarily; more likely, however, it refers back to the same place name in the immediately preceding passage.[67] The personal name appears to present more serious problems, for it is obviously different from the corresponding personal names in Matt 9:9–13 and parallels. It is clear, however, that Luke (or the pre-Lukan tradition) could not simply repeat the name "Levi," for this would betray the fact that the two passages were variants of the same story; it was necessary, therefore, to use some other name. The choice may have been based on irony: the name in Hebrew means "the righteous one" or "the pure one," which contrasts strikingly with his designation as a "sinner" and one of the "lost."

It is also relevant that the story of Zacchaeus has the same general literary structure as Matt 9:9–13 and parallels and pictures essentially the same kind of situation, the same criticism of Jesus, and the same type of reply by Jesus.

V

The fifth point to be noted is that the specific identification of one of the Twelve as a tax collector is problematic, to say the least. Only Matthew (10:3), in listing the Twelve, refers to Matthew as "the tax collector"; the other lists simply include his name with no further identification.[68] It may also be of some significance that, although Mark and Luke list Matthew after Bartholomew and *before* Thomas, who is followed by James the [son] of Alphaeus, the first gospel lists Matthew *after* Thomas, who follows Bartholomew, and immediately before James the [son] of Alphaeus; in other words, the Gospel of Matthew places Matthew one step further down on the list than do Mark and Luke and thus in immediate proximity to James the [son] of Alphaeus (Acts here agrees with Matthew,

---

67. Luke 18:35–43: "As he drew near to Jericho ..." See Bultmann, *History of the Synoptic Tradition*, rev. ed., 65–66, for some of the problems.
68. Mark 3:18; Luke 6:15; Acts 1:13b.

although in Acts, Thomas and Bartholomew are reversed). Such variations may be an indication of some intentional tampering with the lists.

Because only the Gospel of Matthew's list identifies Matthew/ Levi as a tax collector and only the Gospel of Matthew has Matthew as the subject of the call story, it is generally agreed that the specific identification of Matthew as a tax collector in the Gospel of Matthew's list of the Twelve is directly or indirectly related to the story of the call of Matthew/Levi.[69] The tradition of the call itself poses difficult and perplexing exegetical problems. There can be little question but that the three accounts are, at least as they now stand in the gospels, intended as variants of the same tradition,[70] yet Mark and Luke report the call of a man named "Levi" (Mark further identifying him as "Levi the [son] of Alphaeus"),[71] while Matthew refers to him as "a man named Matthew." It is also noteworthy that, although Mark does not explicitly identify Levi as a tax collector (he only reports that he was "sitting at the tax office"), Luke directly identifies him as a tax collector, and Matthew indirectly makes the same identification by naming him "Matthew"

---

69. Matt 9:9/Mark 2:14/Luke 5:27–28.

70. Jeremias (*New Testament Theology*, 116 n. 1), however, argues that: "1. The pre-literary tradition reported of both Levi and Matthew that they were publicans; 2. The report that both Levi (Mark 2.14) and Matthew (Matt. 10.3) were among the disciples who accompanied Jesus is similarly pre-literary"; cf. 115, where he asserts that "we know by name no less than three publicans who were numbered among the followers of Jesus" (i.e., Levi, Matthew, and Zacchaeus).

71. The Greek does not explicitly state that Levi was the *son* of Alphaeus, but only that he was *somehow* related to Alphaeus (*Leuin ton tou Halphaiou*). There is some significant manuscript evidence for the name "James the [son] of Alphaeus," but this is probably simply a scribal effort to harmonize this passage with the various lists of the Twelve, where James is unanimously identified as the [son] of Alphaeus (Matt 10:3/Mark 3:18/Luke 6:15/Acts 1:13b). It has sometimes been suggested that Levi and James were brothers, but there is no basis for this other than the indication that both were related to Alphaeus. It might even be suggested that Levi and James are two names for the same person, but, again, there is no actual basis for such a suggestion.

and them, in his list of the Twelve, describing Matthew as "the tax collector."[72]

Many attempts have been made to explain the problems in these passages. One of the more ingenious was proposed by B. W. Bacon, who pointed out that several important manuscripts read "James the [son] of Alphaeus" rather than "Levi the [son] of Alphaeus" in Mark 2:14. He then suggested that some scribe, working from this version of Mark, wrote "the tax collector" into the margin of an early manuscript of Matthew beside the name of "James the [son] of Alphaeus" in Matt 10:2, that, eventually these words somehow got into the text after the name of Matthew rather than that of James (Matthew's name immediately precedes that of James in the Gospel of Matthew's list), and that finally the name in Matt 9:9 was changed from Levi to Matthew to correspond with Matt 10:3.[73] Other proposed solutions have included the suggestion that Levi and Matthew are two names for the same person or that Levi and James were perhaps brothers.[74] Perhaps the best proposal has come from Rudolph Pesch. He argues that the author of Matthew has changed the name from Levi to Matthew because, for this author, a "call" necessarily means a call to discipleship, the "disciples" are identical with the "Twelve," and thus Levi could not have been the subject of a "call" story because he obviously was not one of the Twelve.[75] There are still other possibilities, however. A strong argument can be made, for

---

72. This is one of several reasons for regarding Luke's version of this tradition as secondary in relation to either Matthew's or Mark's or both.

73. Bacon, *Studies in Matthew,* 39–40.

74. For discussion, see, e.g., Duling, "Matthew (Disciple)."

75. Pesch, "Levi-Matthäus (Mc 2.14/Mt 9.9, 10.3)." Jeremias (*New Testament Theology,* 116 n. 1) adds that this exchange of names implies a pre-literary tradition that both Levi and Matthew were tax collectors and that both were followers of Jesus, but this is not necessarily the case, Pesch suggests that perhaps the author's choice of Matthew rather than some other apostle was partly a process of elimination (e.g., different traditions regarding others of the Twelve) and may have been somehow related to the tradition that attributes the authorship of this gospel to Matthew the apostle.

example, that the phrase "a man called Matthew" (*anthrōpon ... Maththaion legomenon*) is not original to the Matthean text and has been added by a scribe (or possibly by the author himself), perhaps for the purpose of associating the story of Levi's call with an earlier identification of Matthew the apostle as a tax collector.[76]

The important point that has been established, however, is that the tradition is ambiguous regarding the exact the identity of the man being called (Levi, Matthew, or perhaps even James), whether he was one of the Twelve, and, indeed, whether he was even a tax collector. The ambiguity reaches still further, however, for Bultmann and others have argued that the entire account of the call of Levi/Matthew is simply a "variation" of the same "motif" found in the accounts of the calls of Simon and Andrew and of James and John[77] and suggested that the "motif" itself, as first worked out in the story of the call of the fishermen, may have "been woven out of an already formulated metaphor of 'fishers of men.'"[78] In other words, if that argument is correct, the narrative details of the story of the call of Levi/Matthew have no historical value whatsoever, and, if the identification of the Apostle Matthew as a tax collector is in any way based upon this story, it, too, is without historical basis.

---

76. In only one other place (17:14) does Matthew use *anthrōpos* absolutely to refer to a particular person; it is possible, therefore, that a scribe (or possibly Matthew himself) has substituted *anthrōpos* in 9:9 for some other word or phrase that originally stood in the text or source. In any case, the final words, "called Matthew" (*Maththaion legomenon*) may well be secondary. Not only does the phrase interrupt the connection between *kathēmenon epi to telōnion* and *kai legei* (Luke: *eipen*) *auto akolouthei moi*, which is unbroken in both Mark and Luke, but it is not characteristic of Matthew's usual style. Elsewhere, when Matthew uses *legomenos* with a proper name, he *always* connects the entire phrase with no interruptions (e.g., Matt 1:16; cf. 2:23; 4:18; 10:2; 26:3, 14, 36; 27:16, 17, 22, 23 [*bis*]), and he *never* places *legomenos* at the end of the phrase, as it is placed here.

77. Matt 4:18–22/Mark 1:16–20; cf. Luke 5:1–11.

78. Bultmann, *History of the Synoptic Tradition*, rev. ed., 28, 386–87; on the "variation of motif" as one example of the "generating power of apophthegms," cf. 61–62; on the specific details in such apophthegms as merely "accidental," cf. 63–64. The "motif" in question here is "the sudden summons from business to 'following'" (28).

VI

The sixth and final point to be noted is the possibility that some or perhaps even all of the references to tax collectors in the gospels are a mistake, based upon a transliteration of an Aramaic word meaning something almost synonymous with "sinners" rather than a translation of the Aramaic word for "tax collectors." The Aramaic word *ṭĕlānê* (from the verb *ṭĕlal*, "to play," "to sport"; cf. *ṭûl*, "to walk about," "to be at leisure," "to enjoy oneself"), is translated by Marcus Jastrow as "[sporters,] night demons, urchins," [79] but the root meaning suggests interesting associations with "sinners" and "harlots"; the contemporary term "playboys" might be a fairly close equivalent. The pronunciation of *ṭĕlānê* would be rather close to that of the Greek word for "tax collectors," that is, *telōnai*. A translator of the Aramaic traditions about Jesus into Greek, perhaps being unfamiliar with the apparently not widely used Aramaic term, may simply have assumed that the reference was to tax collectors. If such an erroneous transliteration was made, it accomplished (either intentionally or unintentionally) two things: (1) it removed or at least lessened the moral offence of associating Jesus with "sporters" (revelers, perhaps associates of prostitutes, even pimps); and (2) it made Jesus appear anti-Zealot and perhaps, by implication, even somewhat pro-Roman in his sympathies. Moreover, such an erroneous transliteration would do much to explain the otherwise highly unusual juxtaposition in the gospels of "tax collectors" with "sinners" and particularly with "harlots" (the juxtaposition with "Gentiles" is more easily understandable); if the reference originally was to *ṭĕlānê*, the juxtaposition becomes intelligible.[80]

---

79. Jastrow, *Dictionary of the Targumim, the Talmud Bibli and Yerushalmi, and the Midrashic Literature*, 1:438, cf. 537, 523.

80. The specification of and emphasis upon "tax collectors" as a group with whom Jesus had particularly intimate associations is surprising, because other occupational groups are not thus specified and emphasized. If the reference is to a "social" class rather than an occupational group, however, this would be more in keeping with other materials in the gospels. It is even possible that *ṭĕlānê* might refer to some sort of male "counterpart" to prostitutes (or possibly even to homosexuals).

Conclusion

Six points have been noted regarding Jesus and the tax collectors: (1) Traditions about Jesus' association with tax collectors are found only in the Synoptic Gospels, being notably absent from the Fourth Gospel. (2) The Synoptic Gospels preserve traditions suggesting that Jesus held a highly negative view regarding tax collectors. (3) The references to intimate contacts between Jesus and tax collectors appear, for the most part, in the form of accusations on the lips of his critics, and it is not at all clear that these accusations are based upon fact. (4) Only two passages actually report that Jesus did, in fact, hold table fellowship with tax collectors, and both of these passages can plausibly be regarded as artificial constructions rather than historical accounts. (5) The specific identification of one of the Twelve as a tax collector is, at best, problematic. (6) It is possible that references to tax collectors in the gospels are the result of an erroneous transliteration into Greek of an Aramaic term meaning something like "playboys." The result of the investigation, then, is that, although it can by means be asserted that Jesus did not associate intimately with tax collectors, neither can it be confidently affirmed that he did. The question must, at least for the present, remain open.

The materials suggesting such intimate association may have developed within the early church on the basis of inferences from the charges of Jesus' critics, or they may have been created for apologetic purposes—perhaps to justify the church's decision to reach beyond the circle of the "righteous" to the "sinners" or for use in the polemic against (Pharisaic) Judaism, or perhaps, in line with Brandon's thesis, as part of a pro-Roman and consequently anti-Jewish apologetic. This last possibility would not, of course, prove the validity of Brandon's portrayal of Jesus, but it would cut the ground from under one of the arguments against that portrayal.

PART FIVE

Post-Crucifixion Appearances, Christian Origins, and Resurrection Faith

Chapter 16

Post-Crucifixion Appearances and Christian Origins

It is regarded as virtually axiomatic in most contemporary New Testament scholarship that Christian faith from its very beginning was firmly rooted in the conviction that God had raised Jesus from the dead—indeed, that without this conviction, Christianity would never have been born. The following statements are typical:

> It is not our concern to argue whether the Resurrection did or did not happen. It is certain that the first Christians *believed* it had happened. There never was a time when Christianity existed … without the Resurrection as the fundamental belief.[1]

> That within a few weeks after the crucifixion Jesus' disciples came to believe this is one of the indisputable facts of history. The whole subsequent history of the church rests upon this fact, and is inexplicable without it.[2]

The almost inevitable implication, of course, is that if the first Christians were in error about this, if God did not raise Jesus from the dead, then Christianity has no real basis and is a delusion, and this implication is made explicit by Paul in 1 Cor 15:14–19.

"Postcrucifixion Appearances and Christian Origins." *JBL* 88,2 (June 1969) 157–65. Copyright © 1969 Society of Biblical Literature. Reprinted with permission.
1. Lindars, *New Testament Apologetic*, 72.
2. Fuller, *Foundations of New Testament Christology*, 142.

Most scholars today also assume that the disciples first came to believe that Jesus had been raised from the dead not because they were unable to find his body in the tomb,[3] but rather because they were convinced that the living Christ had appeared to them.[4] The original basis for the resurrection faith, in other words, was the postcrucifixion "appearances" of Jesus to the disciples, however these "appearances" are to be understood.[5] As one writer puts it:

> All that can finally be said is that the disciples were convinced that Jesus had been raised because they saw something which they could identify as someone, more precisely as Jesus. To this fact all early Christian evidence testifies. ... Historical examination permits us to say only that they were convinced that they had seen Jesus.[6]

Thus it is to be expected that the very earliest form of the Christian kerygma would either include or presuppose a reference to these postcrucifixion "appearances," such as is found, for example, in 1 Cor 15:3–7, which is generally believed to have been derived from a pre-Pauline (perhaps very primitive) kerygmatic or confessional formula:

> For I delivered to you as of first importance what I also received, that Christ died for our sins in accordance with the scriptures, that he was buried, that he was raised on the third day in accordance with the scriptures, and that he appeared to Cephas, then to the twelve. Then he appeared to more than five hundred brethren at one time, most of whom are still

---

3. Apparently, the empty tomb tradition was developed later for apologetic and didactic purposes; see, e.g., Anderson, *Jesus and Christian Origins*, 192–95. This is disputed by some, however; see, e.g., Pannenberg, *Jesus—God and Man*, 99–106.

4. Price, *Interpreting the New Testament*, 301.

5. For a recent attempt to determine just what sort of experiences these "appearances" may have been, see Pannenberg, *Jesus—God and Man*, 92–99.

6. R. M. Grant, *Historical Introduction to the New Testament*, 373; cf. also Leipoldt, "Zu den Auferstehungsgeschichten," 737; and Fuller, *Foundations of New Testament Christology*, 142.

alive, though some have fallen asleep. Then he appeared to James, then to all the apostles.

It is the purpose of this paper, however, to suggest: (1) that the speeches in the early chapter of Acts, as well as certain other parts of the New Testament, reflect a very early form of the Christian kerygma in which there is no thought at all of any postcrucifixion "appearances" of Jesus; (2) that traditions of such "appearances" developed subsequent to the actual beginnings of Christianity; and (3) that these traditions were not initially intended to serve as a basis for the resurrection faith. Thus, if it is to be argued that Christianity from the very first was grounded in the resurrection faith, then some basis for this faith other than the postcrucifixion "appearances" of Jesus must be found.

I

The origin of the speeches in Acts is one of the as yet unresolved problems of New Testament study. Some scholars have maintained that the speeches in the early chapters of the book are based upon primitive, perhaps Aramaic, sources and thus represent a very early form of the kerygma.[7] Others insist that these speeches were composed by the author of Luke-Acts and reflect only the faith of the late first-century church and the specific concerns of the author.[8] An intermediate position is taken by still others, who argue that, while the speeches in their finished form are the products of the author, "they nevertheless can be safely regarded as enshrining primitive liturgical and kerygmatic formulae as well as traditional testimonia or proof texts."[9] It is this intermediate position that will be adopted in the discussion to follow. Thus, where the christology of the speeches is demonstrably and substantially different from that of the author of Luke-Acts as expressed else-

---

7. See, e.g., Dodd, *Apostolic Preaching and Its Development*, 17–20.

8. See esp. Dibelius, *Studies in the Acts of the Apostles*, 165–74 (and the full discussion, 138–85).

9. Fuller, *Critical Introduction to the New Testament*, 126; cf. his *Foundations of New Testament Christology*, 20.

where, it can be assumed that this christology is pre-Lukan.[10] And a careful comparative analysis of this pre-Lukan christology or, rather, of these pre-Lukan christologies[11] should lead to some at least tentative conclusions regarding their chronological and/or logical position in the developing thought of the early church.[12]

Except in Acts 10:39–41 and 13:30–31, the speeches in question contain no explicit references to any postcrucifixion "appearances" of Jesus, though they do speak repeatedly of his resurrection from the dead. To be sure, there are statements about "witnesses" (*martyres*) to the resurrection (1:22; 2:32; 3:15; 4:33; 5:32; 10:39–41; 13:31), and it is clear from his reports of the postcrucifixion "appearances" to the disciples (Luke 24:13–53) and his account of the "ascension" (Acts 1:1–12) that the author of Luke-Acts regards these "witnesses" as "eyewitnesses." The theme of "witness," however, which nearly always in Acts means witness to Jesus' resurrection, dominates the entire book of Acts, as it does in a lesser way the Third Gospel, and almost certainly reflects a specific concern of the author rather than traditional materials that he may have utilized. Not only does the theme occur in speeches, both kerygmatic and non-kerygmatic, through the book of Acts (1:8, 22; 2:32; 3:15; 4:20; 5:32; 10:39–41; 13:31; 20:21, 24; 22:15, 18, 20; 23:11; 26:16), but it also appears in four narrative sections (4:33; 8:25; 18:5; 28:23), all of which apparently derive from the author's own hand. The author wants to insist as vigorously as possible, no doubt for theological and apologetic reasons, that Jesus actually was raised from the dead and that he was seen by a particular

---

10. Cf. the discussion in Moule, "Christology of Acts," 166–72.

11. John A. T. Robinson ("The Most Primitive Christology of All?" 139–40) maintains that the speeches "contain at least two incompatible Christologies," that neither of them is the Christology of the author of Luke-Acts, and that "both are products of a much more primitive stage in the Church's thinking."

12. It is important to note at this point that any given passage in Luke-Acts may reflect more than one stage in the developing christology of the early church. Lindars (*New Testament Apologetic*, 35–36) points out that "we must be prepared to find examples of very varied age and importance side by side in a single speech."

group of people who were divinely appointed as witnesses to the resurrection.[13] Thus, these Lukan statements about "witnesses" to the resurrection should not be regarded as evidence for a pre-Lukan tradition of postcrucifixion "appearances" of Jesus.

The two passages in the speeches that do refer explicitly to postcrucifixion "appearances" of Jesus pose a special problem. Acts 13:30–31, which forms part of Paul's sermon in Antioch of Pisidia, reads, "But God raised him from the dead; and for many days he appeared (*ōphthē*) to those who came up with him from Galilee to Jerusalem, who are now his witnesses to the people." Here, the presence of the "witness" motif, the idea of Jesus appearing "for many days" (cf. Acts 1:3), and the emphasis on Galilee and Jerusalem[14] all betray specifically Lukan concepts and concerns, and it is probable, therefore, that these verses derive from the author of Luke-Acts rather than from pre-Lukan traditions. It might be argued that the use of the term *ōphthē* for "he appeared" reflects a pre-Lukan tradition, because this is the same term used in the earlier Pauline account of the postcrucifixion "appearances" (1 Cor 15:5–8). Such an argument has no real validity, however, for the term occurs a number of times in Luke-Acts, almost always refers to the "appearance" of a "supernatural" being (see Luke 1:11; 24:34; Acts 2:3; 7:2, 30, 35; 9:17; 13:31; 16:9; 26:16) and is the regular Lukan term for "appearances" of the risen Christ (Luke 24:34; Acts 2:3; 9:17; 13:31; 26:16). The other passage in a speech that refers explicitly to postcrucifixion "appearances" of Jesus, Acts 10:39–41, comes from Peter's sermon to Cornelius:

> And we are witnesses to all that he [i.e., Jesus] did both in the country of the Jews and in Jerusalem. They put him to death by hanging him on a tree; but God raised him on the third day and made him manifest; not to all the people but to us who were chosen by God as witnesses, who ate and drank with him after he rose from the dead.

---

13. This argument is convincingly presented by Talbert, *Luke and the Gnostics*, 17–32.

14. Talbert, *Luke and the Gnostics*, 22–30.

Here, again, we find the specifically Lukan idea of a particular group of people appointed by God as witnesses to the resurrection. Here, also, the reference to eating and drinking with Jesus after the resurrection reflects a characteristic Lukan tendency to emphasize the materiality or corporeality of the resurrection, likely in an attempt to combat a growing docetic attitude in the church.[15] Thus, it is best to regard this passage, too, as a Lukan construction.

If, then, we eliminate from the speeches in the early chapters of Acts all statements about "witnesses" to the resurrection, as well as the two specific reference to postcrucifixion "appearances" of Jesus, as deriving from the author of Luke-Acts, we are left with a series of internally consistent kerygmatic formulations that make no mention directly or indirectly, of any postcrucifixion "appearances" of Jesus. These formulations must be regarded as pre-Lukan, because the author himself so obviously believes that there were such "appearances'" and that they constituted "proof" of the resurrection (Acts 1:3). We can only conclude, then, that the speeches in the early chapters of Acts reflect a primitive form of the kerygma that knows nothing of any postcrucifixion "appearances" of Jesus.

This conclusion finds support elsewhere in the New Testament. For example, unless we accept the "longer ending" (Mark 16:9–20) as authentic,[16] it is quite possible to read Mark, which most scholars continue to regard as the earliest of the gospels,[17] as containing no references to any postcrucifixion "appearances" of Jesus.[18]

---

15. Talbert, *Luke and the Gnostics*, 30–32; cf. also Talbert, "Anti-Gnostic Tendency in Lucan Christology."

16. William R. Farmer has recently argued in an unpublished paper read before the Southwestern Section of the Society of Biblical Literature on March 16, 1968, that there really are not adequate textual, linguistic, or theological grounds for rejecting the "longer ending," but this goes against the views of the vast majority of contemporary scholars.

17. This has recently been disputed by several writers; see esp. Farmer, *Synoptic Problem: A Critical Analysis*.

18. It is possible to interpret 16:7 and 14:28 as referring not to a postcrucifixion "appearance" but rather to the expected "parousia"; see the discussion in Kümmel, *Promise and Fulfilment*, 77–79.

Indeed, except for Paul's statement in 1 Corinthians 15 and the "appearance" stories in the gospels and Acts, the New Testament as whole is completely silent about any postcrucifixion "appearances" of Jesus. Moreover, even Wolfhart Pannenberg, who himself believes that the resurrected Jesus actually was "seen" by members of the primitive Christian community, acknowledges that it is only the Pauline report that has any real value for the historian:

> The appearances reported in the Gospels, which are not mentioned by Paul, have such a strongly legendary character that one can scarcely find a historical kernel of their own in them. Even the Gospels' reports that correspond to Paul's statements are heavily colored by legendary elements, particularly by the tendency toward underlining the corporeality of the appearances.[19]

It is necessary, therefore, to examine the Pauline statement in an attempt to trace the history of the "appearance" traditions.

II

Most scholars agree that 1 Cor 15:3–7 is based on pre-Pauline (perhaps very primitive) kerygmatic or confessional materials.[20] Some believe that the passage exhibits Semitic linguistic and stylistic features and point to a *Sitz im Leben* in the earliest Palestinian church,[21] but this is disputed by others.[22] In this passage, Paul asserts that the risen Christ appeared (*ōphthē*) to Cephas, then to the twelve, then to more than five hundred brethren, then to James, then to all the apostles. It is highly significant, however, that Paul includes himself among those to whom Christ "appeared," evidently making no real distinction between his own experience and

---

19. Pannenberg, *Jesus — God and Man*, 89.

20. See, e.g., Conzelmann, "On the Analysis of the Confessional Formula in I Corinthians 15:3–5," 18, and the literature cited in n. 17.

21. See, e.g., Jeremias, *Eucharistic Words of Jesus*, 101–3.

22. Conzelmann ("On the Analysis of the Confessional Formula in I Corinthians 15:3–5," 18–20, 22) examines Jeremias' arguments and concludes that the original language of the formula was Greek, not Semitic.

that of the others except that his was "last of all."[23] Furthermore, he speaks elsewhere of an "abundance" (*hyperbolē*) of "visions" (*optasiai*) and "revelations" (*apokalypseis*) of the Lord (2 Cor 12:1; cf. v. 7),[24] thus implying, no doubt, that at least in his own case the "appearance" of the risen Christ was not limited to one occasion.[25] This leads to the further observation that Paul apparently understands the resurrection of the dead, and thus also the resurrection of Jesus (for him the two are strictly parallel; see, e.g., Phil 3:21; Rom 6:8–11; 8:29), not as the mere resuscitation of a corpse but rather as a radical transformation into what he calls a "spiritual body" (*sōma pneumatikon*; see 1 Cor 15:35–57). This, again, lends support to the view that the risen Christ could "appear" whenever, wherever, and to whomever he chose. The "appearances," in other words, need not have been limited to a specific interim period between the "resurrection" and the "ascension," as Luke-Acts portrays them. Unfortunately, the Pauline testimony is generally read in light of the later accounts of the gospels and Acts, rather than *vice versa*, and this may lead to a distortion of what Paul is actually saying.

Most significant of all, however, is the fact that for Paul the crucial thing about the "appearances" was not so much their "historicity" (though he assumed this) as it was the identity of those who saw the risen Christ[26] and the implications of these "appearances" for those individuals and for the church as a whole. Whenever Paul refers to his own experience of "seeing" the Lord, he is at-

---

23. See also 1 Cor 9:1; Gal 1:12, 16; and 2 Cor 12:1.

24. Emanuel Hirsch ("Zum Problem des Osterglaubens," 295–302) has pointed out that the *ōphthē* of 1 Corinthians 15 is not etymologically distinguishable from the *optasiai* of 2 Cor 12:1 and apparently refers to the same type of experience.

25. See, e.g., Althaus, *Die Wahrheit des kirchlichen Osterglaubens*, 16–17; Wilckens, "Der Ursprung der Überlieferung der Erscheinungen des Auferstandenen," 85–86.

26. Conzelman ("On the Analysis of the Confessional Formulas in I Corinthians 15:3–5," 23) observes: "According to Paul's intention, the emphasis lies on the 'last' appearance. It is important that the original reference to Cephas and the twelve can be enlarged to such a series."

tempting to legitimize either his own credentials as an apostle (1 Cor 9:1; 2 Cor 12:1) or the validity of his particular version of the Christian gospel (Gal 1:12, 16). The passage now under consideration is no exception. Paul's initial concern in 1 Corinthians 15 is not to establish the fact that Christ has been raised from the dead or that Christians are to be raised at the last day (these points are raised beginning in v. 12 almost as an afterthought), but rather to insist as strongly as possible upon the validity of his own interpretation of the gospel.[27] He does this by appealing to the agreement between his message and that of the pre-Pauline church (vv. 3a and 11) and by asserting that he, like the others, has "seen" the Lord and is therefore qualified to be an apostle (vv. 4–10). Even the appeal in v. 6 to the more than five hundred brethren "most of whom are still alive, though some have fallen asleep," is not an invitation to the readers to consult these brethren and thus convince themselves that Christ actually was raised from the dead (this would hardly have been feasible for Paul's readers in Corinth because most of the brethren presumably still lived in Palestine); rather, it is but another way of saying that there has been from the very first, and still is, a large group of people who preach precisely the same gospel as does Paul himself.[28] The *Sitz im Leben*,

---

27. Conzelman ("On the Analysis of the Confessional Formulas in I Corinthians 15:3–5," 24–25) suggests that Paul's real point is that "one cannot have the proclamation of the resurrection without the proclamation of the death." The Corinthians had concluded: "If Christ is risen, so are also his people." Paul, however, maintains that the resurrection of Christians is still future.

28. Karl Barth has argued that the list of eyewitnesses was included by Paul not to prove the fact of the resurrection but to show, by defending his own credentials as an apostle, that the proclamation of the risen Christ was in line with the preaching of the first apostles; see his *Church Dogmatics*, IV:335; cf. also his *Die Auferstehung der Toten*, 74ff. Rudolf Bultmann ("New Testament Mythology," 39) disagrees, maintaining that Paul does here attempt "to prove the miracle of the resurrection by adducing a list of eyewitnesses." Anderson (*Jesus and Christian Origins*, 211) suggests that what is involved here is not proof or legitimation; rather, "it is made plain that the Easter faith and message are indissolubly linked to the Easter testimony of the original disciples, and so are bound to a fixed and circumscribed place in history and not to any hazy mythical realm."

therefore, for Paul's statement about the "appearances" of the resurrected Christ is to be located in the conflict between him and
other Christians over his version of the gospel and his claim to
apostleship.[29]

III

With this fact clearly in mind, it is now possible to outline a tentative reconstruction of the history of the "appearance" traditions. The earliest form of the kerygma, reflected particularly in
the speeches in the early chapters of Acts but also at other places
in the New Testament, knows nothing at all of any postcrucifixion "appearances" of Jesus. Such traditions first flourished
in the context of disputes over leadership and authority within
the Christian community. In much the same way as the ancient
Hebrews depended upon theophany traditions to legitimate particular places of worship, the early Christians developed and used
christophany traditions to legitimize the leadership of particular
individuals and groups within the church.[30]

It has been suggested[31] that the earliest recoverable such tradition (1 Cor 15:5–6) spoke of "appearances" to Peter,[32] then to the
twelve,[33] and then to more than five hundred brethren,[34] while a
later alternative tradition (1 Cor 15:7) mentioned "appearances"

---

29. See, e.g., Schoeps, *Paul*, 70–74.

30. See Wilckens, *Die Missionsreden der Apostelgeschichte*, 74 ff., and "Der
Ursprung der Überlieferung der Erscheinungen des Auferstandenen,"
esp. 63–81.

31. See Fuller, "Resurrection of Jesus Christ," 13–16.

32. The gospels contain no direct narrative of this appearance, but
there are perhaps traces of it in Mark 16:7, Luke 24:34; 22:31, and John
21:15–19; moreover, some scholars believe that one or more of the following passages, though now located in the earthly life of Jesus, originally
were derived from postcrucifixion "appearance" stories: Mark 8:27–33
and parallels; Mark 9:2–8 and parallels; Luke 5:1–11; and Matt 16:17–19.
See, e.g., Bultmann, *History of the Synoptic Tradition*, 257–61; Stauffer, *New
Testament Theology*, 31; Fuller, "Resurrection of Jesus Christ," 14–15.

33. This is reflected in various ways in such passages as Mark 16:7;
Matt 28:16–20; Luke 24:36–53; and John 20:19–23.

34. This is not reflected directly in the gospel tradition, though some
would find a variant of it in the Pentecost tradition (Acts 2:1–4).

to James,[35] then to all the apostles,[36] then perhaps to a larger group.[37] It appears, then, that the two traditions were identical, except that the later one substituted James for Peter as the first person who "saw" the risen Jesus. Such a substitution might easily have occurred when James replaced Peter as the leader of the Jerusalem church.[38] When Paul later became involved in disputes over his apostolic authority, he, like the earlier leaders, began to talk about his own experience of having "seen" the Lord. At a somewhat later date the "appearance" tradition was further elaborated in such a way as to stress the corporeality of the risen Christ and perhaps used to combat the growing docetic tendencies within the church. As the stories finally appear in the gospels, their primary function is that of attesting to the reality of Jesus' resurrection from the dead, and their original role of legitimizing the leadership of particular individuals and groups has largely disappeared.

Such a reconstruction leaves unexplained the reference in 1 Cor 15:6 to the more than five hundred brethren, as well as some of the accounts in the gospels, particularly the "appearances" to the women (Matt 28:9–10; John 20:11–18), to the two travelers on the Emmaus road (Luke 24:13–35), and to Thomas (John 20:24–29), but the following suggestions can be offered. It is quite possible that the reference to the more than five hundred brethren might reflect a kind of "democratizing" tendency in the early church, perhaps in reaction against the exclusive claims of various would-be leaders. The stories of "appearances" to women (which are

---

35. There is no mention of such an "appearance" elsewhere in the New Testament, but it is perhaps implied by the tradition that James and the other brothers of Jesus did not follow Jesus during his lifetime (see Mark 3:21, 31–35; John 7:5) but were among the early Christians (see Acts 1:14).

36. This perhaps corresponds to "the twelve" of the earlier tradition.

37. It is assumed that this last "appearance" has disappeared from the later tradition.

38. See Klein ("Galater 2:6–9 und die Geschichte der Jerusalemer Urgemeinde"), who describes a kind of "power struggle" in the Jerusalem community; he believes that Galatians was written at a time when James and John were rising leaders and Peter was declining. See also Brandon, *Jesus and the Zealots*, 158–69.

absent from Paul's statement) may represent simply further developments, under the influence of already current "appearance"
stories, of the "empty tomb" traditions; or it may be that they reflect an attempt to legitimize a place of prominence in the church
for Mary Magdalene and perhaps certain other women,[39] and
possibly even for the son or sons of one or more of the women.[40]
As for the "appearances" to the two travelers to Emmaus and to
Thomas, these accounts have clearly theological and apologetic
motifs[41] and probably developed relatively late, though it is possible that they reflect earlier attempts to legitimize the leadership
of particular individuals in the church.

This proposed reconstruction of the history of the "appearance" traditions does not necessarily imply, of course, that the
first reports of Jesus' postcrucifixion "appearances" were simply
fabricated by the Christians, though this may well have been the
case in some instances. Rather, it implies that the "appearance"
stories followed and, and at least in part, resulted from the resurrection faith; they did not precede and form the basis for this faith.
Indeed, given the prior existence of this faith, plus the apparent
eschatological fervor of the primitive church and the well-attested
presence of manifold ecstatic phenomena among the Christians, it
should not be at all surprising that a Stephen, for example, would
exclaim in a moment of stress and rapture, "Behold, I see the
heavens opened, and the Son of man standing at the right hand
of God" (Acts 7:56).[42] Once the precedent was established, how-

---

39. There is some confusion in the accounts as to the identity of the
women who "saw" the risen Jesus.

40. Here, again, the problem of identity appears. Matthew's account
would suggest that it is James and Joseph (James and Joses, the brothers
of Jesus?) who are involved, but there may be reflections elsewhere of
other traditions in which the concern is for James and John (the sons of
Zebedee).

41. See, e.g, Anderson, *Jesus and Christian Origins*, 228–29, 236–37.

42. This is not necessarily to argue for the authenticity of this particular tradition, but simply to suggest the kind of situation in which such
an experience might be expected to have occurred. Perhaps the cultus,
however, would be the most likely context for the "appearances."

ever, such experiences would tend to become widespread in the church; and eventually the church, as it became increasingly more "institutionalized," would find it necessary to discourage these experiences at the individual level but, at the same time, to appropriate the traditions of the experiences for its own theological, apologetic, and administrative purposes.

Chapter 17

Christian Origins and Resurrection Faith

I

Contemporary New Testament scholarship is increasingly in agreement that the resurrection faith preceded the first christological formulations of the primitive Palestinian church, both logically and chronologically. Norman Perrin, for example, asserts that "the starting point for New Testament Christology is not the message of the historical Jesus—not even the implicit Christology of that message—but the theologizing of early Christianity," and he then adds that "the first step taken by the Church in her theologizing" was "a post-Easter step taken in response to" the conviction that Jesus had been raised up by God.[1] There is considerable disagreement, however, as to just why and how this resurrection faith arose.[2] The so-called objective view holds that it was the event of Jesus's resurrection that produced the faith,[3] while the subjective view regards the faith as, perhaps, the mythologi-

---

"Christian Origins and Resurrection Faith." *JR* 52,1 (January 1972) 41–55. Copyright © 1972 University of Chicago Press. Reprinted with permission in *TUSR* 10 (1970–73) 48–59. Reprinted with permission.

1. Perrin, "Recent Trends in Research in the Christology of the New Testament," 231–32.

2. See, e.g., Moule, "Introduction," 2–4.

3. See, e.g., Moule, *Phenomenon of the New Testament*, 13; he insists that "the birth and rapid rise of the Christian Church ... *remain an unsolved enigma for any historian who refuses to take seriously the only explanation offered by the Church itself*," namely, the resurrection of Jesus, and quotes with approval from Niebuhr, *Resurrection and Historical Reason*, 15: "Naturalizing the gospel history only succeeds in making it sentimental."

cal expression of a new understanding of the real significance of Jesus' message and activity.[4] Willi Marxsen has recently clarified the problem somewhat, however, by suggesting that, regardless of what did or did not happen to the crucified Jesus, the original resurrection faith must be regarded as an interpretation, an inference, a deduction on the part of the followers of Jesus. He observes that "no individual of the primitive community ever claimed to have seen or experienced Jesus' resurrection as an event, a fact, a happening." The most that is claimed is that the grave where Jesus was buried had been found empty or that certain persons had seen Jesus after his death. It must follow, therefore, "that when the *kerygma* claims that the resurrection actually happened as an event (perhaps also by providing a date 'on the third day'), it is expressing a belief—or perhaps we ought to say more precisely that it is expressing *merely* a belief, without specifying witnesses, and what is more, without being in the least able to specify witnesses."[5] We may quite legitimately ask, therefore: Of what was the original resurrection faith an interpretation? On the basis of what data or evidence did the followers of Jesus infer or deduce that he had been raised from the dead?

Traditionally, Christians have appealed to the empty tomb and the postcrucifixion "appearances" of Jesus as the twin bases for the resurrection faith. Today, however, a great many scholars believe that the empty-tomb tradition is a relatively late development, motivated largely by apologetic and didactic needs, without any real basis in historical fact.[6] And I have recently argued elsewhere

---

4. See, e.g., Bultmann, "New Testament and Mythology," 42: "The real Easter faith is faith in the word of preaching which brings illumination. If the event of Easter Day is in any sense an historical event additional to the event of the cross, it is nothing else than the rise of faith in the risen Lord, since it was this faith which led to the apostolic preaching. The resurrection itself is not an event of past history."

5. Marxsen, "Resurrection of Jesus as a Historical and Theological Problem," 15–49, esp. 17–31; cf., more recently, his *Resurrection of Jesus of Nazareth*.

6. See, e.g., Anderson, *Jesus and Christian Origins*, 192–95; but, for an opposing view, cf., e.g., Moule, "Introduction," 6–11; and Pannenberg, *Jesus—God and Man*, 99–106.

that the "appearance" tradition, far from preceding and forming the basis for the resurrection faith, as is usually assumed, actually followed and resulted from this faith and was motivated in large measure by the desire to legitimize the leadership of particular individuals and groups within the early Church.[7] If, then, both the empty-tomb tradition and the "appearance" tradition are secondary developments, as I believe them to be, the original resurrection faith must have had some other basis, and it is this other basis that we must now seek. To this end, I suggest that we attempt to retrace the history of the resurrection faith *in reverse*, beginning with the well-developed expression of that faith in the theology of Luke-Acts and working back toward its origin. Admittedly, our conclusion will be largely hypothetical and tentative, but this is necessarily true to a greater or lesser degree of all historical reconstruction:

> All historical narrative is at once a synthesis and a hypothesis. It is a synthesis inasmuch as it combines the mass of known facts in an account of the whole; it is a hypothesis insomuch as the relations that it establishes between these facts are neither evident nor verifiable by themselves. To unite the facts into an ensemble and relate them is in practice one and the same process. For it goes without saying that the grouping of facts will differ according to the idea one wants to give of their relation. Everything then depends upon this ... and upon the degree of creative imagination of the historian and upon his general conception of human affairs. This amounts to saying that in its highest and most essential expression history is a conjectural science, or, in other words, a subjective science.[8]

I would add that "in its highest and most essential expression history is" an *art* and not a science at all.

---

7. Walker, "Postcrucifixion Appearances and Christian Origins," chap. 16 in this volume.

8. Pirenne, "What Are Historians Trying to Do?" 94–95.

II

The author of Luke-Acts presents Jesus' resurrection from the dead and his ascension into heaven as two separate and successive events, and it is this view that became the "orthodox" Christian belief. Because this separation is not prominent elsewhere in the New Testament, however,[9] and because it apparently presupposes a number of exegetical, theological, and perhaps liturgical developments within the early Christian community,[10] it is now generally believed that the resurrection and the ascension were originally thought of as simultaneous occurrences or, rather, as alternative ways of talking about the same occurrence.[11] Many scholars, therefore, maintain that the dominant motif in the most primitive resurrection faith was Jesus' exaltation.[12] Some speak of God's act whereby Jesus was enthroned in heaven as Lord and/or Messiah and entered upon his kingly rule,[13] while others regard the Son of Man christology as more primitive and speak of Jesus' exaltation as Son of Man.[14]

It has recently been suggested, however, that a very important distinction must be made between "exaltation," "enthronement," or "glorification," on the one hand, and mere "ascension," "assumption," or "translation," on the other hand, and that behind the exaltation christology can be found traces[15] of a still more primitive view in which the resurrection is seen, not as Jesus' ex-

---

9. But see John 20:17.

10. See, e.g., James M. Robinson, "Ascension," 246–47.

11. Barnabas Lindars (*New Testament Apologetic*, 42 n. 2) claims that "this is now an axiom of New Testament critical scholarship."

12. See, e.g., Acts 2:22–36; 13:33; Rom 1:3–4; Phil 2:9; Heb 1:3–13; 8:1; John 3:14; 12:32, 34.

13. See, most recently, Hayes, "Resurrection as Enthronement."

14. See, e.g., Perrin, "New Beginnings in Christology," 495; cf. also his "Mark XIV.62"; "Son of Man in Ancient Judaism and Primitive Christianity"; *Rediscovering the Teaching of Jesus*, 164–99; "Son of Man in the Synoptic Tradition"; and "Recent Trends in Research in the Christology of the New Testament."

15. See, e.g., Acts 3:20–21; cf. also Mark 2:18–20; Acts 1:9–11.

altation or enthronement, but rather his assumption into heaven, there to wait in a state of essential inactivity until the impending Parousia, at which time he will be manifested as Messiah or Son of Man.[16] And it is highly significant that the far-reaching step from the earlier assumption christology to the later exaltation christology can best be accounted for on the basis of three factors at work in the life of the early church:[17] frustrated eschatological expectations, "pneumatic" phenomena,[18] and scriptural exegesis. The Parousia had not occurred as anticipated, and this created a major crisis for Christian faith, but the continuing growth and spread of the church, accompanied by what was understood as the activity of the "Holy Spirit," implied that something crucial had happened, so the Christians looked to their Scriptures and found an answer in Psalm 110:1: "Yahweh says to my lord: 'Sit at my right hand, till I make your enemies your footstool.'" Jesus had not merely been assumed into heaven to await his exaltation at the Parousia, as they had previously supposed; he had, rather, at the

---

16. See, e.g., John A. T. Robinson, "The Most Primitive Christology of All?" and *Jesus and His Coming*, 143–50; Hahn, *Titles of Jesus in Christology*, 129–35; Fuller, *Foundations of New Testament Christology*, 142–81; Perrin, "Recent Trends in Research in the Christology of the New Testament," 222. This distinction is rejected, however, by, e.g., Knox, *Humanity and Divinity of Christ*, 8 n. 2; and Conzelmann, *Outline of the Theology of the New Testament*, 67–68.

17. See, e.g., Perrin, "Recent Trends in Research in the Christology of the New Testament," 222; he points out that "the linking of christological developments with factors at work in the life and experience of early Christianity ... has come to be a major emphasis in recent work."

18. The question of terminology becomes particularly problematic at this point. "Charismatic" is not explicit enough to describe the phenomena to be discussed, especially because, in its contemporary usage, it tends to place the emphasis upon the "personality" of the person or persons involved rather than upon the "gift" or "endowment" that the term actually suggests. "Ecstatic" is much better than "charismatic" and actually is quite appropriate in this case, if it is properly defined, but some might object to it on the grounds that it is too explicit and suggests some degree of mental "derangement." For these reasons, I have chosen, somewhat reluctantly, to use the more neutral term "pneumatic" in most instances. On "ecstasy," see, e.g., Oepke, "ἔκστασις, ἐξίστημι."

moment of his assumption, been exalted to the right hand of God, where he was now exercising his kingly rule, but the Parousia must be delayed until the subjugation of his enemies.[19]

Assuming the validity of the reconstruction thus far, we may now ask: What produced the earlier view that Jesus had been assumed into heaven to await his exaltation at the Parousia? And my suggestion is that, given the general religious and theological milieu in which Jesus' followers lived and thought, this more-primitive form of the resurrection faith can best be accounted for on the basis of precisely the same kinds of factors that later brought the shift to the exaltation Christology: namely, frustrated eschatological expectations, pneumatic phenomena, and scriptural exegesis. Indeed, in light of the circumstances, both general and particular, it might even be maintained that the appearance of the resurrection faith in its primitive form as well as its later development was virtually inevitable.

III

The frustrated eschatological expectations of Jesus' followers are obvious. Despite a bewildering variety in detail, there was widespread anticipation in first-century Judaism of God's decisive intervention in history and human experience and the final triumph of his will and manifestation of his rule, perhaps in the form of the "Kingdom of God" (or "Kingdom of Heaven") or the "New Age," and many believed that this "good time coming" would be preceded or ushered in by some human or superhuman personage or personages sent or raised up by God.[20] Indeed, some expected the return to earth of some such illustrious figure of the past as Moses or Elijah.[21] Whether Jesus made any specific messianic or quasi-messianic claims for himself, either explicit or implicit, is at this point immaterial, although if he did make such claims, subse-

---

19. This has been convincingly argued by Fuller, *Foundations of New Testament Christology*, 129–35; and, most recently, Perrin, "Recent Trends in Research in the Christology of the New Testament," 222–23.

20. See, e.g., Perrin, *Kingdom of God in the Teaching of Jesus*, 160–69.

21. See, e.g., Fuller, *Foundations of New Testament Christology*, 46–49.

quent developments become more easily understandable. There clearly was at least some speculation during his lifetime about his identity or role,[22] and there is good reason to believe that he was regarded by some of his contemporaries as the expected eschatological prophet who would herald the coming of the end and that he himself "understood his mission in terms of eschatological prophecy."[23] Moreover, the sources indicate quite unmistakably that Jesus himself was, if not an "ecstatic," at least a "charismatic type,"[24] and the appearance of such a pneumatic or spirit-filled individual was bound to suggest that the last days were dawning, because "the idea of a special outpouring of the Spirit was part of the general expectation" for the end time.[25] Finally, of course, Jesus did, without question, announce that the Kingdom was coming, and all of his message and activity apparently were related to this announcement.[26] On the basis, then, of his message, activity, and personal charisma, Jesus' followers came to believe that the Kingdom was imminent, but their expectations were frustrated by the course of subsequent events. Jesus, the prophet of the Kingdom, was put to death, and the Kingdom did not come.

This might well have marked the end of the influence of Jesus, but, for some reason, it did not. Just as the influence of John the Baptist, who apparently also announced the coming of the

---

22. See, e.g., Mark 6:14–16 and parallels; and Mark 8:27–30 and parallels.

23. See, e.g., Fuller, *Foundations of New Testament Christology*, 125–31.

24. See, e.g., Barrett, *Holy Spirit and the Gospel Tradition*, esp. 2–4, 113–21; cf. also van Unnik, "Jesus the Christ." Note also the almost certainly authentic traditions: (1) that Jesus performed exorcisms; (2) that he was accused of being in league with "Beelzebul" (Mark 3:22 and parallels); (3) that his family apparently considered him "beside himself" (Mark 3:21, 31–35; the verb used here is cognate to the noun from which the English words "ecstasy," "ecstatic," and "ecstaticism" are derived); and (4) that he functioned as a "prophet," which would have been meaningless without the assumption that he "possessed the Spirit" (or, better, that the Spirit "possessed him").

25. Lindars, *New Testament Apologetic*, 54; cf. e.g., Sjöberg, "Between the Old and New Testaments," 11–13.

26. See, e.g., Perrin, *Rediscovering the Teaching of Jesus*, 54.

Kingdom and who may also have been a charismatic type, continued long after his death, and some of his followers evidently claimed messianic status for him,[27] so the influence of Jesus continued and increased after his death. In part, this must have been simply because he made such an impression upon his followers that they could not easily ignore, forget, or dismiss him as a deluded fanatic,[28] but a further reason, and perhaps the primary reason, must surely have been the appearance of pneumatic phenomena, perhaps similar to those that characterized his own life, among his followers shortly after his death. Indeed, it may well be that this was the major difference between the followers of Jesus and the followers of John the Baptist: the former "possessed the Spirit," and the latter did not.[29]

IV

It is clear that such phenomena as prophecy, glossolalia, "faith healing," and visions dominated the worship of the church at Corinth a quarter of a century after the time of Jesus and that these phenomena were attributed to the working of the Holy Spirit,[30] but it is not certain whether such phenomena were present also in the most primitive Palestinian community. The early chapters of Acts claim that they were, but the late date of Acts, together with the author's obvious interest in the working of the Spirit, suggests the possibility that beliefs and practices of the later Hellenistic church have been read back into the earlier period. It is very difficult to assess the value of Acts as a historical source,[31] but C. K. Barrett has defended the essential historicity

---

27. See, e.g., Farmer, "John the Baptist," 962.

28. See, e.g., Enslin, *From Jesus to Christianity*, 1–16; cf. his *Prophet from Nazareth*.

29. See, e.g., Acts 18:24–19:7. Note the tradition that John's disciples fasted, but Jesus' did not (Mark 2:18 and parallels), and see Käsemann, "Beginnings of Christian Theology," who suggests that "legalism" and "enthusiasm" were mutually exclusive approaches to religion in the first-century Judeo-Christian context.

30. See, e.g., 1 Corinthians 12–14 and 2 Cor 12:1–13.

31. See, e.g., Haenchen, "Book of Acts as Source Material."

of this particular motif in Acts, arguing quite cogently that the New Testament as a whole "points to a corporate reception of the Spirit as the beginning of the apostolic ministry of the Church,"[32] and Rudolf Bultmann agrees that "the earliest Church knew that it had been given the *Spirit*, that gift of the end of days which, according to the Jewish view, had departed from Israel with the last of the prophets, but whose impartation was promised for the end of days."[33] Bultmann is not certain "whether the manifestation of the Spirit in ecstasy and speaking in tongues (1 Corinthians 14), which later played so great a role in Hellenistic congregations, had already appeared in the earliest Church,"[34] but T. W. Manson, Hans Conzelmann, and others believe that it had.[35] In the absence of any real evidence to the contrary, therefore, it appears reasonable to conclude that the references in the first part of Acts to "pneumatic ecstasy" in the primitive Palestinian church are based, at least in part, upon reliable traditions and describe "a genuine experience of early Christianity."[36]

---

32. Barrett, *Holy Spirit and the Gospel Tradition*, 1–2.

33. Rudolf Bultmann, *Theology of the New Testament*, 1:41; cf. Käsemann, "Beginnings of Christian Theology"; and his "On the Subject of Primitive Christian Apocalyptic," where he speaks of the "post-Easter enthusiasm" of the primitive Palestinian community.

34. Bultmann, *Theology of the New Testament*, 1:41.

35. T. W. Manson, "Corinthian Correspondence (1)," 203–5; Conzelmann, *Outline of the Theology of the New Testament*, 37–38; cf. also, e.g., Haenchen, "Book of Acts as Source Material," 261–62, who regards the Pentecost story as one of the "traditional materials" in Acts. For possible historical precedents within Judaism to the early Christian glossolalia, see, e.g., Phillips, "Ecstatics' Father," 183–94, esp. 190; and Andrews, "Tongues, Gift of," 672. For a general study of glossolalia, see, e.g., Currie, "'Speaking in Tongues.'"

36. Spivey and Smith, *Anatomy of the New Testament*, 245. Obviously, we cannot at this point attempt to say just how and why these phenomena first appeared among Jesus' followers after his death, any more than we can explain similar phenomena throughout the history of Christianity (even among Presbyterians and Episcopalians today!) and in other religions. It may well be, however, that the precedent of Jesus himself was a major factor, although this possibility must be worked out on another occasion.

Apparently, then, Jesus' proclamation of the coming of God's Kingdom, together with his activity and his personal charisma, had led his followers to believe that they were living in the last days. This belief had been shattered initially by Jesus' death, but the pneumatic phenomena that began to manifest themselves shortly after the crucifixion convinced the disciples that the eschatological outpouring of the Spirit, which had begun in Jesus' own life, was being continued among them, that the Kingdom was indeed near at hand, as Jesus had said, and that they were, in fact, living in the last days, as they had believed before Jesus' death. This meant that Jesus had not been mistaken after all; his message and activity were vindicated by the subsequent course of events: not, however, his resurrection from the dead, as they later came to believe, but the gift of the Spirit. This, I would suggest, was the earliest form of Christian faith, and I believe that this reconstruction of Christian origins can be supported by examining the "Pentecostal" sermon attributed to Peter in the second chapter of the Acts of the Apostles.[37]

Barnabas Lindars has suggested that the first "Petrine" sermon in Acts 2:14–40 actually consists of two originally separate speeches or, more likely, of "two different ranges of scriptural material" that were used by the early Church. The Pentecost material in vv. 14–21, 38–40 includes the quotation of and Christian commentary on Joel 2:28–32, while the resurrection material in vv. 22–36 is a quotation of and Christian commentary on Ps 16:8–11.[38] To be sure, each of these blocks of material has "its own exegetical history," and each, apparently, is the end product of "a process of

---

37. I am assuming that, although the speeches in Acts, in their present form, were created by the author of Luke-Acts, those speeches in the early chapters of Acts "nevertheless can be safely regarded as enshrining primitive liturgical and kerygmatic formulae as well as traditional testimonia or proof texts" (Fuller, *Critical Introduction to the New Testament*, 126). For a discussion of the problem, see, e.g., Feine and Behm, *Introduction to the New Testament*, 117–20.

38. Lindars, *New Testament Apologetic*, 36–37; cf. Perrin, *Rediscovering the Teaching of Jesus*, 23–24.

some complexity,"[39] but it is highly significant that we find in the Pentecost material traces of what must have been a very primitive form of Christian faith,[40] which bases itself exclusively upon the gift of the Holy Spirit and contains no reference whatsoever to Jesus' resurrection, either as an exaltation to kingly status or as an assumption into heaven.[41] The argument, based on Joel 2:28–32, is simply that the outpouring of the Spirit shows that the "day of the Lord" is at hand. The fact that the author of Luke-Acts finds it necessary to insert the resurrection material in such an artificial manner surely indicates that the earlier Pentecost material originally did not refer to any resurrection of Jesus, and, in my opinion, it is inconceivable that any primitive Christian preaching would have failed to mention the resurrection unless the resurrection faith had not yet appeared among Jesus' followers, which is what

---

39. Lindars, *New Testament Apologetic*, 37.

40. Apparently, the quotation of Joel 2:28–32 in Acts 2:17–21, 39 is based upon the Septuagint rather than the Hebrew text, but this is not necessarily a serious objection to the antiquity of the underlying theology; see, e.g., Lindars, *New Testament Apologetic*, 35–36: "All it means is that, in Luke's Greek-speaking milieu, the change to the exclusive use of this recension of the Septuagint has already taken place. ... There are of course a few places where relics of previous forms of the text remain. ... We must be prepared to find examples of very varied age and importance side by side in a single speech." Actually, the quotation in Acts differs more from both the Masoretic and Septuagint texts than those two texts differ from one another and probably should be regarded, therefore, as a *pesher* adaptation rather than a *verbatim* quotation; see, e.g., Lindars, *idem.*, 14–17, who points out striking similarities between early Christian exegesis and the *pesher* commentaries produced by the Qumran community, in which considerable freedom was exercised with regard to the wording of the Old Testament passages concerned; cf. also, e.g., Perrin, "Mark XIV.62"

41. Note that Shlomo Pines (*The Jewish Christians of the Early Centuries of Christianity*) believes that an Arabic text that he has studied contains materials reflecting a form of early Jewish Christianity, and he gives no indication in his discussion of that text that these Jewish Christians displayed any interest at all in traditions about Jesus' resurrection. Cf., however, Kraft, Review of Shlomo Pines, *The Jewish Christians of the Early Centuries of Christianity*, 330: "Whether the source is as significant for the period of Christian origins as Pines would like to believe must await its full publication and systematic examination."

I must therefore assume to have been the case here. Apparently, Jesus' followers at first based their renewed expectation of the imminent coming of the Kingdom, not on the resurrection faith, but rather on their possession of the Spirit, that is, on the appearance of pneumatic phenomena among them shortly after Jesus' death.

But what about Jesus himself? How did it come about that Jesus, the martyred prophet of the Kingdom, came to be regarded as the bearer of the coming Kingdom? How did it happen that the "proclaimer" became the "proclaimed"?[42] What produced the earliest form of the resurrection faith? Obviously, the sources do not allow certainty at this point, because they all assumed their present form long after the appearance of this faith, but we have already seen that the shift from the early assumption christology to the later exaltation christology apparently was made with the aid of and on the basis of scriptural exegesis, and I now suggest that, given the general religious and theological milieu in which Jesus' followers lived and thought, the most primitive form of the resurrection faith can itself best be explained as the result of exegetical developments that had their impetus and origin in the pneumatic experiences of Jesus' followers after his death.

V

Several features of the general religious and theological milieu should be noted. *First*, and this is often overlooked, there never would have been a time when Jesus' followers regarded death as the final and absolute end of Jesus. Even the ancient Hebrews apparently believed in a vague kind of existence after death,[43] and, by the first century, the idea of the resurrection of the dead was apparently widely accepted not only by apocalyptic enthusiasts but also by the Pharisees and others[44] and by Jesus himself,[45] and

---

42. This, of course, is the problem posed most significantly in recent times by Rudolf Bultmann (see, e.g., his *Theology of the New Testament*, 1:33–37).

43. See, e.g., Gaster, "Dead, Abode of the," 787–88

44. See, e.g., Davies, *Paul and Rabbinic Judaism*, 299–303.

45. See, e.g., Strawson, *Jesus and the Future Life*.

this idea was accompanied by the notion of future rewards and punishments. *Second*, as Eduard Schweizer has pointed out, the idea that a "Righteous One" who humbled himself or voluntarily accepted suffering and death in obedience to God would be rewarded either on earth or in heaven was apparently well established, and it appears that the early Christian understanding of Jesus was influenced by this idea.[46] *Third*, it was popularly believed that such a Righteous One might escape the usual human experience of death and be assumed bodily into heaven or, perhaps, be assumed into heaven immediately after death;[47] indeed, as James M. Robinson has observed, the ascension of dignitaries of the past was "an increasingly popular and detailed motif" in first-century Jewish thought.[48] *Fourth*, and finally, as has already been pointed out, there was ample precedent for the belief that a particularly illustrious figure who had ascended to heaven, such as Moses or Elijah, might return to earth to precede or usher in the end time, and it is clear that the primitive Palestinian church was greatly influenced in its understanding of Jesus by the traditions about Moses and Elijah.[49]

It was in the context of such ideas and expectations that the followers of Jesus sought and found answers to their questions about Jesus and his relationship to what they were presently experiencing and what they anticipated in the near future, and, apparently, it was in their Scriptures that they sought and found these answers.[50] Some of the exegetical developments that led from the

---

46. Schweizer, *Lordship and Discipleship*, 22–41; for a more detailed discussion, cf. his *Erniedrigung und Erhöhung bei Jesus und seinen Nachfolgern,* chaps. 5–7.

47. See, e.g., Schweizer, *Lordship and Discipleship*, 27–28.

48. James M. Robinson, "Ascension," 245, lists: Enoch, Elijah, Levi, Baruch, Ezra, Moses, Zephaniah, Abraham, Isaiah, Adam, and even Raphael.

49. See, e.g., Fuller, *Foundations of New Testament Christology*, 167–73.

50. See, e.g., Perrin, *Rediscovering the Teaching of Jesus*, 23: "It is evident that the earliest Christians made most significant use of the Old Testament in their theologizing. They developed major aspects of their belief and expectation from Old Testament texts, interpreting the texts in the light of their experience and their experience in the light of the

original "pneumatic and eschatological enthusiasm" to the most primitive form of the resurrection faith are, no doubt, forever lost, and others are hopelessly entangled in the maze of later theologizing, but traces of some still remain. A detailed analysis is beyond the scope of this paper and must be worked out on another occasion, but a brief summary of several that are reflected in the speeches in the early chapters of Acts is in order.

VI

Barnabas Lindars has observed that the most primitive use of Scripture by Jesus' followers was in terms of "the argument from *literal fulfillment*":

> The Bible says that such and such will happen, and it *has* happened. This is the most direct exegesis. It has a simplicity and forestalls criticism and precludes further argument.[51]

This is surely correct; but it is not correct, in my opinion, that this argument from literal fulfillment was first used to demonstrate the messiahship of Jesus or that "in the New Testament this argument is only used in connection with the Resurrection."[52] I have already suggested that the followers of Jesus first appealed to the Jewish Scriptures for an explanation of the pneumatic phenomena that they began to experience after Jesus' death and that they found an explanation in Joel 2:28–32: the outpouring of the Spirit confirmed Jesus' announcement that the last days had arrived. Only subsequently did they seek in the Scriptures an understanding of the role and significance of Jesus himself. Traces of at least three such exegetical developments can be detected in the early chapters of Acts, and it is quite probable that these, to some extent, represent parallel or overlapping attempts by the primitive church to reach

---

texts. The Christian practice here paralleled that of the Qumran scribes and, like those scribes, the Christians read the Old Testament texts as strictly relating to themselves and their experiences, and they exercised very considerable freedom in regard to the wording of the texts."

51. Lindars, *New Testament Apologetic*, 33.
52. Lindars, *New Testament Apologetic*, 33.

a proper understanding of Jesus rather than a strictly chronological or logical succession.

First, in light of Jesus' own charismatic or pneumatic activity, and against the background of popular ascension traditions in first-century Judaism and particularly the tradition about Elisha receiving the spirit of Elijah when the latter was taken up into heaven,[53] the followers of Jesus became convinced, apparently on the basis of Ps 68:19a (18a in English), that it was none other than the crucified Jesus who had given his own Spirit to them and that he, therefore, like Elijah, must have been taken to heaven.[54] In the context of first-century Jewish thought, this would also have implied the possibility and perhaps even the probability of his return from heaven in the end time, and, because the end time had already begun with the outpouring of the Spirit, this return would be very soon. Apparently, Ps 68:19a was sometimes read or paraphrased as: "Thou didst ascend the heights, leading captives in thy train, and giving gifts to men," and, at least among the followers of Jesus, the "gifts" were understood as spiritual gifts or the gifts of the Spirit.[55] Lindars observes that "the evidence is slighter, and the results less certain" regarding the use of Ps 68:19a by the primitive church "than in the case of Ps 110:1" which he regards as the earliest such *testimonium* used by the church; he also maintains that "this time we cannot use the argument from literal fulfillment to achieve certainty that the Psalm verse was actually used in the most primitive phase" and concludes, therefore, that "it is more probable that it enters into the discussions at a slightly later stage."[56] I suggest, on the contrary: (1) that the meager evidence for the use of Ps 68:19a by the primitive church can

---

53. 2 Kings 2; cf. also the reference to Moses' spirit being given to the elders in Num 11:16–30.

54. See, e.g., Acts 2:33; cf. also Acts 5:31 and Eph 4:8, where Ps 68:19a (18a in English) is applied to Jesus.

55. See, e.g., Lindars, *New Testament Apologetic,* 51–59; obviously, however, Lindars would not agree with my reconstruction in full, because he regards the resurrection faith as both chronologically and logically prior to the idea of the gift of the Spirit.

56. Lindars, *New Testament Apologetic,* 51.

best be attributed to the fact that a major part of the christology reflected in such usage was very soon superceded and, to some extent, suppressed by subsequent christological developments; (2) that a form of the argument from literal fulfillment was used in connection with Ps 68:19a with reference to the gift of the Holy Spirit; and (3) that Ps 68:19a may well have been, therefore, one of the earliest *testimonia* used by the followers of Jesus, perhaps preceded only by Joel 2:28–32.

Second, Deut 18:15–19, which speaks of a "prophet like Moses" whom God will "raise up," was initially applied, perhaps even during Jesus' own lifetime, to his historical activity among the Jews; but, given the historical fact of his death, the "raising up" almost inevitably came to be interpreted as a raising from the dead or, perhaps at first, simply as a raising up to heaven.[57] It is true, as Lindars points out, that the use of the Deuteronomy passage in Acts 3:22–26 is most likely based upon the Septuagint rather than the Hebrew text,[58] but this does not necessarily affect my argument regarding the antiquity of the christology reflected here.[59] The point is that we find here a presentation of Jesus that does not mention his resurrection and that could quite easily have developed into the idea of that resurrection. Surely, the non-resurrection christology must be more primitive than the resurrection christology, and surely the Deuteronomy passage would not have been used as the basis of a non-resurrection christology if the resurrection christology had already appeared! I suggest, therefore, that the development of the resurrection faith in its most primitive form was based in part upon a Christian exegesis of Deut 18:15–19.[60]

---

57. See Acts 3:22–26.

58. Lindars, *New Testament Apologetic*, 207.

59. See n. 40 above.

60. Other features of Acts 3:12–16 also suggest that it reflects a very primitive strand in the christological thought of Jesus' followers (see, e.g., J. A. T. Robinson, "The Most Primitive Christology of All?"; and Fuller, *Foundations of New Testament Christology*, 167–73).

Third, it was argued on the basis of Ps 16:8–11, that Jesus, because he was the "Holy One,"[61] must have been raised from the dead.[62] Lindars asserts that the main point of the argument in Acts 2:22–32 is that Psalm 16 cannot refer to David, who was *not* raised from the dead but that it can and does refer to Jesus, who *was* raised, and that Jesus, therefore, must be the Messiah.[63] I suggest, on the contrary, that the original argument can better be summarized as follows: Psalm 16 cannot refer to David, who was only a prophet and was not raised from the dead; Jesus, however, is the Holy One; the Psalm, therefore, refers to him, and he must, accordingly, have been raised from the dead. The passage in Acts assumes the position that Jesus' resurrection is necessitated by his identity, not *vice versa* (v. 24).[64]

Other examples could be cited, and those just mentioned need further elaboration, but perhaps enough has been said to provide at least a basis of plausibility for my thesis that, given the general religious and theological milieu in which the followers of Jesus lived and thought, the birth of the resurrection faith can be accounted for on the basis of three factors at work in the life and experience of the first Christians: frustrated eschatological expectations, pneumatic phenomena, and scriptural exegesis.

---

61. See, e.g., Fuller, *Foundations of New Testament Christology*, 167–73.

62. See Acts 2:22–32.

63. Lindars, *New Testament Apologetic*, 38–45.

64. For a highly illuminating and suggestive discussion of the primitive Christian use of Psalm 16 along somewhat similar lines, see Boers, "Psalm 16."

Bibliography

Ackroyd, Peter R., and Barnabas Lindars, eds. *Words and Meanings: Essays presented to David Winton Thomas on his retirement from the Regius Professorship of Hebrew in the University of Cambridge.* Cambridge: Cambridge University Press, 1968.

Alexander, Loveday C. "Sisters in Adversity: Retelling Martha's Story." Pp. 197–213 in Levine and Blickenstaff, *Feminist Companion to Luke.*

Althaus, Paul. *Die Wahrheit des kirchlichen Osterglaubens. Einspruch gegen Emanuel Hirsch.* Gütersloh: C. Bertelsmann, 1940.

Anderson, Hugh. *The Gospel of Mark.* NCB. London: Oliphants, 1976.

_____. *Jesus and Christian Origins: A Commentary on Modern Viewpoints.* New York: Oxford University Press, 1964.

Andrews, Elias. "Tongues, Gift of." Pp. 671–72 of *IDB* 4.

Anonymous. "καθηγητής, οῦ, ὁ." *EDNT* 2:222.

_____. "Josephus and Jesus." *Time* 99,9 (February 28, 1972) 55.

Attridge, Harold W. "'Heard because of His Reverence' (Heb 5:7)." *JBL* 98 (1979) 90–93.

Bacon, Benjamin W. *Studies in Matthew.* New York: Henry Holt and Company, 1930.

Bailey, John Amedee. *The Traditions Common to the Gospels of Luke and John.* NovTSup 7. Leiden: E. J. Brill, 1963.

Barrett, C. K. *The Gospel according to St John: An Introduction with Commentary and Notes on the Greek Text.* London: S.P.C.K., 1955.

_____. *The Gospel according to St John: An Introduction with Commentary and Notes on the Greek Text.* 2nd ed. Philadelphia: Westminster Press, 1978.

_____. *The Holy Spirit and the Gospel Tradition.* London: S.P.C.K., 1947.

_____. "Stephen and the Son of Man." Pp. 32–38 in Eltester and Kettler, *Apophoreta.*

Barth, Karl. *Church Dogmatics.* 5 vols. Edinburgh: T & T Clark, 1956–69.

_____. *Die Auferstehung der Toten. Akademische Vorlesung über I. Kor. 15.* 2nd ed. Munich: C. Kaiser, 1930.

_____. "Recapitulation Number Three." *ChrCent* 77,3 (January 20, 1960) 72–76.

Bartsch, Hans-Werner, ed. *Kerygma and Myth: A Theological Debate.* 2 vols. London: S.P.C.K., 1953–62.

_____. *Kerygma und Mythos. Ein theologisches Gespräch.* 6 vols. Hamburg: Reich & Heinrich (vol. 2: Hamburg-Volksdorf: Herbert Reich Evangelischer Verlag), 1948–64.

Baumbach, Günther. "Zeloten und Sikarier." *TLZ* 90 (1965) 727–40.

Beare, Francis Wright. *The Gospel according to Matthew: Translation, Introduction, and Commentary.* New York: Harper & Row, 1981.

Best, Ernest. *The Temptation and the Passion: The Marcan Soteriology.* SNTSMS 2. Cambridge: Cambridge University Press, 1965.

Best, Ernest, and R. McL. Wilson, eds. *Text and Interpretation: Studies in the New Testament Presented to Matthew Black.* Cambridge and New York: Cambridge University Press, 1979.

Bietenhard, Hans. "ὄνομα, ὀνομάζω, ἐπονομάζω, ψευδώνυμος." Pp. 242–83 in *TDNT* 5.

Black, Matthew. *An Aramaic Approach to the Gospels and Acts.* 3rd ed. Oxford: Clarendon Press, 1967.
————. "The Christological Use of the Old Testament in the New Testament." *NTS* 18 (1971–72) 1–14.
————. "Jesus and the Son of Man." *JSNT* 1 (1978) 4–18.
————. "The 'Son of Man' in the Teaching of Jesus." *ExpTim* 60 (1948–49) 32–36.
————. "The Son of Man Problem in Recent Research and Debate." *BJRL* 45 (1962–63) 305–18.
Boers, Hendrikus W. "Psalm 16 and the Historical Origin of the Christian Faith." *ZNW* 60 (1969) 106–10.
————. "Where Christology Is Real: A Survey of Recent Research on New Testament Christology." *Int* 26 (1972) 300–327.
Boobyer, George H. "Mark 11,10a and the Interpretation of the Healing of the Paralytic." *HTR* 47 (1954) 115–20.
————. "The Secrecy Motif in St. Mark's Gospel." *NTS* 6 (1959–60) 222–35.
Bornkamm, Günther. "End-Expectation and Church in Matthew." Pp. 15–51 in Bornkamm, Barth, and Held, *Tradition and Interpretation in Matthew.*
————. *Jesus of Nazareth.* New York: Harper and Brothers, 1960.
Bornkamm, Günther, Gerhard Barth, and Heinz Joachim Held. *Tradition and Interpretation in Matthew.* Philadelphia: Westminster Press, 1963.
Borsch, Frederick H. *The Christian and Gnostic Son of Man.* SBT 2nd series 14. Naperville: Alec R. Allenson, 1970.
————. *The Son of Man in Myth and History.* Philadelphia: Westminster Press, 1967.
Bousset, Wilhelm. *Kyrios Christos. Geschichte des Christusglaubens von den Anfängen des Christentums bis Irenaeus.* 5th ed. Göttingen: Vandenhoeck & Ruprecht, 1965.
Bowman, J. W. "The Background of the Term 'Son of Man.'" *ExpTim* 59 (1947–48) 283–88.
Braaten, Carl E., and Roy A. Harrisville, eds. *The Historical Jesus and the Kerygmatic Christ: Essays on the New Quest of the Historical Jesus.* New York and Nashville: Abingdon Press, 1964.
————. *Kerygma and History: A Symposium on the Theology of Rudolf Bultmann.* New York and Nashville: Abingdon Press, 1962.
Brandon, S. G. F. *Jesus and the Zealots. A Study of the Political Factor in Primitive Christianity.* Manchester: Manchester University Press, 1967.
Brown, Raymond E. *The Birth of the Messiah: A Commentary on the Infancy Narratives in Matthew and Luke.* Garden City, NY: Doubleday and Company, 1977.
————. *The Epistles of John: Translated with Introduction, Notes and Commentary.* AB 30. Garden City, NY: Doubleday and Company, 1982.
————. *The Gospel according to John (i–xii): Introduction, Translation and Notes.* AB 29. Garden City, NY: Doubleday and Company, 1966.
————. *The Gospel according to John (xiii–xxi): Introduction, Translation and Notes.* AB 29A. Garden City, NY: Doubleday and Company, 1970.
Brownlee, William H. *The Midrash Pesher of Habakkuk.* SBLMS 24. Missoula, MT: Scholars Press, 1979.
Bruce, Alexander Balmain. "The Synoptic Gospels." P. 191 in Nicoll, *Expositor's Greek Testament*, vol. 1.
Buchanan, George Wesley. "Current Synoptic Studies: Orchard, the Griesbach Hypothesis, and Other Alternatives." *RL* 46 (1977) 415–25.

_____. "Has the Griesbach Hypothesis Been Falsified?" *JBL* 93 (1974) 550–72.

Bultmann, Rudolf. "ἀφίημι, ἄφεσις, παρίημι, πάρεσις." Pp. 509–12 in *TDNT* 1.

_____. "The Christological Confession of the World Council of Churches." Pp. 273–90 in Bultmann, *Essays, Philosophical and Theological*.

_____. "Die Bedeutung des geschichtlichen Jesus für die Theologie des Paulus." Pp. 188–213 in Bultmann, *Glauben und Verstehen*, vol. 1.

_____. *Essays, Philosophical and Theological*. New York: The Macmillan Company, 1955.

_____. *Existence and Faith: Shorter Writings of Rudolf Bultmann*. New York: Meridian Press, 1960.

_____. *Glauben und Verstehen. Gesammelte Aufsätze*. 4 vols. Tübingen: J. C. B. Mohr (Paul Siebeck), 1933–1960.

_____. *The Gospel of John: A Commentary*. Ed. R. W. N. Hoare and J. K. Riches. Philadelphia: Westminster Press, 1971.

_____. *The History of the Synoptic Tradition*. Oxford: Basil Blackwell, 1963.

_____. *The History of the Synoptic Tradition*. Rev. ed. New York and Evanston: Harper & Row, 1969.

_____. "Is Exegesis without Presuppositions Possible?" Pp. 289–96 in Bultmann, *Existence and Faith*.

_____. *Jesus and the Word*. New York: Charles Scribner's Sons, 1958.

_____. "The New Approach to the Synoptic Problem." *JR* 6 (1926) 337–62. Reprinted as pp. 35–54 in Bultmann, *Existence and Faith*.

_____. "New Testament and Mythology: The Mythological Element in the Message of the New Testament and the Problem of its Re-interpretation." Pp. 1–44 in Bartsch, *Kerygma and Myth*, vol. 1.

_____. "The Primitive Christian Kerygma and the Historical Jesus." Pp. 15–42 in Braaten and Harrisville, *Historical Jesus and Kerygmatic Christ*.

_____. "Reich Gottes und Menschensohn." *TRu* n.s. 9 (1937) 1–35.

_____. Review of Schubert M. Ogden, *Christ without Myth*. *JR* 42 (1962) 226.

_____. "The Study of the Synoptic Gospels." Pp. 5–76 in Bultmann and Kundsin, *Form Criticism*.

_____. *Theology of the New Testament*. 2 vols. New York: Charles Scribner's Sons, 1951–55.

Bultmann, Rudolf, and Karl Kundsin. *Form Criticism: Two Essays on New Testament Research*. New York: Harper and Brothers, 1962.

Buri, Fritz. "Entmythologisierung oder Entkerygmatisierung der Theologie." Pp. 85–101 in Bartsch, *Kerygma und Mythos*, vol. 2.

Burkett, Delbert. *The Son of Man in the Fourth Gospel*. JSNTSup 56. Sheffield: JSOT Press, 1991.

Burkitt, F. C. *The Gospel History and Its Transmission*. Edinburgh: T. and T. Clark, 1906.

Burney, C. F. *The Poetry of Our Lord: An Examination of the Formal Elements of Hebrew Poetry in the Discourses of Jesus Christ*. Oxford: Clarendon Press, 1925.

Buttrick, David G., ed. *Jesus and Man's Hope*. 2 vols. Pittsburgh: Pittsburgh Theological Seminary, 1970–71.

Campbell, J. Y. "The Origin and Meaning of the Term Son of Man." *JTS* 48 (1947) 145–55.

_____. "Son of Man." Pp. 230–32 in Richardson, *A Theological Word Book of the Bible*.

Campenhausen, Hans von. *The Formation of the Christian Bible*. Philadelphia: Fortress Press, 1972.

Carlston, Charles Edwin. "A *Positive* Criterion of Authenticity?" *BR* 7 (1962)
    33–44.
Carter, Warren. "Getting Martha Out of the Kitchen: Luke 10:38–42 Again." Pp.
    214–31 in Levine with Blickenstaff, *Feminist Companion to Luke.*
Casey, Maurice. *Son of Man: The Interpretation and Influence of Daniel 7.* London:
    S.P.C.K., 1979.
Ceroke, C. P. "Is Mk 2,10 a Saying of Jesus?" *CBQ* 22 (1960) 369–90.
Clark, Kenneth W. "The Transmission of the New Testament." Pp. 617–27 of *IB*
    12.
Coakley, J. F. "The Anointing at Bethany and the Priority of John." *JBL* 107 (1988)
    241–56.
Cohen, Shaye J. D. "Epigraphical Rabbis." *JQR* 72 (1981) 1–17.
Colpe, Carsten. "ὁ υἱὸς τοῦ ἀνθρώπου," Pp. 400–77 in *TDNT* 8.
Colwell, E. C. "A Definite Rule for the Use of the Article in the Greek New
    Testament." *JBL* 52 (1933) 12–21.
Conzelmann, Hans. *Jesus: The Classic Article from RGG Expanded and Updated.*
    Philadelphia: Fortress Press, 1973.
_____. "Jesus Christus." Col. 619–53 in Galling, et al., *Die Religion in Geschichte
    und Gegenwart,* vol. 3.
_____. "On the Analysis of the Confessional Formula in I Corinthians 15:3–5."
    Int 20 (1966) 15–25.
_____. *An Outline of the Theology of the New Testament.* London: S. C. M. Press,
    1969.
_____. "Present and Future in the Synoptic Tradition." Pp. 26–44 in Funk, *God
    and Christ.*
_____. *The Theology of St. Luke.* New York: Harper & Row, 1960.
Cope, Lamar. "The Synoptic Problem in the Light of Redaction Criticism: The
    Phenomenon of Redaction Overlap." Unpublished paper, 1971.
Coppens, Joseph. *La relève apocalyptique du messianisme royal,* vol. 3: *Le Fils de
    l'homme néotestamentaire.* BETL 55. Leuven: Uitgererij Peeters/Leuven
    University Press, 1981.
_____. "Le Fils de l'homme dans l'évangile johannique." *ETL* 52 (1976) 28–81.
Corley, Bruce, ed. *Colloquy on New Testament Studies: A Time for Reappraisal and
    Fresh Approaches.* Macon, GA: Mercer University Press, 1983.
Cranfield, C. E. B. *The Gospel according to Saint Mark.* CGTC. Cambridge:
    Cambridge University Press, 1959.
Cribbs, F. Lamar. "The Agreements that Exist between Luke and John." *SBLSP* 9
    (1979) 1:215–61.
_____. "St. Luke and the Johannine Tradition." *JBL* 90 (1971) 422–50.
_____. "A Study of the Contacts that Exist between St. Luke and St. John."
    SBLSP 3 (1973) 2:1–93.
Cullmann, Oscar. *The Christology of the New Testament.* 2nd ed. London: SCM
    Press, 1963.
_____. "Dissensions within the Early Church." *USQR* 22 (1967) 83–92.
_____. *Jesus and the Revolutionaries.* New York: Harper and Row, 1970.
_____. *Salvation in History.* New York: Harper and Row, 1967.
_____. *The State in the New Testament.* Rev. ed. London: SCM Press, 1963.
Currie, Stuart D. "'Speaking in Tongues': Early Evidence outside the New
    Testament Bearing on 'Glōssais Lalein.'" *Int* 19 (1965) 274–94.
D'Angelo, Mary Rose, "Reconstructing the 'Real' Women from Gospel Literature:
    The Case of Mary Magdalene." Pp. 105–28 in Kraemer and D'Angelo,
    Women & Christian Origins.

Dahl, Nils Alstrup. "The Problem of the Historical Jesus." Pp. 138–71 in Braaten and Harrisville, *Kerygma and History*.

Dauer, Anton. *Johannes und Lukas: Untersuchungen zu den johanneisch-lukanischen Parallelperikopen Joh 4, 46–54/Lk 7, 1–10—Joh 12, 1–8/Lk 7, 36–50, 10, 38–42—Joh 20, 19–29/Lk 24, 36–49.* FB 50. Würzburg: Echter Verlag, 1984.

Davies, William D. *Paul and Rabbinic Judaism: Some Rabbinic Elements in Pauline Theology.* 2nd ed. London: S.P.C.K. Press, 1955.

_____. "A Quest to Be Resumed in New Testament Studies." Pp. 35–72 in Marty, *New Directions in Biblical Thought*. Originally published in *USQR* 15 (1960) 83–98.

De Jonge, Marinus, ed. *L'Évangile de Jean: Sources, redaction, théologie.* BETL 44. Gembloux: J. Duculot, 1977.

Denaux, Adelbert, ed. *John and the Synoptics.* BETL 101. Leuven: University Press/ Uitgeverij Peeters, 1992.

Descamps, A.-L., and André de Halleux, eds. *Mélanges bibliques en homage au R. P. Béda-Rigaux.* Gembloux: J. Duculot, 1970.

Dibelius, Martin. *From Tradition to Gospel.* New York: Charles Scribner's Sons, 1934.

_____. *Studies in the Acts of the Apostles.* London: SCM Press, 1956.

Dilthey, Wilhelm. *Pattern & Meaning in History: Thoughts on History & Society.* Ed. and intro. H. P. Rickman. 1st Harper Torchbook ed. New York: Harper & Brothers, 1962.

Dodd, C. H. *According to the Scriptures: The Sub-Structure of New Testament Theology.* New York: Charles Scribner's Sons, 1953.

_____. *The Apostolic Preaching and Its Development: Three Lectures with an Appendix on Eschatology and History.* New York: Harper and Brothers, 1944.

_____. "The Earliest Sources for the Life of Jesus." Unpublished lecture at Cambridge University, 1937.

_____. *Historical Tradition in the Fourth Gospel.* Cambridge: Cambridge University Press, 1963.

_____. *History and the Gospel.* New York: Charles Scribner's Sons, 1938.

_____. *The Interpretation of the Fourth Gospel.* Cambridge: Cambridge University Press, 1953.

_____. *The Old Testament in the New.* FBBS 3. Philadelphia: Fortress Press, 1963.

Doeve, J. W. *Jewish Hermeneutics in the Synoptic Gospels and Acts.* Assen: von Gorcum, 1953.

Donahue, John R. "Tax Collectors and Sinners: An Attempt at Identification." *CBQ* 33 (1971) 39–61.

Duling, Dennis C. "Matthew (Disciple)." ABD 4:618–22.

Duncan, George Simpson. *Jesus, Son of Man: Studies Contributory to a Modern Portrait.* London: Nisbet, 1947.

Dungan, David L. *The Sayings of Jesus in the Churches of Paul: The Use of the Synoptic Tradition in the Regulation of Early Church Life.* Philadelphia: Fortress Press, 1971.

Ebeling, Gerhard. *The Nature of Faith.* Philadelphia: Muhlenberg Press, 1961.

_____. *The Problem of Historicity in the Church and Its Proclamation.* Philadelphia: Fortress Press, 1967.

_____. *Theology and Proclamation: Dialogue with Bultmann.* Philadelphia: Fortress Press, 1966.

_____. *Word and Faith.* Philadelphia: Fortress Press, 1963.

Edwards, George R. *Jesus and the Politics of Violence.* New York: Harper and Row, 1972.

Eichrodt, Walther. "Zum Problem des Menschensohns." *EvT* 19 (1959) 1–3.

Ellis, E. E., and M. Wilcox, eds. *Neotestamentica et Semitica: Studies in Honour of Matthew Black*. Edinburgh: T & T Clark, 1969.

Eltester, W., and F. H. Kettler, eds. *Apophoreta. Festschrift für Ernst Haenchen zu seinem siebzigsten Geburtstag am 10. December 1964*. BZNW 30. Berlin: Alfred Töpelmann, 1964.

Enslin, Morton Scott. *From Jesus to Christianity*. Boston: Beacon Press, 1964.

_____. "Marcion, Gospel of." Pp. 262–63 in *IDB* 3.

_____. *The Prophet from Nazareth*. New York: McGraw-Hill Book Company, 1961.

Epstein, Isidore. "Midrash." Pp. 376–77 in *IDB* 3.

Evans, Owen E. "Kingdom of God, of Heaven." Pp. 17–26 in *IDB* 3.

Farmer, William R. "Basic Affirmation with Some Demurrals: A Response to Roland Mushat Frye." Pp. 303–22 in Walker, *Relationships among the Gospels*.

_____. "An Historical Essay on the Humanity of Jesus Christ." Pp. 100–126 in Farmer, Moule, and Niebuhr, *Christian History and Interpretation*.

_____. "John the Baptist." Pp. 955–62 in *IDB* 2.

_____. "The Post-Sectarian Character of Matthew and Its Post-War Setting in Antioch or Syria." *PRSt* 3 (1976) 235–47.

_____. "A Proposed Methodology for Redaction Criticism of the Gospels." Unpublished Paper, 1974.

_____. "Redaction Criticism and the Synoptic Problem." Pp. 239–50 in *The Society of Biblical Literature One Hundred Seventh Annual Meeting Seminar Papers*, vol. 1. Society of Biblical Literature, 1971.

_____. *The Synoptic Problem: A Critical Analysis*. New York: The Macmillan Company, 1964.

_____. "Who are the 'Tax Collectors and Sinners' in the Synoptic Tradition?" Unpublished paper read before *Studiorum Novi Testamenti Societas*, 1958.

Farmer, William R., ed. *New Synoptic Studies: The Cambridge Gospel Conference and Beyond*. Macon, GA: Mercer University Press, 1983.

Farmer, William R., C. F. D. Moule, and R. R. Niebuhr, eds. *Christian History and Interpretation: Studies Presented to John Knox*. Cambridge: Cambridge University Press, 1962.

Fee, Gordon D. "Modern Text Criticism and the Synoptic Problem." Pp. 154–69 in Orchard and Longstaff, *J. J. Griesbach*.

Feine, Paul, and Johannes Behm. *Introduction to the New Testament*. Ed. Werner Georg Kümmel. Nashville: Abingdon Press, 1966.

Fitzmyer, Joseph A. "κύριος, κυριακός." Pp. 328–31 in *EDNT* 2.

_____. "Another View of the 'Son of Man' Debate." *JSNT* 4 (1979) 58–68.

_____. "The Contribution of Qumran Aramaic to the Study of the New Testament." *NTS* 20 (1974) 382–407.

_____. *The Gospel according to Luke (I–IX): Introduction, Translation, and Notes*. AB 28. Garden City, NY: Doubleday and Company, 1981.

_____. "New Testament Κύριος and Maranatha and Their Aramaic Background." Pp. 218–35 in Fitzmyer, *To Advance the Gospel*.

_____. "The New Testament Title 'Son of Man' Philologically Considered." Pp. 143–60 in Fitzmyer, *A Wandering Aramean*.

_____. "The Priority of Mark and the 'Q' Source in Luke." Pp. 131–70 in Buttrick, *Jesus and Man's Hope*, vol. 1.

_____. Review of Matthew Black, *An Aramaic Approach to the Gospels and Acts*. *CBQ* 30 (1968) 424–28.

_____. "The Semitic Background of the New Testament Κύριος-Title." Pp. 115–42 in Fitzmyer, *A Wandering Aramean.*

_____. *To Advance the Gospel: New Testament Studies.* New York: Crossroad Publishing Company, 1981.

_____. *A Wandering Aramean: Collected Aramaic Essays.* Missoula, MT: Scholars Press, 1979.

Foakes Jackson, F. J., and Kirsop Lake, eds. *The Beginnings of Christianity,* part I: *The Acts of the Apostles,* vol. I: *Prolegomena,* I: *The Jewish, Gentile, and Christian Backgrounds.* London: Macmillan, 1920.

Formesyn, R. E. C. "Was There a Pronominal Connection for the 'Bar Nasha' Selfdesignation?" *NovT* 8 (1966) 1–35.

Fosdick, Harry Emerson. *The Man from Nazareth as His Contemporaries Saw Him.* New York: Harper and Brothers, 1949.

Freed, Edwin D. "The Son of Man in the Fourth Gospel." *JBL* 86 (1967) 402–9.

Fuchs, Ernst. *Studies of the Historical Jesus.* SBT 42. London: SCM Press, 1964.

Fuller, Reginald H. "Classics and the Gospels: The Seminar." Pp. 173–92 in Walker, *Relationships Among the Gospels.*

_____. *A Critical Introduction to the New Testament.* London: Gerald Duckworth & Company, 1966.

_____. *The Foundations of New Testament Christology.* New York: Charles Scribner's Sons, 1965.

_____. *The Mission and Achievement of Jesus: An Examination of the Presuppositions of New Testament Theology.* SBT 12: Chicago: Alec R. Allenson, 1954.

_____. *The New Testament in Current Study.* New York: Charles Scribner's Sons, 1962.

_____. "The Resurrection of Jesus Christ." *BR* 4 (1960) 8–24.

Fuller, Reginald H., et al. *Longer Mark: Forgery, Interpolation, or Old Tradition? Protocol for the Eighteenth Colloquy, 7 December 1975.* Berkeley, CA: The Center for Hermeneutical Studies in Hellenistic and Modern Culture, 1976.

Fuller, Reginald H., E. P. Sanders, and Thomas R. W. Longstaff. "The Synoptic Problem: After Ten Years." *Perkins Journal* 28 (1975) 63–74.

Funk, Robert W., ed. *God and Christ: Existence and Province.* JTC 5. Tübingen: J. C. B. Mohr (Paul Siebeck)/New York: Harper & Row, 1968.

Galling, Kurt, et al., eds. *Die Religion in Geschichte und Gegenwart. Handwörterbuch für Theologie und Religionswissenschaft.* Vol. 3. 3rd ed. Tübingen: J. C. B. Mohr (Paul Siebeck), 1959.

Gaster, Theodor H. "Dead, Abode of the." Pp. 787–88 in *IDB* 1.

Gelston, A. "A Sidelight on the 'Son of Man.'" *SJT* 22 (1969) 189–96.

Giblin, Charles H. "Reflections on the Sign of the Manger." *CBQ* 29 (1967) 110–15.

Giles, Pauline. "The Son of Man in the Epistle to the Hebrews." *ExpTim* 86 (1974–75) 328–32.

Gnilka, Joachim, ed. *Neues Testament und Kirche. Für Rudolf Schnackenburg.* Freiburg, Basel, and Vienna: Verlag Herder, 1974.

Goguel, Maurice. *The Life of Jesus.* New York: The Macmillan Company, 1933.

Goodspeed, Edgar J. *A Life of Jesus.* New York: Harper and Brothers, 1950.

Goulder, Michael D. *Midrash and Lection in Matthew: The Speaker's Lectures in Biblical Studies 1969–71.* London: S.P.C.K., 1974.

Grant, Frederick C. "Was the Author of John Dependent upon the Gospel of Luke?" *JBL* 56 (1937) 285–307.

Grant, Robert M. *A Historical Introduction to the New Testament.* New York: Harper & Row, 1963.

Guignebert, Charles. *Jesus*. London: Kegan Paul, Trench, and Trubner, 1935.

Gundry, Robert H. *Matthew: A Commentary on His Literary and Theological Art*. Grand Rapids: William B. Eerdmans Publishing Company, 1982.

_____. "On True and False Disciples in Matthew 8.18–22." *NTS* 40 (1994) 433–41.

Haenchen, Ernst. "The Book of Acts as Source Material for the History of Early Christianity." Pp. 258–78 in Keck and Martyn, *Studies in Luke-Acts*.

Hahn, Ferdinand. *The Titles of Jesus in Christology: Their History in Early Christianity*. London: Lutterworth Press, 1969.

Hammann, Konrad. *Rudolf Bultmann: A Biography*. Salem, OR: Polebridge Press, 2013.

Hare, Douglas R. A. *The Son of Man Tradition*. Minneapolis: Fortress Press, 1990.

Harner, Philip B. "Qualitative Anarthrous Predicate Nouns: Mark 15:39 and John 1:1." *JBL* 92 (1973) 75–87.

_____. *Understanding the Lord's Prayer*. Philadelphia: Fortress Press, 1975.

Haufe, Günter. "Das Menschensohn-Problem in der gegenwärtigen wissenschaftlichen Diskussion." *EvT* 26 (1966) 130–41.

Hayes, John H. "The Resurrection as Enthronement and the Earliest Church Christology." *Int* 22 (1968) 333–45.

Heekerens, Hans-Peter. *Die Zeichen-Quelle der johanneischen Redaktion. Ein Beitrag zur Enstehungsgeschuichte der vierten Evangeliums*. Stuttgart: Verlag Katholisches Bibelwerk, 1984.

Hengel, Martin. *Die Zeloten. Untersuchungen zur jüdischen Freiheitsbewegung in der Zeit von Herodes I. bis 70 n. Ch.* AGJU 1. 2nd ed. Leiden: E. J. Brill, 1976.

_____. Review of S. G. F. Brandon, *Jesus and the Zealots*. *JSS* 14 (1969) 231–40.

_____. *Was Jesus A Revolutionist?* FBBS 28. Philadelphia: Fortress Press, 1971.

Hennecke, Edgar. *New Testament Apocrypha*. 2 vols. Ed. Wilhelm Schneemelcher. Philadelphia: Westminster Press, 1963–65.

Héring, Jean. *Le royaume de Dieu et sa venue: Étude sur l'espérance de Jésus et de l'apôtre Paul*. Paris: Alcan, 1937.

Higgins, A. J. B. "Is the Son of Man Problem Insoluble?" Pp. 70–87 in Ellis and Wilcox, *Neotestamentica et Semitica*.

_____. *Jesus and the Son of Man*. London: Lutterworth Press, 1964.

_____. "Son of Man-*Forschung* since 'The Teaching of Jesus.'" Pp. 119–35 in Higgins, *New Testament Essays*.

_____. *The Son of Man in the Teaching of Jesus*. SNTSMS 39. Cambridge: Cambridge University Press, 1980.

Higgins, A. J. B., ed. *New Testament Essays: Studies in Memory of Thomas Walter Manson*. Manchester: Manchester University Press, 1959.

Hirsch, Emanuel. "Zum Problem des Osterglaubens." *TLZ* 65 (1940) 295–302.

Hodgson, Peter C. "The Son of Man and the Problem of Historical Knowledge." *JR* 41 (1961) 91–108.

Hooker, Morna D. "Is the Son of Man Problem Really Insoluble?" Pp. 155–68 in Best and Wilson, *Text and Interpretation*.

_____. *The Son of Man in Mark: A Study of the Background of the Term "Son of Man" and Its Use in St. Mark's Gospel*. London: S.P.C.K., 1967.

Horgan, Maurya P. *Pesharim: Qumran Interpretations of Biblical Books*. CBQMS 8. Washington: The Catholic Biblical Association of America, 1979.

Hoskyns, Edwyn, and Noel Davey. *The Riddle of the New Testament*. London: Faber and Faber, 1931.

Howard, Wilbert F. "The Gospel according to St. John: Introduction and Exegesis." Pp. 437–811 in *IB* 8.

Huffmon, Herbert Bardwell. "Names, Religious Significance of." Pp. 619–21 in *IDBSup*.

Iber, G. "Überlieferungsgeschichtliche Untersuchungen zum Begriff Menschensohn in Neuen Testament." Ph.D. Diss., Heidelberg, 1953.

Jastrow, Marcus. *A Dictionary of the Targumim, the Talmud Babli and Yerushalmi, and the Midrashic Literature with an Index of Scriptural Quotations.* 2 vols. New York: Title Publishing Company, 1950.

Jeremias, Joachim. "Abba." Pp. 11–65 in Jeremias, *Prayers of Jesus.*

_____. *The Central Message of the New Testament.* New York: Charles Scribner's Sons, 1965.

_____. "Die älteste Schicht der Menschensohn-Logien." *ZNW* 58 (1967) 159–72.

_____. *The Eucharistic Words of Jesus.* 3rd ed. New York: Charles Scribner's Sons, 1966.

_____. *Jerusalem in the Time of Jesus: An Investigation into Economic and Social Conditions during the New Testament Period.* Philadelphia: Fortress Press, 1969.

_____. "Kennzeichen der *ipsissima vox* Jesu." Pp. 86–93 in Jeremias, *Synoptische Studien.*

_____. "The Lord's Prayer in the Light of Recent Research." Pp. 82–107 in Jeremias, *Prayers of Jesus.*

_____. *New Testament Theology: The Proclamation of Jesus.* New York: Charles Scribner's Sons, 1971.

_____. *The Parables of Jesus.* Rev. ed. New York: Charles Scribner's Sons, 1963.

_____. *The Prayers of Jesus.* SBT 2nd series 6. Naperville, IL: Alec R. Allenson, 1967.

_____. "The Present Position in the Controversy concerning the Problem of the Historical Jesus." *ExpTim* 69 (1957–58) 333–39. Reprinted as pp. 15–20 in Jeremias, *Problem of the Historical Jesus.*

_____. *The Problem of the Historical Jesus.* Philadelphia: Fortress Press, 1964.

_____. *Unknown Sayings of Jesus.* London: S.P.C.K., 1957.

_____. "Zöllner und Sünder." *ZNW* 30 (1931) 293–300.

Jeremias, Joachim, ed. *Synoptische Studien. Alfred Wikenhauser zum siebzigsten Geburtstag am 22. Februar 1953 dargebracht von Freunden, Kollegen und Schülern.* Munich: Karl Zink Verlag, 1953.

Joest, Wilfried, and Wolfhart Pannenberg, eds. *Dogma und Denkstrukturen.* Göttingen: Vandenhoeck und Ruprecht, 1963.

Johnson, Sherman E. "Matthew: Introduction." Pp. 213–50 in *IB* 8.

Jüngel, Eberhart. *Paulus und Jesus. Eine Untersuchung zur Präzisierung der Frage nach dem Ursprung der Christologie.* Tübingen: J. C. B. Mohr (Paul Siebeck), 1962.

_____. *Paulus und Jesus. Eine Untersuchung zur Präzisierung der Frage nach dem Ursprung der Christologie.* 2nd ed. Tübingen: J. C. B. Mohr (Paul Siebeck). 1964.

Kähler, Martin. *The So-Called Historical Jesus and the Historic, Biblical Christ.* Ed. and intro. Carl E. Braaten. Philadelphia: Fortress Press, 1964.

Käsemann, Ernst. "The Beginnings of Christian Theology." Pp. 82–107 in Käsemann, *New Testament Questions of Today.*

_____. "Das Problem des historischen Jesus." *ZTK* 51 (1954) 125–53.

_____. "Die Anfänge christlicher Theologie." *ZTK* 57 (1960) 162–85.

_____. *Essays on New Testament Themes.* SBT 41. London: SCM. Press, 1964.

_____. *New Testament Questions of Today.* Philadelphia: Fortress Press, 1969.

_____. "On the Subject of Primitive Christian Apocalyptic." Pp. 108–37 in
  Käsemann, *New Testament Questions of Today*.
_____. "The Problem of the Historical Jesus." Pp. 15–47 in Käsemann, *Essays
  on New Testament Themes*.
_____. "Sentences of Holy Law in the New Testament." Pp. 66–81 in
  Käsemann, *New Testament Questions of Today*.
_____. *The Testament of Jesus: A Study of the Gospel of John in the Light of Chapter
  17*. Philadelphia: Fortress Press, 1968.
Keck, Leander E. "Oral Traditional Literature and the Gospels: The Seminar." Pp.
  103–22 in Walker, *Relationships among the Gospels*.
Keck, Leander E., and J. Louis Martyn, eds. *Studies in Luke-Acts: Essays Presented
  in Honor of Paul Schubert*. Nashville and New York: Abingdon Press, 1966.
Kee, Howard Clark. *Jesus in History: An Approach to the Study of the Gospels*. 2nd
  ed. New York: Harcourt Brace Jovanovich, 1977.
Kee, Howard Clark, Franklin W. Young, and Karlfried Froehlich. *Understanding
  the New Testament*. 2nd ed. Englewood Cliffs, NJ: Prentice-Hall, Inc., 1965.
Keener, Craig S. *The Gospel of John: A Commentary*. 2 vols. Peabody, MA:
  Hendrickson Publishers, 2003.
George A. Kennedy, "Classical and Christian Source Criticism." Pp. 125–55 in
  Walker, *Relationships among the Gospels*.
Kilpatrick, G. D. "Acts vii.56: Son of Man?" *TZ* 21 (1965) 209.
_____. "Again Acts vii.56: Son of Man?" *TZ* 34 (1978) 232.
_____. *The Origins of the Gospel according to St. Matthew*. Oxford: Clarendon
  Press, 1946.
_____. "Some Thoughts on Modern Textual Criticism and the Synoptic
  Gospels." *NovT* 19 (1977) 275–92.
Kingsbury, Jack Dean. *Matthew: Structure, Christology, Kingdom*. Philadelphia:
  Fortress Press, 1975.
Kistemaker, Simon. *The Gospels in Current Study*. Grand Rapids: Baker Book
  House, 1972.
Kittel, Gerhard. "ἀββᾶ." Pp. 5–6 in *TDNT* 1.
Klassen, William. "Jesus and the Zealot Option." *CJT* 16 (1970) 12–21.
Klassen, William, and Graydon F. Snyder, eds. *Current Issues in New Testament
  Interpretation: Essays in Honor of Otto A. Piper*. New York: Harper and Row,
  1962.
Klein, Günter. "Galater 2:6–9 und die Geschichte der Jerusalemer Urgemeinde."
  ZTK 57 (1960) 275–95.
Knohl, Israel. "The Messianic Son of Joseph: 'Gabriel's Revelation' and the Birth
  of a New Messianic Model." *BAR* 34,5 (Sept/Oct 2008) 58–62.
Knox, John. "Acts and the Pauline Letter Corpus." Pp. 279–97 in Keck and
  Martyn, *Studies in Luke-Acts*.
_____. *Chapters in a Life of Paul*. New York and Nashville: Abingdon-
  Cokesbury Press, 1950.
_____. *The Death of Christ: The Cross in New Testament History and Faith*. New
  York: Abingdon Press, 1958.
_____. *The Humanity and Divinity of Christ: A Study of Pattern in Christology*.
  Cambridge: Cambridge University Press, 1967.
_____. *Marcion and the New Testament: An Essay in the Early History of the
  Canon*. Chicago: University of Chicago Press, 1942.
Koester, Helmut. *Ancient Christian Gospels: Their History and Development*. London:
  SCM Press/Philadelphia: Trinity Press International, 1990.

_____. "History and Development of Mark's Gospel: From Mark to Secret Mark and Canonical Mark." Pp. 35–57 in Corley, *Colloquy on New Testament Studies.*

_____. *Introduction to the New Testament*, vol. 2: *History and Literature of Early Christianity.* Philadelphia: Fortress Press/New York: Walter de Gruyter, 1982.

_____. "Response." Pp. 29–32 in Fuller, et al., *Longer Mark.*

Kraemer, Ross Shepard, and Mary Rose D'Angelo, eds. *Women & Christian Origins.* New York and Oxford: Oxford University Press, 1999.

Kraft, Robert A. Review of Shlomo Pines, *The Jewish Christians of the Early Centuries of Christianity according to a New Source. JBL* 86 (1967) 329–30.

Kuhn, Karl Georg. "βασιλεύς, βασιλεία, βασίλισσα, βασιλεύω, συμβασιλεύω, βασίλειος, βασιλικός, C: מלכות שמים in Rabbinic Literature." Pp. 571–74 in *TDNT* 1.

Kümmel, Werner Georg. *Introduction to the New Testament.* Rev. ed. Nashville: Abingdon Press, 1975.

_____. *Promise and Fulfilment: The Eschatological Message of Jesus.* Naperville, IL: Alec R. Allenson, 1957.

Kysar, Robert. *John.* Minneapolis: Ausburg Publishing House, 1986.

_____. "John, the Gospel of." *ABD* 3:912–31.

_____. *John, the Maverick Gospel.* Atlanta: John Knox Press, 1976.

Ladd, George Eldon. *Jesus and the Kingdom: The Eschatology of Biblical Realism.* New York: Harper and Row, 1964.

Lane, William L. *The Gospel according to Mark: The English Text with Introduction, Exposition, and Notes.* Grand Rapids: William B. Eerdmans Publishing Company, 1974.

Lapin, Hayim. "Rabbi." Pp. 600–602 in *ABD* 5.

Le Déaut, Roger. "Apropos a Definition of Midrash." *Int* 25 (1971) 259–82.

Leipoldt, Johannes. "Zu den Auferstehungsgeschichten." *TLZ* 73 (1948) 737–42.

Leivestad, Ragnar. "Der apokalyptische Menschensohn. Ein theologisches Phantom." *ASTI* 6 (1968) 49–105.

_____. "Exit the Apocalyptic Son of Man." *NTS* 18 (1971–72) 243–67.

Lenski, R. C. H. *The Interpretation of St. Matthew's Gospel.* Columbia, OH: Wartburg Press, 1943.

Levine, Amy-Jill. "Introduction." Pp. 1–22 in Levine with Blickenstaff, *Feminist Companion to Luke.*

Levine, Amy-Jill, with Marianne Blickenstaff, ed. *A Feminist Companion to John.* Feminist Companion to the New Testament and Early Christian Writings 4–5. 2 vols. London and New York: Sheffield Academic Press, 2003.

_____. *A Feminist Companion to Luke.* Feminist Companion to the New Testament and Early Christian Writings 3. London and New York: Sheffield Academic Press, 2002.

Lietzmann, Hans. "Notizen." *ZNW* 22 (1923) 153–54.

Lindars, Barnabas. *New Testament Apologetic: The Doctrinal Significance of the Old Testament Quotations.* London: SCM Press, 1973.

_____. "Re-enter the Apocalyptic Son of Man." *NTS* 22 (1975–76) 52–72.

_____. "The Son of Man in the Johannine Christology." Pp. 43–60 in Lindars and Smalley, *Christ and Spirit in the New Testament.*

Lindars, Barnabas, and Stephen S. Smalley, eds. *Christ and Spirit in the New Testament: In Honour of Charles Francis Digby Moule.* Cambridge: Cambridge University Press, 1973.

Lindsey, Robert L. *A Hebrew Translation of the Gospel of Mark.* N.p., n.d.

_____. "A Modified Two-Document Theory of Synoptic Dependence and Interdependence." *NovT* 6 (1963) 239–63.

_____. *A New Approach to the Synoptic Gospels.* Jerusalem: Dugworth Publishers, 1971.

Linton, Olof. "Evidence of a Second-Century Revised Edition of St. Mark's Gospel." *NTS* 14 (1968) 321–55.

Lohse, Eduard. "ῥαββί, ῥαββουνί." Pp. 961–65 in *TDNT* 6.

Lohse, Eduard, Christoph Burchard, and Berndt Schaller, eds. *Der Ruf Jesu und die Antwort der Gemeinde. Festschrift für Joachim Jeremias.* Göttingen: Vandenhoeck & Ruprecht, 1970.

Lord, Albert B. "The Gospels as Oral Traditional Literature." Pp. 33–91 in Walker, *Relationships among the Gospels.*

Macquarrie, John. *The Scope of Demythologizing: Bultmann and His Critics.* New York: Harper and Brothers, 1960.

Maddox, Robert. *The Purpose of Luke-Acts.* FRLANT 126. Göttingen: Vandenhoeck & Ruprecht, 1982.

Manson, T. W. "The Corinthian Correspondence (I)." Pp. 190–209 in Manson, *Studies in the Gospels and Epistles.*

_____. "The Foundation of the Synoptic Tradition: The Gospel of Mark." Pp. 28–45 in Manson, *Studies in the Gospels and Epistles.*

_____. "The Gospel according to St. Matthew." Pp. 68–104 in Manson, *Studies in the Gospels and Epistles.*

_____. "The Life of Jesus: A Study of the Available Materials." *ExpTim* 53 (1942) 248–51. Reprinted as pp. 13–27 in Manson, *Studies in the Gospels and Epistles.*

_____. "The Quest of the Historical Jesus—Continued: A Commemoration Day Address delivered at Westminster College, Cambridge, in 1949." Pp. 3–12 in Manson, *Studies in the Gospels and Epistles.*

_____. *Studies in the Gospels and Epistles.* Ed. Matthew Black. Philadelphia: Westminster Press, 1962.

_____. *The Teaching of Jesus; Studies in Its Form and Content.* 2nd ed. Cambridge: Cambridge University Press, 1935.

Manson, W. "The Son of Man and History." *SJT* 5 (1952) 113–22.

Marlow, Ransom. "The *Son of Man* in Recent Journal Literature." *CBQ* 28 (1966) 20–30.

Marshall, I. H. "The Synoptic Son of Man Sayings in Recent Discussion." *NTS* 12 (1966) 327–51.

Marty, Martin E., ed. *New Directions in Biblical Thought.* New York: Association Press, 1960.

Marxsen, Willi. *Mark the Evangelist: Studies on the Redaction History of the Gospel.* Nashville: Abingdon Press, 1969.

_____. "The Resurrection of Jesus as a Historical and Theological Problem." Pp. 15–49 in Marxsen et al., *Significance of the Message of the Resurrection.*

_____. *The Resurrection of Jesus of Nazareth.* Philadelphia: Fortress Press, 1970.

Marxsen, Willie, et al. *The Significance of the Message of the Resurrection for Faith in Jesus Christ.* Ed C. F. D. Moule. SBT 2nd series 8. Naperville, IL: Alec R. Allenson, 1968.

McArthur, Harvey K. "Basic Issues: A Survey of Recent Gospel Research." *Int* 18 (1964) 38–55.

McArthur, Harvey K., ed. *New Testament Sidelights: Essays in Honor of Alexander Converse Purdy.* Hartford: The Hartford Seminary Foundation Press, 1960.

McCasland, S. Vernon. *The Pioneer of Our Faith: A New Life of Jesus.* New York, Toronto, and London: McGraw-Hill, 1964.

McCown, C. C. "Jesus, Son of Man: A Survey of Recent Discussion." *JR* 28 (1948) 1–12.

Meeks, Wayne A. "Hypomnēmata from an Untamed Sceptic: A Response to George Kennedy." Pp. 157–72 in Walker, *Relationships among the Gospels.*

Metzger, Bruce M. *The Text of the New Testament: Its Transmission, Corruption, and Restoration.* New York: Oxford University Press, 1964.

Meyer, Arnold. *Jesu Muttersprache. Das galiläische Aramäische in seiner Bedeutung für die Erklarung der Reden Jesus und der Evangelien überhaupt.* Freibrug: J. C. B. Mohr, 1896.

Michel, Otto. "τελώνης." Pp. 88–105 in *TDNT* 8.

Miller, Merrill P. "Midrash." Pp. 593–97 in *IDBSup.*

Miller, Robert J. *Born Divine: The Births of Jesus & Other Sons of God.* Santa Rosa, CA: Polebridge Press, 2003.

Moloney, Francis J. *The Johannine Son of Man.* Rome: Libreria ateneo salesiano, 1976.

————. "The Reinterpretation of Psalm VIII and the Son of Man Debate." *NTS* 27 (1980–81) 656–72.

Montefiore, C. G., and H. Loewe. *A Rabbinic Anthology: Selected and Arranged with Comments and Introductions.* Cleveland: Meridian Books/New York: Jewish Publication Society of America, 1963.

Moody, Dale. "God's Only Son: The Translation of John 3:16 in the Revised Standard Version." *JBL* 72 (1953) 213–19.

Moore, George Foot. *Judaism in the First Centuries of the Christian Era: The Age of the Tannaim.* 3 vols. Cambridge, MA: Harvard University Press, 1927–30.

Moule, C. F. D. "Introduction." Pp. 2–4 in Marxsen et al., *Significance of the Message of the Resurrection.*

————. "The Christology of Acts." Pp. 159–85 in Keck and Martyn, *Studies in Luke-Acts.*

————. "Neglected Features in the Problem of 'the Son of Man.'" Pp. 413–28 in Gnilka, *Neues Testament und Kirche.*

————. *The Origin of Christology.* Cambridge: Cambridge University Press, 1977.

————. *The Phenomenon of the New Testament: An Inquiry into the Implications of Certain Features of the New Testament.* Naperville, IL: Alec R. Allenson, 1967.

Moule, C. F. D., ed. *The Significance of the Message of the Resurrection for Faith in Jesus Christ.* SBT 2nd series 8. Naperville, IL: Alec R. Allenson, 1968.

Mowinckel. Sigmund. *He that Cometh: The Messiah Concept in the Old Testament and Later Judaism.* New York and Nashville: Abingdon Press, 1956.

Neirynck, Frans. "John and the Synoptics." Pp. 73–106 in de Jonge, *L'Évangile de Jean.*

————. *L'Évangile de Noël selon S. Luc.* Études religieuses 749. Brussels: Pensée Catholique/Paris: Office Général du Livre, 1961.

Neusner, Jacob, ed. *The Study of Judaism: Bibliographical Essays.* New York: KTAV Publishing House, 1972.

Nicoll, W. Robertson, ed. *The Expositor's Greek Testament*, vol. 1. Grand Rapids: William B. Eerdmans Publishing Company, 1951 reprint of 1912 original.

Niebuhr, Richard R. *Resurrection and Historical Reason: A Study of Theological Method.* New York: Charles Scribner's Sons, 1957.

O'Day, Gail R. "The Gospel of John: Introduction, Commentary, and Reflections." Pp. 491–865 in *NIB* 9.

O'Rourke, John J. "The Synoptic Problem Is a 'Can of Worms.'" Unpublished
    paper presented at 1975 annual meeting of Society of Biblical Literature.
Oepke, Albrecht. "ἔκστασις, ἐξίστημι." Pp. 449–60 in TDNT 2.
_____. "ἐπιστάτης." Pp. 622–23 in TDNT 2.
Ogden, Schubert M. *Christ without Myth: A Study Based on the Theology of Rudolf
    Bultmann.* New York: Harper and Brothers, 1961.
Orchard, Bernard. "J. A. T. Robinson and the Synoptic Problem." NTS 22 (1976)
    346–52.
Orchard, Bernard, and Thomas R. W. Longstaff, eds. *J. J. Griesbach: Synoptic
    and Text-critical Studies 1776–1976.* Cambridge and New York: Cambridge
    University Press, 1978.
Outler, Albert C. "'Gospel Studies' in Transition." Pp. 17–29 in Walker,
    Relationships among the Gospels.
Owen, H. P. "Stephen's Vision in Acts 7.55–56." NTS 1 (1954–55) 224–26.
Painter, John. "The Enigmatic Johannine Son of Man." Pp. 3:1869–87 in van
    Segbroeck et al., *Four Gospels 1992.*
Pannenberg, Wolfhart. *Jesus—God and Man.* Philadelphia: Westminster Press,
    1968.
Parker, Pierson. "Luke and the Fourth Evangelist." NTS 9 (1962–63) 317–36.
_____. "The Meaning of 'Son of Man.'" JBL 60 (1941) 151–57.
Parvis, Merrill M. "Text, NT." Pp. 594–614 in IDB 4.
Peabody, David B. "The Late Secondary Redaction of Mark's Gospel and the
    Griesbach Hypothesis: A Response to Helmut Koester." Pp. 87–132 in
    Corley, *Colloquy on New Testament Studies.*
Peake, Arthur S. "The Messiah and the Son of Man." Pp. 220–37 in Arthur S.
    Peake, *The Servant of Yahweh: Three Lectures Delivered at King's College,
    London, during 1926 together with The Rylands Lectures on Old Testament and
    New Testament Subjects.* Manchester: Manchester University Press, 1931.
Perrin, Norman. "The Creative Use of the Son of Man Traditions by Mark."
    USQR 23 (1968) 357–65. Reprinted as pp. 84–93 in Perrin, *Modern Pilgrimage.*
_____. *The Kingdom of God in the Teaching of Jesus.* Philadelphia: Westminster
    Press, 1963.
_____. "The Literary *Gattung* 'Gospel'—Some Observations." ExpTim 82
    (1970–71) 4–7.
_____. "Mark XIV.62: The End Product of a Christian Pesher Tradition?" NTS
    12 (1965–66) 150–55. Reprinted with "Postscript" as pp. 10–22 in Perrin,
    Modern Pilgrimage.
_____. *A Modern Pilgrimage in New Testament Christology.* Philadelphia:
    Fortress Press, 1974.
_____. "New Beginnings in Christology: A Review Article." JR 46 (1966)
    491–96.
_____. "Postscript" to "Mark XIV.62: The End of a Christian Pesher Tradition?'
    Pp. 18–22 in Perrin, *Modern Pilgrimage.*
_____. "Recent Trends in Research in the Christology of the New Testament."
    Pp. 217–33 in *Transitions in Biblical Scholarship.* Ed. J. Coert Rylaarsdam.
    Chicago: University of Chicago Press, 1968. Reprinted as pp. 41–56 in Perrin,
    Modern Pilgrimage.
_____. *Rediscovering the Teaching of Jesus.* New York and Evanston: Harper &
    Row, 1967.
_____. "Son of Man." Pp. 833–36 in IDBSup.

_____. "The Son of Man in Ancient Judaism and Primitive Christianity: A Suggestion." *BR* 11 (1966) 17–26. Reprinted with "Postscript" as pp. 23–40 in Perrin, *Modern Pilgrimage*.

_____. "The Son of Man in the Synoptic Tradition." *BR* 13 (1968) 3–25. Reprinted as pp. 57–83 in Perrin, *Modern Pilgrimage*.

_____. "The Use of *(Para)didonai* in Connection with the Passion of Jesus in the New Testament." Pp. 204–12 in Lohse, Burchard, and Schaller, *Der Ruf Jesu und die Antwort der Gemeinde*. Reprinted with "Postscript" as pp. 94–103 in Perrin, *Modern Pilgrimage*.

_____. *What Is Redaction Criticism?* GBS. Philadelphia: Fortress Press, 1969.

_____. "The Wredestrasse Becomes the Hauptstrasse: Reflections on the Reprinting of the Dodd Festschrift." *JR* 46 (1966) 296–300.

Pesch, Rudolf. "Levi-Matthäus (Mc 2.14/Mt 9.9, 10.3). Ein Beitrag zur Lösing eines alten Problems." *ZNW* 59 (1968) 40–56.

Pesch, Rudolf, and Rudolf Schnackenburg with Odilo Kaiser, eds. *Jesus und der Menschensohn. Für Anton Vögtle*. Freiburg: Verlag Herder, 1975.

Phillips, Anthony. "The Ecstatics' Father." Pp. 183–94 in Ackroyd and Lindars, *Words and Meanings*.

Pike, Diane Kennedy, and R. Scott Kennedy. *The Wilderness Revolt: A New View of the Life and Death of Jesus Based on Ideas and Notes of the Late Bishop James A. Pike*. Garden City, NY: Doubleday & Company, 1972.

Pines, Shlomo. *The Jewish Christians of the Early Centuries of Christianity according to a New Source*. Jerusalem: Central Press, 1966.

Pirenne, Henri. "What Are Historians Trying to Do?" Pp. 87–100 in *The Philosophy of History in Our Time: An Anthology*. Ed. Hans Meyerhoff. Garden City, NY: Doubleday and Company, 1959.

Price, James L. *Interpreting the New Testament*. New York: Holt, Rinehart, and Winston, 1961.

Quesnell, Quentin. *The Mind of Mark: Interpretation and Method through the Exegesis of Mark 6,52*. Analecta Biblica 38. Rome: Pontifical Biblical Institute, 1969.

Reed, Barbara E. "'Do You See This Woman?': A Liberative Look at Luke 7.36–50 and Strategies for Reading Other Lukan Stories against the Grain." Pp. 106–20 in Levine with Blickenstaff, *Feminist Companion to Luke*.

Richardson, Alan. *The Political Christ*. Philadelphia: Westminster Press, 1973.

Richardson, Alan, ed. *A Theological Word Book of the Bible*. New York: The Macmillan Company, 1957.

Riesenfeld, Harald. *Jésus transfiguré: l'arrière-plan récit évangélique de la transfiguration de Notre-Seigneur*. Copenhagen: E. Munksgaard, 1947.

Robinson, James M. "Ascension." Pp. 245–47 in *IDB* 1.

_____. "The Formal Structure of Jesus' Message." Pp. 91–110 in Klassen and Snyder, *Current Issues in New Testament Interpretation*.

_____. *Kerygma und historischer Jesus*. Zürich: Zwingli Verlag, 1960.

_____. *A New Quest of the Historical Jesus*. SBT 25. London: SCM Press, 1959.

_____. "The Problem of History in Mark, Reconsidered." *USQR* 20 (1965) 131–47.

_____. "The Recent Debate on the 'New Quest.'" *JBR* 30 (1962) 198–208.

Robinson, John A. T. *Jesus and His Coming: The Emergence of a Doctrine*. New York and Nashville: Abingdon Press, 1957.

_____. "The Most Primitive Christology of All?" *JTS* n.s. 7 (1956) 177–89. Reprinted as pp. 139–53 in Robinson, *Twelve New Testament Studies*.

_____. *Twelve New Testament Studies*. SBT 34. Naperville, IL: Alec R. Allenson, 1962.

Sahlin, H. "Die Früchte der Umkehr." *ST* 1 (1947) 54–68.

Sanders, E. P. *The Tendencies of the Synoptic Tradition*. SNTSMS 9. Cambridge: Cambridge University Press, 1969.

Sandmel, Samuel. *The Hebrew Scriptures: An Introduction to Their Literature and Religious Ideas*. New York: Alfred Knopf, 1963.

_____. *We Jews and Jesus*. New York: Oxford University Press, 1965.

Schmid, Josef. *Das Evangelium nach Lukas*. 4th ed. Regensburg: Friedrich Pustet, 1960.

Schmidt, Karl Ludwig. "βασιλεύς, βασιλεία, βασίλισσα, βασιλεύω, συμβασιλεύω, βασίλειος, βασιλικός, E: The Word Group βασιλεύς κτλ. in the NT." Pp. 576–93 in *TDNT* 1.

Schmidt, Nathaniel. "Recent Study of the Term 'Son of Man.'" *JBL* 45 (1926) 326–49.

Schnackenburg, Rudolf. "Der Menschensohn im Johannesevangelium." *NTS* 11 (1964–65) 123–37.

_____. "Der Sinn der Versuchung Jesu bei den Synoptikern." *TQ* 132 (1952) 297–326.

Schneemelcher, Wilhelm, ed. *Festschrift für Günther Dehn zum 75. Geburtstag am 18. April dargebracht*. Neukirchen-Vluyn: Erziehungsverein, 1957.

Schneider, Gerhard. *Das Evangelium nach Lukas*. 2 vols. ÖTK 3. Gütersloh: Mohn, 1977.

Schniewind, Julius. *Die Parallelperikopen bei Lukas und Johannes*. Leipzig: O. Brandstetter, 1914.

_____. *Die Parallelperikopen bei Lukas und Johannes*. 2nd ed. Hildesheim: George Olms, 1958.

Schoeps, Hans-Joachim. *Jewish Christianity: Factional Disputes in the Early Church*. Philadelphia: Fortress Press, 1969.

_____. *Paul: The Theology of the Apostle in the Light of Jewish Religious History*. London: Lutterworth Press, 1961.

Schreiber, Johannes. "Die Christologie des Markusevangeliums. Beobachtungen zur Theologie und Komposition des zweiten Evangeliums." *ZTK* 58 (1961) 154–83.

_____. *Theologie des Vertrauens. Eine redaktionsgeschichtliche Untersuchung des Markusevangeliums*. Hamburg: Furche-Verlag, 1967.

Schrenk, Gottlob, and Gottfried Quell. "πατήρ, πατρῷος, πατριά, ἀπάτωρ, πατρικός." Pp. 945–1022 in *TDNT* 5.

Schulz, S. Q. *Untersuchungen zur Menschensohn-Christologie im Johannesevangelium. Zugleich ein Beitrag zur Methodengeschichte der Auslegung des 4. Evangelium*. Göttingen: Vandenhoeck & Ruprecht, 1957.

Schürmann, Heinz. "Beobachtungen zum Menschensohn-Titel in der Redequelle. Sein Vorkommen in Anschluss- und Einleitungswendungen." Pp. 124–47 in Pesch and Schnackenburg, *Jesus und der Menschensohn*.

_____. *Das Lukasevangelium*, vol. 1: *Kommentar zu Kap. 1, 1–9, 50*. HThKNT 3. Freiburg: Herder, 1969.

_____. "Zur Traditionsgeschichte der Nazareth-Perikope Lk 4, 16–30." Pp. 191–205 in Descamps and de Halleux, *Mélanges bibliques en homage au R. P. Béda-Rigaux*.

Schüssler Fiorenza, Elisabeth. *But She Said: Feminist Practices of Biblical Interpretation*. Boston: Beacon Press, 1992.

_____. "Eschatology of the NT." Pp. 271–77 in *IDBSup*.

_____. "A Feminist Critical Interpretation for Liberation: Martha and Mary (Luke 10:38–42)." *Religion and Intellectual Life* 4 (1986) 21–36.

Schweitzer, Albert. *The Quest of the Historical Jesus: A Critical Study of Its Progress from Reimarus to Wrede.* Macmillan Paperbacks ed. New York: The Macmillan Company, 1961.

Schweizer, Eduard. "Der Menschensohn (Zur eschatologischen Erwartung Jesu)." *ZNW* 50 (1969) 185–209. Reprinted as pp. 56–84 in Schweizer, *Neotestamentica.*

_____. *Erniedrigung und Erhöhung bei Jesus und seinen Nachfolgern.* Zurich: Zwingli Verlag, 1955.

_____. *Erniedrigung und Erhöhung bei Jesus und seinen Nachfolgern.* 2nd ed. Zurich: Zwingli Verlag, 1962.

_____. *The Good News according to Luke.* Atlanta: John Knox Press, 1984.

_____. *The Good News according to Matthew.* Atlanta: John Knox Press, 1975.

_____. *Lordship and Discipleship.* Rev. ed. of Schweizer, *Erniedrigung und Erhöhung.* SBT 28. London: SCM Press, 1960.

_____. *Neotestamentica: Deutsche und Englische Aufsätze 1952–1963: German and English Essays 1951–1963.* Zurich and Stuttgart: Zwingli Verlag, 1963.

_____. "The Son of Man." *JBL* 79 (1960) 119–29.

_____. "The Son of Man Again." *NTS* 9 (1962–63) 256–61. Reprinted as pp. 85–92 in Schweizer, *Neotestamentica.*

Schweizer, Eduard, et al. *Spirit of God.* New York: Harper and Brothers, 1961.

Scofield, C. I., ed. *The Holy Bible.* "The Scofield Reference Bible." New ed. New York: Oxford University Press, 1917.

Shanks, Hershel, "Is the Title '*Rabbi*' Anachronistic in the Bible?" *JQR* 53 (1963) 337–45.

_____. "Origins of the Title '*Rabbi.*'" *JQR* 59 (1968) 152–57.

Shepherd, Massey H., Jr. "Response." Pp. 46–52 in Fuller, et al., *Longer Mark.*

Sidebottom, E. M. *The Christ of the Fourth Gospel in the Light of First-Century Thought.* London: S.P.C.K., 1961.

Simon, Marcel. *St. Stephen and the Hellenists in the Primitive Church.* New York: Longmans, Green, 1958.

Sjöberg, Eric. "Between the Old and New Testaments." Pp. 7–23 in Schweizer, et al., *Spirit of God.*

_____. *Der verborgene Menschensohn in den Evangelien.* Lund: C. W. K. Gleerup, 1955.

Smalley, Stephen S. "The Johannine Son of Man Sayings." *NTS* 15 (1968–69) 278–301.

Smith, Charles W. F. "Lord's Prayer." Pp. 154–58 in *IDB* 3.

Smith, Dwight Moody, Jr. *The Composition and Order of the Fourth Gospel: Bultmann's Literary Theory.* New Haven and London: Yale University Press, 1965.

_____. *John among the Gospels: Some Dimensions of the Problem.* 2nd ed. Columbia, SC: University of South Carolina Press, 2001.

Smith, Graham. "The Matthaean 'Additions' to the Lord's Prayer." *ExpTim* 82 (1970–71) 54–55.

Smith, M. S. "The 'Son of Man' in Ugaritic." *CBQ* 45 (1983) 59–60.

Smith, Morton. *Clement of Alexandria and a Secret Gospel of Mark.* Cambridge: Harvard University Press, 1973.

_____. *Jesus the Magician.* New York: Harper and Row, 1978.

_____. *The Secret Gospel: The Discovery and Interpretation of the Secret Gospel according to Mark.* New York: Harper and Row, 1973.

_____. "Zealots and Sicarii, Their Origins and Relation." *HTR* 64 (1971) 1–19.

Spivey, Robert A., and D. Moody Smith, Jr. *Anatomy of the New Testament: A Guide to Its Structure and Meaning*. New York: Macmillan and Company, 1969.

Stauffer, Ethelbert. *New Testament Theology*. New York: Macmillan Publishing Company, 1955.

Stein, Robert H. "The Proper Methodology for Ascertaining a Markan Redaction History." *NovT* 13 (1971) 181–98.

_____. "The 'Redaktionsgeschichtliche' Investigation of a Markan Seam (Mc 1 21f.)." *ZNW* 61 (1970) 70–94.

Stendahl, Krister. *The School of St. Matthew and Its Use of the Old Testament*. Philadelphia: Fortress Press, 1968.

Strawson, William. *Jesus and the Future Life: A Study in the Synoptic Gospels*. Philadelphia: Westminster Press, 1959.

Strecker, Georg. "The Passion- and Resurrection Predictions in Mark's Gospel (Mark 8:31; 9:31; 10:32–34)." *Int* 22 (1968) 421–42.

Streeter, Burnett Hillman. *The Four Gospels: A Study of Origins Treating of the Manuscript Tradition, Sources, Authorship, & Dates*. Rev. ed. London: Macmillan and Company, 1930.

_____. *The Four Gospels: A Study of Origins Treating of the Manuscript Tradition, Sources, Authorship, & Dates*. 5th ed. London: Macmillan Company, 1936.

Talbert, Charles H. "An Anti-Gnostic Tendency in Lucan Christology." *NTS* 14 (1967–68) 259–71.

_____. *Luke and the Gnostics: An Examination of the Lucan Purpose*. Nashville and New York: Abingdon Press, 1966.

Talbert, Charles H., and Edgar V. McKnight. "Can the Griesbach Hypothesis Be Falsified?" *JBL* 91 (1972) 338–68.

Taylor, Vincent. "Luke, Gospel of." Pp. 180–88 in *IDB* 3.

_____. *The Names of Jesus*. New York: St. Martin's Press, 1953.

_____. *The Passion Narrative of St. Luke: A Critical and Historical Investigation*. Ed. O. E. Evans. New York and London: Cambridge University Press, 1972.

Teeple, Howard M. "The Origin of the Son of Man Christology." *JBL* 84 (1965) 213–50.

Thackeray, H. St. John. *Josephus: The Man and the Historian*. New York: KTAV Publishing House, 1967.

Thompson, William G. "An Historical Perspective in the Gospel of Matthew." *JBL* 93 (1974) 243–62.

_____. *Matthew's Advice to a Divided Community (Mt 17,22–18,35)*. Analecta Biblica 44. Rome: Pontifical Biblical Institute, 1970.

_____. "Reflections on the Composition of Mt 8:1–9:34." *CBQ* 33 (1971) 365–88.

Tödt, H. E. "Excursus II: Discussion of the Concept of the Heavenly Son of Man in Acts 7:56." Pp. 303–5 in Tödt, *Son of Man in the Synoptic Tradition*.

_____. *The Son of Man in the Synoptic Tradition*. Philadelphia: Westminster Press, 1965.

Tollers, Vincent, and John R. Maier, eds. *The Bible in Its Literary Milieu: Contemporary Essays*. Grand Rapids: William B. Eerdmans Publishing Company, 1979.

Townsend, John T. "Rabbinic Sources." Pp. 64–77 in Neusner, *Study of Judaism*.

Tuckett, Christopher. "The Present Son of Man." *JSNT* 14 (1982) 58–81.

Tyson, Joseph B. "Sequential Parallelism in the Synoptic Gospels." *NTS* 22 (1976) 276–308.

_____. *A Study of Early Christianity*. New York: Macmillan Company, 1973.

_____. "The Synoptic Problem Should be Solvable." Unpublished paper presented at 1975 annual meeting of Society of Biblical Literature.

Van Segbroeck, F., Christopher M. Tuckett, Gilbert Van Belle, and Jozef Verheyden, eds. *The Four Gospels 1992: Festschrift Frans Neirynck.* 3 vols. BETL 100. Leuven: Leuven University Press/Uitgeverij Peeters, 1992.

van Unnik, W. C. "Jesus the Christ." *NTS* 8 (1962) 101–16.

Vermes, Geza. "Appendix E: The Use of בר נש/בר נשא in Jewish Aramaic." Pp. 310–30 in Black, *An Aramaic Approach.*

_____. *Jesus the Jew: A Historian's Reading of the Gospels.* London: Collins, 1973.

_____. "The Present State of the 'Son of Man' Debate." *JJS* 29 (1978) 123–34.

_____. "The 'Son of Man' Debate." *JSNT* 1 (1978) 19–32.

Vielhauer, Philipp. *Aufsäze zum Neuen Testament.* Munich: Kaiser Verlag, 1965.

_____. "Ein Weg der neutestamentlichen Theologie? Prüfung der Thesen Ferdinand Hahns." *EvT* 25 (1965) 24–72. Reprinted as pp. 141–98 in Vielhauer, *Aufsäze zum Neuen Testament.*

_____. *Geschichte des urchristlichen Literatur. Einleitung in das Neue Testament, die Apokryphen und die Apostolischen Väter.* Berlin and New York: Walter de Gruyter, 1975.

_____. "Gottesreich und Menschensohn in der Verkündigung Jesu." Pp. 51–79 in Schneemelcher, *Festschrift für Günther Dehn.* Reprinted as pp. 55–91 in Vielhauer, *Aufsäze zum Neuen Testament.*

_____. "Jesus und der Menschensohn. Zur Diskussion mit Heinz Eduard Tödt und Eduard Schweizer." *ZTK* 60 (1963) 133–77. Reprinted as p. 92–140 in Vielhauer, *Aufsäze zum Neuen Testament.*

_____. "Jewish-Christian Gospels." Pp. 1:118–39 in Hennecke, *New Testament Apocrypha.*

Vögtle, Anton. *Das Evangelium und die Evangelien. Briträge zur Evangelienforschung.* KBANT. Düsseldorf: Patmos-Verlag, 1971.

Vööbus, Arthur. "Syriac Versions." Pp. 949–54 in *IDBSup.*

Voss, Gerhard. *Die Christologie der lukanischen Schriften in Grundzügen.* StudNeot 2. Bruges: Desclée de Brouwer, l965.

Walker, William O., Jr. "Introduction: The Colloquy on the Relationships among the Gospels." Pp. 1–15 in Walker, *Relationships among the Gospels.*

Walker, William O., Jr., ed. *The Relationships among the Gospels: An Interdisciplinary Dialogue.* TUSR 5. San Antonio: Trinity University Press, 1978.

Weeden, Theodore J. *Mark—Traditions in Conflict.* Philadelphia: Fortress Press, 1971.

West, H. Philip, Jr. "A Primitive Version of Luke in the Composition of Matthew." *NTS* 14 (1967) 75–95.

Wevers, J. W. "Theodotion." Pp. 618–19 in *IDB* 4.

Wilckens, Ulrich. "Der Ursprung der Überlieferung der Erscheinungen des Auferstandenen." Pp. 56–95 in Joest and Pannenberg, *Dogma und Denkstrukturen.*

_____. *Die Missionsreden der Apostelgeschichte. Form- und traditionsgeschichtliche Untersuchungen.* Neukirchen[-Vlyn]: Neukirchener Verlag, 1961.

Winter, Paul. Review of Norman Perrin, *Rediscovering the Teaching of Jesus. DL* 89 (1968) 784.

Wolfe, Charles. "The Use and Abuse of Textual Criticism for Solving the Synoptic Problem." Unpublished paper presented at 1976 annual meeting of Society of Biblical Literature.

Woodward, Kenneth L., and Ann Schumacher. "Easter 1966—A Quest for the True Jesus." *Newsweek* 48,15 (April 11, 1966) 71–73.

Zahrnt, Heinz. *The Historical Jesus.* New York and Evanston: Harper and Row, 1963.

Zeitlin, Solomon. "A Reply." *JQR* 53 (1963) 345–49.

_____. "The Title *Rabbi* in the Gospels Is Anachronistic." *JQR* 59 (1968) 158–60.

Index of
Modern Authors

About the Author

William O. Walker, Jr. (Ph.D., Duke University) is Jennie Farris Railey King Professor Emeritus of Religion at Trinity University in San Antonio, Texas, where he served as a member of the faculty and as an administrator from 1962 until his retirement in 2002. The author of *Paul and His Legacy* (2015) and *Interpolations in the Pauline Letters* (2001), he has served as co-author, editor, associate editor, or assistant editor of a number of other books, including *The HarperCollins Bible Dictionary* (1996), and has published more than sixty articles on New Testament topics. He is a member of Studiorum Novi Testamenti Societas, the Society of Biblical Literature, the Catholic Biblical Association of America, and is a Fellow of Westar Institute.

CPSIA information can be obtained
at www.ICGtesting.com
Printed in the USA
BVHW09s1002241018
531100BV00030B/1876/P